The Drama of Preaching

The Drama of Preaching

Participating with God in the History of Redemption

ERIC BRIAN WATKINS

WIPF & STOCK · Eugene, Oregon

THE DRAMA OF PREACHING
Participating with God in the History of Redemption

Wipf & Stock
An Imprint of Wipf and Stock Publishers
199 W. 8th Ave., Suite 3
Eugene, OR 97401

www.wipfandstock.com
Funded by the Afbouw Foundation.

PAPERBACK ISBN: 978-1-4982-7859-1
HARDCOVER ISBN: 978-1-4982-7861-4
EBOOK ISBN: 978-1-4982-7860-7

Manufactured in the U.S.A.   JANUARY 30, 2017

Sponsored by STICHTING AFBOUW KAMPEN

For the Church

"For in the cross of Christ, as in a magnificent theater, the inestimable good-
ness of God is displayed before the whole world."

—JOHN CALVIN
COMMENTARY ON THE GOSPEL ACCORDING TO JOHN,
2.73 (RE. JOHN 13:31)

Contents

Acknowledgments | ix

Abbreviations | xii

Introduction | xiii

1   Continuing an Unfinished Discussion: The Redemptive-Historical Preaching Debates Yesterday and Today | 1

2   The Drama of Redemption and Redemptive-Historical Preaching | 24

3   Hebews 11: Setting the Stage | 64

4   Hebrews 11: A Theatre of Martyrs | 82

5   Application or Imitation? Reconsidering the *Sine Qua Non* of Preaching | 114

6   Imitating the Saints: A Case Stude in Hebrews 11 | 135

7   Preaching the Christ-Centered Drama of Redemption in the Postmodern Scene | 153

Summary and Conclusion | 189

Appendix: Samenvatting (Dutch Summary) | 197

Bibliography | 203

Names Index | 225

Subject Index | 231

Scripture Index | 251

Acknowledgments

By God's grace, this slightly revised version of my PhD dissertation on preaching is the crescendo of eighteen years of academic work, toward the goal of serving Christ's church. He alone truly knows the many joys and sorrows, trials and triumphs that have attended this journey. The grace He has given me along the way to complete this task has been abundant and free, and my heart is overwhelmed with gratitude. As a servant of God's word, I have profited both from the studies contained herein, as well as the many experiences by which I have been taught along the way. My sincere hope is to contribute something helpful to the contemporary discussions about preaching, thus edifying the church and bringing glory to our Triune God.

I cannot express deeply enough my gratitude to Dr. C.J. (Kees) de Ruijter, my first promoter, for his guidance, correction, and encouragement along the way. It would be difficult to recall a time we met together in which he did not pray for me, my family, and the church I serve. His sincere concern for the latter two evidenced that I was far more to him than just a student—but rather a brother and a son in the faith. While I am grateful that Kees was willing to guide me as a student, I am particularly grateful for his nudging me to consider the particular implications of redemptive-historical preaching in a postmodern context, and the strengths and weaknesses of the "drama of redemption" rhetoric. If this study has any practical benefit, it is largely due to his influence. Through and through, Kees showed himself to be a pastor-scholar, whose love for the church informed our academic discussions at every turn. I could not have hoped for a more patient and supportive promoter to learn from and with during my studies. It has truly been a pleasure to work with him.

I would also like to express my gratitude to my second promoter, Dr. P.H.R. (Rob) van Houwelingen. His knowledge of the biblical text, and materials related to the book of Hebrews was both helpful and encyclopedic. Nearly every conversation or e-mail we exchanged led to his making additional suggestions of books or articles I should read, and trails I should pursue. He also proved to be an excellent conversation partner, catching numerous mistakes along the way, and challenging my conclusions when they were less than convincing. This book has been greatly enriched by his contributions.

Thanks are also due to members of my reading committee: Drs. Gerrit Immink, Dennis Johnson, and Gert Kwakkel. I am particularly grateful for the advice, correction, and encouragement by Drs. Johnson and Kwakkel, whose suggestions, both in style and substance, have surely improved the quality of this book. Additional feedback was given to me at the time of my defense from Drs. Egbert Brink, Hans Burger, George Harinck, and Kees van Dusseldorp. Though I was unable to synthesize all of the suggestions made by my various reviewers, I am sincerely grateful not only for their insights, but for the very kind and gracious manner in which they communicated with me.

Various members of the faculty and staff of the Theological University in Kampen (Broederweg) graciously helped and served me along the way. I am particularly grateful to Geert Harmanny, Marjolijn Palma, and Arjo Riemer in the TUK library who very patiently put up with a somewhat clumsy American trying his best to find his way around the library. Their kind assistance saved me countless hours, and made my work in Kampen far more efficient. Koos Tamminga very graciously worked on the summary in Dutch (Samenvatting).

I am sincerely grateful to Wipf and Stock Publishers and to its patient and helpful editorial staff for accepting this work for publication, and for kindly allowing me to produce a small number of copies for my graduation, as required by the university. The printing of this monograph was made possible by a gracious donation from the Afbouw foundation in Kampen. I am also grateful for the help of Dr. William den Hollander, who edited a final version of the manuscript, and also helped me format it to Wipf and Stock requirements. In the end, any remaining mistakes are solely my responsibility.

Traveling back and forth to Holland, attending conferences, and purchasing the books needed to complete this process was not cheap. I am deeply grateful to the Midgett family for financially supporting this project, and ever more for their prayers and encouragement over the years. I am also grateful to Dr. Wolter Rose, who very kindly opened his home to me, providing a very comfortable *tweedehuis* in Kampen. Rev. Joel Fick was a steady conversation partner along the way, and his brotherly encouragement was a breath of fresh air.

I must offer my sincere gratitude to the members, elders, and deacons of Covenant Presbyterian Church in St. Augustine, Florida. Week after week, they have both endured and enjoyed the benefits of having a full-time pastor doing part-time PhD work in preaching. Though I would like to think I am a better preacher as a result of my studies, there were many times I was confident that they needed more of their pastor than I was able to give. The completion of this book owes in no small part to their patience, encouragement, and support. Their willingness to give me a paid study sabbatical in 2013 was simply one token of their co-laboring with me in this endeavor. I thank them for practicing what I preach. That the church has grown spiritually and numerically during these years is evidence of the grace of God at work in and through his church, and for that grace I am deeply grateful.

Lastly, I have the privilege of honoring my wife, Heather. Of the twenty years we have been married, I have spent eighteen working toward one degree after the next. When I began the PhD program, we were starting a new church together, and had just adopted the second of our two dear children. Only God truly knows how graciously and faithfully Heather has supported and encouraged me through this process. Her love and faithfulness have covered a multitude of my failures, and her friendship has meant more to me than any degree ever will. She and our children, Kirra and Carl, have made countless sacrifices over the years of my studies, yet have proven to be my most reliable counselors and inspiring encouragers. My mother (who now lives with us) has taught me since my childhood the values of hard work and perseverance. May God grant our family continued love, joy, and peace as we glorify and enjoy our covenant-keeping God together. And yes, kids, Daddy is finally done with his dissertation.

—Eric B. Watkins
St. Augustine, October 2016

Abbreviations

ASV—American Standard Version
BAGD—Bauer, W., et al., *Greek-English Lexicon of the New Testament and Other Early Christian Literature.* 2d ed. Chicago, 1979
CTJ—*Calvin Theological Journal*
ESV—English Standard Version
EvQ—*Evangelical Quarterly*
HC—Heidelberg Catechism
KJV—King James Version
L&N—*Greek-English Lexicon of the New Testament: Based on Semantic Domains*, edited by J.P. Louw and E.A. Nida. 2d ed. New York, 1989
LSJ—Liddell, H.G., et al., *A Greek-English Lexicon.* 9th ed. Oxford, 1996
NASB—New American Standard Bible
NBG—Nederlandse Bijbelgenootschap
NBV—Nieuwe Bijbelvertaling
NIV—New International Version
NKJV—New King James Version
NLT—New Living Translation
NPNF—*Nicene and Post-Nicene Fathers.* Series 1
P&R—Presbyterian & Reformed Publishing
RSV—Revised Standard Version
SwJT—*Southwestern Journal of Theology*
TDNT—*Theological Dictionary of the New Testament*, edited by G. Kittel and G. Friedrich. Translated by G. W. Bromiley. 10 vols. Grand Rapids, 1964–1976
VC—*Vigiliae christianae*
WCF—Westminster Confession of Faith
WLC—Westminster Longer Catechism
WSC—Westminster Shorter Catechism
WTJ—*Westminster Theological Journal*

Introduction

PREACHING IS DRAMATIC. THROUGH it God both speaks and acts. In a manner of speaking, God *preached* the world into existence.[1] By this spoken word, he called into being that which formerly did not exist. By this same spoken word, God not only upholds all things (Heb 1:3), but also, in particular, redeems and re-creates humanity into his own image through the preaching of the gospel.[2] Preaching, thus, is a part of God's unfolding drama of redemption in which he speaks and acts out his purposes in history from creation to consummation. From one generation to the next, to bear the responsibility of preaching God's word is both a remarkable privilege and a tremendous challenge. This is increasingly true in the context of postmodernism and its struggles to retain confidence in history, authority, and morality—losses which come with profound consequences for preaching. Yet these challenges are not altogether new, nor are they insurmountable.

Many of the time-tested Christian confessions hold preaching in high regard. For example, the Second Helvetic Confession, one of the loftier expressions of preaching, says that preaching, when faithfully performed is nothing less than the word of God.[3] According to this confession, when preachers faithfully preach God's word—*God himself is speaking and acting.* Thus, preaching has always been at the heart of the church. However, where theological matters are important, they are frequently surrounded by clouds of controversy. This is certainly true of preaching. A working definition of preaching might be as follows: preaching is rightly proclaiming the word of God in such a way as to declare clearly and authoritatively what man is to believe concerning God, as well as the duty God requires of man.[4] Other nuanced definitions for preaching have varied in homiletic reflection over the centuries.[5] This variety underscores both the importance and the complex-

1. Horton, *Pilgrim Theology*, 346.

2. HC 27–28. Cf. WSC 88.

3. Second Helvetic Confession Art. 1.

4. This working definition is based upon 2 Tim 2:15 and WSC 3.

5. Perhaps most recognizable in our day is the definition of preaching as the explication and application of God's word. A simple definition, however, is neither given by Scripture nor easily determined from church history. See, for instance, Dargan's recognition of the difficulty in pinpointing the birth of Christian preaching in definitive and paradigmatic form. In his view, the apostolic model is the "regulative basis for Christian

ity of preaching. Often, these complexities have led to debates from which have come both sweet and bitter fruit. One particular debate from the last century seems to have found something of a rebirth in recent hermeneutic and homiletic discussions. It is what we shall refer to as the "redemptive-historical"[6] preaching debate.

In the 1930s in the Netherlands, this particular debate ensued over hermeneutic and homiletic questions, and would have lasting effects upon many churches inside and outside the Netherlands. The RH debate centered upon questions of how the Bible ought to be preached and thus properly connected to the people of God today, particularly from Old Testament narrative texts. Chief among those questions was how the person and work of Jesus Christ ought to be preached from Old Testament narratives, and equally the question of making legitimate application from the same Old Testament narratives. This nuanced debate wrestled over the question of application—or what was more precisely referred to as *exemplaristic*[7] application, which reduced biblical characters to moral examples in abstraction from the person and work of Christ. Both the supporters of the RH approach and those labeled as exemplaristic generally agreed on the importance of preaching Christ as the center of Scripture (though nuances abounded on each side). Key to the debate, however, was the question of to what extent Old Testament characters could function as examples. The RH side pushed back strongly, arguing that what often occurred in preaching was a violation of the intention of the biblical text, which, in their view, was to display the redemptive work of God in history. This will be further developed in chapter five, but, simply put, the priority of respecting a historical text for where it stood in the plot-line of history lay at the heart of the RH side of the debate. Those on the other side appreciated this concern, but responded quite defensively that the RH advocates were coming close to creating a novel

---

preaching at all times"; Dargan, *A History of Preaching*, 1.25. Ronald Wallace takes the view that, "The earliest Christian preaching took the form of a simple conversational, practical, and pastoral homily, based on the text which had been read, and often following the varied topics suggested by the text, with little concern to attain a satisfying rhetorical structure"; *New International Dictionary*, 479. Xavier Leon-Defour, while noting the complexity of defining preaching, suggests, "To preach in our day is to announce the event of salvation as well as to exhort or teach"; *Dictionary of Biblical Theology*, 449.

6. This is the English translation of the Dutch *heilshistorisch*. Hereafter, RH.

7. B. Holwerda is credited with coining this term when he labeled a particularly moralistic strain of preaching "exemplaristic" (exemplarisch in Dutch); Holwerda, *Gereformeerd mannenblad*, 27. See also his "De heilshistorie in de prediking," available in English at http://www.spindleworks.com/library/holwerda/holwerda.htm. See also the discussion in Greidanus, *Sola Scriptura*, 19–21.

approach to preaching—one that over-emphasized history to the point of excluding the exemplaristic contribution of biblical characters.

Though numerous biblical texts were focused on during this debate, a text that received considerable attention from both sides was Hebrews 11. This was likely due to the recognition that a homiletic approach to the Old Testament, in order for it to be deemed biblically viable, needed to be consistent with the way in which the New Testament both hermeneutically and homiletically utilizes the Old Testament. The book of Hebrews, and Hebrews 11 in particular, was a virtual epicenter of both—inspired hermeneutic and inspired homiletic. Though each side of the RH debate sought to be "biblical" in its approach to preaching, it would be an understatement to say that a consensus was *not* reached.[8] In some areas, the preaching debates that began in the 1930s would make progress and come to clearer expression in the decades that followed. Regrettably, however, there were other areas of the debate that never reached a mature conclusion, including the particular issues related to preaching from the hall of faith found in Hebrews 11, and, perhaps more precisely, the issue of homiletic application. This problem remains central to current discussions of RH preaching.

Fast-forward numerous decades, and we see an eventual decline in Dutch materials related to this debate in the Netherlands. This is likely due to the long shadow of World War II, internal struggles within the churches, and the changing theological scene in the Netherlands and beyond. In 1988, C. Trimp, at that time professor of Homiletics at the Theologische Universiteit Kampen in the Netherlands, made a sincere plea for further reflection and development on both the hermeneutical and homiletical side of the debate.[9] It could be said that today, while the echo of that debate is heard in many churches both inside and outside of the Netherlands, there is still a great need for the church to wrestle not only with the questions of the past, but questions of the future, particularly as they relate to the influences of

8. This preaching debate was part of a significant struggle within the Gereformeerde Kerken in Nederland (GKN). The issues were significant enough that in 1944, another denomination was formed, the Gereformeerde Kerken in Nederland (vrijgemaakt) (GKv). It would be far too simplistic, however, to reduce the reason for the new denomination to the preaching debate. It was much more comprehensive than that. For two accounts of this struggle in English, see Van Reest, *Schilder's Struggle*, and Van Dijk, *My Path to Liberation*. Both works are translations of Dutch volumes.

9. Trimp, *Heilsgeschiedenis en prediking*. This book was translated into English in 1996 under the title *Preaching and the History of Salvation*. The book not only gives a helpful summary of key aspects of the debate, but also pleads for the revisiting of some of the questions that remain unanswered. This monograph owes part of its motivation to Trimp's volume, as well as the way in which the current climate of homiletics, particularly in North American churches and seminaries, seems to be repeating many of the same steps of the RH debates that took place in the Netherlands.

postmodernism upon the church and its preaching. The homiletic community is in need of additional conversation partners, nuanced reflection, and
contemporary translation of some of the older questions and concerns.[10]

Still, we are left wondering if Trimp's request for a furthering of the
conversation remains unanswered. In a variety of ways, his request for
advancing the worthwhile aspects of the discussion about RH hermeneutics and preaching is being responded to, both inside the Netherlands and
outside of it. One indirectly related form of advancement may be seen in
the "drama of redemption"[11] paradigm, which, while not being explicitly a
rehearsal of the same questions from the earlier debate, is nonetheless remarkably similar in many of its concerns. In short, the DR paradigm views
the Bible as a unified, redemptive drama in which God is not simply the author but the main actor. At the same time, he is not alone; he has granted the
church a scripted role that she must learn to faithfully perform (improvise)
on the world stage—what Calvin called the "theatre of God's glory."[12] In our
understanding, the DR paradigm moves beyond the RH model, while bearing a particular concern for the need to communicate the substance of the
biblical message in ways that we will suggest may be helpful for preaching
in a postmodern age.

PURPOSE AND THESIS OF THIS STUDY

The purpose of this monograph will be to suggest the ways in which the
DR paradigm may help to advance the RH preaching debate beyond some
of the earlier obstacles and subsequent caricatures. In particular, our thesis
is that a wedding of the RH and DR ideas may help overcome the false dilemma between preaching that is focused on the work of Christ revealed
in redemptive history, and preaching that is focused on homiletic application. Thus, a union between the RH and DR paradigms could potentially
overcome this regrettable dilemma, and create a faithful, fresh, and fruitful
approach to preaching the gospel in a postmodern age.

10. A point that is affirmed by Baars, "Heilshistorische prediking," 10–15.

11. This term shall be used throughout the monograph, and is a synthesis of terms/
ideas taken from several authors. See below for further details. Hereafter "DR."

12. Calvin *Inst.*, 1.6.2.

NECESSITY OF THIS STUDY

Literary contributions to the discussion of how to interpret and apply the Scripture are as old as the canon itself. Various homiletic approaches have developed alongside these discussions in an attempt to answer the questions of the day, and contemporary questions both echo and replace older ones. It is our conviction that revisiting an old discussion that had a strong emphasis on the importance of *history* (RH), and building upon it with a newer one that embodies a fresh approach to the question of homiletic *application* (DR), will hopefully address important contemporary homiletic questions while enhancing confidence and effectiveness in preaching. Our hope, in the end, is that this monograph will address these issues in a way that is helpful to the church, and faithful to the one who continues to speak and act through the ministry of his inspired word.

PLAN OF THIS STUDY

Having introduced the purpose, necessity, and plan of this study in the Introduction, Chapter 1 will survey the current status of the discussion related to redemptive-historical preaching, bridging the gap from the past to the present, thus showing the continuing relevance of the RH preaching debate. Chapter 2 will more fully introduce the DR paradigm, as well as the particular ways in which it can be employed as an enhancement beyond the RH preaching paradigm and its challenges. It will also address possible objections to the proposed synthesis. In chapters 3 and 4, we will look specifically at Hebrews 11 as an exegetical case study in synthesizing the DNA of the RH and DR paradigms. Chapter 5 will focus on the important issues of homiletic application and imitation. Chapter 6 will continue this discussion, particularly addressing the idea of imitating the saints found in Hebrews 11. In chapter 7 we will apply our homiletic proposal particularly to the concern of preaching in a postmodern context and its sophisticated struggles with history, authority, and morality. Lastly, our summary and conclusion will tie the various threads together, respond to potential objections, and make an earnest plea to recognize the strengths and the weaknesses of the RH and DR paradigms, thus forging from the two a nuanced homiletic method to be faithfully improvised in the drama of preaching.

PRESUPPOSITIONS AND THEOLOGICAL POINT OF VIEW

As with all monographs, so also this one is influenced by the author's pre-suppositions and theological point of view. Thus, rather than let the reader try to discern these between the lines, it may be helpful to state them here. This monograph is written from a theological point of view that might be described as Protestant, evangelical, and confessionally Reformed. That is to say, the author adheres to orthodox, Protestant creeds and confessions, and in particular has taken ordination vows as a minister in the Orthodox Presbyterian Church, in which the Westminster Confession and Catechisms are the theological standards. Along with these the author also affirms the substance of the Three Forms of Unity (Belgic Confession, Heidelberg Catechism, Canons of Dordt). Lastly, and perhaps most importantly, the author presupposes the unity, integrity, and authority of Scripture, and its abiding relevance for the church and world today.

1

Continuing an Unfinished Discussion
The Redemptive-Historical Preaching Debates Yesterday and Today

WHAT HAS BECOME OF RH preaching? Did Trimp's plea for a reconsideration of some of the important questions from the earlier debate go unanswered?[1] Arie Baars puts it well by asking, "Has RH preaching gone out with the tide?"[2] In this chapter we shall consider the current climate of interest in RH preaching, both inside and outside the Netherlands. We will suggest that interest in RH preaching has waned in the Netherlands since the earlier debates, and we will consider some of the reasons why this is the case. We will then look at the way in which there appears to be a surge of interest in RH preaching (and matters related to it) outside the Netherlands. Related to this second point, we will demonstrate that the interest in RH preaching is not limited simply to *preaching* per se, but extends also to other theological branches, such as hermeneutics, systematic, and historical theology.

---

1. Trimp's efforts to continue the discussion, or at least particular nuances of it, are best expressed in one of his more popular homiletic works, *Klank en weerklank*. Note that this book comes three years after his original plea in *Heilsgeschiedenis en prediking*.

2. Baars, "Heilshistorische prediking," 15 (trans. mine).

INTEREST IN REDEMPTIVE-HISTORICAL PREACHING IN THE NETHERLANDS

It is fair to say that the level of interest in RH preaching in the Netherlands (the so-called "birthplace" of the movement) has waned considerably since the earlier decades of its inception. Evidence for this is found not only in Trimp's attempt to revive the discussion, but also in the academic material that has been published on preaching in recent decades.[3] This is not to say that there is *no* interest in RH preaching, for in fact the opposite is the case. There are currently both academic and popular attempts to continue discussions related to RH preaching; however, in the contexts where these efforts continue, there has clearly been development from the older expressions of RH preaching to what it is now. This is most immediately seen in the work of Trimp's successor, Kees (C.J.) de Ruijter, and his numerous homiletic publications. The most recent, *Horen naar de Stem van God*, is an attempt to address several of the issues Trimp raised in the twilight of his career, such as the place of the Trinity in homiletic reflection and, perhaps more importantly, the idea of focusing on the immediate needs and situation of the hearer in preaching.[4]

Further attempts to not only revitalize, but also advance the discussion in the Netherlands can be seen in recent PhD dissertations. Kees van Dusseldorp, for instance, has developed a homiletic approach that weaves together certain threads of the RH preaching paradigm with current trends in narrative theology.[5] Additionally, Jos Douma's 2008 dissertation, *Veni Creator Spiritus*, develops and advances some of Trimp's homiletic concerns, with particular emphasis on the role of the Holy Spirit (an attempt to correct a perceived overemphasis on Christology at the expense of pneumatology), as well as reflecting further on the role of the hearer in preaching.[6] Still,

---

3. De Ruijter discusses Trimp's efforts to revive the discussion in the 1980's in "Gods verbondswoord," 156. See also Bos, *Identificatie-mogelijkheden*, 69. Bos seems to agree with Sidney Greidanus, who suggests several reasons why the conversation burned out rather quickly and remained somewhat dormant thereafter; Greidanus, *Sola Scriptura*, 52–55.

4. De Ruijter, *Horen naar de stem van God*; see especially chapter three on the role of the Trinity in preaching. De Ruijter's views about preaching, especially as he attempts to address Trimp's concern to give more adequate attention to the needs of the hearer, have not gone unchallenged, even by those within the RH tradition. See Douma's interaction in *Hoe gaan wij verder?*, 84–88. Douma is reacting particularly to an earlier homiletic work that focused greater attention on the hearer. Cf. De Ruijter, *Preken en horen*.

5. Van Dusseldorp, *Preken tussen de verhalen*.

6. Douma, *Veni Creator Spiritus*; see pg. 53 in particular for his clear sense of carrying the mantle of Trimp's concerns.

there is a sense in which many in the Netherlands who are familiar with the early debate and its representatives would see the RH paradigm as being somewhat *ouderwets* (old-fashioned), and would respectfully relegate it to the well-respected but virtually untouched trophy case of the past. We would like to now consider a few reasons why that may have become the case, since doing so will help us appreciate not only why interest in RH preaching may have waned in the Netherlands, but also why it may be finding traction in other places for largely different reasons.

In order to appreciate the rise and fall of RH preaching in the Netherlands, it needs to be seen in its historical and ecclesiastical context. To a large extent, developments in RH preaching were embodied particularly in one, modestly sized denomination, the Gereformeerde Kerken in Nederland (vrijgemaakt) (hereafter GKv). This denomination was born in the context of a difficult ecclesiastical controversy and the long, dark shadow of a world war.[7] The new denomination began in 1944 as an offshoot of the Gereformeerde Kerken in Nederland (hereafter GKN). One of its foremost leaders was Klaas Schilder, a well-educated and prolific pastor-theologian-churchman. Schilder attained a heroic persona within the denomination. Biographers depict him as a brilliant theologian and churchman who stood against a rushing tide of issues that threatened the church. He bravely opposed the atrocities of World War II and, like many pastors in that period, ministered in a context of fear, sacrifice, and deep loss.[8] Though Schilder's theological views were embraced by some and rejected by others, his principled, tireless, and self-sacrificial nature would seem to justify many of the laudable things that have been said of him. Numerous churches, pastors, and congregants followed the leadership of Schilder through a large controversy which became known as the "Vrijmaking" (liberation).[9]

At the heart of this ecclesiastical controversy was the doctrine of the covenant and the particular concern for the proper way to address the baptized people of God through preaching. Much has been written on this subject, and it is not our intention to repeat what has been written elsewhere. Still, the long and tense debate surrounding issues related to Abraham Kuyper's view of the covenant are an undeniable part of the justification for the new denomination in 1944. Concerns over the nature of the covenant, baptism, and assurance of salvation all intersected in this debate, not simply questions about preaching. But perhaps the real tipping point was the fact

7. Kuiper, "Vrijmaking of wederkeer," 11–43.

8. Schilder biographies abound. For a recent and extensive biography, see Van Rijswijk, De Jong, Van de Kamp, and Boersma, *Wie is die man?*. For a short English introduction, see Faber, "Klaas Schilder's Life and Work."

9. Van Deursen, *The Distinctive Character of the Free University*, 203.

that those who did not embrace Kuyper's view of the covenant felt that it was being imposed upon them in a way that was conscience-binding beyond the church's established polity.[10] While it is not our intention to evaluate the ecclesiastical issues within that debate, it could be suggested that one of the reasons why RH preaching may have waned so quickly is that it was born in the context of this largely inward-facing, ecclesiastical debate.[11]

Another key background against which the development of RH preaching also needs to be seen is the modernistic, critical approach to the Bible, with its attack upon the Bible's history, unity, and integrity. Advocates of the RH preaching paradigm saw themselves as defending a consistently Reformed, orthodox response to the higher critical paradigm insofar as the RH approach sought to stress the continuity and integrity of the Bible, and especially the importance of *history*. Emphasizing the covenantal continuity of the Bible was not simply perceived as the most proper way to approach the Bible homiletically; it was also seen as a significant *apologetic* tool to help keep the foundation of the church from being swept away by the swiftly moving tide of modernism.

This apologetic concern can be illustrated by the way in which some of the early advocates of RH preaching saw a threat in the writings of Karl Barth and the "neo-orthodox" approach to theology, as well as others who were effectively stripping the Bible of its historical character and reducing it to subjective, existential, religious encounters with God. Sermons from the higher critical and neo-orthodox points of view were perceived as effectively rewriting the confessional script of the church and radically (if not subtly) reducing the content of preaching to subjective application. Many Reformed theologians of that day found these strange winds to be as threatening to the spiritual peace and welfare of the churches in Europe as the world wars were to its physical peace and welfare. Schilder, for instance, did his PhD dissertation in Germany, writing on the topic of paradox.[12] The idea of paradox is well-known in Barth's writings. Schilder developed a clear suspicion of Barth's theology and others whose theological formulations were implying a dubious critique of the historical reliability of the Bible and by implication the nature

---

10. Article 31 of the Church Order was central to this discussion and the formation of the new church. Selderhuis, *Handboek Nederlandse kerkgeschiedenis*, 811–13. See also Veenhof, "Church Polity in 1886 and 1944," 459–64.

11. For a short summary of this debate in Dutch, see Te Velde, "*De Vrijmaking gepeild*," 17–24. See also Jongeling, De Vries, and Douma, *Het vuur blijft branden*. Particular concerns about trends toward political and experimental (politieke en bevindelijke) preaching are expressed in the same volume by Douma in "Kerk zijn," 142–6.

12. Schilder, *Zur* Begriffsgeschichte *des "Paradoxon."*

of the church's theological stances.[13] The RH hermeneutic and its emphasis on *history* became both a pastoral and theological way of equipping the church to respond to the formidable foes of the so-called "higher criticism" of the Bible on the one hand, and the subtle, and therefore difficult to address, theological nuances of neo-orthodoxy on the other.

Thus, when we consider the intra and extra-ecclesiastical context of the early development of the RH preaching paradigm, we need to recognize its complexity. It would be too simplistic to identify it as something that myopically developed *within the church*, as though pressures and issues outside the church (political, philosophical and theological) had no influence.[14] But these issues would not remain at the forefront of the church's life forever. The flame of those original concerns would eventually cool, as the new denomination began to take on its own identity and confront new challenges. But what became of preaching?

Again we return to Schilder and his legacy. Schilder is the obvious and well-known father of the RH movement.[15] In spite of all the commendable things that might be said about him, however, his work was not always easy to follow. This perspective is acknowledged by those within Schilder's tradition who are sympathetic to his views.[16] Many of Schilder's sermons are like masterfully artistic paintings,[17] yet they are not always easily read, either in Dutch or in English translations. Thus, the early fruit of one of the leading pioneers of the RH preaching paradigm in the Netherlands remained somewhat hidden behind a lofty, poetic, yet esoteric vocabulary which may have caused subsequent generations to describe RH preaching as being antiquated and inaccessible.

It may also be fair to suggest that not only was Schilder somewhat difficult to read; but also the movement itself, especially within the Netherlands, has been characterized (if not caricatured) as being a lofty, overly intellectual approach to preaching. As we shall demonstrate, RH preaching was developed as a pointed reaction to psychologizing and subjectivizing

13. Harinck, "Inleiding," 12.

14. Hyun, *Redemptive-Historical Hermeneutics and Homiletics*, 78.

15. While Schilder is well-known to many who are interested in RH preaching, too few are aware of some of the distinct contributions on the subject by homileticians such as B. Holwerda, M.B. Van 't Veer, C. Veenhof, H.J. Schilder, C. Trimp, and C.J. de Ruijter, as well as others whose particular contributions will resurface at various points throughout this monograph.

16. Van Bekkum notes that, "Schilder is not always easy to follow," in "Op de tweesprong van kerk en wereld," 23 (trans. mine); see also pg. 19. Faber confirms the same in "Klaas Schilder's Life and Work," 6.

17. This is a bit of a pun as Schilder's name means "painter" in Dutch.

preaching paradigms, as well as those that might be described as moralistic or exemplaristic. In doing so, it also reacted rather strongly to the
traditionally embraced "uitleggen en toepassen" (explication and application) approach to preaching.[18] This exposition and application approach to
preaching was the dominant paradigm during that time. We must highlight
the important fact that sympathizers with the RH preaching paradigm believed sermons that focused on the subjective life of the believer and her
keeping of the commandments inevitably weakened the believer's ground
of assurance, as it located the source of assurance more on the believer's
obedience than upon the finished work of Christ. To state it simply, those
who favored the RH preaching paradigm and left the GKN to join the GKv,
did so in part as a pastoral attempt to guard the liberty of pastors to hold
varying views of the covenant and, perhaps just as importantly, to protect
the doctrine of the believer's assurance of salvation. As D. van Dijk reflects
in his own path toward becoming a GKv pastor, "The ultimate reason for all
the uncertainty in our people's hearts lay in an error they were making: they
sought the requisite certainty in themselves rather than in God's promises."[19]
And further:

> Once I had come to these insights, they made quite a difference
> in how I went about my work as a minister—in my visits to the
> sick, in my catechism classes, and especially in preaching . . .
> Such a change in insight with regard to the meaning of the cov-
> enant for the life of the congregation had definite implications
> for how we preach.[20]

This illustrates the fact that discussions around RH preaching were insepa-
rably connected to complex yet important pastoral and theological issues,
not just the issues of moralism and exemplarism.

Several particular factors need to be noted. The first is that what developed in the place of the paradigms perceived by RH preachers as being
overly subjective, became in the eyes of many an *over*-emphasis on the objective facts of history.[21] RH sermons were often seen as brilliant, intensely

18. The emblem of the "explication and application" (uitleggen en toepassen) paradigm at that time was found in the homiletic of Hoekstra, *Gereformeerde homiletiek*.

19. Van Dijk, *My Path Toward Liberation*, 209–15.

20. Ibid., 213–4.

21. "In the so-called redemptive-historical vision of preaching it is a basic fact that
the sermon only does justice to the (historical) text while the whole of Scripture and
especially its emphasis on the coming of Christ stands central. The strong one-sided
focus on the coming of Christ as the bridge across the historical distance between the
historical Bible-stories and the community of today was at the same time a factor that
hindered the further development of this important vision of preaching"; De Ruijter,

exegetical, and very God-centered; but could also be perceived as flying high over the hearts and lives of God's people without necessarily touching down upon the practical realities of daily life.[22] Second, there were numerous inconsistencies within the movement that called its coherence and credibility into question. Schilder, for instance, decried the exemplaristic use of Scripture as a means of making positive or negative comparisons in a moralistic manner. Yet his own preaching would occasionally betray his methodology.[23] An additional difficulty came with attempting to apply Schilder's idea of locating all texts in their historical plot-line. Many Old Testament texts could not always be easily located in their exact historical context per the RH method, and even Schilder's own *Christus in Zijn Lijden* evidences the tension of locating every text in the gospel narratives in a perfectly straight plot-line.[24]

Eventually, a tension developed between those who were committed to a pure expression of RH preaching and those who sought for greater application or relevance in preaching.[25] This distance would slowly increase over subsequent decades in the Netherlands, as RH preaching was perceived as an idealistic reaction to certain trends and excesses within the church of the past, rather than as a model that would necessarily be the homiletic way of the church's future.[26] Many, even within the GKv, would eventually treat the RH preaching model with the respectful sentiment that one would show their grandparents. In time, RH sermons, along with much of the literature surrounding the RH debate, were regarded nostalgically rather than as urgently needed preaching tools with contemporary relevance and efficacy. New issues began to take center stage with the GKv, and in this light we

---

Horen naar de stem van God, 112n34 (trans. mine).

22. Krabbendam's near-infamous critique of RH preaching as being like a plane flying high above the realities of this life illustrates our point. See his "Hermeneutics and Preaching," 232–6.

23. This criticism was most notably leveled against Schilder for the negative examples he employed from Scripture to describe certain leaders within the church. See Berkouwer, "Verval der Exegese," 273; see also Schilder, "Bijbel en Relativisme," 250, cited in Renninger, "The New Testament Use of the Old Testament Historical Narrative," 23.

24. Greidanus, *Sola Scriptura*, 176–7.

25. C. Trimp recognized this as a legitimate concern; "The Relevance of Preaching," esp. 3–4.

26. Rein Bos viewed RH preaching as becoming too predictable (voorspelbaar), and as failing to answer the question of how the people today connect with the text of yesterday through the sermon. In the end, RH sermons remained overly objective; Bos, *Identificatiemogelijkheden*, 74, 77–78.

might suggest that the heightened attention to RH preaching slowly began to fade to the background.[27]

In summary, the RH preaching debates in the Netherlands took strongest root in a relatively small church that was struggling to keep its identity within a changing, fractured world. The long shadow of World War II and a variety of inter-ecclesiastical dynamics kept much of the church's focus inward. The great desire to be the "true church" created a fortified climate of corporate theological introspection. In other words, the RH preaching debate was a good and fruitful debate in many ways, but it could easily be suggested that it produced a reactionary homiletic method that focused on the needs of the baptized, and yet may have failed to produce a homiletic paradigm that focused on the evangelistic needs of the *un*baptized. This focus effectively guaranteed that the growth of the church, and the love for RH preaching, would have to come from within—or the church would not grow. In this light, we will suggest here (and develop more fully later) that the RH preaching paradigm remains in need of a more outward focus, as well as additional conversation partners.[28]

INTEREST IN REDEMPTIVE-HISTORICAL PREACHING OUTSIDE THE NETHERLANDS

In light of the comments in the previous section, it is a small irony that the current climate of interest in RH hermeneutics and preaching is arguably stronger outside the Netherlands than within it. At this point, a careful distinction needs to be made between the distinctively Dutch version of the RH paradigm and its broader use outside the Netherlands. As noted above, even those who were labeled as "exemplaristic" in the RH preaching debates, were, generally speaking, sympathetic to many of the RH concerns, particularly the importance of seeing Christ in all of Scripture and of locating a text, as much as possible, in its place in history. Both sides in the Netherlands agreed with that. The particular point of contention was on the use of biblical characters as examples, whether positive or negative, in what was perceived as "moralistic" ways that violated the intention of the biblical text. Thus, especially for those unfamiliar with the nuances of the

27. For additional suggestions as to why this appears to be the case in the Netherlands, see Baars, "Heilshistorische prediking in deze tijd," 14–15. Baars concludes his article by suggesting that there are still important aspects of redemptive-historical preaching that are worth considering.

28. This sentiment is expressed by the current president of the Theologische Universiteit Kampen (the theological university associated with the GKv), Mees te Velde, "Vrijgemaakte vreemdelingen," 176–7.

RH debate, there are many (see below) who might be identified as RH in the broad sense of the term, but not in the narrow sense as defined by advocates like Schilder, Holwerda, Van 't Veer, and Van Dijk.[29]

In non-Dutch speaking contexts, interest in Dutch-Reformed theologians such as Herman Bavinck, Abraham Kuyper, and Geerhardus Vos has caused pastors and theologians to reflect more on the theological developments in the Netherlands. Herman Bavinck studies have seen a significant resurgence of interest, particularly as a result of the republication (in English) of his four-volume systematic theology, beginning with the *Prolegomena* in 2003.[30] Though a large percentage of Abraham Kuyper's work has been translated into English for some time, there is currently a strong amount of interest in his work in several ecclesiastical and academic circles, as is expressed in the *Neo-Kuyperian* school of thought and related theological projects.[31] Herman Ridderbos has become well-recognized in the English-speaking world as a representative of the RH paradigm, especially outside the Netherlands. This is an irony to many in the GKv tradition, as Ridderbos chose to remain in the GKN and not join Schilder and the GKv.[32] While these important Dutch theologians have in one way or another indirectly fueled the current climate of interest in RH hermeneutics and preaching, it is toward the particular contributions of Geerhardus Vos that we must now turn our attention.

Vos's influence has been felt in numerous directions. He had a significant hand in bringing Kuyper and Bavinck to Princeton for their Stone Lectures.[33] Vos was also influential for the work of Louis Berkhof[34] and Herman Ridderbos.[35] Vos's *Biblical Theology* made a landmark contribution to the sci-

29. Henceforth, we shall refer to this narrow understanding of the RH paradigm in Holland as "RHD" (=Redemptive Historical Dutch).

30. Bavinck, *Reformed Dogmatics Vol. 1.* Laurence O'Donnell refers to this translation project as Bavinck's "immigration" to America; O'Donnell, *Kees Van Til*, 6.

31. We do not mean to imply that Kuyper ought to be described as an RH preacher. It would be more fitting to align him with the puritan doctrine/application approach to preaching; see Kuyper, *Our Worship*, esp. 185–204. Still, interest in Kuyper has generated lateral interest in figures like Schilder and even the development of RH preaching in Kuyper's generation.

32. For a conciliatory article on Herman Ridderbos as a RH exegete, see Roukema, "Heilshistorische exegese: Herman Ridderbos," 53–72. See also Ridderbos, "The Redemptive-Historical Character of Paul's Preaching," 44–60.

33. Published as Kuyper, *Lectures on Calvinism*, and Bavinck, *The Philosophy of Revelation*.

34. According to Muller, "Berkhof notes his use of Bavinck but registers especially the importance of the theology of Geerhardus Vos to his own development"; in his Preface to Berkhof, *Systematic Theology*, vii.

35. Ridderbos, *Paul*, leaned heavily upon Vos, and Ridderbos apparently

ence of hermeneutics, and perhaps just as important is his magnum opus, *The Pauline Eschatology*.[36] Vos is reputed as being a bulwark in the development of Reformed biblical theology, and is hallowed as the "father of the amillenial view of eschatology in America."[37] His exegetical method is an unambiguous embodiment of an RH hermeneutic. He is well known for his metaphor in which he describes the history of revelation as a rose seed that slowly grows into a fully bloomed, beautiful rose.[38] For Vos, the opening chapters of Genesis introduce the story line of the Bible in seed form, particularly the *protoeuangelion*. That seed is viewed as having fully blossomed in the climax of redemptive history, the work of Jesus Christ in his death and particularly his resurrection. Important for Vos is the idea that all the DNA of the maturely blossomed rose is latent within the rose seed itself. The difference between one and the other, in his view, is not a difference in substance, but a difference in maturity—history. This organic metaphor is not something invented by Vos but inherited and developed from the Reformed theological tradition, and particularly the influence of Bavinck.[39]

What is of note, however, is that not all who have come to appreciate Vos's work are from a distinctively Dutch-Reformed background.[40] Rather, Vos represents a viable alternative to the significant influence of dispensationalism that has towered over the landscape of evangelical hermeneutics and homiletics.[41] Vos's notable reception of late in various ecclesiastical circles ought to be seen against the background of dispensationalism's approach to the unity of Scripture, and its implications especially for preaching

acknowledged to Marianne Radius (the daughter of Geerhardus and Catherine Vos), "a great dependence upon her father in his own thinking." See J.T. Dennison, Jr., *The Letters of Geerhardus Vos*, 81n208.

36. Vos, *The Pauline Eschatology*.

37. This ascription seems to have first appeared with Gaffin, "Geerhardus Vos and the Interpretation of Paul," 228. The same comment has been made several times by James T. Dennison, Jr; see J.T. Dennison Jr., "The Bible and the Second Coming," 57; J.T. Dennison Jr., *The Letters of Geerhardus Vos*, 66; and J.T. Dennison Jr., "Geerhardus Vos," 82–92.

38. Vos, *Biblical Theology*," 7–8; see also Vos, "The Idea of Biblical Theology as a Science and Discipline," 11.

39. For an in-depth treatment of the organic metaphor in Bavinck, see Eglinton, *Trinity and Organism*, particularly chapter 3, "Bavinck's Organic Motif."

40. Vos began his teaching career in the Christian Reformed Church at what would become Calvin Seminary. He later moved to Princeton to teach there, and transferred his ministerial credentials into the PCUSA.

41. Poythress notes Vos's influence on those who sought to develop covenant theology in contrast to Dispensational hermeneutics and its implications for Old Testament teaching and preaching in his *Understanding Dispensationalists*, 40.

from the Old Testament.[42] Vos's biblical-theological (RH) star has undoubtedly been recently seen against this sky. Dispensational hermeneutics have caused many to wrestle with the homiletic implications of the Old Testament for the church.[43] Challenges to preaching from the Old Testament, and particularly the issue of moralistic preaching, have come from those inside and outside of dispensational circles.[44] The particular difficulty within dispensationalism is the hermeneutical struggle to see the gospel in the warp and woof of the Old Testament. In short, when Christ and the gospel are not seen as the base-note of the Old Testament, moralistic (Christ-*less*) preaching will inevitably take its place. Apart from a Christ-centered emphasis, as Goldsworthy notes, "Much that passes for application of the Old Testament to the Christian life is only moralizing."[45]

This struggle has sparked an interest in RH exegetes such as Vos and others, whose approach to the Bible stresses the unity of the Old and New Testaments, and a Christ-centered focus within each.[46] Thus, whereas dispensational hermeneutics have often fostered moralistic preaching, especially from the Old Testament, by contrast, RH hermeneutics often have fostered Christ-centered preaching. Vos's RH heirs have sought to redress these issues both hermeneutically and homiletically. It is worthwhile to think further about some of those whom Vos influenced, both directly and indirectly.

Vos taught at Princeton for thirty-nine years (from 1893–1932). He had many notable American Presbyterian pastors and theologians as

42. Holwerda well-summarizes the main issue within Dispensationalism on this point: "When Jewish Israel did not accept Jesus as Messiah, the fulfillment of Old Testament prophecy was interrupted. During this interruption the gospel went out to the Gentiles and the church was formed, but dispensationalists hold that this was not God's original purpose and that it does not fulfill the Old Testament promises for the simple reason that the Church is not Israel"; Holwerda, *Jesus and Israel*, 4–5.

43. See, for instance, the unanswered questions raised by Rosscup about seeing Christ in the Old Testament in his "Hermeneutics and Expository Preaching," 102–103. Many of the questions are also raised with a covenantal or RH approach to the Old Testament, though the answers are notably different. For helpfully balancing nuances from a "Progressive Dispensational" point of view, see Pelton, *Preaching with Accuracy*, esp. 41–44.

44. For a list of additional problems, see Gibson, "Challenges to Preaching the Old Testament," 24. Kaminski argues, "This exegetical fallacy, called moralizing, assumes the main point of the OT story is to teach a moral principle"; Kaminski, "Preaching From the Historical Books," 62.

45. Goldsworthy, *The Goldsworthy Trilogy*, 25.

46. Craig Blaising notes that "many dispensationalists have welcomed these developments [from biblical theology] as clarifying insights into the normal function of literary language and its interpretation;" Blaising, "Dispensationalism: The Search for Definition," 31.

students.[47] Though the early decades of Vos's work seemed to draw only modest attention, his posthumous influence has had a much broader scope.[48] His real influence on the pulpit is not simple to trace, but can be seen in the writings of homileticians such as Edmund Clowney and Dennis Johnson. Clowney's *Preaching and Biblical Theology* is heavily dependent upon Vos.[49] Clowney's influence perpetuates this family tree in numerous directions. Dennis Johnson's recent work on homiletics is a thorough, contemporary attempt to embody an unambiguously RH model from a Vosian perspective.[50] Clowney's influence on Timothy Keller is well known, and perhaps embodied most clearly in the Doctor of Ministry course they taught together on preaching at Reformed Theological Seminary, Orlando.[51] Keller's recent book on preaching also makes frequent allusion to Clowney, and expresses an appreciative interaction with Clowney throughout.[52]

Vos's legacy is also notable in the work of several theologians who have not focused on homiletics per se, but upon other aspects of theology. Richard Gaffin Jr.'s long career at Westminster Seminary has been marked by teaching and preaching to several generations of pastors and theologians in a Vosian perspective, and includes editing a number of Vos's works, as well as being involved in the current project of translating Vos's four-volume *Dogmatiek*.[53] Various biographical works on Vos illustrate not simply his influence but also the surge of academic interest in (re)discovering Vos.[54] Vos's influence on the Reformed apologist Cornelius Van Til is significant, though often under-appreciated. John Muether helpfully notes the impact of Vos's covenant theology on Van Til's philosophy of revelation and histo-

47. J. Gresham Machen, John Murray, Cornelius Van Til, and Ned B. Stonehouse were just a few. Richard Lints has an even longer list in his *The Fabric of Theology*, 182–3n90.

48. For the influence of Vos on a particular denomination, see C.G. Dennison, "Geerhardus Vos and the Orthodox Presbyterian Church," 67–90. James Dennison (brother of Charles) has since started a seminary built around the distinctives of Vos's theological method. See http://www.nwts.edu/statement.htm.

49. Clowney, *Preaching and Biblical Theology*.

50. Johnson, *Him We Proclaim*.

51. Available online at https://itunes.apple.com/nl/itunes-u/preaching-christ-in-postmodern/id378879885. Keller also dedicates his book *The Prodigal God* to Clowney.

52. Keller, *Preaching*, esp. 6, 60, 71.

53. Vos, *Reformed Dogmatics*. See also Vos, *Redemptive History and Biblical Interpretation*. Gaffin has also written about Vos in numerous places.

54. See J.T. Dennison Jr., *The Letters of Geerhardus Vos*, 13–86. See also the prominent place given to Vos by Richard Barcellos, *The Family Tree of Reformed Biblical Theology*. George Harinck is currently working on a biography of Geerhardus Vos that will appear in the *American Reformed Biographies* series.

ry.[55] The point we are trying to make here is that through Vos, many have discovered and sought to perpetuate a hermeneutical approach to the Bible which must be seen as RH, even outside the realm of homiletics.

However, Vos's hermeneutical approach has had significant homiletic implications for those who have embraced it. Thus again we feel the irony that a surge of interest in RH hermeneutics and homiletics is developing outside of the Netherlands. While some are familiar with the RH developments in the Netherlands, many are not and are discovering the RH model through authors like Vos and those who have followed after him. The RH family tree is, therefore, broad with diverse branches and deep roots. While certain branches seem to be growing more quickly than others, the tree is a long way from dead. It is remarkably alive and teeming with new life. This can be further demonstrated by looking at other sides of the RH family tree.

The family tree of RH homiletics begins to branch out to those whom we might describe as having an interest in RH preaching and hermeneutics, but not necessarily descending directly from Vos's side of the family tree of biblical theology. Bryan Chapell, for instance, expresses dependence upon the Dutch-Reformed family tree of biblical theology in the development of his *Christ-Centered Preaching*.[56] The work of Australian Graeme Goldsworthy has done much to vitalize interest in contemporary questions related to RH preaching and hermeneutics.[57] Both Chapell's and Goldsworthy's homiletic works have gained significant attention internationally.

Finally, we should not fail to mention the very important work of Sidney Greidanus. His 1970 Th.D. dissertation *Sola Scriptura* on the RH preaching debates is almost single-handedly responsible for the broader awareness among English speakers of the RH preaching debates that took place in the Netherlands. He has subsequently published numerous books on the topic of Christ-centered preaching.[58] Although his writings have received criticism from both Dutch and English speaking advocates of RH preaching,[59] his work still retains a very significant place in discussions

---

55. Muether, *Cornelius Van Til*, 129, 172, respectively. William D Dennison's apologetic method is framed around insights from Cornelius Van Til and Geehardus Vos; W.D. Dennison, *Paul's Two-Age Construction and Apologetics*.

56. Chapell, *Christ-Centered Preaching*.

57. Among Goldsworthy's many important works, we would highlight the importance of his distinctive homiletic effort in Goldsworthy, *Preaching the Whole Bible*.

58. We will list the two works of Sidney Greidanus we think are most important: *The Modern Preacher and the Ancient Text*, and perhaps more importantly, *Preaching Christ from the Old Testament*.

59. See the early Dutch reviews of Sidney Greidanus' *Sola Scriptura* by Jonker, *Gereformeerd weekblad*, 350–1; Geertsema (with response by Greidanus), *Mededelingen van de vereniging voor calvinistische wijsbegeerte*, 7–12; Trimp, *De Reformatie*, 337–9. See

about RH preaching. Though we intend to interact with nuances of Greidanus' work at various points, we cannot overstate the importance of his
writings for the English-speaking world. Nearly every English work on RH
homiletics expresses some aspect of dependence and appreciation, whether
positive or negative, upon Greidanus' dissertation. It is a bit of an academic
concern that so many writers and preachers are effectively dependent upon
one source (Greidanus) as their primary filter for describing and understanding this important homiletic debate. We could only imagine that if
Greidanus were rewriting the book today, after years of reflection, he might
nuance certain things. We would add to this that there are certainly other
voices which would enlarge our perception of the debate, but those voices
are not heard due to language barriers. Thus, a temptation exists to see the
debate myopically or to miss certain nuances— or even worse, to create
regrettable caricatures and unnecessary dichotomies when describing RH
preaching.[60] It is hoped that this monograph, in spite of its imperfections,
might shed a little light on a few of these perceptions that shall be addressed
in subsequent chapters.

HOMILETICS IN THE CONTEXT OF OTHER
THEOLOGICAL DISCIPLINES

Homiletics is a specific theological discipline but it is not an isolated one. In
order for it to be properly approached, it must be done in cooperation with,
and submission to other theological disciplines. We have in mind here the
disciplines of exegetical theology, systematic theology, and even historical
theology. Homiletics, which is a subset of practical theology, must be seen
as a flower that grows in the field among these other disciplines. In this light,
not only can we imagine the most proper approach to homiletics, we can
also see the way in which the revival of interest in RH preaching branches

---

also C.G. Dennison, "Some thoughts on Preaching," 3–9.

60. Terry Johnson's critique seems to reflect many of the frequently expressed concerns. So he says, "The problem with the redemptive-historical extremists is three-fold.
First, the ethical thrust of the New Testament, which is not inconsiderable, disappears.
All preaching becomes about Jesus and the cross, that is, about justification by faith.
Everything else is a footnote to justification. As a consequence, preaching becomes
predictable, cliché, and boring. Flights of redemptive-historical fancy become com-
monplace, as texts are twisted to say what they do not say, forced to teach what they do
not teach, while what they do teach is lost"; Johnson, "Preaching the Point." In addition,
Timothy Bayly portrays RH preaching as being unconcerned with appeals to the heart
and treating every verse as if it were John 3:16; Bayly, "Covenant Succession and the
Emasculation of the Church," 137.

out into the other disciplines, as practical theology cannot ultimately or healthily be separated from them.

Beginning with exegetical theology, we cannot help but reiterate that the current interest in RH *homiletics* is wed to an interest in RH *hermeneutics*. But, as many have pointed out, what some call RH (or "salvation-historical"), others refer to as biblical theology.[61] Both of these terms have been used by authors with various meanings. This terminology was developed at the turn of the twentieth century in the context of difficult debates between advocates of the higher-critical approach to the Bible and its more conservative defenders. Theologians would subsequently employ the term and nuance its intended meaning. The same is true of the term "biblical theology." While Vos and many RH theologians employ the term in a particular way, there is also a large school of "biblical theologians" who employ the term quite differently from Vos.[62]

More to our point is the fact that there are numerous books (homiletic works, commentaries, monographs, etc.) that employ a hermeneutic that might be described as RH, while actually showing little, if any, familiarity with the RH preaching debates in the Netherlands. Some of them also show little to no dependence upon theologians such as Vos, Ridderbos, and Bavinck, though such dependence is likely. In certain examples, we find authors make use of theologians such as Vos only in some of their works, but then seem to perpetuate an exegetical approach that is notably consistent with the RH paradigm. We could take, for example, the recent *Reformed Expository Commentary* series. This series is self-consciously attempting to embody an RH approach to the Bible, yet is not quoting repeatedly from what we might call RH sources (certainly not Dutch ones). We note with interest this statement in the series introduction:

> . . . these commentaries are *redemptive-historical* in their orientation. We believe in the unity of the Bible and its central message of salvation in Christ. We are thus committed to a Christ-centered view of the Old Testament, in which its characters, events, regulations, and institutions are properly

61. Vos's own vocabulary makes this point; see Vos, "The Idea of Biblical Theology as a Science and Discipline," 21–22. For a review of the topic in a GKv oriented homiletic that makes the connection between Vos and "Biblical Theology," see Houtman, *This Is Your God*, 91–93.

62. For a discussion of the various uses of the "Biblical Theology" vocabulary outside of Vos, see Barr, "Definitions: The Many Faces of Biblical Theology," 1–18. Brevard Childs interestingly distinguishes the "older school" of Biblical Theology (including Vos) from the "newer school" by their method of treating history (e.g., Oscar Cullmann); Childs, "Current Models for Biblical Theology."

understood as pointing us to Christ and his gospel, as well as giving us examples to follow in living by faith.[63]

Alongside this could be placed the recent *Gospel in the Old Testament* series which is written in a Vosian trajectory, and is "committed to the proposition that the Bible, both Old and New Testaments, is a unified revelation of God, and that its thematic unity is found in Christ."[64] Something similar could be said of the prolific writings of G.K. Beale, who quotes from more recognized RH authors at times and whose writings reflect more generally obvious RH concerns. The point here is that we ought not to reduce RH hermeneutics to a short list of Dutch authors, but recognize rather that many contemporary theologians are approaching Scripture in the light of RH concerns, and that this is seen in much recent exegetical work.

We could add to this the recent discussions about the relationship between biblical and systematic theology, a discussion that also is being juxtaposed to questions about RH hermeneutics and preaching. Regarding systematic theology, we agree with Vos that, "Dogmatics is the crown which grows out of all the work that biblical theology can accomplish."[65] Without biblical theology there would not be systematic theology; or, to say it differently, it is impossible to achieve a healthy systematic theology apart from employing a biblically sound hermeneutical approach.[66] To the extent that the RH hermeneutic is biblical, it is essential for forming proper exegetical conclusions about particular texts—hence, systematic theology. We note with delight the attempts in recent decades (for instance the work of authors such as Michael Horton and Richard Gamble, etc.)[67] to consider doing systematic theology with an approach that seeks to do justice to broader understanding of RH hermeneutics (*à la* Herman Ridderbos, Vos, etc.). It is

---

63. Taken from Phillips, *Hebrews*, xii (emphasis original).

64. See the series introduction in Duguid, *Living in the Gap Between Promise and Reality*, x.

65. Vos, "The Idea of Biblical Theology as a Science and Discipline," 24.

66. John Murray, a student of Vos, attempted to synthesize Vos's biblical theology into his approach to systematic theology; see Murray, "Systematic Theology," 1–21. Richard Gaffin, following Murray, perpetuates the same motif; see Gaffin, "Systematic Theology and Biblical Theology," 32–50.

67. Richard Gamble identifies his recent three-volume systematic project as an attempt to perpetuate the RH insights and methodology of Vos, alongside the benefits of systematic and historical theology; see Gamble, *The Whole Counsel of God*, 1.xxxiii. The first volume is replete with references to Vos. Similarly, Michael Horton's recent systematic theology seeks to frame its structure around the doctrine of the covenants, and sees itself as standing in the direct shadow of Vos's RH insights; Horton, *The Christian Faith*, 27–30.

interesting that even Vos himself wrote a systematic theology.[68] While each of these authors ought to be appreciated for their unique contributions, it is undeniable that they are systematicians who employ an RH hermeneutic.

We would also mention here the important way in which systematic theology is effectively the logical conclusion of biblical theology. Consider the crucial way in which the creeds of the church help to embody the "faith once for all delivered to the saints."[69] To put it differently, the Bible does not simply commend the idea of teaching hermeneutics, but also of teaching the "sound doctrine"[70] that is derived from sound hermeneutics. It is with these thoughts in mind that we recognize the inseparable relationship of RH hermeneutics to recent work and discussions in systematic theology. The revived interest in the former has sparked important discussions about the latter. Without systematic theology, biblical theology would be a lone flower in a garden without variety, with no fence to protect it. Thus, while assessing the renewed expressions of interest in RH hermeneutics, we must also consider the way in which that discussion has been carried on in the arena of systematic theology, and the way in which systematic theology protects and supports both those who preach and those to whom they preach.[71]

THE NEWNESS OF REDEMPTIVE-HISTORICAL PREACHING

The last area we address is that of historical theology. We suggest here that the resurgence of interest in RH hermeneutics and homiletics has raised some intriguing questions from a historical theological perspective. How truly new is the RH paradigm of preaching? Can it be found with the church fathers, the Reformers, or Protestant orthodox theologians? Is the RH hermeneutic consistent with the creeds and catechisms of the church? Did Vos, Schilder, or those in their generation really introduce something "new" to the Reformed theological world? Would sermons, commentaries, or other exegetical works from these various periods reveal a similar sort of preaching paradigm? While some of these questions have been addressed, we might suggest that others warrant further investigation. Yet these questions, while very important, do not trump what must be the first question: "Is this RH preaching paradigm biblical?" Anthony Selvaggio answers this way:

68. Vos, *Dogmatiek: Vol. 1 Theologie, Anthropologie; Vol. 2 Soteriologie; Vol. 3 Christologie; Vol. 4 Ecclesiologie, Media Gratia, Eschatologie.*

69. Jude 3.

70. I Tim. 1:10; Titus 1:9; 2:1.

71. Van der Welle, "Preken. Ook voor leken?" 13.

What we now refer to as Biblical Theology or the Redemptive-Historical approach has been with the church since the dawn of the New Testament era. However, it is my contention that the controversy in the Netherlands was the genesis event for the modern development of the approach and also served to fuel the modern debate over how to preach the Old Testament in the Reformed church.[72]

We would suggest that historically speaking, it is very important to recognize that Vos was not the first one to liken the covenant promise of the Bible as a development of a seed into a flower. Schilder and Holwerda were not the first to oppose moralistic, overly subjective preaching, and Clowney was not the first to argue for preaching Christ from all of Scripture.[73] None of these theologians were Copernican revolutionaries. They were modern reformers at best.

Recent explorations in historical theology are proving that the RH preaching paradigm is better likened to a slowly growing family tree than a spontaneous big bang. Richard Barcellos puts it well, "Does Reformed Theology have to wait until Vos to find adherents to a more redemptive-historical approach to Scripture?"[74] While there are certainly varying opinions on the question of the newness of RH preaching, it is the position (and underlying assumption) of this monograph that it is not a *de novo* homiletic approach. Rather, we contend that the RH homiletic approach has a biblical foundation and historical antecedents. In saying this, we readily acknowledge the danger of anachronism, one that reads something contemporary *back* into previous documents. While that danger ought to be borne in mind, it is at the same time true and proper to admit that those who have argued for an RH approach to hermeneutics and homiletics have done so foremost from Scripture itself and secondly from the timely deposits of church history (creeds, commentaries, sermons, etc.). Additionally, historical-theological

---

72. Selvaggio, "An Answer to the Challenge of Preaching the Old Testament," 172n10.

73. Though following and building upon Clowney's work, perhaps the most thorough and persuasive defense of the contemporary expression of RH preaching from an exegetical point of view is Johnson's *Him We Proclaim*. See especially chapters 3, 6, 9, and 10. Tae-Hyeun Park's recent and impressive dissertation notes that some of the questions now being asked about Puritan preaching were sparked by similar questions that surfaced in the RH preaching debates in the Netherlands; see Park, "The Sacred Rhetoric of the Holy Spirit," esp. 9–11.

74. Barcellos, *The Family Tree of Reformed Biblical Theology*, 2. His dissertation bears out his answer to the question—no. We note with appreciation the article of John Fesko in which he demonstrates the antiquity of biblical theology; Fesko, "The Antiquity of Biblical Theology," 443–77.

investigations have demonstrated continuity between the RH sermons of
the last century and sermons from various points along the trail of church
history.[75] Awareness of this must check, if not dispel, the idea that RH
preaching is altogether *new*.

Even with these qualifications, there is no question that both advocates
and critics of RH preaching (and its twin sister, biblical theology) treat the
movement as being relatively young. In describing the preaching debates
in the Netherlands, it was and still is somewhat popular to describe the debate as beginning in a certain time-period—typically the 1930s with the
work of Klaas Schilder, *Christus in zijn lijden*.[76] For example, John Carrick
states, "The original controversy, which began in the Netherlands in 1930
with the publication of Schilder's *Trilogy*, continued into the early 1940's
and subsequently faded."[77] Carrick's perspective is not unique, as there are
certainly others who hold to this view. Sidney Greidanus, upon whom Carrick's description of the RH preaching debates in the Netherlands is im-
mensely dependent, makes a similar observation. Greidanus also describes
the inception of the debate as occurring in the 1930s.[78] According to Greidanus, "Schilder might be called the initiator of the redemptive-historical
approach."[79] Huijser, a critic of Schilder and the RH approach, called Schilder in 1950 the "auctor intellectualis" (intellectual author) and the "Urhe-
ber" (spiritual father) of this "*novelty in Reformed homiletics.*"[80]

Still, this point of view is not so simple. Many in the GKv tradition
would see the historical description in a similar light but would nuance it.
Trimp, for instance, notes that it is particularly with the work of B. Holwerda in 1940 and 1942 respectively that the debate takes on a more formal
character. It is in his article "De Heilshistorie in de Prediking" that Holwerda introduces the term "*exemplarische*" (exemplaristic).[81] This term would
prove to have far-reaching significance, as it labeled the preaching method
that would be contrasted with RH preaching. Yet in the very article in which

---

75. Hyun, *Redemptive-Historical Hermeneutics and Homiletics*, 34–43. For a short
treatment of the subject as it relates to Luther and Calvin, see Bos, *We Have Heard
that God Is With Us*, 120–6. Greidanus offers two lengthy, balanced chapters on "The
History of Preaching Christ From the Old Testament" in *Preaching Christ From the Old
Testament*, 69–176.

76. Schilder, *Christus in zijn lijden* (3 vols.); published in English as *Christ and His
Sufferings*.

77. Carrick, *The Imperative of Preaching*, 114.

78. Greidanus, *Sola Scriptura*, 1.

79. Ibid., 40.

80. Ibid., 40 (emphasis added).

81. Holwerda, "De heilshistorie in de prediking," especially 82.

we find the so-called genesis of the terminology that ignites the RH preaching debate, Holwerda himself grounds the discussion in developments that go back to the first part of the twentieth century, citing in particular an article of J. Ridderbos that appeared in 1922, and referencing issues that were clearly at play well before the 1930s.

Trimp also argues that prior to the RH preaching debate that began in the 1930s, many of the concerns that became associated with the RH debate had been discussed in preceding centuries.[82] He discusses the development of these ideas as they relate to homiletics in Luther and Calvin. Regarding the former he notes, "Luther spoke of a direct presentation of Christ and Christian doctrine in the Old Testament stories."[83] Trimp does not anachronistically suggest that Luther was an RH preacher. He also does not in any way deny Luther's use of *exemplum* as a category of application in preaching. Yet Trimp notes that while Luther (as also Calvin) sought to distance himself from the allegorical method, at the same time Luther also employed an approach to the Old Testament that was, generally speaking, Christocentric.[84] This approach to the Old Testament lies at the heart of the RH preaching debate.

Trimp's point about a Christocentric hermeneutic in the time of the Reformation is upheld by numerous authors, not only in connection narrowly with the RH preaching debates, but especially within the family tree of biblical theology. John Fesko, for instance, notes the way in which the early Reformers (i.e. Luther and Calvin) contain Christocentric nuances that ought to be seen in the long line of hermeneutical and homiletical concern that come to clearer expression in later centuries.[85] Fesko traces this line backwards to the early church, including fathers such as Irenaeus.[86] He also traces the work into the post-Reformation developments in covenant theology. His survey makes the point that while there is something *new* about biblical theology and the RH preaching paradigm; at the same time, there is much about it that is remarkably *old*. The long timeline of church history displays this development. Even such a strong advocate of the RH

---

82. Trimp, *Preaching and the History of Salvation*, 101.

83. Ibid., 110.

84. Childs, *Biblical Theology of the Old and New Testaments*, 45. Daniel Doriani notes that, "Since Luther, Protestant theologians have been wary of the 'imitation of Christ' motif." He suggests this is due to its association with not only sentimental and subjective interpretations, but also, more importantly, the concern for "works-righteousness" oriented preaching; Doriani, *Putting the Truth to Work*, 201.

85. Fesko, "The Antiquity of Biblical Theology," 464.

86. See also J.T. Dennison Jr., "Irenaeus and Redemptive History," 67–72; see also Childs, *Biblical Theology*, 30–33.

paradigm as Geerhardus Vos forces us to live with the reality that covenant theology is not born in a moment but develops slowly and organically in the theological and pastoral family tree of church history.[87] Should not the same be said of RH preaching?

Vos notes the relative newness of the discipline of biblical theology by referring to the "birth" of biblical theology that took place under the dark star of higher critical scholarship.[88] Vos's interaction with this school, and especially its strong anchor in Germany, reminds us in some ways of the early work and concerns of Klaas Schilder. George Harinck notes that on the one occasion when Schilder was able to meet Vos, Schilder expressed great interest in Vos's work on the history of covenant theology. "Well now, I have seen him; the author of this remarkable brochure about the covenant concept in the older reformed [theologians]."[89] Schilder then reflects on their discussion about the article and issues in covenant theology. It is easy to appreciate the ways in which Schilder might have found a friend in Vos. One cannot help but note the irony of the two supposed "fathers" of the RH paradigm sitting in the same room, neither truly aware of the legacy they would leave behind. Vos, like Schilder, was not simply an exegete, but also an apologist for orthodox, Protestant theology. Much of their writings was effectively in response to the attacks of higher criticism, which seemed on the one hand to recognize the historical continuity of the Bible's theological narrative, but on the other hand sought to dismiss it out of hand on the basis of higher-critical assumptions and exegesis. To these challenges Vos and Schilder responded with a covenant theology that was rigorously exegetical and *historically* self-conscious.[90]

Vos's most unambiguous historical piece, "The Doctrine of the Covenant in Reformed Theology," is a sweeping overview of the development of covenant theology from the time of the early Reformers into the period

87. Vos, "The Doctrine of the Covenant in Reformed Theology," 234–67. Vos uses "organic" language throughout to describe the slowly developing nuances of covenant theology within the Reformed tradition. One cannot help but hear an echo of the way in which Vos also describes the "organic" development of covenant theology within Scripture itself.

88. For a recent survey of the development of biblical theology, including Vos's role, see Bray, "Biblical Theology and From Where It Came," 194–208.

89. Harinck and Van Omme, "Schilders Amerikaanse reis van 1939," 298 (trans. mine). Schilder is referring to Vos's "De verbondsleer in de gereformeerde theologie" (="The Doctrine of the Covenant in Reformed Theology").

90. We would not imply by this that there were no distinctions between their covenant theologies. There certainly were, perhaps beginning with the issue of the covenant of works. For an interesting yet critical analysis of Vos's understanding of covenant and election by someone in the GKv tradition, see Faber, *American Secession Theologians on Covenant and Baptism*, 15–54.

of Protestant Scholasticism. While Vos does not identify the various theologians as being RH or biblical theological authors, he does note the long and nuanced approach to covenant theology that sought to harmonize both the unity and diversity of the Bible's covenant theology. Vos's article might be described as his attempt to sketch the family tree of Reformed, covenant theology, and to implicitly demonstrate the way in which his own covenant theology stood in the shadow of the countless giants that came before him.[91] The higher critical school of thought wrongly divided the Bible into an overly fragmented collection of books rather than seeing it as a single, unified, and harmonious book (made up of many books) that ultimately tells one story of the promise-making, covenant-keeping God of the Bible and his singular plan to bring his kingdom climactically into the world through the life, death, and resurrection of his Son. Thus, the family tree of Reformed, covenantal theology is composed of time-tested branches and tender new shoots. The RH paradigm needs to be seen as a branch upon this family tree, not as a rogue offshoot, but an organic development within a movement nourished by various soils, and refined by its interactions with higher-criticism, dispensationalism, and now postmodernism (which we will more fully address in chapter 6).

SUMMARY: THE DISCUSSION CONTINUES

In this chapter we have tried to demonstrate that while interest in RH preaching has waxed and waned in ecclesiastical circles in the Netherlands, it is actively growing in other places around the world in various ways.[92] Renewed interest in stalwart theologians such as Bavinck, Kuyper and Vos has promoted research into the RH hermeneutical paradigm, and its homiletic counterpart. At the more popular level, the works of well-known authors such as Tim Keller and Bryan Chapell have generated an interest in a Christ-centered approach to preaching that has clear family ties to the RH preaching paradigm that came out of the GKv. In this light, we agree with James Eglinton: "Without Vos the preaching of Bryan Chapell or Tim Keller is hard to imagine. Foreigners that seek a Christocentric, biblical hermeneutic and homiletic often end up with the Dutch tradition by way of Vos."[93]

---

91. Might Schilder have been interested in finding the same in Vos's article?

92. Hyun has ably demonstrated the significant influence of RH hermeneutics in Korea; Hyun, *Redemptive-Historical Hermeneutics and Homiletics*, 26.

93. Eglinton, "Schilder als exportproduct," 189 (trans. mine).

While the work of Klaas Schilder is perhaps the best known of the GKv theologians,[94] it is still likely that many who are discovering RH preaching through the more popular academic trails[95] are doing so without significant knowledge of the RH developments in the GKv. Thus, there is a regrettable sense, especially as it relates to the science of homiletics, that many of the same issues are being revisited in virtual ignorance of the groundwork that has already been laid. To say it differently, much of the homiletic material being currently produced on preaching from the Old Testament (especially that which addresses issues of preaching Christ from the Old Testament and the question of application in preaching) is effectively creating or *recreating* the wheel of the RH preaching debate that took place in the Netherlands.

It is in light of these things that we can say that the drama of RH preaching continues. In both theologically Reformed circles and broadly evangelical circles, questions about preaching Christ from all of Scripture, and the issue of proper *application* in preaching, seem to be raising the level of interest in RH preaching both directly and indirectly. Finally, the particular challenge of postmodernism has caused the church to wrestle not only with preaching paradigms of the past, but also with the question of developing preaching paradigms that will prove useful in the future. It is at this point that we shall introduce our proposal of a homiletic paradigm that weds what we think is the best fruit of RH preaching with one of its distant cousins—the drama of redemption paradigm.

94. We should not fail to recognize the important contributions of theologians such as J. Douma, J. Van Bruggen, and S.G. de Graaf (who never joined the GKv), whose works have been translated into English; yet these authors appear to be somewhat less known than Schilder.

95. We have in mind here particular groups such as The Gospel Coalition and its recent interest in Christ-centered preaching.

2

The Drama of Redemption and Redemptive-Historical Preaching

IN THE PREVIOUS CHAPTER we surveyed a number of examples that demonstrate a revival of interest in RH preaching and subjects related to it. In this chapter we elaborate that idea more fully by developing a hermeneutical and theological approach that we believe is compatible with RH preaching and, when combined with it, has remarkable potential to serve the church homiletically. The paradigm we wish to develop is the *Drama of Redemption* (DR). It should be clarified at the outset that this paradigm is not our creation, but rather one that we are attempting to *synthesize* with RH preaching. What is suggestively new or creative about this chapter (and this monograph) is the attempt to self-consciously wed the RH and DR paradigms into a creative and effective homiletic model in a postmodern age. In order to accomplish this, we shall begin by defining the DR paradigm according to some of its leading advocates. Second, we shall discuss the biblical use of the drama metaphor. Third, the historical development of the paradigm is sketched. Fourth, we discuss the application of the paradigm within the field of homiletics. Finally, we will suggest several cautions concerning the DR paradigm in particular.

Numerous authors have advocated language that fits into the DR paradigm, yet for our purposes we will be interacting significantly with the work of Kevin Vanhoozer and Michael Horton as leading contemporary representatives of the paradigm. Each of these authors has earned a respectable reputation in the academic world, both inside and outside their own ecclesiastical and theological contexts, and thus serve as helpful conversation partners. While their writings build upon the work of others, we find certain nuances in these two authors that we believe will prove to be particularly insightful contributions for the field of homiletics. Though we do not intend to look at Vanhoozer and Horton in isolation from others who are advocating a similar theological and rhetorical paradigm, we do want to highlight their particular influence upon the orientation of this and subsequent chapters.

DEFINING THE DRAMA OF REDEMPTION

The DR paradigm may be defined as a hermeneutical and theological metaphor in which the Triune God is the author of the Spirit-directed script (Scripture) as well as its primary actor in Christ, who authoritatively calls man to creative yet faithful participation (covenant obedience) in the historically unfolding kingdom of God upon the world stage of God's glory. It is important to highlight that in our adoption of the DR metaphor, it is exactly that—a metaphor that we find helpful for a number of reasons; but not a triumphant metaphor, or even *the* dominant biblical metaphor. The Bible employs many metaphors to be sure, and while we find a particular benefit to the drama metaphor both theologically and homiletically, its importance should not be overstated.

The above definition needs to be illustrated and unpacked in several ways. First, the rhetorical value of the phrase "drama of redemption" has surfaced in numerous theological monographs as a helpful means of wedding orthodoxy and orthopraxy. Michael Horton uses the DR vocabulary throughout his *A Better Way: Rediscovering the Drama of God-Centered Worship*,[1] as well as in his more academic *Covenant and Eschatology: The Divine Drama*. The former is an argument for seeing worship through the lens of covenant theology. The second book is part of a four-volume series in which the drama metaphor is frequently employed as an innovative way of thinking about Christology, soteriology, ecclesiology, and eschatology. Commenting on the four-volume project as a whole in the last book of the series, *People and Place*, Horton helpfully notes, "Further, this project has consistently defended an analogical account of the theological statements, appealing to the metaphor of drama to express the dynamic interplay between eschatology and history in the diverse covenantal administrations."[2]

---

1. Horton, *A Better Way*; see also his *Christless Christianity*, 25, 55, 147.

2. Horton, *People and Place*, ix; for additional references to the drama metaphor, see esp. 40 and 98.

In the introduction ("The Dogma is the Drama: A Theology for Pilgrims on the Way") to his systematic theology, Horton summarizes the importance of the drama vocabulary for his emphasis on a practical approach to theology by saying, "The inextricable connection of faith and practice in terms of drama, doctrine, doxology, and discipleship has evident corollaries in every philosophy, religion, and culture. The drama determines the big questions as well as the answers. The doctrines are convictions that arise in light of that drama."[3] Drama vocabulary peppers the work throughout, thus wedding theology, faith, and practice. The same could be said of his more popular *Pilgrim Theology*, which appears to be based on his larger volume, *The Christian Faith*. Drama language permeates *Pilgrim Theology*, including a fairly programmatic definition of theology: "Theology is the *lived*, social, and *embodied* integration of drama, doctrine, doxology, and discipleship."[4] Of key interest for us is the way in which Christ coming into the world to accomplish redemption and bring about the reality of his kingdom is viewed as the pinnacle of the biblical drama; underscored is the fact that this drama is something in which the church plays a vital part, and is not merely a passive spectator.[5]

In a book dedicated to the question of moving beyond the Bible to theology, Kevin Vanhoozer introduces the DR paradigm this way: "Going beyond the Bible biblically is ultimately a matter of participating in the great *drama of redemption* of which Scripture is the authoritative testimony and holy script."[6] For Vanhoozer, the DR language is derived from, if not effectively equal to, "canonical-linguistic theology."[7] This phrase is important to Vanhoozer's overall project, as it suggests that the canon of Scripture is both normative and thus determinative for the Christian life and worldview (in contrast to the cultural-linguistic emphasis of postmodernism). Thus, Vanhoozer proposes, "The burden of the present work is to commend the canonical-linguistic approach to theologians for its turn to practice, for

---

3. Horton, *The Christian Faith*, 15.

4. Horton, *Pilgrim Theology*, 70 (emphasis added).

5. Ibid., 18. See also the appendix, "From Drama to Discipleship: Applying the Coordinates to Key Doctrines," 474–8.

6. Vanhoozer, "A Drama of Redemption Model," 156–7 (emphasis added).

7. This appears to be a pun, offering an alternative to the "cultural-linguistic" theological paradigm found in the writings of George Lindbeck and postmodern hermeneutics. Embedded within the "canonical-linguistic" is the idea of reading the Bible as one book with a unified story full of linguistic nuances. "At the heart of the canonical-linguistic approach is the proposal that we come to know God by attending to the uses to which language of God is put in Scripture itself. Scripture's own use of Scripture is of particular interest, for the cradle of Christian theology is perhaps best located in the interpretive practice of Jesus and the apostles"; Vanhoozer, *The Drama of Doctrine*, 22.

its emphasis on wisdom, and for its creative retrieval of the principle *sola scriptura*."[8] Further combining the normative role of Scripture with the idea of participation, he says, "Canonical-linguistic theology gives scriptural direction for one's fitting participation in the drama of redemption today."[9] Regarding the particular accent of a *lived* theology, Vanhoozer states, "The drama of doctrine is about refining the dross of textual knowledge into the gold of Christian wisdom by putting one's understanding of the Scriptures into practice . . . The proper end of the drama of doctrine is wisdom: lived knowledge, a performance of the truth."[10] Vanhoozer's approach to theology is not simply one of conveying theological propositions, but communicating theology in the same dramatic sense in which it was first revealed (the drama of Scripture). Thus, in addition to conveying truth, Vanhoozer wants to incorporate the idea of "participation" in his theological endeavor, underscoring that Scripture was given to elicit a certain response from its recipients. Therefore, the theological enterprise must unite, rather than divide, orthodoxy and orthopraxy.

The above emphasis may help to explain the importance of the term "drama" over other similar terms (e.g. story, narrative, etc.). Vanhoozer's preference for the term is due to several reasons. The first is that a drama, in contrast to a story, is seen and not just heard. "While it is true that much of the Bible is written in the form of a story, narratives and dramas represent stories differently. Narratives require narrators and recount their tales in the first or third person. Dramas, by contrast, show rather than tell."[11] The ability to see or show is very important in this discussion, as the DR paradigm builds upon the presupposition that God has both spoken and acted in history.[12] Theology, therefore, must not remain isolated or abstracted; it is meant to be seen and lived-out practically in the life of the church and the world.[13] Vanhoozer refers often to a perceived weakness in epic (propositional) approaches to theology. In his words, "The main problem with epic theology, then, is that it opts out of the drama altogether and takes an

8. Ibid., 16.

9. Ibid., 22.

10. Ibid., 22.

11. Ibid., 48.

12. D.A. Carson rightly notes that this is the necessary foundation of biblical interpretation. Carson also admits that while this reasoning is somewhat circular, it is impossible for hermeneutics to be presupposition-less; see Carson, *Collected Writings on Scripture*, 21, 36.

13. De Graaf wrestles with this tension, suggesting that the Biblical story ought to be told in a way that draws people into the story, yet he also argues against dramatizing the story; De Graaf, *Verbondsgeschiedenis*, 1.

external, spectator's perspective upon the contemplated play."[14] In this sense the story of theology is told, but not lived. Vanhoozer is clearly reacting to this type of theological approach, especially in his *The Drama of Doctrine*.

It is thus important to recognize that the DR paradigm is developed against the background of epic approaches to theology which tend to be more abstract or propositional in nature. We would express caution here, however, lest this concern be misrepresented. Vanhoozer is not suggesting the DR paradigm is a move against or away from propositions or propositional theology (neither are we), but rather a move *beyond* mere propositions to a theological approach that is wed to living out theology.[15] "The Bible is not reducible to abstract *scientia*, but must always be seen as *sapientia*—wisdom to be lived."[16] It is the *abstracting* of doctrine that concerns Vanhoozer, and which the DR paradigm seeks to redress. The truth of Christianity was not meant simply to be believed, but rather "felt, done, and loved."[17]

An analogy can be seen between propositional theology and epic approaches to literature, movies, etc. Each preserves the ability for the reader/viewer to remain at a safe distance from the story. They are spectators, passively witnessing the story as it is told or unfolded before them. Even a dramatic play has this potential. But the particular type of drama we are advocating in the DR paradigm is an *interactive drama* in which the audience does not simply witness the drama, but also participates within it. The drama of the Bible is a story to be joined, not simply described or summarized by abstract propositions that keep its readers at a safe, unaffected distance. Thus, the DR approach to theology is concerned not simply to state theology in propositional form, but to show the church how to live out its theology, thus narrowing the divide between practical and theoretical theology.[18]

This concern to see a move in theology from the bare communication of systematic propositions to lived-out appropriations is shared and echoed in defining statements by other advocates of the DR paradigm. Horton employs the term in a similar definition to Vanhoozer, saying, "Theology is the church's reflection on God's performative action in word and deed and its

---

14. Ibid., 86.

15. Cf. Jensen, Review of *The Drama of Doctrine*, 297.

16. Ibid., 276.

17. Ibid., 288.

18. C.J. de Ruijter notes the regrettable distance between these two theological poles; De Ruijter, *Meewerken met God*, 11. We should also observe that older theological works like Calvin's *Institutes* and Bavinck's *Dogmatics* certainly bear a warm and "practical" tone, insisting upon and embodying both orthodoxy and orthopraxy; Gleason, *Herman Bavinck*, 469.

own participation in the *drama of redemption*."[19] We note again the importance of the term "participation." While the church is clearly to reflect on the words and works that God has done in history, it is not enough to stop there. The task of theology is not completed when it has simply described God, or even the manner in which God has entered into history creatively and redemptively; it is completed when it calls the church into a proper relationship with God that includes living out the intended consequences of what God has revealed in his biblical script. Theology is thus inherently *practical*. To the extent that theology is consistent with the Bible, it must constantly remember that it was always given in the context of God's covenantal dealing with man. On this we quote Vos at length:

> The historical character of revelation may be found in its *eminently practical aspect*. The knowledge of God communicated by it is nowhere for purely intellectual purposes. From beginning to end it is knowledge intended to enter into the actual life of man, to be worked out by him in all its practical bearing . . . God has not revealed himself in a school, but in the covenant; and the covenant as a communion of life is all-comprehensive, embracing all the conditions and interests of those contracting it.[20]

Thus, a significant contribution of the DR paradigm is to further demonstrate within the context of a theological methodology that Scripture cannot be simply categorized or cauterized. Rather, it was intended to play a vital role in shaping the way in which people not only believe in God, but also obey God in a vital relationship.[21]

In this context, we find Vanhoozer's "post-propositional" approach to be a fairly provocative, yet innovative theological method that wishes to resist the temptation to reduce the church's theological approach to the Bible to that of mere information gathering and dissemination. The drama metaphor is employed in a way that attempts to guard both the divine and human role in the development and appropriation of theology. The language of "participation" is key, but it is not intended to suggest that human participation in the divine drama in any way upstages the primacy of God's speaking and acting. To put it differently, what is suggested here is that the Bible reveals a divinely inspired drama in which the canon of Scripture is

19. Horton, *Covenant and Eschatology*, 276 (emphasis added).

20. Vos, "The Idea of Biblical Theology as a Science and Discipline," 10 (emphasis added).

21. This is well-captured in the language of WSC 3. Q. "What do the Scriptures principally teach?" A. "The Scriptures principally teach what man is to believe concerning God and what duty God requires of man."

the governing script of the dynamic relationship between God and humanity. The biblical drama, as with theology, begins with God and not with man. It is a drama that is first conceived in the mind of God, yet historically speaking, begins at creation and ends at the consummation of the ages.[22] It has a particular climax in view—the coming of God in Christ in the fullness of time[23] to play his part in the drama of redemption by fulfilling in both word and deed all that is necessary for the salvation of his people, and to also draw them into a renewed story of life that repairs their sin-stained, misguided stories of death.

It is here that the DR paradigm proves to be uniquely compatible with the RH approach to Scripture. In our view it is both important and helpful to view the Bible as revealing one large unfolding drama, with God's own words and deeds framing both the beginning and the end of the story.[24] As Horton puts it, "Like a good play, Scripture possesses a single, unified meaning."[25] God's plan to bring Christ into the world in the fullness of time is the over-arching metanarrative that shapes the micro-narratives of the Old and New Testaments. It is a promise that begins in Genesis 3:15 with the *protoeuangelion*, finds its preliminary fulfillment in the death and resurrection of Christ, and is ultimately consummated in the eternal kingdom. Yet all along the way, God is speaking and acting the promises into fulfillment. He continues this ministry of speaking and acting in the fullest sense in the incarnation when the Word is made flesh.[26] Vanhoozer highlights the way in which Christ becoming incarnate is the garb he dons for his main performance in history.[27] The church is now clothed in the righteousness of Christ, having put off its garments of sin and shame.[28] It is called to continually put on Christ and, being dressed in him, will continue to perform the Spirit-inspired script in the world until the curtain closes at the consummation of the ages and we are climactically clothed in righteousness.[29] This dramatic summary of the history of redemption is well captured in the words of Michael Williams:

22. Vanhoozer recognizes this as a common denominator among "narrative-of-redemption" approaches; Vanhoozer, "A Drama of Redemption Model," 158.

23. Gal 4:4.

24. See G.K. Beale's helpful chapter "The Redemptive-Historical Storyline of the Old Testament" in *A New Testament Biblical Theology*, esp. 29–30; see also his summary of the storylines of the Old and New Testaments, 166–8.

25. Horton, *Covenant and Eschatology*, 171.

26. John 1:14.

27. Cf. Phil 2:5–8.

28. Col 3:9–14.

29. 2 Cor 5:4.

There is far more to doctrine than simply a propositional content. There is instruction for the acting out of the will and purpose of God as the church lives in the light of *the already* of the
biblical drama of Israel, Jesus, and the birth of the early church,
and *the not yet* of the return of Christ and the coming of the
heavenly Jerusalem to earth.[30]

In Vanhoozer's words, "The drama of redemption ends, as with most comedies, with everyone on stage at a wedding banquet."[31]

Such a comprehensive view of the Bible accounts for both the unity
and diversity of the books of the Bible, as well as the various literary genres
that comprise it. This emphasis within the DR paradigm (and the overlapping idea of "canonical-linguistic" theology) is what lies at the heart of the
RH hermeneutic, as it seeks to do justice to the covenantal unity of Scripture
that culminates in the person and work of Christ. At the same time, the
RH model recognizes *the importance of history*, and thus does not view the
entire Bible as revealing the same thing in the same way. Rather, the Bible
is a progressively unfolding message that displays unity on the one hand,
and dramatic development on the other. Both the DR and RH paradigms
seem concerned with this sensitivity to an over-arching metanarrative (a
redemptive, covenantal drama), while recognizing the way in which the biblical story slowly, progressively develops like scenes in a play. While the two
paradigms are distinct from one another, they seem to share overlapping
concerns, or common DNA.

THE DRAMA OF SCRIPTURE

In this section we would like to develop the idea that viewing the content
of Scripture through the lens of drama comports well with the content of
Scripture in a variety of ways. We do not intend to suggest by this that Scripture explicitly employs the drama metaphor, but rather that the metaphor
seems to do justice to various nuances of Scripture. Numerous authors have
attempted to summarize the over-arching content of Scripture as being
something like a redemptive drama. N. T. Wright likens the entire Bible to
a five-act play or drama.[32] The five acts according to Wright are as follows:

30. Williams, "Theology as Witness," 16.

31. Vanhoozer, *The Drama of Doctrine*, 457.

32. Wright, "How Can the Bible Be Authoritative?" 11. Wright's use of the drama
metaphor is in many ways helpful and illuminating. But to the extent that he uses it to
address the question of the Bible's authority, we find this article vaguely disappointing,
in that it seems to reduce the authority of the Bible to the authority of a play in which

Act 1 Creation

Act 2 Fall

Act 3 Israel

Act 4 Jesus

Act 5 Church age

In many respects, Wright's proposal has served as a reference point for others who have reflected on similar ideas. Other stratifications of the same paradigm have been offered, and Wright's proposal, though helpful, has been justifiably critiqued. Wells, for instance, sees a weakness in Wright's suggestion that the church age is the last act and argues instead for the eschaton as the final act.[33] Wells' suggestion would thus imply six acts in contrast to Wright's five, as follows:

Act 1 Creation

Act 2 Fall

Act 3 Israel

Act 4 Jesus

Act 5 Church age

Act 6 Eschaton

Stephen Nichols proposes a more simple dramatic structure:[34]

Act 1 Creation

Act 2 Fall

Act 3 Redemption

Act 4 Restoration

By contrast, Bartholomew and Goheen amplify, rather than shorten, Wright's model by adding to and nuancing it, even beyond that of Wells.[35] Their proposal is as follows:

Act 1 God Establishes his Kingdom: Creation

Act 2 Rebellion in the Kingdom: Fall

Act 3 The King Chooses Israel: Redemption Initiated

　　Scene 1 A People for the King

---

we are "invited" to participate.

33. Wells, *Improvisation*, 52.

34. Nichols, *Welcome to the Story*, 26–28.

35. Bartholomew and Goheen, *The Drama of Scripture*, 26–27.

Scene 2 A Land for His People

Interlude A Kingdom Story Waiting for an Ending: The Intertesta-mental Period

Act 4 The Coming of the King: Redemption Accomplished

Act 5 Spreading the News of the King: The Mission of the Church

Scene 1 From Jerusalem to Rome

Scene 2 And into All the World

Act 6 The Return of the King: Redemption Completed

The nuances contributed by Wells, and especially by Bartholomew and Go-heen are important, in that they account for the eschaton as an extension of the Bible's redemptive drama.[36] They also attempt to draw more attention to the greater complexity of the various biblical epochs. Thus it would seem that the six-act paradigm does greater justice to the whole of the biblical story over against the four and five-act proposals. As was noted earlier by Vos and others, the Bible is not only "full of dramatic interest," it is also eschatologically oriented, concluding with a consummate "And they lived happily ever after." Thus, any stratification of acts that does not account for the eschaton would appear deficient.

On the other side of history (the inception of the drama at creation), it is important to note that the drama of the Bible does not ultimately begin simply with creation, but with the intra-Trinitarian plan of God to accomplish all the things that happen in history. This pre-creation dynamic is often referred to as the *pactum salutis* (covenant of redemption), and has been argued for and against by theologians from varying angles.[37] Regarding this idea of a stage-setting plan within the Trinity, Köstenberger and Swain suggest, "The *pactum salutis* teaches us that the story which unfolds on the stage of history is the story of an intra-Trinitarian fellowship of salvation, a fellowship that reaches back 'before the world began' (John 17:5) and

36. Bartholomew and Goheen also note that Richard Middleton and Brian Walsh were the first to add a sixth act to N.T. Wright's five act analogy; cf. Middleton and Walsh, *Truth is Stranger Than It Used to Be*, 182, 215.

37. For an excellent introduction to the idea of the covenant of redemption, see VanDrunen and Clark, "The Covenant Before the Covenants," 167–96. Vos outlines the development of the *pactum salutis* in "The Doctrine of the Covenant in Reformed Theology," 245–53. Others have expressed reluctance to referring to an intra-Trinitarian covenant per se. Karl Barth, for instance, rejected the idea on the basis that it created a dualism of wills within the Trinity; Barth, *Church Dogmatics IV*, 65–66. For a thorough interaction with various reservations about the idea of a *pactum salutis*, see Loonstra, "Verkiezing-Verzoening-Verbond," esp. chapters 5, 12.

that continues even to 'the hour' of Jesus' cross, resurrection and ascension (John 17:1)."[38]

If the idea the intra-Trinitarian plan rightly serves is that which occurs before the curtain of history rises, it might be suggested that the Bible's dramatic structure is as follows:

*Before the Curtain Rises: Trinitarian Plot and Casting of Characters

Act 1 Creation

    Scene 1 Creation in General

    Scene 2 The Creation of Man in Detail

Act 2 Life in Paradise to Paradise Lost

    Scene 1 Before the Fall

    Scene 2 After the Fall

Act 3 From Patriarchs to the Exodus

Act 4 Life in the Land to the Loss of the Land

    Scene 1 Conquest and Dominion

    Scene 2 Covenant Failure and Expulsion

*Interlude: Stage-Setting During the Intertestamental Period

Act 5 Jesus: the *Denouement* of History

    Scene 1 Birth to Baptism

    Scene 2 Baptism to Cross

    Scene 3 Resurrection to Ascension

Act 6 Church Age

    Scene 1 From Jerusalem to Rome

    Scene 2 From Rome to the Ends of the World

Act 7 The Eschaton

    Scene 1 The Return of the King

    Scene 2 Victory and Final Judgment

*Standing Ovation: The Eternal Celebration of the Glorified King and His Kingdom

This proposed stratification is simply a creative suggestion for applying the drama metaphor to the major epochs of Scripture. We would highlight again that while the drama metaphor is only that—a metaphor—the scenes

38. Köstenberger and Swain, *Father, Son and Spirit*, 170.

of the biblical drama unfold on various stages, each of which occurs in particular historical contexts. Related to this, each covenantal administration that occurs in history (and thus each scene within the drama of redemption) is effectively an outworking of the covenant that occurs "before the curtain rises" in the eternal plan of the Triune God.[39] This is true not simply from the perspective of God's ordaining all things that come to pass,[40] but in particular of the work of Christ that is described as fulfilling all that the Father sent him to do.[41]

In addition, to the extent that drama is both speaking and acting for the purpose of displaying the realities of life, an analogy can be seen in the word and deed nature of biblical revelation. The Bible clearly depicts God as both speaking and acting. As noted previously, God's speaking and acting are the very foundation of revelation itself. Creation is capable of being described in dramatic terms as it is brought about by God's speech-acts, and all of creation continues to testify to its subordinate role to the one whose glory is revealed in every dramatic detail.[42] In addition, Adam was created in the *imago Dei* in such a way that we might appropriately say that all that he was created to do was to be a spirited, creative mimicking of God's knowledge, righteousness, holiness, and dominion over the creatures.[43] After the fall, a heroic drama ensues in which God reveals himself as the divine rescuer, who enters upon the stage of redemptive history to speak and act on behalf of his people. What God does in the history of Israel is nothing less than a display of his power and glory, not only before his people Israel, but also before his enemies. This display is but a preview of the coming of God in Christ Jesus, the epicenter of redemptive history.[44]

It is in the coming of Christ that we find the drama of God's redemption reaching its climactic expression.[45] God comes, clothed in the frail garments of humanity,[46] intent upon perfectly performing every word of

39. Horton, *Covenant and Eschatology*, 13. Cf. Heb 13:20.

40. Eph 1:11; WSC 7.

41. John 17:3; Heb 10:5–10.

42. Ps 19 makes us think along these lines.

43. WSC 10.

44. N.T. Wright sees this as the heart of Christ's prophetic ministry—retelling the story of Israel with himself at its center; Wright, *Jesus and the Victory of God*, 199. We shall address the topic of typology in a subsequent section.

45. Sayers, *Creed or Chaos?*, 5.

46. We do not mean in any way to imply a docetic view of the incarnation. Christ was, we believe, fully God and fully man, yet without sin. Still, in the incarnation the eternal Word *became* flesh. As Vanhoozer notes, "The Son is the principal actor: God became fully man, and hence historical, on the world stage"; Vanhoozer, *The Drama of*

God's inspired script (the law) and enduring the fullness of the wages of our sin—the tragic death of a martyr. As Ryken has pointed out, the gospel may be compared to a U-shaped comedy, in which the narrative moves through various, successive stages, the mission itself seeming at a moment to be severely threatened, if not thwarted, by the death of Christ.[47] Yet God, in his irrepressible power, overcomes his and his people's enemy through his triumph over death itself in the resurrection. The U is completed as he who has come from the eternal glory of his Father in heaven returns there, and does so climactically with his rescued bride at his side, there to join him in the eternal bliss of life in communion with the triune God.[48]

In this context, it is provocative to think about the ministry of Jesus and his relationship to the Old Testament. Jesus appears to fulfill his ministry in fairly dramatic ways, even if his actions do not constitute drama in the technical sense. The signs that he performed were often done as a means to synthesize the relationship between the words and works of God. So, for instance, in John 6 Jesus not only proclaims the "bread of life" message, he also dramatically provides bread for the people, and refers to himself as the "true bread" that has come down from heaven. Vos has rightly pointed out that often, when Jesus uses the adjective "true" (ἀληθινόν), as in John 6:32, Jesus is not contrasting that which is true with that which is false, but is rather contrasting that which is true with that which was temporary, typological, and provisional.[49] God had given the people bread to eat in the wilderness. It was not false bread, but bread that symbolized the coming of the one who would enter the world and offer his body and blood for the life of his people. Jesus is that true bread, and thus his body is "true food" and his blood "true drink" (John 6:55).

Jesus also spoke in parables. Parables, unlike other forms of teaching, make a point by telling a story into which the reader or listener is called to imaginatively participate. Kenneth Bailey makes the point well in saying, "A Parable is not a delivery system for an idea. It is not like a shell casing that can be discarded once the idea (the shell) is fired. Rather, a parable is a house in which the reader or listener is invited to take up residence. The reader is encouraged to look out on the world from the point of view of the story."[50] The stories Jesus told, whether actual or parabolic, were always designed to draw the listener *into* the drama of the story as an empathiz-

---

Doctrine, 106.

47. Ryken, Wilhoit, and Longman III, "Comedy as Plot Motif," 160–1.

48. Reeves, *Delighting in the Trinity*, 94.

49. Vos, "'True' and 'Truth' in the Gospel of John," esp. 345–7.

50. Bailey, *The Cross and the Prodigal*, 87.

ing participant. The story became not simply *a* story but *their* story. In this respect, Jesus continues the long line of Old Testament revelation that often invoked dramatic actions of word and deed as a means of cultivating a sense of continuity between the past and the present participants—they were a part of the same story. This idea could be illustrated from a number of Old Testament rituals.

Circumcision was not simply a sign of the covenant in a general sense, but a perpetual reminder that God had made a covenant promise to Abraham *and to his descendants* (Gen 17:7). Two chapters earlier God both made and confirmed promises to Abraham through what he said and by his passing through the animals that were symbolically torn in half. The fact that God passed through the animals rather than Abraham signified that it would ultimately be God himself (not Abraham) who would lay down his life for the satisfaction of the covenant promise. Word and deed were dramatically bound to one another and reinforced one another. What the word said, the sign showed.[51] Thus, God "swore by himself" (Heb 6:13) and confirmed the promise to Abraham and his children by oath. The rite of circumcision created trans-generational continuity within the covenant community, so that the recipient could effectively say, Abraham's story is *my* story. Galatians 3:29 thus affirms that believers are Abraham's children—participating in the same promise through faith and union with Christ (Gal 3:26).

The Passover displayed the realities of the covenant in both word and deed. As often as it was celebrated, it was to remind the people of Israel, whether young or old, that they too had been brought out of the bondage of Egypt by the power of God who passed by them in judgment when he struck down the enemies of his people.[52] The implication is that the Passover was to create a sense of solidarity between the past and the present, one generation and another (Exod 12:26–27). The participant was to think of it not simply as a story, but *their* story. The language of "participation" is used in connection with the Passover and the Lord's Supper (the New Testament counterpart to the Passover). One who partakes in the covenant meal by faith is *participating* in the blood of the lamb or the blood of Christ, as it were (1 Cor 10:16). The ritual meals create solidarity with something in the past, while perpetuating that experience in the life and faith of the participant in the present.[53]

Joshua 4 offers a similarly intriguing example of this. The Israelites were told to take up twelve stones from the midst of the Jordan river as they

51. HC 66; WCF 27:1–3.

52. Horton, *People and Place*, 106.

53. Johnson, *Walking with Jesus through His Word*, 217.

were passing through, and to set them up on the other side as a memorial to what God had done in delivering and preserving them. Yet the memorializing of the event was not simply for that generation. So the text of Joshua 4:21–24 reads:

> And he said to the people of Israel, "When your children ask their fathers in times to come, 'What do these stones mean?' then you shall let your children know, 'Israel passed over this Jordan on dry ground.' For the LORD your God dried up the waters of the Jordan for you until you passed over, as the LORD your God did to the Red Sea, which he dried up for us until we passed over, so that all the peoples of the earth may know that the hand of the LORD is mighty, that you may fear the LORD your God forever."

Of particular interest is the fact that the text states that the stones are there to show "you" what the LORD did for "you." Future participating generations were not to think of the memorial as simply a reminder of what God did for the prior generation who actually passed through the Jordon, but rather to think of it as though God had actually done it *for them*—as though they were the very ones who passed through the Jordon. They were not simply rehearsing a story, but *their* story. They were to find their life *in the story*, and then continue to live in the light of that story. Many other features of Israel's worship and rituals operate on a similar level. They called the people of God to dramatically embody the events of the past in a way that recreated the stage upon which those events first took place. But now they were the participants in the story, and thus the redemptive-plot was perpetuated in and through them.

In the Old Testament, prophets were frequently called upon to perform various theatrical displays before the people of Israel as a means of communicating a scripted message. Ezekiel is commanded by God to perform several oddly dramatic spectacles before Israel, culminating in chapter 12 in which it is made clear that his actions were signs of what God was about to do to for Israel (Ezek 12:11). Hosea is commanded to marry a prostitute and to have children by her in order to show the nation not only what they had become, but even more importantly, how God's grace would triumph over their sin and judgment. Isaiah's three years of nakedness were to be a sign of God's judgment through famine (Isa 20:1–6). Ryken refers to Jeremiah as the master of such "street theater" for his many performances (Jer 13:1–7; 17:19–27; 19; 27; 32:1–25; 51:59–64).[54] These peculiar Old Testament

---

54. Ryken, *Dictionary of Biblical Imagery*, 857.

episodes of dramatic activity were employed by God as a means of acting out either what the people had done or what God himself would do.

It is important to note that by the time of the New Testament, generally speaking, the Greek theater was a thing of the past.[55] That does not mean that New Testament authors were unfamiliar with theatrical plays or comedies, as is evidenced by occasional quotations or allusions to such plays, such as Paul's quotation of Menander's play, *Thais,* in 1 Corinthians 15:33.[56] The New Testament employs terms that bear theatrical connotations. In particular, the use of the terms such as theater (θέατρον), mimic (μιμέομαι), and hypocrite (ὑποκριτής), had a back-drop in theatrical contexts, though by the time of the New Testament they were employed in notably different and nuanced ways. Paul's use of θέατρον in 1 Cor 4:9 is worth considering. "For I think that God has exhibited us apostles as last of all, like men sentenced to death, because we have become a spectacle (θέατρον) to the world, to angels, and to men."[57] The apostles are viewed here as a spectacle on display before the world, angels, and men.[58] Hanswulf Bloedhorn says of the term theater (θέατρον) used here, "Later documents attest to the use of *theatron* as a term for the artistic practice of role-playing before spectators, i.e. for theatrical performance as such and its organization (1 Cor. 4:9)."[59] Hodge views this use of theater (θέατρον) as functioning metonymically, and comments, "Such were the sufferings of the apostles that men and angels gazed on them with wonder, as people gaze on a spectacle in a theater."[60] Kistemaker suggests that Paul's use of term here likely reflects on the scene in Acts 19:29–31, where Gaius and Aristarchus were dragged into the theater to be spectacles to the crowd, a regrettable fate sometimes experienced by criminals.[61] He further notes, "Anyone and everyone could be present to watch the execution of slaves and criminals. Paul's statement that he is a

55. Ferguson, *Backgrounds of Early Christianity,* 90.

56. Menander would be categorized as "new comedy" for its focus on the realities of everyday life, and predictable "stock" characters. For the distinctions between old and new comedy, see Dugdale, *Greek Theatre in Context,* 11–18. The behavior of characters displayed in plays like that of Menander were designed to draw attention to what was socially acceptable and unacceptable behavior; Ibid., 157.

57. Referring to Heb 10:33 and 1 Cor 4:9, "In both of these passages the emphasis is on how the persecution of believers make them a show or a theater of faith, to the world and to angels"; Ryken, Wilhoit, and Longman III, "Theater," 856–7.

58. On the idea of "angels as audience" see Heb 13:1 and 1 Pet 1:12.

59. Bloedhorn, "Theatre," 383.

60. Hodge, *1&2 Corinthians,* 72. The idea of a dramatic spectacle is recognized by LSJ, 787.

61. See *TDNT,* 3.42 for a helpful discussion of the correspondence between the NT use of θέατρον and its cognates.

spectacle to the world, therefore, is no exaggeration."[62] According to Thiselton, the pastoral implication of this should have had a humbling effect upon the Corinthians, who were safely postured as mere spectators to Paul and the apostle's sufferings, yet called by Paul to imitate him in his sufferings for Christ (1 Cor 4:16).[63]

In Hebrews 10:32–33, the church as a whole is viewed in a similar light, as becoming a spectacle of humiliating martyrdom: "But recall the former days when, after you were enlightened, you endured a hard struggle with sufferings, sometimes being publicly exposed (θεατριζόμενοι) to reproach and affliction, and sometimes being partners with those so treated." In this context, θεατριζόμενοι ought to be defined as, "To cause someone to be publicly exposed as an object of shame or disgrace."[64] The idea of shame is significant here. Shame was something that the converts to Christianity would have undoubtedly experienced, whether they were Jewish or Gentile. This shame was not simply familial, nor was it in any way tame. The author of Hebrews seems to be making the point that the shame experienced by the congregation was both public and harsh.

However, to the extent that they experienced such shame, not only were they identifying with one another, and participating in the sufferings of one another; even more so, they were identifying with and participating in the sufferings and shame of Christ himself (Heb 13:12–13). As Croy notes, "Shame was encountered but disdained by Jesus."[65] Cockerill says that this language of "being partners" with those who are suffering parallels the work of Christ described in Hebrews 2:14, where Christ becomes man in order that he might share in our suffering.[66] An interesting suggestion is made by Jones, who suggests that as soon as these early converts were baptized they were immediately exposed to trials and temptations.[67] This would make for a provocative and interesting parallel not only with Jesus, who was

62. Kistemaker, *1 Corinthians*, 139.

63. Thiselton, *The First Epistle to the Corinthians*, 360. Grosheide notes that these living theaters of martyrdom and suffering commonly took place for the sake of amusing spectators; Grosheide, *De eerste brief aan de kerk te Korinthe*, 128.

64. L&N 25.201 (pg. 311). Luke Johnson notes that the term θεατριζόμενοι is a *hapax legomenon* in the New Testament; Johnson, *Hebrews*, 269. θεατρίζω occurs outside the New Testament according to *BAGD*, 353.

65. Croy, *Endurance in Suffering*, 73.

66. Cockerill, *The Epistle to the Hebrews*, 501; cf. *BAGD*, 353.

67. Jones, *Let's Study Hebrews*, 178. John Brown makes the same observation, and includes that often it was the case that those sent to such "theaters" were often forced to fight with one another or against wild animals for the sake of entertaining those who looked on; Brown, *Hebrews*, 480. If we adopt an early dating for Hebrews, Brown's suggestion would be pressing the language too literally.

likewise tempted and tried immediately following his own baptism (Matt 3–4), but also with the nation of Israel, who was led into the wilderness to be tested and tried immediately following her "baptism" (1 Cor 10:2) in the Red Sea. It is possible that the author of Hebrews similarly intends for these redemptive-historical parallels to serve as a form of pastoral comfort illustrating their union with Christ and the Old Testament people of God.

O'Brien notes the way in which this theatrical language of shame was figuratively used to describe someone who was made a spectacle or held up to public derision.[68] Johnson highlights the intended negative (humiliating) connotation of this language in the fact that Christians were being treated like the publically scorned actors who were not well thought of during this stage of antiquity. Of this he says, "Given the low repute of actors in the honor-shame calculus of antiquity, and given the involuntary nature of 'being put on display' suggested by the passive form of the verb, we are justified in reading the display as a sort of shaming."[69]

It is quite remarkable, as Moffat notes, that in spite of the fact that this early congregation was exposed to such humiliating public shame, they abandoned neither their confession nor one another.[70] To the contrary, they bore one another's burdens (10:33) and exemplified an interest in one another's sufferings in a way that had become a marvelous display of grace, perseverance, and love.[71] This is the paradoxical theater of martyrdom that was witnessed by antiquity on the stage of redemptive history. Phillips puts it well by saying, "This was the display of faith by which Christians turned the ancient world upside down."[72]

Thus, the author of Hebrews, while exhorting the congregation to continue on in faithful perseverance, also compliments them on their "past

68. O'Brien, *The Letter to the Hebrews*, 384. Bruce provides an interesting discussion of the various ways in which this language could have been applied to Christians more likely before than after A.D. 65, when a large-scale persecution of Christians broke out; Bruce, *The Epistle to the Hebrews*, 267–70. His citations from antiquity would seem to support the idea of a pre-65 date for the book of Hebrews. Ellingworth notes that the reference is too vague to be emphatically attached to the persecution of Nero; Ellingworth, *The Epistle to the Hebrews*, 547. For support of the same, see Moffat, *A Critical and Exegetical Commentary on the Epistle to the Hebrews*, 153.

69. Johnson, *Hebrews*, 269.

70. Moffat, *Hebrews*, 155.

71. Schilder seems to capture this accent well and succinctly by saying, "The people of the world should ascertain in the life of the church a graphic depiction of good, redeemed lives in the fear of God"; Schilder, "De kerk in het wereldtheater," 44 (trans. mine).

72. Phillips, *Hebrews*, 383. Similarly, Paul Veyne notes that the moral solidarity of the church and its preserving through adversity "altered profoundly the moral texture of the late Roman world"; Veyne, *A History of Private Life*, 260.

performance"[73] of faithfulness under pressure. Lane notes the way in which being publicly martyred (the idea behind θεατριζόμενοι) "vividly expresses the public abuse and shame to which the members of the congregation had been exposed."[74] This language was used not only of Christians, but also of the Jews in general in regard to much of the suffering they had experienced. Philo has an interesting, extra-biblical use of this vocabulary, employing both "theater" (θέατρον) and "mimicking" (μιμέομαι) to describe the way in which early non-Christian Jewish martyrs identified with the martyrdom of their faithful Jewish ancestors by becoming a living theatre of religious martyrdom.[75] However, Hughes notes that the persecution in view in Hebrews is distinctively anti-Christian and not anti-Semitic.[76] Van Bruggen connects the language to the martyrdom that the newly converted Jews to Christianity would have experienced as a result of their conversion.[77] While this is plausible, it is difficult in our opinion to ascertain with certainty whether or not the persecution in view was something that came from the Jews or from the imperial Gentile authorities (i.e. Emperor Claudius in A.D. 49). The latter seems more likely in our view, as the Jews rarely had the power to effect such public scenes as Hebrews (and Acts) seem to describe. Nevertheless, Van Bruggen is right in noting that the members of the congregation were effectively considered to be "godslasteraars" (blasphemers) in the eyes of their hostile persecutors, whether Jew or Gentile.[78] By their confession of faith, they became participants in a theater of martyrdom.

In a similar vein, the language of "imitation" (μιμέομαι) is suggestively a summons to act in a way that reflects the prior performance of another. In secular parlance, it was sometimes connected to art or drama, where copying an original specimen was the goal.[79] According to Michaelis, the noun μῖμος means "above all the actor, the mime."[80] Mimes often imitated the scenes of daily life, and were a living display of the realities around them, both good and bad. In the theaters of antiquity, actors imitated persons

73. Hagner, *Encountering the Book of Hebrews*, 171.

74. Lane, *Hebrews 9–13*, 299. For similar support of this idea, see Van Bruggen's comments in Van de Kamp *Hebreeën*, 263.

75. Philo *Flacc.* 72. Philo's language sounds strangely similar to that of Hebrews 11. Josephus records similar statements in *Ag. Ap.* 1.43.

76. Hughes, *A Commentary on the Epistle to the Hebrews*, 428.

77. Van Bruggen, in Van de Kamp, *Hebreeën*, 263.

78. Ibid., 263.

79. *TDNT* 4.660n2.

80. Ibid., 660. Similarly, William D. Furley defines *mimos* as, "In the first place the actor in the popular theatre, the play itself in which he—alone or with a small number of others—portrays human types by words and gesture"; Furley, "Mimos," 921.

from real life or other actors, and thus gave a "fitting" performance of their part in the drama.[81] Paul uses similar language as he commands the church to imitate himself (1 Cor 4:16; 11:1),[82] imitate God (Eph 5:1), be imitators of the apostles, "of the Lord" (1 Thess 1:6), and even of "the churches" (1 Thess 6:12). With this language, Paul appears to be summoning the church to remember the parts played by those who have gone before them as live performers on stage in the living-theater of God's redemption, whether those actors are Old Testament saints,[83] apostles, other Christians, or especially Jesus, and through faith and obedience to *imitate* them. In doing so, Paul does not abstract these street-performers from their redemptive-historical context or from the community of which they are part—the church.

Consistent with the discussion above regarding the idea of "being publicly exposed" (θεατριζόμενοι) in Hebrews 10:33 is the use of μιμηταὶ (imitators) in Hebrews 6:12 ". . . so that you may not be sluggish, but *imitators* of those who through faith and patience inherit the promises." In context, the author of Hebrews reminds the congregation of their love and service toward the saints, and pleads with them to remain steadfast so that through "faith and patience" they might inherit the promises and, in doing so, "imitate" those who have done the same. We find this language to be similar to the usage of μιμέομαι (to imitate) outside the New Testament. Michaelis's comments on the use of μιμηταὶ (imitators) in Hebrews are apt as he suggests, "It is a summons to keep the faith in one's own life and death."[84] In the context of Hebrews, this means imitating those who, by faith and perseverance, inherit the promises. Thus, in a way similar to dramatic usage, the idea of imitation can be suggested as a pastorally effective heuristic device.[85] A faithful mimicking is called for as those who endure a variety of trials for the faith do so against the backdrop of others who have performed similar roles. This language in Hebrews 6:12 likely anticipates the argument of Hebrews 11, which we will develop in chapter 5.

Finally, the term ὑποκριτής, from which the word "hypocrite" is derived, has antecedents in the realm of acting; yet by the time it came into use in biblical parlance bore a consistently negative connotation.[86] It is likely that the term originally had something of a more neutral meaning, suggest-

---

81. Harris, *Theater and Incarnation*, 53; Vanhoozer, *The Drama of Doctrine*, 252–63.

82. *TDNT* confirms that this is a frequent feature of Paul's preaching; *TDNT* 6.667; cf. 2 Thess 3:7 where this seems to be a standard expectation.

83. Cf. Heb 6:12, and especially Heb 11.

84. *TDNT* 6.666.

85. Again, we are not insisting that the New Testament vocabulary here is explicitly dramatic, but that it comports well with the heuristic function of the drama metaphor.

86. *TDNT* 8.566.

ing that the one doing the acting was simply interpreting an event, story, etc.[87] The biblical usage bears a decidedly negative connotation, implying that the hypocrite (ὑποκριτής) was deceitfully proclaiming something that he or she was not practicing in reality. Thus, their message was false.[88] It needs to be highlighted that these terms that have been discussed, though appearing to have theatrical connotations, were ultimately borrowed from the everyday life and culture with which the various New Testament congregations would have been familiar in one fashion or another. The usage of these terms does not imply that the New Testament authors were thinking in self-consciously dramatic terms. They do, however, support the idea that the world of the New Testament overlapped a culture that was familiar with plays, comedies, and public spectacles. It is this last category that most likely informs the New Testament usage of theatrical terms. Though not a drama per se, the Christian church was a spectacle before a watching world. It was called to mimic those who had been faithful, and to avoid those who hypocritically wore the mask of religion while denying its reality in Christ.

In summary of this section, we hope to have shown that the drama metaphor, while not explicitly biblical, nonetheless appears to have biblical analogies and can, in a guarded way, serve an illustrative purpose. Thus, it seems fitting and pastorally helpful to employ the DR paradigm as a heuristic device for communicating biblical truth. To view and describe (and hence preach) through the lens of a dramatic metaphor seems consistent with those who, like Vos, view the Bible as being "full of dramatic interest."[89] To read the story is to live the story. To preach the story is not simply to tell the story of redemption, but to draw hearers into that story as faithful participants. Subsequent chapters will afford us the opportunity to apply the drama metaphor more precisely, especially as it relates to preaching. But before doing that, we would like to briefly review the use of the drama metaphor in church history. Simply put, our goal in the next section is to illustrate the use of the drama metaphor by a few key theologians, and to acknowledge objectively the love-hate relationship the church seems to have with the idea of drama in theological parlance.

---

87. "In Attic, then, ὑποκρίνομαι means "to act." The actor's job is to present the drama assigned to him by artistic reciting accompanied by mime and gestures . . . ."; *TDNT* 8.560.

88. Of the eighteen times the word is used in the New Testament, not a single one of them is neutral, let alone positive. See also L&N 766, and *BAGD* 845 for the same definition, both of which see the idea of "acting" as prominent.

89. Vos, *Biblical Theology*, 17.

THE DRAMA OF REDEMPTION AND REDEMPTIVE-HISTORICAL PREACHING   45

HISTORICAL USE OF THE DRAMA METAPHOR

The language of theater as a means of communicating and illustrating theology is foreign neither to the history of the church, nor to key Reformed
theologians. It is well recognized that the church has had a love-hate relationship with the theatre. Harris notes that Augustine, following Plato,
compared the theatre to a plague, and that the early church often embodied
this disdain for the theater.[90] Von Balthasar puts it even more pointedly, saying that Augustine "saw the struggle between the church and the theatre as
an allusion to the great conflict between the two principles of world history,
that is, the City of God and the secular state."[91] Yet whereas many in the
early church found the theater difficult to embrace and shunned it, Calvin
seems to have found in it a redeemable means by which to describe God's
work in creation and occasionally in the church.[92]

Calvin employed the theater metaphor frequently in describing the created order as the "theater of God's Glory."[93] He also referred to the world as a
"glorious theater,"[94] "most beautiful theater,"[95] and "this magnificent theater
of heaven and earth replenished with numberless wonders."[96] In book 1 of
his *Institutes* he states, "For our salvation was a matter of concern to God in
such a way that, not forgetful of himself, he kept his glory primarily in view,
and therefore, created the whole world for this end, that it may be a theater
for his glory."[97] This theater language was part of his apologetic method, arguing that every human that God has made is surrounded by the theatrical
display of God's glory in creation. Yet, for Calvin, sin has so affected humanity that much of the play is lost upon us apart from God's redemptive plan
to restore our ability to perceive more clearly God's glory in creation and in
the church.[98] Though Calvin's "theater" vocabulary predominantly occurs
in the context of viewing the created order as a theatrical venue, there are

90. Harris, *Theater and Incarnation*, 69–70.

91. Von Balthasar, *Theo-Drama*, 1.157.

92. We want to avoid overstating this idea. It would be anachronistic to say that
Calvin employed the DR paradigm. Our goal is to simply illustrate that the drama
metaphor has been employed at least in isolated or incidental contexts within the Reformed tradition.

93. Calvin, *Inst.* 1.6.2; cf. 1.5.1; 1.5.8; 1.14.20; 2.6.1; 3.9.2; 3.20.23.

94. Calvin, *Inst.* 1.5.8.

95. Calvin, *Inst.* 1.14.20.

96. Calvin, *Inst.* 2.6.1.

97. Schreiner, *The Theater of His Glory*, 5, citing Calvin, CO 8:294.

98. Ibid., 107.

rare occurrences that suggest that he considered the church's worship as a divinely directed theater within the larger world-theater of God's glory.

Thus, in discussing the way in which we are to receive the grace of Christ, Calvin rejects the idea of venerating saints or appealing to them as intercessors. Rather, Calvin sees the saints as onlookers or spectators watching the drama of our redemption in history. He says, "Consequently, they attend sacred assemblies, and the church is for them *a theater* in which they marvel at the varied and manifold wisdom of God (Ephesians 3:10)."[99] In a similar fashion, Calvin describes the church as a sacred theater of which the angels are spectators. In his comments on Psalm 138:1 he says, "The solemn assembly is, so to speak, a *heavenly theater*, graced by the presence of attending angels; and one reason why the cherubim overshadowed the ark of the covenant was to let God's people know that the angels are present when they come to worship in the sanctuary."[100]

To view the Bible as revealing a multi-faceted drama with God's kingdom as the metanarrative is not overly innovative, nor particularly contrary to RH hermeneutics. As noted above, Geerhardus Vos described the Bible as being "full of dramatic interest."[101] In many ways, his RH hermeneutical approach to the Bible is an implementation of the drama idea. To say it differently, for Vos the real drama of the Bible is bound to the covenant itself. It is God's slowly unfolding plan to redeem lost sinners from their destruction-bent courses. The plan unfolds like a dramatic story in which the plot is slowly developed, the characters slowly yet punctually introduced, and the climax of the story—God's coming in Christ—happens at just the right time. This is the climactic emphasis of Galatians 4:4; history is seen as being pregnant, virtually bursting with climactic readiness for the coming of the Son of God into history to do for humanity what it could not do for itself—namely, reverse the curse brought about by sin. Schilder clearly sees the idea of drama in the incarnation of Christ and his redemptive work.[102] Regarding the humanity of Christ, he says:

> 'True man' signifies thus: genuine man. Not half-man, not almost-man, not sublimated man, not man in a different history, a so-called 'higher' [man], not man-like, but a real man, *able to act with and in a drama*, which falls within the same framework

---

99. Calvin, *Inst.* 2.6.1 (emphasis added).

100. Calvin, *Commentary on the Book of Psalms*, 199 (emphasis added).

101. Vos, *Biblical Theology*, 17.

102. Trimp, *Heilsgeschiedenis en Prediking*, 61.

of time and space as [that] in which Adam and we had and have
our own drama.[103]

Vos's metaphor in which he describes the coming of Christ into the
world as a seed slowly developing into a rose seems to aptly parallel the drama metaphor. Just as a seed naturally and organically develops, so also does
a good dramatic plot. Each successive scene is built upon the prior scene. It
is neither a mere replay of the former scene, nor is it a plot-spoiler that gives
away all of the climactic details to be revealed later at the perfect time. Yet
when the climax of the plot happens, and the success of the drama's hero is
revealed, then, and only then, do all the previous details make sense. Just as
with watching a movie a second time, knowing the ending helps to explain
many of the confusing, loose details that appeared to be disconnected or
unrelated. The same is true with the Bible, especially as understood through
an RH lens. There is a real sense in which Christians learn to read their Bible
backwards, allowing the end of the story to explain and clarify the details
that were introduced and slowly developed.[104] The Bible reveals a well-
developed drama, and not a detail of it is wasted. But many of the details
cannot be properly understood apart from seeing how the story ends—how
the drama comes to its own climactic finish. In this sense, we agree with and
are greatly helped by Vos's famous line, "eschatology precedes soteriology."[105]
In the context of our current reflection, we infer from this that the unfolding
drama of the Bible (soteriology) is informed by its dramatic climax (eschatology). The latter interprets the former, but the former brings the latter
about. The goal of revelation is the consummation of the covenant, just as
the goal of every dramatic rescue is the wonderful relationship that seems
to emerge at the end of the story. As Webster puts it, "Biblical theology is a
kind of anatomy of the historical unfolding of God's dealings with creatures,
a rendering of the temporal work of God."[106] This is what the Bible reveals
and, in this sense, the Bible truly is "full of dramatic interest." Kline says, "All
Scripture is covenantal, and the canonicity of all the Scripture is covenantal.
Biblical canon is covenantal canon."[107] The canon is shaped by the drama of
the covenant.

103. Schilder, *Heidelbergsche Catechismus*, 2.113 (trans. mine); cf. Runia, *Het hoge
woord in de Lage Landen*, 123.

104. Johnson, *Him We Proclaim*, 159.

105. Vos, *The Pauline Eschatology*, 60. And similarly, "The New Testament writers
in their attempt to grasp the content of the Christian salvation make the future the
interpreter of the present, eschatology the norm and example of the soteriological experience"; Vos, "The Eschatological Aspect of the Pauline Conception of the Spirit," 212.

106. Webster, "Principles of Systematic Theology," 69.

107. Kline, *The Structure of Biblical Authority*, 75.

In more recent decades since the time of Vos, the idea of drama has become a point of real interest. Beyond the authors we have introduced as primary for our purposes, it is important to recognize the vital work of theologians such as Von Balthasar. He is arguably a significant author upon whom both Vanhoozer and Horton lean, and with whom both frequently interact. In the words of Wells, "The theologian who has given the most consideration to the notion of theology as drama is Hans Urs von Balthasar."[108] His five-volume *Theo-Drama* is a seminal work on the interaction between drama and theological endeavor. Intensely important in his project is the idea of drama being the performance of theology. Thus he says, "Performance requires that one come up with a unified vision embracing both the drama (with the author's entire creative contribution) and the art of the actors (with their very different creative abilities)."[109] The recognition of the author's creative intention in the script is key; but the importance of the creative *performance* of the script is also key. This language seems to lend itself well to the nuances we find in Vanhoozer and Horton. It is important to underscore the simplicity of this nuance of drama as the *performance* of the biblical script. We would concur with Von Balthasar in saying, "Drama means action."[110] Thus, the church's enterprise of theological formation and communication is entirely dramatic for Von Balthasar. Dogmatic theology is, in his view, "dramatic at its core."[111]

Additionally, Von Balthasar sees the Bible itself as unfolding a theocentric drama. According to him, what is unique about the Bible is that it is "the testimony of Scriptures, which asserts the uniqueness of the drama enacted by God with his creation."[112] He views the Bible as not simply a stale, passive record of what God has done, but a living, active participant in the drama of God's redemption.[113] Jesus Christ is seen as the hermeneutical key that explains both the Old and New Testament.[114] In addition, he views Jesus as being "God's interpretation of himself in history."[115] Finally, he notes how too often in theology the focus tends to be upon the work of Christ, to the exclusion of the work of the Father and the Spirit. For Von Balthasar,

108. Wells, *Improvisation*, 46.

109. Von Balthasar, *Theo-Drama*, 1.298.

110. Ibid., 1.451.

111. Ibid., 2.51.

112. Ibid., 2.78.

113. Ibid., 2.112; cf. Heb 4:10–11.

114. Ibid., 2.91.

115. Ibid., 2.91. In a similar light, Hans Burger suggests, "Although Father, Son and Spirit as three divine actors are all mentioned, Jesus Christ has the central position"; Burger, *Being in Christ*, 256.

the climax of the covenant drama is emphatically bound to the Triune God whose purpose in history was to stage the redemption of people who would later enjoy eternal life.[116] In his own words, "The Son brings his mission to a close at the point where everything enters into the Triune life."[117]

Added to the important, voluminous contributions of Von Balthasar is the pithy work of Dorothy Sayers. If the former might be likened to a wieldy battle-axe of theo-dramatic vocabulary, the latter is a sharp little dagger. Sayers's single volume, *Creed or Chaos*, referenced in numerous books (including the works of Horton and Vanhoozer), articulates something along the DR line of thought. *Creed or Chaos* is not simply insightful; it is piercingly provocative. Sayers is well-known for her juxtaposition of drama and dogma. In her words, "It is the neglect of drama that makes for dullness. The Christian faith is the most exciting drama that ever staggered the imagination of man—and the dogma *is* the drama."[118] Significant to her articulation of this theological drama is the overwhelming way in which God is not simply the central actor in the drama, but that he becomes the paradoxical victim and hero. Sayers finds this to be the most confrontational truth of Christianity, and she seems almost offended by any means of communicating this theo-drama in dispassionate ways that fail to do justice to the fascinating drama of God's redemption in Christ. So she says:

> So this is the outline of the official story—the tale of the time when God was the under-dog and got beaten, when He submitted to the conditions He had laid down and became a man like the men He had made, and the men He had made broke Him and killed Him. This is the dogma we find so dull, this terrifying drama of which God is the victim and the hero.[119]

She has stale preaching and dry orthodoxy in mind when she pointedly says, "Let us, in Heaven's name, drag out the Divine Drama from under the dreadful accumulation of slipshod thinking and trashy sentiment heaped upon it, and set it on an open stage to startle the world into some sort of vigorous reaction."[120] We cannot help but appreciate her rattling tone. Her words seem to capture a sentiment that we find important to authors such as Horton and Vanhoozer—the idea of the Bible's drama being full of life and intended to be both lived and communicated in a creative, passionate way that befits the glory of the divine drama itself. Her pointed remarks

---

116. Von Balthasar, *Theo-Drama*, 3.139.

117. Ibid., 3.521.

118. Sayers, *Creed or Chaos?*, 3 (emphasis original).

119. Ibid., 5.

120. Ibid., 24.

to preachers are as unsettling as they are challenging. With a sheer lack of inhibition she says, "If Christian ministers really believe it [i.e. the dogma they preach] is only an intellectual game for theologians and has no bearing upon human life, it is no wonder that their congregations are ignorant, bored and bewildered."[121]

More recent authors such as N.T. Wright have found a place for the drama vocabulary as a means of communicating the nature of the Bible's authority. We quote him at length:

> The authority of the Bible is the authority of a love story in which we are invited to take part. It is, in that sense, more like the 'authority' of a dance in which we are invited to join; or a novel in which, though the scene is set, the plot well developed, and the ending planned and in sight, there is still some way to go, and we are invited to become living, participating, intelligent, and decision-making characters in the story as it moves toward its destination.[122]

It is appropriate at this point in which we are reviewing the historical development of the drama metaphor within the context of the church to briefly mention something about the move from modernism to postmodernism. This is important because if it were not for the hermeneutical, epistemological, and theological conundrums and contributions articulated within strains of postmodernism, it is arguable that many of our primary authors (Horton, Vanhoozer, etc.) would not be engaged in their current work. In other words, it is largely against the backdrop of postmodernism, in particular, that the DR rhetoric has been developed. Thus, postmodernism is the contemporary context in which the DR metaphor has come to thrive. To fail to recognize the distinct context of postmodernism will inevitably lead to devaluing the significance of the DR metaphor, especially as it relates to preaching.

In contrast to modern and subsequent postmodern theological trends that effectively reduced the narrative of Scripture to a religious history of human invention without any certain divine authorship or authority,[123] the DR paradigm is self-consciously advocating a view that returns God to the

---

121. Ibid., 31.

122. Wright, *Simply Christian*, 186.

123. De Ruijter, *Horen naar de stem van God*, 69. Goldsworthy describes the movement saying, "Postmodernism . . . grows out of the philosophy of the death of God. It is a form of literary atheism that cannot accept that the author's intention is recoverable. The death of the author means of course the death of both the divine and human authors"; Goldsworthy, *Preaching the Whole Bible*, 68.

place of being the one whose authoritative words and redemptive deeds occupy center stage *in history*.[124] In this sense, the DR paradigm serves an apologetic purpose, in that it argues for both the integrity and continuity of the Bible from a canonical point of view.[125] Boersma summarizes Vanhoozer's goal well by saying, "In short, Vanhoozer wishes to recover the role of the imagination over against a stale propositionalism and at the same time, wants us to hold firmly to the canon as the regulative principle that guides our interpretation."[126] This can be illustrated through several recent historical examples that help form the backdrop both of postmodernism and, more importantly, the DR paradigm.

The historical-critical movement that once dominated the landscape of biblical criticism was, in many respects, very modern (in the sense of pre-dating the advent of postmodernism), but has waned in recent decades.[127] Critics of the movement, both inside and outside the conservative, evangelical world, have recognized that advocates of the historical-critical movement were no less free from theological presuppositions and circular reasoning than those advocating biblical inerrancy.[128] Suspicious of even modern secular presuppositions, Ricoeur asks, "Who interprets? The theologian or the philosopher? The preacher or is it already the exegete? Without a doubt there is no such thing as an innocent interpretation."[129] Furthermore, postmodernism's utter recalcitrance toward propositional theology has ironically criticized even the field of biblical criticism, effectively finding itself adrift on a sea of intellectual skepticism—a skepticism that has subsequently left a giant void.[130] Negative aspects of Enlightenment thinking have

124. This, again, is the distinct move from the "cultural-linguistic" turn of postmodernism back to a "canonical-linguistic" approach to Scripture and its norms.

125. Pelton, "A Canonical center is an attempt to articulate a unified story"; Pelton, *Preaching with Accuracy*, 122.

126. Boersma, "On Baking Pumpkin Pie," 241.

127. For example, "Schleiermacher realized that we today cannot understand the ancient biblical texts simply by using the objective methods of literary and historical criticism"; Braaten and Jenson, *A Map of Twentieth-Century Theology*, 115.

128. Vanhoozer, *Remythologizing Theology*, esp. 17 for his critique of Bultmann on this point.

129. Ricoeur, *Figuring the Sacred*, 139.

130. This is well illustrated by Charles Bartow, "How is the word of God known here at the end of the 20th century? Who gets to name God? Can human beings speak for God? How can we distinguish between our wishful thinking about God and legitimate construals? What will prevent us from confusing God's word of comfort with our own idolatrous longings? Does anybody believe anymore that this is remotely possible? Does God still speak?"; Bartow, *God's Human Speech*, xii. Biezeveld puts it similarly, "In a world without God, has speaking about God lost any manner of obviousness?"; Biezeveld, "Uitgedaagd tot nieuw spreken over God," 11 (trans. mine).

had the effect of opening a drain in the bottom of a bathtub. A downward spiral has begun, leaving a vacuum of intellectual doubt, and those doubts have implied changes in the theological method for Bible-believing evangelicals as well as skeptics. Williams summarizes this well:

> Change is coming to evangelical theology as evangelicals are beginning to recognize something of the validity of the post-modern critique of enlightenment rationalism, its ghettoization of the knowing subject and the production of an epistemology that often is more of an impediment to knowing than either a servant to or explanation of knowing. We are finally beginning to get it: what one sees is a product of who one is and where one stands in relation to reality.[131]

Older, modernistic hermeneutical methods that attempted to embrace the higher critical approaches to the Bible while still allowing for some form of quasi-pietistic biblical "application" have only enlarged the gap between the Bible and the reader.[132] Lessing's ditch has only become harder to cross, and many other well-known modern biblical projects have suffered a similar blow at the hands of postmodernism.[133] We could list here Adolf von Harnack's reduction of biblical content to kernel and husk (personal application and historical propositions), as well as Bultmann's reduction of the Bible to Kerygma and Myth (existential application versus the facts of Scripture). Harnack and Bultmann well-represent a generation of biblical critics who struggled with confidence in the integrity of Scripture, and therefore its "facts," yet still wanted to hold on to the Bible as a guiding religious book with ethical and existential implications.[134] Thus, for Harnack, the unwanted "husks" of Scripture (so-called historical facts, theological propositions, etc.) were peeled away from the tender kernels that remained after higher

---

131. Williams, "Theology as Witness," 72.

132. Gadamer discusses the difficulty of presuppositions in modern theologians such as Bultmann and Schleiermacher; Gadamer *Truth and Method*, 331–3. It is interesting to note how, especially with Schleiermacher's influences from German pietism, "application" becomes the dominant existential feature, even when historical and hermeneutical confidence is lost; see esp. 333. This will be further addressed in a subsequent chapter dealing with application in preaching.

133. See chapter 6 below for a fuller treatment of Lessing's views and their implications for preaching in a postmodern context.

134. Vanhoozer refers to Bultmann's demythologizing approach in *Kerygma and Myth* as "the quintessential example of the distinctly modern first theology that characterizes much twentieth-century Protestant Liberalism"; Vanhoozer, *Remythologizing Theology*, 13. John Wilson argues that Harnack's book *What is Christianity?* is one of the most widespread, readable, and influential theological works of its time; Wilson, *Introduction to Modern Theology*, 135.

criticism ravaged the field of biblical scholarship, and for Bultmann, the Bible's historical propositions and implicit theology were shelved alongside other "mythical" works.

What was left of modernism's hermeneutical and theological endeavor is little more than the empty shell that has become postmodernism and its subjective hermeneutics. It is in this context that we find Vanhoozer particularly helpful in his proposal of a virtual reversal of the postmodern paradigm which exalts the reader's authority over the authority of the biblical text. Horton's appreciation of Vanhoozer's contribution at this point is well-noted when he says, "In this light, we could concur with Vanhoozer, who has posed an intriguing reversal of postmodern theory in which the reader as lord (*over*standing) is displaced by the reader as servant (*under*standing)."[135] As a response to the tired problem of how to cross the gap between the world of today and the events of Scripture, the DR paradigm begins with the idea that the reader *already* lives her life within the drama that the Bible reveals. The challenge, then, is in learning to faithfully participate in the process of interpretation and in coherently living out the Bible's theology. To the extent that we find ourselves to be participants *in the drama*, we do not exaggerate a sense of discontinuity from the drama itself. Nor do we exalt ourselves over the story as though merely functioning as exalted spectators and critics. In Horton's words, "While the church is not the master of the text, it is the amphitheater in which the Word creates the reality of which it speaks, the place where a valley of dry bones becomes a resurrected community."[136]

If postmodernism has proven anything, it has proven that hermeneutical and epistemological autonomy do not exist, and that neither the Biblicist nor the skeptic has an easy claim upon truth. Each has to live with the burden of its own presuppositions and acknowledge their own non-neutrality.[137] Every interpreter of the Bible and history does so from the perspective of an informed narrative (or drama), whether realized or sublime. Everyone is living in a dramatic story; the only question is which one, and whether or not the story is coherent and tenable.[138] In this sense, the distinct hermeneutical presupposition of the DR paradigm is one that does not exaggerate the

---

135. Horton, *Covenant and Eschatology*, 202. For similar appreciation, see Lancaster, "Dramatic Enactment of Christian Faith," 123; see also Jensen, Review of *The Drama of Doctrine*, 227.

136. Horton, *People and Place*, 98.

137. For a helpful summary of this hermeneutical conundrum or "circle" see Osborne, *The Hermeneutical Circle*, 376.

138. Nancey Murphy and Brad Kallenberg helpfully describe this dilemma with an interesting pun, "Constructing the Cartesian theater" in "Anglo-American Postmodernity," esp. 27–31.

distance from the biblical text (script) but rather underscores *participation within* the story of the text. Vanhoozer articulates this as the distinct purpose of Scripture, "Scripture has a role—a speaking, acting part—in the drama of redemption precisely as divine discourse. Scripture not only conveys the content of the gospel but is itself caught up in the economy of the gospel, as the means by which God draws others into his communicative action."[139]

De Ruijter says something similar regarding God's role in crossing the bridge of history, "It is God himself who through his own speech-acts bridges the distance with the Bible and the reader, and calls the reader to the use of Scripture through the hearing of the Word."[140] In this view of Scripture, the Bible is not reducible to that which conveys theological content or propositions, but must rather be seen as a divine means of self-revelation and also *incorporation* of others into God's historically unfolding drama.

Thus, according to Vanhoozer, it is the reduction of theology to mere propositions (largely divorced or abstracted from their canonical context) that has exposed the Achilles heel of orthodoxy, and in some ways capitulated to modernism's theological approach. Along the lines of this critique he says, "The heart of the critique consists in the claim that propositionalist theology, while claiming to be biblical, is actually modernist in its epistemology inasmuch as it buys into modernity's reduction of knowledge to information and into modernity's myth that rationality is universal."[141] It is to this concern that Vanhoozer is responding with a particular goal to defend orthodoxy in the context of recognizing the Bible's redemptive narrative, as well as its unambiguous pastoral goal: orthopraxy.[142] This is accomplished in the DR paradigm by the work of the Holy Spirit that draws the Christian into the Scriptural drama through union with Christ.[143] On this point, Vanhoozer says, "Christian participation is rather pneumatic: those who participate in the theo-dramatic missions do so through union with Christ, a union that is wrought by the Spirit yet worked out in history by us."[144] Nichols puts this idea in a similar light, "We who have read the story, we who have been brought into the story through our union with Christ and by his work, we who love the story, also live the story."[145] Such a work of uniting people securely with the work of Christ wrought by his part

---

139. Vanhoozer, *The Drama of Doctrine*, 48, 70; cf. Heb 4:10–11.

140. De Ruijter, *Horen naar de stem van God*, 105 (trans. mine).

141. Vanhoozer, *The Drama of Doctrine*, 87.

142. Jensen, Review of *The Drama of Doctrine*, 227.

143. Vanhoozer, *The Drama of Doctrine*, 210.

144. Vanhoozer, *The Drama of Doctrine*, 366.

145. Nichols, *Welcome to the Story*, 141.

in the drama of redemption can only be accomplished through the work of the Holy Spirit. The drama of redemption revealed in Scripture is both revealed by the Spirit and invigorated by the Spirit. Apart from the work of the Spirit, the drama falls flat.

REDEMPTIVE-HISTORICAL PREACHING AND THE DRAMA OF REDEMPTION

In this penultimate section we would simply like to connect the dots between the DR paradigm presented thus far and RH preaching. What we hope to have shown by now is that the drama metaphor is pastorally effective for communicating biblical content and is with historical precedence. While the danger of anachronism is recognized, we hope to have cautiously avoided that pitfall by attempting to paint a backdrop for the use of the drama metaphor in exegetical, theological, and historical strokes. Now we would like to suggest a few ways in which the DR paradigm shares notable points of symmetry with the RH paradigm, but more importantly, has the ability to advance the RH preaching paradigm beyond some of its previous and current struggles.

To begin, according to the advocates of the DR paradigm referenced thus far, the idea of the gospel as the over-arching, dramatic, covenantal metanarrative is the hermeneutic key to Scripture. The unfolding drama of redemption within the canon is what gives Scripture its shape, function, and authoritative voice. The Bible, in this view, is authoritative not because man (including the church) says it is, but because God is its author. This presupposition overshadows both the DR and RH paradigms. More importantly, it is worked out homiletically as the RH paradigm begins with the idea of God's word as covenant revelation, with the primary accent falling upon God's redemptive plan to save his people through the work of Christ. The person and work of Christ is the interpretive lens through which the rest of the Bible is to be understood.[146] In contrast to modernism and postmodernism, neither the DR paradigm as we are advocating it, nor the RH paradigm, begin with man. They each begin with God. God is the author of the script; the Holy Spirit is the director of the script through the ministry of the word, and Christ comes as the climactic *denouement* of the drama in the fullness of time to give his

146. Richard Hays has convincingly argued for the New Testament's adaption of a "figural" reading of the Old Testament, and that in particular this is the way the gospel writers read and proclaimed the Old Testament, seeing Jesus as its goal and interpretive lens. He also argues that the historical-critical model, refusing to read the New Testament on its own hermeneutical terms, has failed to appreciate the particular literary genre which the Bible actually embodies; Hays, *Reading Backwards*, 2–6.

Spirit.[147] The Spirit's role in the drama of redemption is of perpetual significance from beginning to end. As Wells rather eloquently puts it:

> As for the Spirit, the incorruptible 'witness' who registers all things objectively, he is also the 'love of God poured forth'. . . throughout the entire drama; he is profoundly involved from within, right to the very end, and 'with sighs too deep for words' he moves the tangled drama on toward its solution, 'the glorious freedom of the children of God.'[148]

The goal at this point is to juxtapose the primary concerns of the RH preaching paradigm in a fairly natural way with the DR paradigm. Both are concerned to see the unfolding of God's redemptive plan, climaxing in Jesus Christ, as the primary message of Scripture.[149] Both view God's part in the drama as the main point or epicenter of the story.[150] Both also wish to do justice to the way in which not every story in the Bible is effectively the same story; but rather, each story needs to be understood in the light of its canonical or RH context.[151] Yet again, the various stories (dramas) are not to be treated as isolated, independent stories, disconnected from the whole, any more than a scene from a play was meant to be understood outside the context of the broader drama of which it is a part. In Gibson's words, "If the Old Testament is Act One of the drama and the New Testament is Act Two, we could hardly preach Act One without some testimony or reference to the fact that Act Two (its fulfillment) has now taken place."[152] The parts interpret the whole and the whole interprets the parts. But the main interpreter is God himself, who teaches us to interpret his dramatic word through the analogy of faith. In De Graaf's words, "The Scriptures are a unity. The Old Testament is the book of the coming Christ; the New Testament of the Christ who has come."[153] Thus, as we shall illustrate more fully in subsequent chapters, the New Testament itself would seem to require a

147. Piper, "Jesus Christ as Denouement in the Theater of God," 133.

148. Wells, *Improvisation*, 50.

149. WCF 8:5. See also Goldsworthy, *Preaching the Whole Bible*, 60. Greidanus' cautions about an exaggerated Christocentricity at the expense of a proper theocentricity are duly noted; Greidanus, *Sola Scriptura*, 176–7.

150. Bullmore, "The Gospel and Scripture," 52.

151. Goldsworthy, in a similar vein, affirms canonical unity while protecting textual nuances. So he says, "The unity of the canon is a dogmatic construct stemming from Christology." He goes on to give a helpful list of ways to unpack this, along with cautions that keep the treatment of each text from sounding the same; Goldsworthy, *Gospel-Centered Hermeneutics*, 251–2. See also Young, *The Art of Performance*, 161–2.

152. Gibson, *Preaching the Old Testament*, 176.

153. De Graaf, *Verbondsgeschiedenis*, 4 (trans. mine).

dramatic, Christ-centered hermeneutic of the Old Testament.[154] We believe these concerns overlap significantly in both the RH and DR paradigms, and in that sense, while the two paradigms are obviously different, they share certain elements of common DNA.

The striking difference between the two paradigms is arguably the most fascinating and homiletically promising. In chapter one the critical observation was made that one of the likely reasons that the RH preaching debate in the Netherlands stalled and was unable to resolve certain homiletical tensions, was its *over*-reaction to poorly done, moralistic application, including the troublesome division of doctrine from application. In addition to this, it also did not effectively fuel a sufficiently missional outlook for the church. It is here that we find that the DR paradigm helps the RH preaching paradigm to take a step out of the mud in which it has been trapped. Inasmuch as early Dutch RH preachers and homileticians wished to overcome the doctrine/application or objective/subjective dualistic dilemma, we would propose that a viable option may be found in the contemporary DR paradigm. The doctrine/application and objective/subjective approach to homiletics in many ways reflects the same dualism that the DR paradigm is reacting to in the area of theology. Thus, the endeavor here is not to rewrite the church's homiletic or theological tradition, nor to oppose it. That said, there may be a way in which at least the rhetorical means of communicating, both in the area of theology as well as homiletics in particular, may be helpfully advanced by the use of the drama metaphor and the DR paradigm as a whole. A case in point would be locating the church's role in the context of preaching.

In our view, the RH preaching paradigm (particularly the early Dutch version) was not altogether consistent or helpful when dealing with the question of where the church *fits in* to the sermon. In many respects, the church regrettably became much like the passive spectator described in the DR paradigm—the pitfall of the modern theological approach. This passive spectator would watch the drama of redemption unfold and come gloriously to its climax in Christ. But what was the church's part? What role did it play? What did God expect of the church in response? Were spectators merely to give a faithful applause to the concrete acts of God in history displayed before them in the sermon? Are such imperatives as "looking to," "contemplating," "rejoicing in," "resting in," even "believing" sufficient to satisfy the wonderful complexity of New Testament imperatives and the broader idea of participating in the work of the kingdom of God? It is here

154. Johnson rightly portrays this as the theme of the Bible that both harmonizes the Old and New Testaments, and also "unlocks" the Bible as a whole for the modern preacher; Johnson, *Him We Proclaim*, 9.

that we believe the DR paradigm has the ability to enhance the contemporary discussion of the RH preaching paradigm further, particularly in a postmodern context. A sermon is much more than a creative display of God's redemption as something merely to be believed; it is also a summons to active participation in the drama of redemption by the life-giving Spirit of God through the preaching of the Word.

Worth highlighting is the nuanced use of the language of participation. This term is not intended to purport in any way that man *helps* God accomplish redemption, even though man is called to fittingly participate in God's *display* of redemption. The Bible's dramatic revelation is clearly one that intends to draw the church into the drama of the redemption that God is continuing to write until the curtain closes at the end of history. Every hearer of the sermon is called to faithful, creative performance of the life (role) God has given us in this world. We must, in Horton's words, learn to ". . . surrender our trivial scripts in order to be written into God's unfolding drama. And then we go out into the world to live out our new role in this play."[155] Every sermon, including an RH one, needs to show Christians how they ought to live out their role in the drama—how they themselves also become living spectacles before the watching world. In Horton's words, "When Christ is proclaimed in his saving office, the church becomes a theatre of death and resurrection."[156]

While not upstaging God with our own petty performances, we nonetheless need to faithfully fulfill whatever it is that God has scripted for us in his word and through his Spirit. As De Ruijter puts it, "Preaching is defined, in this light, as Spirit-innovated work through the concrete script for the current act in the actual scene of the drama of God's salvation."[157] In this sense the DR paradigm faults the RH paradigm (especially RHD) implicitly for not more fully developing the church's role in the drama of the end of the age—especially the Great Commission. But much more important than simply rendering an implicit critique of the RH preaching paradigm, the DR paradigm gives a spirited breath of fresh air to invigorate preachers with an approach that strongly unites the text and church, orthodoxy and orthopraxy. The peculiar contribution of this approach is that it does not presume an exaggerated distance between Scripture and the church or between doctrine and application. Rather, it starts with the presupposition of an inclusive script (Scripture) that intends to identify the proper role of

155. Horton, *Christless Christianity*, 205.

156. Ibid., 141.

157. De Ruijter, *Horen naar de stem van God*, 118 (trans. mine).

every person in God's drama of redemption—beginning with God, yet also including his covenant partners.[158]

CAUTIONS AND CONCLUSION

While we are deeply grateful and indebted to the various advocates of the DR paradigm and their particular contributions, we want to suggest a few cautions and potential objections. First, while we greatly appreciate the implementation of metaphors such as drama, theater, etc., to describe the Bible's unfolding message and the church's role within the plan of God in history, we want to suggest that the metaphor should not be pressed too far.[159] It is only a metaphor. As noted by others, there are certain places where the metaphor is very helpful, and other places where it breaks down. For instance, ironically, one of the hardest places to apply the metaphor is in identifying the pastor/preacher's role.[160] Is he a director? (No, that is the Holy Spirit).[161] Is he a stagehand? Something else? Various authors who attempt to develop the DR paradigm struggle to identify exactly what the analogous role to the pastor would be in the theater.[162] This simply illustrates for us that like all metaphors, even the drama metaphor breaks down and has limitations. We do not believe this limitation is fatal, but it serves as a caution not to press the metaphor too far.

Secondly, the DR paradigm, and particularly Vanhoozer's formulation, seems to come close to rendering a broad-scale critique of the time-tested method of systematic theological endeavor. We have noted that for Vanhoozer, the Bible cannot be reduced to that which simply conveys content. In this light, he mildly distances himself from traditional approaches to systematic theology and what he describes as the "epical approach" to theological propositions. Vanhoozer critiques (without abandoning) the traditional approach to systematic theology as being potentially reductionistic—lifting biblical ideas out of their historical, narrative context and folding them into a system of propositions, divorced from the context and implied pastoral

---

158. Trimp, *Heilsgeschiedenis en prediking*, 12–17. We should note here an important term in Trimp's work "omgang" which in English might rendered as concourse, intercourse, or fellowship. It captures the idea of "covenant partnership" perhaps better than the English "covenant partners" conveys.

159. For the same concern, see Williams, "Theology as Witness," 22.

160. This concern about the pastor's role in particular is shared by others; cf. Jensen, Review of *The Drama of Doctrine*, 228.

161. Vanhoozer, *The Drama of Doctrine*, 33, 448.

162. This somewhat vague application of "director" to the office of pastor is well-illustrated in Mason, "Back to (Theo-drama) School," esp. 19.

intent. According to Vanhoozer, "The main problem with epic theology, then, is that it opts out of the drama altogether and takes an external, spectator's perspective upon the contemplated play."[163] In a review of Vanhoozer's book, Williams seems to summarize, if not overstate, Vanhoozer's concern by saying:

> The propositionalist reading of the Bible—looking for truth-statements—denies any relevance to the form of Scripture. The action of the drama of redemption is drained away; the text of Scripture is de-dramatized as the narrative—the biblical story is treated merely as a delivery system for a deposit of doctrinal truth, a truth which is itself conceived of in ahistorical terms.[164]

In this regard, we would suggest a bit of caution, lest the proverbial baby be thrown out with the bath water. We agree, in general, with the concerns expressed regarding epic, or propositional theology, as Vanhoozer puts it, but our concerns are focused more on the ways in which theology is communicated, rather than the substance itself.[165] In fairness, it is arguable that even those theologians who wrote what Vanhoozer describes as "epic" systematic theologies would affirm the importance of wedding orthodoxy and orthopraxy. And does not such a theologian as Bavinck prove at least a mild exception to Vanhoozer's broad critique of modern systematic theologies?

Additionally, we find it difficult at times to distinguish Vanhoozer's critique of the former (rhetoric) from the latter (substance) and are concerned that the very thing Vanhoozer is hoping to preserve—the church's theology (theology as summary of the biblical script)—may be vitally threatened by an over-reaching critique of the traditional formulations of theology. The irony of this would be to unnecessarily re-script the theological identity of the church. Nevertheless, the particular value of Vanhoozer's work for us is that it helps communicate (even defend) theology in a way that is sensitive to the narrative of postmodern rhetoric and its particular interest in the rhetoric of drama. A similar note of appreciation, ironically, might be ascribed to earlier methods of communicating systematic theology and preaching; they also were a product of their time and rhetoric, and served an important purpose in their own day, in part by comporting to rhetorical norms in vogue at that time. Thus, while the rhetorical effects of the DR paradigm are particularly helpful in the current theological environment,

163. Vanhoozer, *The Drama of Doctrine*, 86.

164. Williams, "Theology as Witness," 17.

165. We wonder if Williams is being hyperbolic when he suggests that, "The propositionalist reading of the Bible denies any relevance to the form of Scripture"; Ibid., 17.

caution should warn against too quickly dismissing the rhetorical appropri-
ateness of a previous generation, lest they are anachronistically judged by
the measuring stick of contemporary rhetoric. The same could and should
be said of preaching from a different era.

Our third concern is an outworking of the second. Does Vanhoozer's
rewriting of the theological-rhetorical script potentially require too many
qualifications? In other words, while attempting to help dig the contemporary
theological enterprise out of the ditch dug by postmodernism, does the DR
paradigm effectively avoid falling into the same ditch? For instance, when
reading through Vanhoozer's seminal work, *The Drama of Doctrine*, we find
ourselves wondering, which theological script *in particular* should the church
perform? Vanhoozer speaks over and over about the importance of sound
doctrine, right theology (orthodoxy), as well as rightly-practiced theology
(orthopraxy), but it is not entirely clear which theological confession or tradition Vanhoozer is advocating as the right one. In this sense, his confessional
allegiance is much more open-ended than that of other DR advocates (e.g.
Horton). It appears that Vanhoozer's theo-dramatic rhetoric could potentially
be adopted by any number of different theological/confessional traditions,
and that the language of "creative improvisation" could be misapplied in a
way that might create a tension with confessional orthodoxy.[166]

We do not wish to overstate this last concern by suggesting that Vanhoozer is arguing for a relativistic approach to orthodoxy or orthopraxy by
any means, or even that his DR rhetoric implies a "one-size fits all" theological approach. Still, we could wish for a bit more confessional clarity as
to *which* doctrinal/confessional system is required by the DR paradigm he
is advocating. Ignoring these sorts of questions leaves the DR paradigm
open to perhaps too many forms of application, and, ironically, theological
vagueness. A vague confessional allegiance leads to a vague script, which
in turn is difficult to perform. We close with the potent words of Dorothy
Sayers on the importance of dogmatic clarity:

> It is the dogma that is the drama—not beautiful phrases, nor
> comforting sentiments, nor vague aspirations to loving-kind-
> ness and uplift, nor the promise of something nice after death—
> but the terrifying assertion that the same God who made the

---

166. This concern is raised by Sarah Lancaster from a feminist point of view in her
"Dramatic Enactment of Christian Faith," 125–6. This is also expressed from a different
perspective by Congar, "On Baking Pumpkin Pie," 254. Vanhoozer anticipates many
of these concerns; yet the caution about the potential abuse or over-application of the
DR rhetoric seems apt, especially as the DR idea is applied in the realm of practical
theology.

world lived in the world and passed through the grave and gate
of death.[167]

Homiletically speaking, a sermon's content needs to be measured on
a confessional scale.[168] This is an important qualification, as new hermeneutical and homiletical paradigms will come and go, as further scholarly
insights are developed, and as different challenges confront the church. If
the exegesis that forms the content of the sermon contradicts the church's
creedal or confessional theology, either the content of the sermon needs
to be reconsidered, or perhaps one's creedal commitments need to be revised or reformed. Nevertheless, creeds and confessions form something of
a theological fence around the yard of preaching. Inside the fence, there is
safety and freedom; but when sermons lead the church outside the boundaries of accepted creedal and confessional commitments, there is danger,
and the steps of the sermon ought to be carefully retraced. We believe these
insights have been well suggested and defended by many authors, including
Horton and Vanhoozer.[169]

Insofar as there is no such thing as a private interpretation of Scripture, we concur with the importance of an ecclesial, and thus confessional
reading of Scripture.[170] Confessional theology aids the preacher in helping
congregants to understand not only the scriptural text, but also the *text* of
the world stage upon which they live out their textually driven, theologically
informed lives.[171] In short, confessional theology helps guarantee that our
sermon-directed performances of the inspired script are not rogue performances, but are done in harmony with and submission to the community
of faith from one generation to the next, thus embodying the theological
catholicity of the church. Apart from such confessional integrity and clar-

167. Sayers, *Creed or Chaos*, 24.

168. Richard Lints notes that in the absence of confessional boundaries, "We often
refashion the text in our own image—a thoroughly postmodern thing to do"; Lints,
"The Vinyl Narratives," 97.

169. Vanhoozer suggests, "The pastor's all-important role is to lead the people of God
to mount local performances for the kingdom of God. As assistants to the Spirit-director,
pastors must avail themselves of the resources of church theology—creedal, confessional,
and congregational—as they seek to shape the church's performance in new cultural
and intellectual scenes"; Vanhoozer, *The Drama of Doctrine*, 33; see also 413. Likewise
Horton, *Christless Christianity*, 154, "The creed leads to deeds; doctrine fuels doxology,
generating love and service to the saints as well as to our unbelieving neighbors."

170. This very important idea will be more fully developed in chapter 6.

171. Van der Welle, "The competency to do so [i.e. preach effectively] you can learn,
so that you, as a theologian can translate the Bible (the script) and the tradition of your
church (the stage) into the language of the people of your own age"; Van der Welle,
"Preken," 13–14 (trans. mine).

ity, sermons may lose their rudder, and creativity may slip into *subversion* of the inspired script, rather than *submission* to it, thus leaving the church aimlessly adrift upon the sea of postmodern transience. In this context it is hoped that the DR paradigm could be a viable contribution to the work of homiletics, particularly when wed to nuances of the RH paradigm. In the next chapter, we will begin applying this suggestion in the specific context of looking at Hebrews 11 as a test case for our proposed synthesis of the DR and RH paradigms.

3

Hebrews 11
Setting the Stage

IN THE PREVIOUS CHAPTER we examined the drama metaphor in theological and pastoral rhetoric and juxtaposed it with the RH preaching paradigm. One of our goals was to demonstrate how the DR vocabulary might be employed as a helpful metaphor for describing the content of Scripture and to describe, in particular, overlapping affinities it shares with RH hermeneutics. In this chapter, we would like to apply a homiletic synthesis of DR and RH ideas in an exegetical context. We intend to do this by utilizing Hebrews 11 as a case study or, perhaps better put, a test case for how our homiletic proposal comports with a well-known and important chapter of the Bible—one of particular interest for discussions about RH preaching. It should be pointed out that in many respects, this chapter of the monograph and the following chapter are two sides of the same coin.

In this chapter we intend to offer a brief exegetical treatment of Hebrews 11 with particular sensitivity to how the covenantal work of God in both the DR and RH paradigms is being displayed in the lives of those listed in the hall of faith. To be clear, it is not our goal to offer a thorough exegetical commentary on Hebrews 11. Rather, our intention is to highlight certain exegetical nuances that shed light on past and present questions regarding the homiletic use of Hebrews 11, and the particular question of whether or not Hebrews 11 can be understood in a Christocentric manner. The thesis of this chapter is that Hebrews 11, properly understood, calls upon the "cloud of witnesses" to testify in nuanced ways to how the substance of the new covenant promises was not simply revealed *to* the Old Testament saints, but was also revealed *through* them. This latter accent harmonizes the overlapping concerns of the DR and RH paradigms particularly well. In order to accomplish our goals for this chapter we intend first to briefly summarize the various approaches to Hebrews 11. Second, we will look carefully at what may be a hermeneutical key to Hebrews 11 as found in the first two verses of the chapter. Third, we will consider the structure of Hebrews 11 as it relates to the pastoral intent of the book. Fourth, we will reflect upon what the saints received from God according to Hebrews 11:2. Fifth, we will consider the import of Hebrews 12:1–2 for understanding Hebrews 11. Finally, we will look in careful detail at the numerous faithful witnesses in Hebrews 11 to discern their key contributions within the historically unfolding drama of redemption. Subsequent chapters will address the important issue of homiletic application from Hebrews 11.

VARIOUS APPROACHES TO HEBREWS 11

Why Hebrews 11? This book, whose authorship is unknown,[1] is generally recognized as belonging to a first-century congregation, likely coming from a Jewish background and undergoing a variety of trials and struggles as a result of their faith.[2] Though its recipients are under a variety of pressures, the particular temptation before them is that of denying their profession of faith and returning to the visible ministries of the Old Covenant. The author of Hebrews takes great pains to show how the things to which the congregation is tempted to return, particularly those things of the Old Covenant, have been fulfilled in Christ. We would suggest that nearly everything the author of Hebrews touches in the Old Testament, he turns into a revelation of the person and work of Christ in some fashion or another.[3] Jesus is the lens through which the author of Hebrews reads the Old Testament. Thus, the congregation cannot return to the types and shadows that have been fulfilled in Christ. He alone is to be the object of their faith and trust. Thus, the book of Hebrews offers us not only a test case in hermeneutics; it is also a test case in the homiletic or pastoral use of the Old Testament

1. For a thorough list of proposals, see Laansma, "Hebrews," 187. Origin is well-known for his third-century quip, "As for who has written it, only God knows"; cited in Ehrman, *A Brief Introduction to the New Testament*, 300. For a recent scholarly attempt to demonstrate that Barnabas, the "son of encouragement," is the author, see De Boer "Tertullian on Barnabas' Letter," 243–63.

2. Guthrie, "New Testament Exegesis of Hebrews," 601; Lane, *Hebrews 1–8*, lxii; see also Lane, *Hebrews 9–13*, 301.

3. France, "The Writer of Hebrews as Biblical Expositor," 246.

from a Christ-centered hermeneutic. As we shall see, Hebrews 11 functions consistently within the hermeneutic of the book as a whole, and gives a helpful overview of the way in which the New Testament approaches the Old Testament from an exegetical and pastoral perspective.[4]

There are also historical reasons why selecting Hebrews 11 as the primary test case for our synthesis between the DR and RH paradigms is preferable. The first is because of the unambiguous position of prominence Hebrews 11 retained in the RH preaching debate in the Netherlands. Hebrews 11 was clearly one of the main texts used.[5] It is ironic that both the exemplaristic and RH sides of the debate used Hebrews 11 to defend their position. The exemplaristic view of Hebrews 11 is arguably the one that has enjoyed the widest appreciation in the history of exegesis and homiletics on Hebrews 11.[6] We could also suggest that it is the most common approach today, in and out of Reformed pulpits. In the exemplaristic approach, the Old Testament saints of Hebrews 11 are held up *primarily* as imitable models of what it means to walk by faith in obedience to God, and the pastoral implication of the chapter is to be like them by following their example of faith, perseverance, and obedience.[7]

By contrast, the RH approach to Hebrews 11 argues that the author of Hebrews neither intended to give a strict definition of faith in the beginning of the chapter, nor did he intend that the *primary* function of the chapter was to hold out examples of faith to be followed. The author of Hebrews, according to the RH view, places the primary accent of Hebrews 11 on God revealing how he worked in history through the faith of his people to bring about that which would be fulfilled in the person and work of Jesus Christ. To be sure, there are abundant nuances that properly belong to the characterizations above, even regarding authors who were lined up in one camp or

4. Anderson, "To see how Hebrews reads the Bible is to learn how we likewise might read it"; Anderson, "The Challenge and Opportunity of Preaching Hebrews," 140.

5. Greidanus lists it among the three central texts of the debate, including 1 Corinthians 10 and James 5; Greidanus, *Sola Scriptura*, esp. 116–7. Commenting on Hebrews 11, Holwerda says, "Not only does Hebrews 11 prove nothing against this view, the whole view of salvation history is foundational to Hebrews 11"; Holwerda, *Begonnen hebbende van Mozes*, 95 (trans. mine). For a compelling critique of Holwerda's narrow view of Hebrews 11, see Trimp, *Heilsgeschiedenis en prediking*, 92. Van 't Veer seems more balanced in saying, "But it is already the case that the nature of faith enters into the foreground here, and not so much the content of faith; nevertheless in Hebrews 11 this is intended redemptive-historically"; Van 't Veer, *Van de dienst des Woords*, 166 (trans. mine). See also Houtman, *This is Your God*, 112.

6. Johnson offers a thorough explanation of this approach to Hebrews 11 in *Him We Proclaim*, 233.

7. See, for instance, the particular application of the exemplaristic approach to Hebrews 11 in Huijser, "'Exemplarische' prediking," 160–82, esp. 180–2.

another within the debate. The most important nuance we will highlight is that there were exemplaristic theologians and pastors who still recognized the priority of redemptive revelation in contrast to what we might call *bare exemplarism*, even though they placed the pastoral accent on the exemplaristic nature of Hebrews 11. On the other side, there were pastors and theologians who, while giving priority to the objective revelation of redemptive history (the RH side), still saw a place for properly deduced imperatives to imitate the lives of the saints in Hebrews 11. Thus, it is not entirely fair or even helpful to refer simply to the exemplaristic or RH sides of this debate without qualification. We admittedly find that many of these over-simplifications muddy the waters of the debate by not recognizing certain laudable nuances of each side. Even worse, to neglect some of these mediating nuances allows for regrettable caricatures of both sides of the debate to be formed and perpetuated without qualification.

Outside of the RH preaching debates in the Netherlands, generally speaking, the majority of interpretative approaches to Hebrews 11 have clearly fallen upon the exemplaristic side. Where nuances exist, they still affirm a primary emphasis on following the examples set before us in the hall of faith. Many of these nuances will come out as we work our way through the chapter. Yet bound to the question of whether or not the saints in Hebrews 11 are given as examples for our imitation is the question: what exactly are the saints *examples* of? In other words, are they being held up as ethical examples? Legal witnesses? Athletes who have finished their own races upon the course we are still running? Are they spectators in a coliseum? These and other explanations have been given in an attempt to understand the particular ways in which the author of Hebrews seems to be employing the hall of faith. Each of these ideas has its own merit, some more than others; but it is only by working through the chapter and looking particularly at the first and last verses of the pericope that we can confidently form an opinion.

TRANSLATION TRAJECTORIES OF HEBREWS 11:1-2

"Ἔστιν δὲ πίστις ἐλπιζομένων ὑπόστασις, πραγμάτων ἔλεγχος
οὐ βλεπομένων. ἐν ταύτῃ γὰρ ἐμαρτυρήθησαν οἱ πρεσβύτεροι."

"Now faith is the substance of things hoped for, the evidence of
things not seen; for by it [faith] the elders were witnessed [to]."[8]

These opening verses to Hebrews 11 have understandably received considerable attention in light of the numerous questions that have plagued expositors and preachers of Hebrews 11. In many respects, the way one translates these two verses will significantly affect the way the rest of the chapter will be interpreted both exegetically and homiletically. Of key significance are the ways in which the two words ὑπόστασις (substance) and ἔλεγχος (evidence) are interpreted. Various translations treat the terms quite differently: the one tradition presents a subjective translation of these foundational words, and subsequently the remainder of the chapter; the other translates the words more objectively, which results in a potentially different approach to the chapter as a whole.[9] We might compare the importance of this exegetical decision to shooting an arrow from a bow. Though subtle nuances might be hard to determine at the release of the arrow, yet in time, those subtle directive nuances will have a significant effect on where the arrow lands. So it is with the translation of Hebrews 11:1-2. A brief sketch of the various translations will reveal the inclination toward an objective or subjective interpretation of these watershed verses. We shall arrange the specimen translations into two categories; the first will be those that translate verses 1-2 more subjectively, the latter will be those that translate them somewhat more objectively.

The majority of translations fall into the first (subjective) category, which is well-demonstrated in the ESV's rendering, "Now faith is the assurance of things hoped for, the conviction of things not seen. For by it the people of old received their commendation." We could add to this the following English translations (NIV, NASB, ASV, RSV, NLT), as well as the Dutch (NBV, and NBG-vertaling 1951). Each of these translations, in one fashion or another, translates ὑπόστασις and ἔλεγχος with a more subjective

---

8. Trans. mine.

9. Van Bruggen dismisses the importance of whether ὑπόστασις is taken objectively or subjectively when he says, "The discussion over the question of whether *hupostasis* indicates an objective certainty (foundation) or a subjective confidence is less than meaningful. Faith is by nature subjective (to trust), but it focuses on certain promises and is thus an objective ground of hope"; in Van de Kamp, *Hebreeën*, 268 (trans. mine).

accent. An alternative is found in the Dutch *Statenbijbel*,[10] as well as the KJV and NKJV, the latter of which says, "Now faith is the substance of things hoped for, the evidence of things not seen. For by it the elders obtained a *good* testimony." William Lane's translation in his commentary expresses this remarkably well. His rendering is, "Now faith celebrates the objective reality [of the blessings] for which we hope, the demonstration of events as yet unseen. On this account the men of the past received attestation by God."[11]

In the majority of English translations, the key word ὑπόστασις is translated with "assurance," "being sure," or "confidence."[12] In a similar and consistent light, ἔλεγχος is translated "conviction," "certainty," etc. The emphasis here suggests that the main accent of faith seems to fall upon what it means in the life or subjective appropriation of the believer. By contrast, the KJV, NKJV, and the Dutch *Statenbijbel* each place the accent on the objective. In other words, whereas the first group of translations suggest that faith is that which resides in the subjective experience of the believer (confidence, assurance, conviction, etc.), the latter group of translations allow for the idea that the faith in Hebrews 11 has more of an emphasis on faith as testimony (as evidence, proof, etc.) to the unseen realities for which believers still hope.[13] For the one group of translations, then, the focus of Hebrews 11 implicitly lends itself to emphasizing the subjective faith of the individual saints; for the other group, the focus tends toward highlighting what is being revealed *through the faith* of each of the saints. Our goal here is not to present a rigid either-or approach, but to show how the objective side of faith in Hebrews 11 is both viable and important in understanding the theological and pastoral purpose of the hall of faith.[14]

10. The view of Hebrews 11:1 was much discussed and debated in the earlier RH debates. It reads, "Het geloof nu is een vaste grond der dingen, die men hoopt, en een bewijs der zaken, die men niet ziet"; "Now faith is the firm foundation of the things for which men hope, and a display of things sought, but not seen" (trans. mine). Though opinions varied, in the end it was arguably inconclusive.

11. Lane, *Hebrews 9–13*, 325.

12. Paul Ellingworth and Eugene Nida note three ways the word ὑπόστασις has been historically rendered: 1. "Substance" as in God's own being as revealed in Christ in 1:3; 2. "Assurance" or "confidence," which they see as the most common; 3. "Guarantee" as it was used in title deeds; Ellingworth and Nida, *A Translators Handbook on the Letter to the Hebrews*, 251.

13. James Thompson, though admitting that this has been a challenging verse in the history of translation, still argues, "The faith of Hebrews 11:1 is thus 'reality' and 'proof,' not subjective experiences"; Thompson, *The Beginnings of Christian Philosophy*, 71.

14. Robert Jewett argues rather forcefully that, "Since the term *elegkos* is never used in the sense of subjective conviction, it thus depicts the objective proving of the reality of the things not seen"; Jewett, *Letter to Pilgrims*, 195.

Our suggestion is that the key words ὑπόστασις and ἔλεγχος in 11:1 allow for an objective accent (one that focuses on ὑπόστασις as revelation) that is consistent with the rest of Hebrews and its theological interpretation of the Old Testament.[15] The first key word, ὑπόστασις, occurs in Hebrews 1:3 and 3:14. In 1:3, the accent is upon the superiority of the revelation of God in Christ: "He is the radiance of the glory of God and the exact imprint of his *nature*[16] (ὑπόστασις), and he upholds the universe by the word of his power . . ."[17] The argument is based on a movement from the lesser to the greater. God revealed covenant promises to the Old Testament saints, yet has perfected that revelation in Christ (a pattern which is suggestively repeated in Hebrews 11:1–12:2). The author's point is to show the superiority of Christ to the covenant promises and ministries of the Old Testament, as they have been "eschatologized" (that is, brought to their consummate fulfillment) in him. Even though God spoke in "many times and in many ways"[18] in the past, Jesus is the climactic Word of God that supersedes the promises, types, and shadows of the past as he fulfills them. But not only is Jesus the fulfiller of God's Word in the flesh, but he is also *God himself* in the flesh, tabernacling among his people.[19] He is the radiant revelation of God himself, the exact χαρακτήρ (imprint), from which we get the English word "caricature," of God's person. Hebrews 1:1–3 is clearly about the revelation of God, not only in his Word, but particularly in Christ, the Word of God incarnate.[20] Thus it would appear that a revelatory emphasis of ὑπόστασις in Hebrews 1:3 seems to be the most natural read.[21] In this light, Rhee suggests,

15. Victor Rhee goes so far as to argue that the subjective accent is altogether wrong. "However, an examination of the exemplars of faith in chapter 11 shows that they had more than a subjective hope; they had an objective hope which they were looking forward to. For this reason, a subjective understanding of *upostasis* is inadequate in defining faith in Heb. 11"; Rhee, *Faith in Hebrews*, 214; cf. also 216.

16. The KVJ and NKJV have "person" in place of "nature."

17. ESV.

18. Heb 1:1.

19. P.H.R. van Houwelingen notes the absence of significant reference to the temple in Hebrews, but numerous references to the tabernacle, in spite of the fact that the temple was arguably still standing at the time of the writing of Hebrews. There are implications in this for the transient nature of the Old Covenant, and its giving way to the better, eschatological ministry of the New Covenant; Van Houwelingen, "The Epistle to the Hebrews," 100; see also Van Houwelingen, "Riddles Around the Book of Hebrews," 157–8.

20. Graham Hughes persuasively argues that the point of Hebrews is: "To hear what the Scriptures have to say about themselves," and to see Christ as the "final content of God's Word"; Hughes, *Hebrews and Hermeneutics*, 56, 58.

21. This point is well argued from several angles by Baugh, "The Cloud of Witnesses in Hebrews 11," 113–32.

"If the objective understanding of *upostasis* and *elegkos* is correct, then the definition of faith in Hebrews 11:1 may be stated as 'Faith is the reality (or substance) of things hoped for, the proof of things not seen.'"[22]

If the only use of the word ὑπόστασις in Hebrews were in 11:1, it would be hard to understand why so many translations go the more subjective route in this verse. We will propose good reasons why the subjective use not only appears in so many translations, and ought not to be dismissed, but also wed to an objective priority. First, there is another use of ὑπόστασις in Hebrews that seems to have a subjective accent.[23] In Hebrews 3:14 we read, "For we have come to share in Christ, if indeed we hold our original *confidence* (ὑπόστασις) firm to the end." The idea of "confidence" is consistently used in the various English translations.[24] While this translation is commendable, what we are called to cling to in this verse is not the idea of faith *in the abstract*, but to remain standing upon the firm foundation of faith—Christ himself.[25] This nuance is picked up in the *Statenbijbel* which renders ὑπόστασις "firm foundation."[26] In other words, the author of Hebrews is pastorally admonishing the community to hold fast to Christ through faith and thus to rest upon him as their firm foundation.[27] He is the "substance of the covenant"[28] and is therefore to remain the object of their faith.[29] Thus, for the author of Hebrews, the idea of those in the community abandoning their confession of faith in Christ was not even to be considered. For this reason, we have to admit that while the subjective implication

22. Rhee, *Faith in Hebrews*, 217.

23. For a helpful treatment of this see Holwerda, *Hebreeën*, 84–89. He discusses the relationship of ὑπόστασις and ἔλεγχος together.

24. We noted an interesting nuance in the Statenbijbel, "For we have become partakers of Christ, if we hold fast to the beginning of this firm foundation to the end" (trans. mine).

25. See O'Brien, "Our preference is to interpret ὑπόστασις in an objective sense, either of 'the basic stance' the author and listeners took when they received the gospel, or 'the reality' of becoming partakers of the messianic identity"; O'Brien, *The Letter To the Hebrews*, 151. O'Brien also suggests. "The objective sense seems to make better sense of the instances of the term in 1:3 and 11:1"; ibid.

26. Trans. mine.

27. Cf. Ps 68:3 in the LXX which renders ὑπόστασις as "foothold" (ESV, NIV, NASB).

28. Clark, "Considered objectively, the substance of the covenant is comprised of God's saving acts in Christ and the explanation of those acts in Christian theology"; Clark, *Caspar Olevian and the Substance of the Covenant*, xviii.

29. A similar idea is found in Heb 6:9, where Christ is the "anchor" of our souls, which, even though hidden from our eyes, continues to keep us secure in our spiritual position, much the same way an anchor hidden underwater secures our position on top of the water.

of Hebrews 3:14 is evident, it cannot be the *only* implication of ὑπόστασις.[30] Historically, Koster notes that early patristic exegesis favored a more objective translation with *substantia*, and that Luther's innovative subjective translation in the Reformation period "introduced a wholly new element into the understanding of Hebrews 11:1," and that this new perspective of faith in Hebrews 11:1 as personal and subjective "has governed Protestant exposition of the passage almost entirely."[31]

We would like to suggest a few more reasons why this discussion about the definition of faith ought to be nuanced, and appreciation for the objective idea ought to be given more consideration. First, ὑπόστασις is not the only noun used to qualify or define faith in Hebrews 11:1. The second noun, ἔλεγχος (evidence), is also arguably a more objective term (perhaps even more than ὑπόστασις).[32] Though ἔλεγχος is a *hapax legomenon* in the New Testament, it is used in extra-biblical Greek of legal matters where objective evidence is presented in order to buttress a case in which those being compelled to make a judgment are not eyewitnesses to the matter in question.[33] Buschel affirms this use of ἔλεγχος by saying, "In Hebrews 11:1, in the well-known characterization of faith, ἔλεγχος means 'proof' or 'persuasion' rather than correction. But it cannot be taken in the sense of subjective persuasion, since this does not correspond to the usage."[34] The subsequent content of Buschel's paragraph goes on to defend the importance of the objective use of ἔλεγχος, yet goes on to translate/paraphrase Hebrews 11:1 as, "Thus faith is confidence in what is hoped for, since it is the divinely given conviction of things unseen."[35] We agree with Buschel's emphasis on ἔλεγχος as "evidence" or "proof" and believe that this is a very important qualification when considering whether or not ὑπόστασις is to be

---

30. Further reason to appreciate the subjective understanding of ὑπόστασις is that in its only other New Testament usages outside the book of Hebrews (2 Cor 9:4; 11:17) the subjective sense also seems stronger.

31. Koster, *TDNT* 8.586. *BAGD* argues strongly against the subjective reading. "The sense 'confidence' or 'assurance' must be eliminated, since examples of it cannot be found. It [the subjective rendering] cannot, therefore, play a role in Hebrews 11:1, where it has enjoyed much favor since Luther"; *BAGD* 847.

32. L&N defines it as, "The evidence, normally based on argument or discussion, as to the truth or reality of something — 'proof, verification, evidence for.' πραγμάτων ἔλεγχος οὐ βλεπομένων 'a proof of the things we cannot see' or 'evidence that what we cannot see really exists' Heb. 11:1." See Baugh's in-depth discussion in "Cloud of Witnesses," 114–6.

33. The term is famously employed in this way by Francis Turretin in his *Institutio Theologiae Elencticae*, translated in English as *Institutes of Elenctic Theology*.

34. Buschel, *TDNT* 2.476.

35. Ibid.

given an objective accent, as in Hebrews 1:3, or subjective, as may appear to be the case in Hebrews 3:14. We believe the context requires an accent on the former—that the faithful in Hebrews 11 *both* subjectively possess *and* objectively reveal the redemptive work of God, thus testifying to the reality of the things that have been revealed and perfected through Christ.[36]

Such a usage of πίστις (faith) is consistent with the New Testament usage of the term. J. Gresham Machen has noted that πίστις has a range of meanings in the New Testament, some being objective while most are subjective, and that caution should be employed when using Hebrews 11:1 as a comprehensive definition of faith. So he says, "These words are not a definition of faith or a complete account of faith: they tell what faith is, but they do not tell *all* that it is, and they do not separate it from all that it is not."[37] Though not conclusive for our study here, examples of the objective use of πίστις may be found elsewhere in the New Testament.[38] The point here is to simply suggest that the New Testament is not unfamiliar with using πίστις as a reference to the objective revelation of God through his words and works in history, and that such a usage is worth considering when approaching Hebrews 11:1 and the revelation on display in the hall of faith. Though exclusively subjective translations of Hebrews 11:1 abound, an objective nuance of the verse is still conceivable (as will be shown below). A wedding of these ideas could throw a very interesting light on the herme- neutic and homiletic intention of Hebrews 11. First, it will be suggested how the structure of Hebrews 11 might also support a view which includes an objective accent of πίστις alongside the subjective.

THE STRUCTURE OF HEBREWS 11

Numerous efforts have been made to propose a structure to Hebrews 11. One of the more creative is that of Victor Rhee who argues for a chiastic struc- ture of the chapter as a whole.[39] Rhee adopts Vanhoye's thesis that the entire

---

36. Simon Kistemaker observes that the author of Hebrews never quotes the words of Christ or other apostles, but exclusively employs the Old Testament as witness to the New Covenant realities that have come in Christ; Kistemaker, "The Psalm Citations in the Epistle to the Hebrews," 113.

37. Machen, *What Is Faith?*, 229 (emphasis added).

38. Jude 3 is perhaps one of the clearer examples, which says, "Beloved, although I was very eager to write to you about our common salvation, I found it necessary to write appealing to you to contend for *the faith* that was once for all delivered to the saints" (emphasis added). See also 1 Tim 1:2; 3:9; 4:1; 6:10, 21. None of these verses necessarily inform the usage of "faith" in Hebrews 11:1, but they do show the potential for a broader semantic range in the NT than simply a subjective understanding of πίστις (faith).

39. Vanhoye, *La Structure Litteraire de L'Epitre aux Hebreux*, 59, 240–2, cited in

book of Hebrews is arranged as a chiasm, with the center of the book being Hebrews 9:11–14. Rhee then builds upon this thesis by suggesting in particular that there is a chiastic structure to Hebrews 11, which places verses 13–16 at the center of the chiasm. While we find this article to be helpful in many ways, and the prospect of a chiasm in chapter 11 to be provocative, we are not convinced of Rhee's proposal for several reasons. First, it makes chapter 11 (and the proposed chiasm) largely disproportionate, placing the center of proposed chiasm very early in the chapter. Second, and more importantly, it fails to account for the important way in which the end of Hebrews 10 and the beginning of Hebrews 12 form a bracket around Hebrews 11. Thus, rather than viewing Hebrews 11 as a chiasm, we would suggest that the boundaries of Hebrews 11 are defined by way of inclusion—opening with faith in 10:37–11:1 and then closing with faith in 11:39—12:2.[40] In our view, the author's comments on Habakkuk 2:4, "the righteous shall live *by his faith*" at the end of chapter 10 form one side of a bracket, and the comments at the beginning of chapter 12, which identify Jesus as "the founder and perfecter *of our faith*" form the other side of the bracket. What comes in the middle is the hall of faith in which the author of Hebrews illustrates how "the just shall live by faith." Their faithful lives not only demonstrate the forward-looking nature of faith, but they are also revelation of the one who is himself the "founder and perfecter" of their faith.[41]

While Hebrews 11 does, in many ways, function as an independent unit, at the same time, it is vital to see it in the context of what comes before and after. Hebrews 10 deals at length with Jeremiah 31, the promise of the New Covenant (verses 1–18), followed by a paraenetic section in which the church is encouraged to draw near to God with language that ought to remind them of their own professions of faith, baptism, and community obligations (verses 19–25). It then proceeds in verses 26–31 into what is arguably the strongest warning in the book of Hebrews, second only to chapter 6. Then, in 10:32–39, the author of Hebrews reminds his audience of the way in which they have already persevered through so much suffering and distress together.[42] Noteworthy is the implementation of the "theater"

Rhee, "Chiasm and the Concept of Faith in Hebrews 11," 327.

40. For a similar suggestion see Guthrie, *The Structure of the Book of Hebrews*, 88. Rhee elsewhere argues for something of a doctrine/paraenesis structure in which 11:1–40 is doctrine, and 12:1–29 is paraenesis; Rhee, *Faith in Hebrews*, 180.

41. Cf. Van Bruggen's comments in Van de Kamp, *Hebreeen*, 250–1.

42. Attridge offers several suggestions as to the particular context of the persecution endured by the church, rightly concluding that while the specifics of their "theatrical" performance are unclear, what is clear is that the community endured public humiliation together; Attridge, *The Epistle to the Hebrews*, 298.

language of verse 33, where the author refers to the community as a "theater of suffering" (θλίψεσιν θεατριζόμενοι).[43] He describes their suffering in a tender, encouraging manner, and then finally brings them to a very important exposition of Habakkuk 2:4.

This section is of significance for understanding Hebrews 11 for several reasons. Already noted is the way in which it helps to form the structural bracket of the *inclusio*, with the second part of the *inclusio* being found in the beginning of chapter 12.[44] Secondly, this brief exposition of the promise that the "righteous shall live by faith" is a preemptive commentary and preliminary introduction to the hall of faith. It is the author's way of staging the heroic performances of those in the hall of faith.[45] The faithful heroes of chapter 11 become living illustrations of the reality of this resurrection promise, as well as legal witnesses to its truthfulness.[46] Furthermore, the orientation of the Habakkuk exposition is clearly eschatological and pastoral in nature.[47] It involves the climactic coming of God in judgment at which point he will separate those who have drifted away in unbelief from those who "have faith and preserve their souls."[48] We can hear an echo of the author's use of Israel in the wilderness in chapters 3 through 4 as an illustration of the consequence of unbelief—they refused to hear God's voice and follow him by faith; they thus died in the wilderness *outside the land*. Yet the promise of the New Covenant offers the hope of a better covenant based upon a better mediator and even better promises. To the extent that the promise is better, so also is the promise of judgment more severe for those who fall away into unbelief. The author's pastoral plea is that the members of the community might see the superiority of the New Covenant ministry of Jesus Christ and cling to him by faith.[49] To the extent that some might be tempted to fall away in unbelief, the author-pastor wants them to see the grave, eschatological consequences of mocking the Son of God who has come to fulfill all the promises of God, including the promise to judge even his own people who rebel against him in unbelief (10:30–31). Thus, the con-

---

43. Cf. chapter 3 above for a fuller exposition of the theatrical reference in Hebrews.

44. Rhee, *Faith in Hebrews*, 181.

45. Westfall, *A Discourse Analysis of the Letter to the Hebrews*, 243.

46. Baugh states, "My understanding of Hebrews 11 proceeds from the author's presentation of the OT believers recorded in the biblical record as recipients of divine testimony to the coming eschatological realities, and thence by faith they became participants in and witnesses to the world to come"; Baugh, "Cloud of Witnesses," 113.

47. Macleod, "The Literary Structure of the Book of Hebrews," 185–97, 196n47.

48. Heb 10:39.

49. This inseparable link between Christology and soteriology is the focal point of Hebrews; Schreiner, *Magnifying God in Christ*, 116–7.

clusion of chapter 10 draws together not only the promise of eschatological judgment for those who fall away, but also promises of eschatological life in the presence of God for those who have persevering faith.[50] These realities are displays of the "things hoped for" (πραγμάτων ἐλπιζομένων) that are "yet unseen" (οὐ βλεπομένων) described in 11:1, and of which the rest of Hebrews 11 offers a panoramic, theatrical display. In these varied contexts of judgment and/or blessing, the saints of Hebrews 11 display what it looks like to be righteous and live by faith in a historical context that previews God's day of visitation.

WHAT THE PEOPLE OF OLD RECEIVED

A few things need to be said about Hebrews 11:2 and the particular issue of what exactly is being said about the hall of faith.[51] Numerous translations render the verse in a way that emphasizes the idea that by faith the Old Testament heroes received their "commendation" (ESV, NIV), "approval" (NASB), "good report or good testimony" (KJV, NKJV). The *Statenbijbel* translates it, "For through their faith the elders have become witnesses."[52] Generally speaking, the accent of these translations suggests that the Old Testament saints were applauded or commended because of their faith. Such an emphasis could certainly lead to a more exemplaristic treatment of the saints in general. Baugh, adopting a different reading of the text, has argued convincingly that while the verb ἐμαρτυρήθησαν can mean to "approve" or to "praise" elsewhere in the New Testament, the consistent usage in the book of Hebrews falls upon the idea of receiving revelation or *being witnessed to*.[53] The verb occurs elsewhere in Hebrews (7:8, 17; 10:15) and five times in chapter 11 (2, 4[2x], 5, 39).[54] The sense is most clearly asserted in 10:15, "And the Holy Spirit also *bears witness* (μαρτυρεῖ) to us."

The emphasis of Hebrews 11:2 thus appears to be that God was not simply commending, but witnessing to the Old Testament saints through various means (1:1), granting them revelation of the things to come, which they received by faith (11:2).[55] As the author says in 4:2, "for good news came"

50. Van Houwelingen, "The Epistle to the Hebrews," 108.

51. Renninger argues that πρεσβύτεροι (literally, "elders") should not be limited to those explicitly mentioned in Hebrews 11 but to all the faithful saints of the Old Testament alluded to in the book of Hebrews; Renninger, "The New Testament Use of Old Testament Historical Narrative," 252.

52. Trans. mine.

53. Baugh, "The Cloud of Witnesses in Hebrews 11," 118–9.

54. Ibid., 118n22; see also Baugh's treatment of the related cognates.

55. *BAGD* inconsistently suggests that in 7:17 the verb should be translated "of

(literally, "was preached")[56] to us just as to them. By faith, the Old Testament saints received and embraced those promises.[57] In this way, they were "witnessed to" by God himself concerning the promises of the covenant. As those who were witnessed to by God, they also become witnesses to us of the same realties. Van Bruggen sees a similar accent when he says, "Through God's witness these people were objective witnesses for us of the things that we hope for and that are not yet seen."[58] Relatedly, O'Brien translates the verse with the sense of commendation, then conversely points out, "It was by faith that the ancients *received testimony* from God."[59] Support for this nuanced rendering of 11:2 is also found in Ellingworth and Nida who suggest that the language "won God's approval" is literally "were witnessed to," i.e., by God. "The meaning may be more precisely "God speaking in Scripture.""[60]

HEBREWS 12:1–2

Turning briefly to Hebrews 12:1–2, we see the other end of the *inclusio*. Many have made the point that Hebrews 11 cannot be properly understood apart from the beginning of chapter 12.[61] That Hebrews 11 is still in view is made clear not only by the conjunction "therefore" (Τοιγαροῦν), but also by the reference to the "cloud of witnesses" in 12:1. The exhortation to set aside those things that might hinder the race of faith (sins and weights), as well as the exhortation to run the race of faith with endurance, are qualified by the manner of running—one with their eyes fixed on Jesus. Ellingworth notes the importance of this Christ-centered focus when he says, "It is remarkable that it is not the Old Testament believers of chapter eleven, whose life of faith is so far unfulfilled (11:40), who are now held up as examples to be followed, but Jesus himself."[62] In this way, the New Covenant community is to imitate the heroic saints who have not only finished their own races of faith, but who did so by looking ahead to the fulfillment of the promises of God in

---

whom it is testified" then in 11:2 "be well spoken of by someone"; *BAGD*, 493. It regrettably does not comment on 10:15.

56. Such is the implication of the aorist passive participle εὐηγγελισμένοι.

57. See Westcott, "The witness is borne to the life which was inspired by faith"; Westcott, *The Epistle To the Hebrews*, 351.

58. Van Bruggen in Van de Kamp, *Hebreeën*, 269 (trans. mine).

59. O'Brien, *The Letter To the Hebrews*, 400 (emphasis added).

60. Ellingworth and Nida, *A Translators Handbook on the Letter to the Hebrews*, 252.

61. Vos, "Running the Race of Faith," 127–8; Dijk, *De dienst der prediking*, 286–7.

62. Ellingworth, *The Epistle to the Hebrews*, 637.

Christ.[63] While the coliseum imagery comes to mind, so also does the idea of legal witnesses, those who have received their approval from God (11:2), and now give their own testimony to the faithfulness of God to keep his promises.[64] The fact that they have finished their own races in faith, despite manifold adversity, testifies to the power of God not only to invigorate the living, but also to give life to the dead. This thought is affirmed at the end of Hebrews 12, where the saints who have entered glory through the veil of death are mentioned in general, and notably Abel, the first 'hero' in Hebrews 11, is mentioned again by name. It is also significant that the author connects Abel's blood to the "sprinkled blood" of Jesus Christ.[65]

According to the author of Hebrews in 12:1–2, Jesus is the "founder and perfecter" (ἀρχηγὸν καὶ τελειωτὴν) of faith."[66] The first term, ἀρχηγὸν, is defined by Delling as, "The hero of a city, who founded it, often gave it its name, and became its guardian."[67] In the Septuagint (LXX), the term was used in reference to the tribal chieftains.[68] In the New Testament, Jesus is called the ἀρχηγὸν τῆς ζωῆς "Author of life" (Acts 3:15) and the ἀρχηγὸν καὶ σωτῆρα "Leader and Savior" of his people (Acts 5:31). The term is used one other time in Hebrews (2:10) and is rendered "founder," "pioneer," or "captain" in various translations. In Hebrews 2:10, it is given a similar meaning as one who initiates a movement. Jesus is the pioneer who opens the way to God for sinners that become righteous in him, and he leads those who have been estranged by sin back into the holy presence of God. In this light the work of Christ, as described in Hebrews, is not simply a movement toward God in general, but a particular fulfillment of all that God promised

63. De Ruijter, "That is the whole story of Hebrews 11. All these people sought it [the promise] through Christ. Yes, also in the Old Testament"; De Ruijter, "Ik geloof," 27 (trans. mine).

64. McWilliams, "The great 'cloud of witnesses' with which the new covenant believers are 'surrounded' comprises those who have borne witness to Christ before his incarnation, of whom we read in chapter 11"; McWilliams, *Hebrews*, 343.

65. We will return to this shortly.

66. Several translations, including the ESV, make this a possessive genitive, and thus translate τῆς πίστεως with "our faith." While this is grammatically possible, we think it is more a consequence of having adopted the subjective approach to 11:1, than it is a necessary interpretation, as is seen in various other translations.

67. *TDNT* 1.487; L&N 36.6 is similar: "a person who as originator or founder of a movement continues as the leader — 'pioneer leader, founding leader.'" Thayer's comments on the use of Hebrews 12:2 are apt, describing Jesus as one "who in the prominence of his faith far surpassed the examples of faith commemorated in Heb. 11"; Thayer, *Thayer's Greek English Lexicon*, 77; see also Schelhaas, "Christus en de historische stoffen in de prediking," 126.

68. Cf. Num 1:16; 2; 3:32, and in particular, the frequent usage in Numbers 7 where the chieftains make offerings of dedication on behalf of their tribes.

in Genesis 3 and later typified through various modes of revelation. In the Garden of Eden God spoke to Adam, but that word was not mixed with faith and perseverance in the covenant. Adam was expelled by God, and this ministry of judgment was attended by cherubim who guarded the way back into the garden (Gen 3:24), thus disallowing Adam to enter in. The book of Hebrews seems to be quite mindful of this as is evidenced by its perpetual exhortation to *enter into God's presence*, as well as the frequent references to the ministry of angels.[69] Furthermore, the idea of Christ as the one who leads his people into the presence of God though his mediatorial work is the over-arching theological theme of the book of Hebrews.[70]

The second key term in 12:2, "perfecter" (τελειωτὴν), is very important in the book of Hebrews. It also bears an eschatological connotation, and refers to the way in which the ministry of Christ supersedes those of the Old Covenant (prophet, priest, king, sacrifice, temple, revelation). All these things are not only "better" (κρείττων) in Christ; in him, they find their perfect fulfillment. This idea of "perfection" is also very important in the book of Hebrews.[71] The law and the Old Covenant ministries to which it was attached are clearly described in Hebrews as being unable to perfect the ones who benefited from their ministry. The effect of this was to leave them in a position of needing something *better* that could only be found in Christ. The pastoral import is strong: whereas certain members of the community were succumbing to numerous pressures to depart from the church and return to the ministries of the Old Covenant, the author-pastor is pleading with them to see that those ministries could never bring about the perfection of the believer nor the consummation of the covenant. Something more, something perfect and eschatological was needed not only to reverse the curse, but also bring about the covenant promise "I will be your God and you will be my people." Such perfection, according to Hebrews, can only be found in Christ. That is why the author-pastor alludes to Christ not only as the "founder and perfecter" of faith, but also as the one upon whom the weary pilgrims of this present evil age must keep their focus. To look away from him will inevitably lead to stopping in one's race of faith and becoming shackled to the "weights" and "sin" which hinder endurance.[72]

69. See particularly chapters 1, 2, 12, and 13.

70. In Hebrews, "To be above the angels is to be God, to be below the angels is to be human." Thus, the Christology of the book of Hebrews is that the one who mediates is the divine God-man. See Bauckham, *Jesus and the God of Israel*, 241.

71. Schreiner notes that in Hebrews, "perfection" is attained through suffering and vindication, and that as particularly embodied in Christ himself; Schreiner, *Magnifying God in Christ*, 115.

72. D.K. Wielenga suggests in a sermon that the language of Hebrews 12:1–2 is a

There is another important connotation of the term "perfecter" (τελειωτὴν) that we wish to address. As has been noted, in the book of Hebrews, Christ has clearly been portrayed as the perfect prophet, priest, and king. He is also the perfect sacrifice. But in what way is he the *perfecter* of faith in Hebrews 12:2? This is an important question, and the way in which it is answered will significantly affect the way the hall of faith is treated in chapter 11 (similar to the suggestion about the way in which the understanding of Hebrews 11:1 affects the rest of the chapter). Our proposal is that Jesus is the "perfecter" of faith in the sense of being the one who fulfills it. He is not simply the object of faith, nor the destination of faith; he is the *fulfillment* of the hall of faith. In other words, as we shall shortly demonstrate, Jesus is the one who amplifies and fulfills the nuances of revelation revealed in each of the heroes in Hebrews 11. Insofar as Jesus is referred to as the perfecter of the ministry and revelation given by the various offices and ministries of the Old Covenant, he is also the perfecter of the testimony given by the "cloud of witnesses" in Hebrews 11. It might be said this way: Jesus is the "better than" Abel, Enoch, Noah, Abraham, Isaac, Jacob, Joseph, etc., in that he fulfills not only what they were hoping for, but that to which their particular lives were witnessing. Jesus is not simply the object of their faith; he is also the one whose very life is being revealed *in* their lives of faith. We might liken the heroes of chapter 11 to facets in a diamond. While each facet is unique, they are yet a part of the same diamond. Each facet captures particular nuances of light, color, etc.[73] yet to look at a facet of a diamond is still to look at the diamond itself. In this respect, Jesus is God's climactic, eschatological Word (Heb 1:2).

Consistent with this, we would express caution in regard to the insertion "our" in Hebrews 12:2 (where Jesus is thus described as the founder and perfect of *our* faith). The possessive pronoun, while a grammatical option, is not required by the text, as is evidenced in the translation variations.[74] Our reservation is not only grammatical, but also theological. To simply call Jesus the author and perfecter "of faith" leaves the text intentionally open to the way in which Jesus is not only the fulfillment of *our* faith (the subjective side of faith), but how Jesus also is the "perfecter" of *the* faith, in the sense of

---

summary of the entire book of Hebrews, let alone chapter 11; Wielenga, "Openbare belijdenis van het geloof," 26.

73. Van Bruggen highlights the particular contributions of those in Hebrews 11, who, though united in faith, each have their own particular "history and scope"; Van Bruggen, "Hermeneutics and the Bible," 168.

74. This is affirmed by Ellingworth and Nida, who suggest, "'Our' may be supplied if Jesus is the source [of faith] but not if he is the example"; Ellingworth and Nida, *A Translator's Handbook on the Letter to the Hebrews*, 290.

perfecting the revelation being revealed in the hall of faith (in an objective manner, consistent with Hebrews 1:1-2).[75] In our view, the author of Hebrews is accenting the way in which Christ is the climax of God's redemptive revelation—his speaking and acting. Even though God has and continues to speak through the saints and prophets of old, his definitive revelation is in Christ, the eschatological Word of God incarnate, and the supreme example of what it means to persevere (12:3). This suggestion seems to be in keeping with the both-and approach to the subjective-objective dilemma of Hebrews 11, and more importantly, the philosophy of revelation set forth in Hebrews as a whole.

In summary, the book of Hebrews seems to require us to view the hall of faith not simply as *ordo salutis* examples to be imitated, but also as *historia salutis* examples of revelation that contribute to the canon by revealing previews of the gospel in their lives of faith.[76] In this way the Old Testament saints were participating in the drama of redemption, embracing and revealing the promises of God by faith. As will be shown more fully later, the same is true for the church today. This is our hermeneutical approach to Hebrews 11 on the basis of the theology of the book as a whole, the pastoral concern of the book, and the brackets formed by the bookends of the "faith" statements found at the end of chapter 10 and the beginning of chapter 12. What remains is to survey the heroes of chapter 11 to demonstrate how their lives of faith participated in and testified to the better things that would come in the person and work of Christ, the founder and perfecter of faith.

75. As Richard Hays notes, Jesus "recapitulates and culminates the testimony of the whole cloud of faithful witnesses rhetorically summed up in chapter 11"; Hays, *The Conversion of the Imagination*, 134.

76. McWilliams suggests, "We must be careful not to turn the *roll* call of faith primarily into a *role* call of faith, as is often done . . . the text is not preaching Abraham or Samson, but Christ"; McWilliams, *Hebrews*, 342 (emphasis original).

4

Hebrews 11

A Theatre of Martyrs

IN THIS CHAPTER, IT is not our intention to examine each of the "by faith" examples in Hebrews 11 in exhaustive detail. Rather, in more of a cursory fashion, we intend to apply the interpretative suggestion above; namely, that each of the heroes of faith listed in Hebrews 11, while displaying a commendable faith, also participated in revealing the better "things to come" with the redemptive work of Christ. This methodology is cautiously related to the idea of typology, in that it suggests that the saints of Hebrews 11 are both examples of faith in the commonly understood sense, but also witnesses to "things to come" through the divinely shaped details of their lives. To look at Hebrews 11 in this light is hardly new. As Goppelt suggests regarding the intention of the author of Hebrews in chapter 11, "No attempt has been made to conceal the fact that . . . they are part of a salvation that has already been experienced and are also shadowy types of the salvation that appeared in Christ."[1] We must grant that much of their testimony can only be understood retrospectively as testifying of Jesus, the founder and perfecter of their faith stories. On this retrospective idea, Greidanus helpfully notes:

> The underlying concern about reading typology retrospectively is that we leave ourselves open to the charge of reading meaning back into the Old Testament text that is not there. But one could counter that typological interpretation is not reading meaning

1. Goppelt, *Typos*, 175.

back into the event described in the text but simply understanding this event in its full redemptive-historical context.[2]

While this caution is apt, at the same time, it does not contradict what
seems to be the interpretive method of Hebrews as a whole; namely, to read
the Old Testament in the light of the coming of Christ and the better things
that came with him.[3] This is not to say that everything in the Old Testament referenced in Hebrews is a type of Christ, but rather that Christ, and
the better (perfect) things brought by him are the interpretive lens through
which the author of Hebrews appears to read Old Testament history.[4] This
method is clearly and importantly distinguished from allegory because of
the profound and necessary emphasis on redemptive *history*.[5] At the same
time, it relates to the idea of typology through the progress of redemptive
history. Thus, the heroes' individual scenes display far more than simply
their own subjective faith experiences in history. They were participants in
revealing God's unfolding redemptive drama as those to whom and through
whom God was speaking.[6] At the same time, the people listed in Hebrews
11 also display what it looks like to walk with God en route to the consummation of the promises of the gospel that find their fulfillment in Christ.[7] As
shall be seen in the following chapter, it is this idea of walking with God in
persevering faith that the congregation is particularly called to imitate. In
order to accomplish our goals for the present chapter, some exegetical comments will be made about each hero of faith, and various commentaries and
published sermons will function as conversation partners along the way,
some offering insights that agree with our thesis, and others that provide differing points of view. Additionally, we will allow other conceptually related
verses to shed light on our passages, according to perspective of the analogy
of faith (letting Scripture interpret Scripture).[8] This is important, for while

2. Greidanus, *Preaching Christ From the Old Testament*, 252.

3. Clowney, *Preaching and Biblical Theology*, 34.

4. Vos views this as the distinction between the preparatory character of the Old
Covenant over against the final character of the New; Vos, *The Teaching of the Epistle
to the Hebrews*, 52. He suggests the author of Hebrews views those living under the old
covenant as living in a "world of shadows"; Ibid., 52.

5. Schilder, "Modern Exemplarisme I," 42.

6. Laansma, "Hebrews," 30.

7. Trimp, *Heilsgeschiedenis en prediking*, 91.

8. We recognize that we are walking a thin line of imputing all that the rest of the
Bible says about an idea in other places into one word or verse. This exegetical fallacy
is referred to as Illegitimate Totality Transfer (ITT). At the same time, it is generally
understood that the Bible interprets itself, and that hard texts are to be understood in
the light of easier texts.

we certainly recognize interpretive distinctions among the New Testament authors, at the same time, there is an essential harmony that binds their interpretive methods—namely, the revelation of the person and work of Christ and the pastoral implications of Old Testament revelation.

CREATION (HEBREWS 11:3)

It is noteworthy that while verse 2 would appear to introduce a long list of *people* (the hall of faith) the section begins rather with a reflection and commentary on our understanding of creation itself. "We" are the first people introduced in the hall of faith, as we "understand *by faith* that the universe was created by the word of God, so that what is seen was not made out of things that are visible." Creation is the necessary foundation of subsequent revelation. According to the author of Hebrews, what is seen in creation was not made out of visible things. We would suggest that this point in Hebrews is much like the apologetic of the Pentateuch itself: the God who has redeemed both Israel and the church is the God of all creation.[9] The "Word of God" language peppers the book of Hebrews, primarily as a redemptive word that culminates in Christ. Here it is posited as not simply the redemptive word, but the *creative* and foundational Word of God that sets all things in motion.

While the point of creation's inception is initially in view, the question of pattern is immediately set before us. The issue the author seems to be addressing is whether or not the things that can be seen were made out of things that were already visible. The answer is in the negative—they were not. The things that exist have been brought into existence by the creative Word of God.[10] That being said, the created things were still patterned *after something*. God, the creator-consummator, is viewed as a masterful painter, without a stroke of his creative energy being wasted. Everything that he creates is intentional and purposeful. Creation itself is infused with an eschatological goal, culminating in the person and work Christ in history to the glory of the Triune God.[11] The first day sets in motion a number of days that must, of necessity, climax in the consummate Sabbath day. In this sense, protology anticipates eschatology, and is mediated, in terms of revelation,

---

9. Kline, *Treaty of the Great King*, 40, 56.

10. Bruce suggests that the role of the Son in creation (1:2) is assumed here in Hebrews 11:3; Bruce, *The Epistle to the Hebrews*, 278–9. This would make for an interesting positioning of the Son as both the creator-author of the creation story, as well as its perfecter (i.e., Hebrews 12:1–2). Ellingworth, however, dismisses the idea that the Son is in view here; Ellingworth, *The Epistle to the Hebrews*, 570.

11. Poythress, *In the Beginning Was the Word*, 98.

through the lens of typology.[12] The protological creation week gives way to a consummate day of rest and doxology for God himself—the Alpha and Omega of creation. That the first creation is patterned after the last/new creation (and not the other way around) is demonstrated from exegetical and theological observations. First, the Bible both begins and ends with garden imagery.[13] But the garden in which the Bible ends is not simply a return to the first garden, but a movement forward to an eschatological garden that far supersedes that of the first garden.[14] The chief illustration of this is that in the new, eschatological garden, neither sin nor death are present, as death itself is said to have died (Rev 20), and the covenant promise of God, "I will be your God and you will be my people" (Rev 21:3) is consummately fulfilled. Adam, in the protological garden, never knew such irrevocable intimacy with God. All that he had that was good could potentially be lost.

In terms of the Christocentric nature of the garden covenant with Adam, several New Testament passages force us to understand that the first Adam was always intended to give way to the person and work of the last Adam. In a similar manner, Romans 5:14 renders a commentary on Adamic revelation, in that it articulates the fact that the first Adam was a type of the last Adam (τύπος τοῦ μέλλοντος), Jesus, who was to come. Accordingly, it is not that Christ, who came last, is patterned after Adam, who came first. But the opposite is the case—the first (protological) Adam is patterned after the last (eschatological).

A similar statement is made by 1 Corinthians 15:45, which juxtaposes both "Adams" with protological and eschatological language. "Thus it is written, 'The first (πρῶτος) man Adam became a living being'; the last (ἔσχατος) Adam became a life-giving spirit." The point we are emphasizing is that a revelatory relationship exists between the design of the first and last Adams. Yet the first is not only patterned after the latter, but also the ministry of the latter definitively supersedes that of the former. Christ's work perfects the work of the first Adam, in as much as the new creation perfects the first, and the eternal Sabbath perfects the initial Sabbath. This is the point of Hebrews 11:3, to show that creation was infused with a destiny that stretched out before it. Hebrews 11:3 is thus foundational to the remainder of the chapter in which the movement from protology to eschatology, and from typology to fulfillment is understood "by faith."

12. For a fruitful study on this topic of typology in the book of Hebrews, see Vos, *The Teaching of the Epistle to the Hebrews*, esp. 55–65. Vos's suggestion that the Old Testament types are patterned after heavenly realities that would enter history with the coming of Christ is remarkable; see esp. 58.

13. Cf. Gen 1–2 with Rev 22.

14. Beale, *A New Testament Biblical Theology*, 639–40.

To have begun with the creation is entirely proper and pastoral. The Pentateuch does the same, and the author of Hebrews, seeking to rescue those who are tempted to return to the shadowy and provisional ministries of the Old Testament, employs an apologetic/exegetical method consistent with that of Moses who showed Israel that the one who redeemed them is the one who has created all things. Creation is the colorful backdrop against which all of God's dealings with man unfold in history—including redemption. It is the theater of God's glory.[15]

CAIN AND ABEL (HEBREWS 11:4)

It is not arbitrary that the first martyr (witness) mentioned in Hebrews 11 is Abel. Abel is the first of many things. He is the first person recorded in Scripture as having offered to God an acceptable sacrifice (Gen 4:4); he is the first person in Scripture to die a martyr's death (Gen 4:8; cf. Matt 23:35); and he is the first person in Scripture to clearly evidence the principle that the "just shall live by faith."[16] Abel's testimony is that not even death can separate those who have faith in the promises of God from receiving those promises (Rom 8:35). At a very basic level, Abel is clearly a commendable example of faith. Yet at a deeper level, he is the first witness to the resurrection, as is indicated by Hebrews 12:24 where Abel is an example of one who, though he died, still speaks, and is counted among the "spirits of the righteous made perfect."

It is remarkable that such dramatic tension should be displayed between these first sons of Adam and Eve—Cain and Abel. As soon as the fall occurred, God promised that another "seed" would be born in time, and that this seed would be bruised by Satan, yet would ultimately crush Satan in triumphant victory.[17] That Eve thinks Cain, her firstborn son, might be the promised seed is suggested from her confession (Gen 4:1) "קָנִיתִי אִישׁ אֶת־יהוה" (literally, "I have acquired a man through the LORD").[18] The sad irony is that Cain clearly was *not* the promised seed of redemption, nor was he in line with the spirit of Christ. He rather proved to be in line with the seed of the serpent. This was evidenced in several ways.

Cain and Abel both bring offerings that are notably the first sacrifice offered by humans after the fall. The chronological language "in the course

15. Cf. the revelation of God's "glory" in creation in Ps 19 with the redemptive glory revealed in Christ, the head of creation, as described in John 1:1–14.

16. Cf. Hab 2:4 with Heb 10:38, as well as Gen 4:10 with Heb 11:4.

17. Gen 3:15.

18. The LXX reads "καὶ εἶπεν Ἐκτησάμην ἄνθρωπον διὰ τοῦ θεοῦ."

of time" (וַיְהִי מִקֵּץ יָמִים), is suggestively like the setting of a stage in which the sacrifices are the main event.[19] Cain, arguably is the central figure of the story, not Abel.[20] Commentators have wrestled with the objective basis of God's accepting Abel and rejecting Cain. The text is not explicit as to God's reason for rejecting Cain.[21] Nor does the Genesis text explicitly refer to the faith of Abel or unbelief of Cain; both can only be deduced by inference. Cain's offering (Gen 4:3) was simply of the "fruit of the ground" and God rejected it.[22] It was neither a blood offering nor an offering of first fruits, and does not appear to have been offered from a posture of faith. Some have suggested that the garments of skin provided by God in Genesis 3:21 occasioned the first animal sacrifice in Scripture, and that by implication, the rejection of Cain's offering lies in that it did not follow the pattern of sacrifice established by God.[23]

Abel, by contrast, implicitly followed God's pattern of sacrifice, and by faith offered a firstborn of his flock (Gen 4:4). Again, the text is not explicit as to why God "had regard for Abel and his offering, but for Cain he had no regard" (Gen 4:4–5).[24] Stedman goes so far as to say, "It is a mistake to read

19. Brueggemann, *Genesis*, 55. The phrase is also used elsewhere of an unspecified period of time, i.e. "in the course of time" (Gen 40:4) and "at the appointed time" (Num 9:2). Gordon Wenham suggests the time marker "in the course of time" likely implies at the end of the first year when harvest occurred; Wenham, *Genesis 1–5*, 103.

20. Eric Peels has convincingly made this point from both the structure of Genesis 4 and from the theological implication of the older brother being upstaged by the younger; Peels, "In het teken van Kaïn," 177.

21. This does not vindicate Brueggemann's suggestion that God acted "capriciously" in rejecting Cain and accepting Abel; Brueggemann, *Genesis*, 55–56.

22. Kuruvilla observes that thus far the "ground" has only been referenced to in regard to the curse (Gen 3:17), Kuruvilla, *Genesis*, 80.

23. Von Rad notes that while the text does not explicitly resolve this riddle, "The only clue one can find in the narrative is that the sacrifice of blood was more pleasing to Yahweh"; Von Rad, *Genesis*, 104. Waltke, by contrast, contends that in the Old Testament, the "tribute" offering was a bloodless sacrifice (cf. Lev 2:14) and suggests the fault with Cain lies in that he did not bring the best (first fruits) but only that which appears to be a token offering; Waltke, *Genesis*, 97. Horton helpfully brings the two ideas together, suggesting that while the tribute offering would be a part of the acceptable sacrifices, Cain fails to bring a blood guilt offering (as did Abel) on this important occasion of the first recorded sacrifice in human history since sin entered the world; Horton, *Pilgrim Theology*, 193.

24. Van Bruggen, for instance, highlights the importance of Abel offering a "firstborn" but still locates the value of Abel's offering in his faith, not so much in the precedent of Genesis 3:21. He does, however, note that Abel's faith was anchored in what God promised to Adam; Van Bruggen, *Hebreeën*, 271; cf. also his sermon on Hebrews 11:4 "Vergeet de dinosaurussen: DENK LIEVER AAN ABEL!" http://vanbruggenpreken. nl/, particularly point 2. Similarly, Van Bruggen says in this connection, "Remembering the saving work of Jesus places us in the row with our forefathers, Adam and Eve .

into this Genesis account any hidden reasons for God's acceptance of Abel's offering and rejection of Cain's."[25] While not wishing to read something artificially into the text, the narrative seemingly suggests that these sacrifices are to be highlighted for their significance, and thus the disposition of the heart seems to be revealed in the type of sacrifice that is offered.

Furthermore, immediately following God's rejection of Cain's offering and acceptance of Abel's, Cain murdered righteous Abel, evidencing that Cain's heart was truly distant from God. Abel alone receives God's approbation, only to be forcefully upstaged by the jealous rage of Cain, which ends in fratricide. It is tragic irony that the first recorded episode of worship ends in death and judgment. Cain proves to be the first murderer in biblical history and sadly, his brother Abel, the first martyr.[26] In connection with this, Cain is the only person from the Old Testament mentioned in the book of 1 John, and that for his murderous example of one we ought not to imitate.[27] Thus, Cain's role is an antagonistic one, as the city of God develops in sharp contrast to the city of man.[28]

That dramatic irony abounds is seen in the fact that it is not unrighteous Cain who dies in the scene but righteous Abel. Where are justice and the promise that the just *shall live*? It is here that Abel's testimony is the strongest, not in life but in death. For even in death, Abel's voice is still heard by God, and God comes in judgment upon Cain. Again, with dramatic irony, the judgment upon Cain is neither total nor immediate. Both must wait: Cain for climactic judgment, Abel for climactic vindication. Yet Abel's faith does not display simply his own righteousness, obedience, and martyrdom. In him, we see the display of another who will actually fulfill the Genesis 3:15 promise of the seed of the woman; one who will offer to God a more acceptable sacrifice on a consummate stage in the "fullness of time" (Galatians 4:4); one whose righteousness, obedience, and martyrdom will exceed that of Abel; and one who will ultimately redeem Abel and those

---

. . ."; sermon on Hebrews 1:1–2a, http://vanbruggenpreken.nl/. C.G. Bos dismisses the importance of blood sacrifice altogether; Bos, "Gods getuigenis over Abel's offer," 6.

25. Stedman, *Hebrews*, 118. Ironically, Stedman, following Bruce, defends the idea that it was over the disposition of the brother's hearts that God accepted the one and rejected the other. But the text does not say that either, a point that is highlighted by Moyise, *The Latter New Testament Writings and Scripture*, 103.

26. Eric Peels rightly affirms that in this narrative, which is as intriguing for what it does not say as what it does say, "a motif occurs which will play a major role in the book of Genesis: the election of the youngest above the oldest (Ishmael – Isaac; Esau – Jacob, Joseph –Judah, etc.)"; Peels, "The World's First Murder: Violence and Justice in Genesis 4:1–16," 37.

27. I am indebted to Rob van Houwelingen for pointing this out to me.

28. Kline, *Kingdom Prologue*, 182.

who join him in the hall of faith.[29] Jesus is the truly faithful son of Eve, as well as the "firstborn of the flock" whose sacrifice will put an end to all sacrifices once and for all (the theme of the book of Hebrews). As with Abel, Jesus is ironically martyred on the world stage of God's glory at the cross. But his death is not the end of him, just as it was not for Abel. Rather, Jesus triumphs over death and its cause (sin) through his resurrection.[30] The author of Hebrews makes a significant connection between Abel and Jesus in 12:24.[31] Whereas the blood of Abel cried out in judgment against Cain, the blood of Christ cries out the opposite for those who have faith in him. It cries out not for justice but for grace, forgiveness, and justification.[32] This is the "better word" spoken by the blood of Christ in contrast to the blood of Abel.

It is hard to overstate the importance of how the author of Hebrews is clearly uniting the testimonies of Abel and Jesus to the resurrection, the former being typological and the latter being the much "better word" in that it is climactic, final, and eschatological. Abel's sacrifice, death, and subsequent *speaking* ministry are eschatologized by Jesus Christ. Jesus is the "better" Abel, of whom the life and ministry of Abel were clearly witnessing. This is the way in which the author of Hebrews sets Abel and Jesus side by side as those who testify to the same heavenly realities (Christ's sacrifice and the hope of the resurrection). While Abel's voice was heard in the days in which God was speaking through his promises, types, and shadows,[33] Jesus speaks in these "last days" (Heb 1:3), and is God's final, consummate Word. He is not simply the one who speaks God's word, but is the Word of God made flesh (John 1), and in him all things are fulfilled, including the revelation first introduced by Scripture's first martyr—righteous Abel.

ENOCH (HEBREWS 11:5-6)

Little is known about the enigmatic figure Enoch. He is hailed as the first in Scripture who was taken up into the presence of God without experiencing

29. This is not to suggest an intentional correspondence between Gen 4:3 and Gal 4:4, but simply an analogy.

30. Abel's drama anticipates the "U" shaped dramatic comedy of the death and resurrection in which the hero must first become the victim. See chapter 2 for further detail on the language of dramatic comedy.

31. Craig Koester sees Hebrews 11–12:24 as one literary unit, and notes, "Initially, Abel's blood speaks, but in the end Jesus' blood speaks even more effectively"; Koester, *Hebrews*, 469.

32. Van Houwelingen, "The Epistle to the Hebrews," 108.

33. HC 19.

death itself. It is not incidental that the author of Hebrews should place Enoch immediately after Abel, not only for chronological reasons, but also for theological reasons. Whereas Abel is the first in Scripture to give clear evidence of death *and resurrection*, Enoch is the first witness in Scripture to the possibility of entering into heaven *apart from death*.[34] Thus, Abel died and was buried, and awaits the final resurrection at Christ's return—which is previewed in the fact that he, though dead, still speaks. Enoch, by contrast to Abel's violent death, is a preview of those who are mysteriously "caught up alive at the Lord's coming."[35] What was so special about Enoch? In order to answer this, it is important to see the way in which Enoch, similar to Abel, must be contrasted with Enoch's counterpart, Lamech. Whereas Abel's contribution to revelation cannot be properly understood apart from the backdrop of the tense conflict with his brother Cain, so also Enoch cannot be properly understood apart from the antithetical behavior of Lamech.

Both Enoch and Lamech are the seventh descendants down the two lines of "seeds" descending from Adam.[36] Noteworthy is the Hebrew use of sevens in the idolatrous confession of Lamech in Genesis 4:24, "If Cain's revenge is sevenfold, then Lamech's is seventy-seven fold." Lamech sees himself for what he is: a proud man in the line of Cain. Whereas God had pledged to bring seven-fold judgment upon anyone who kills Cain (Gen 4:15), Lamech boastfully swears that he will stand in the place of God and be his own avenger. What is more, he will infinitely multiply the wound upon any who seek to injure him. The "seventy-sevenfold" hyperbole of Genesis 4:24 truly highlights Lamech's pride and self-exaltation. In Lamech we see the spirit of the antichrist, the spirit of the age now at work in the sons of disobedience, the proud spirit of Satan himself.

Against this backdrop of unrighteous Lamech is the portrait of faithful Enoch. Enoch is noted as the seventh son of Adam. Hebrew scholars have noted that this literary inclusion of sevens is a way to ask the reader of Genesis to stop and consider how the dramatic story of God's redemptive revelation has unfolded.[37] How are the two seeds promised in Genesis

34. Vos, *Biblical Theology*, 47.

35. Cf. I Thess 4:17.

36. This is simply deduced by counting the generations from Adam to Lamech, and then doing the same with Enoch. See Kline, *Kingdom Prologue*, 184. Jude 14–15 says of Enoch, "It was also about these that Enoch, the seventh from Adam, prophesied, saying, "Behold, the Lord comes with ten thousands of his holy ones, to execute judgment on all and to convict all the ungodly of all their deeds of ungodliness that they have committed in such an ungodly way, and of all the harsh things that ungodly sinners have spoken against him." See also VanderKam, *Enoch*, 2–3.

37. Waltke, *Genesis*, 111–3.

3:15 developing and are we any closer to seeing a climactic resolution? In this context, Lamech represents the seed of the serpent and his kingdom of pride, murder, and rebellion. Enoch stands out in stark, antithetical contrast. Enoch's faith and piety are captured in the very simple phrase, "Enoch walked with God." This language will be used again of Noah in Genesis 6:9, and of Abraham in Genesis 17:1. It is the intimate language of covenant fellowship. It reminds us of the oft-depicted image of God walking with Adam in the Garden of Eden prior to the fall. The idea of walking with God should not be confused with a moment of standing before God in judgment, or even following after God. It is rather the language of communion—a bond with God formed by God's condescending grace, and responded to by the faith of Enoch in the God of the covenant.[38]

Not only does Enoch enjoy intimate fellowship with God, he also functions as a prophet of God.[39] In contrast to Lamech who proclaims himself as king of his own kingdom—a kingdom opposed to the things of God—Enoch prophecies the coming kingdom of God and God's righteous judgment upon all those who rebel against him. He is an early prophet of the latter rains that are to fall in the days of Noah (whose introduction is made immediately following the *translation* of Enoch in Gen 5). Enoch testifies that the just shall live by faith, as he is caught up alive into the presence of God. He also testifies that the wicked shall perish from the earth in an all-consuming wave of judgment. In this way, Enoch has the testimony of "pleasing God," a testimony he had before he was taken by God out of this world into heaven itself. Enoch's commendation is that he "pleased God" by faith, as the author of Hebrews plainly comments in 11:6. Thus, Hebrews 11:6 functions as a parenthetical commentary on all those, in and out of the hall of faith who have been called into vital communion with God himself. If anyone would "draw near to God" he must do so by faith, for without faith it is impossible to do what Enoch did—be "pleasing to God."

NOAH (HEBREWS 11:7)

Noah's contribution to the history of redemption is remarkably clear and frequently tapped, perhaps second only to Abraham in Hebrews 11. Not only did Noah "walk with God" as was previously mentioned, but to Noah was given the revelation that the antediluvian world would be swallowed up in a gulp of divine judgment. The warning comes directly from God himself (Gen 6:13ff). Of particular interest is the fact that Noah was warned

38. This sentiment is well expressed in Phillips, *Hebrews*, 415–7.
39. See Jude 14–15 above.

by God "concerning events not yet seen" (Heb 11:7), that is, the future. All of Noah's actions surrounding the construction of the ark were based not upon what Noah *saw*, but upon what Noah *heard* from God himself. Noah's faith was a forward-looking faith in the word of God. It was also a lively, hard-working faith. The Noah narrative is filled with vigorous action, leading right to the point where God closes the door of the ark, shutting Noah, his family, and all the gathered animals inside. One could easily wonder why such an unusual story is in the Bible in the first place. But this frequently expressed curiosity brings us to the very point of Hebrews 11: the "cloud of witnesses" is testifying not simply to the reality of their own personal faith, but to the promises of God.[40] Noah has forward-looking faith indeed, but the scene he has been drawn into is nothing less than a dress rehearsal for the eschatological day of God's judgment. The flood in Noah's day displays the effect of God's just judgment coming in climactic, dramatic fullness, as well as God's intention to recreate the world in a redemptive righteousness that will supersede the days of Noah and even Eden itself.[41] It is a preview of the day in which all those who are found outside of the shelter that God has provided will be utterly swept away in a wave of judgment. Noah, like Enoch, is called a preacher of righteousness (2 Pet 2:5), in that he does not simply walk with God in quietistic piety, or even build an ark in solitude; rather he builds the ark while proclaiming to the world around him the imminent judgment of God. When that judgment comes, it is only those who are united to Noah that are saved. Noah's family alone represents God's electing purposes to save a people for himself.

Of particular note is the fact that not all those who enter the ark are marked out as having faith with Noah. This is evidenced by the events that unfold with Noah's sons as soon as they exit the ark. The impious display of Noah's sons leads to another division between the blessed and cursed lines. From Noah will descend not only the line of Shem leading to Abraham, but also the line of Ham leading to the Canaanites. The point we wish to emphasize here is the way in which the faithfulness of Noah becomes the means by which those *in Noah* are saved from God's judgment. To the extent that the flood of Noah's day is an epic display of God's judgment, it is also necessarily a preview of the final judgment to come.[42] But it is not simply God's

40. J. Meijer, in an otherwise fairly severe sermon, notes that Noah's faith was anchored both in the direct promises from God, as well as the redemptive promises God made while Adam and Eve were still in the garden of Eden; Meijer, "Noach's geloof," 7.

41. Horton, *Covenant and Eschatology*, 93.

42. Cf. 1 Pet 3:21; see also Rev 20:10,15, where all of God's enemies are cast eternally into a lake of fire. As the Bible often uses water locations as places of judgment (i.e., the crossing of the Red Sea, Jordan River, and other baptismal events), so the flood

judgment that is displayed in the days of Noah, so also is God's salvation for those who are found in the preacher of righteousness who is greater than Noah—Jesus Christ. Just as those in the ark can do or contribute nothing that merits their being in the ark, so is it with those who are in Christ. The judgment of God passes over them because they are hidden in the ark of God's salvation with Noah, the righteous servant of God. Yet even Noah himself must find his perfect righteousness in one whose salvation is *better* than Noah's. Noah's story typifies the greater salvation from judgment that will come in Jesus, and only Jesus can complete and perfect the drama of which Noah is a supporting actor who by God's design has displayed a preview of eschatological realities. In this regard, by faith Noah participates in the revelation of the eschatological things to come in Christ.

ABRAHAM (HEBREWS 11:8-10)

Of all those listed in the cloud of faith in Hebrews 11, Abraham receives the most attention. He is an example of those who, by faith, not only inherit the future promises of God, but he also testifies to the reality of those promises of "things to come" through his faith. This is seen in the first of several descriptions given of Abraham in his pilgrim identity. When God calls Abraham in Genesis 12, he promises Abraham a land that he cannot yet see.[43] Abraham must journey to it by faith on a pilgrimage that will stretch his faith in countless ways. Hebrews 11:8 accents the fact that Abraham was told to "go" and began to do so, even before being told *where*. This is the accent of the language that he "went out, not knowing where he was going." His faith was manifest in his obedience, and he begins to literally walk by faith and not by sight, abandoning all that he knew (people and place) to sojourn in a land that was wholly unknown to him. His gaze was forward and upward.

What is next said about Abraham even further enhances his pilgrim identity. We are told in Hebrews 11:9 that not only did he sojourn by faith, but also that he "lived in tents with Isaac and Jacob, heirs with him of the same promise." That he and the other patriarchs lived in tents underscores the fact that their homes *in the land of promise* were unambiguously temporary. Neither Abraham, Isaac, or Jacob ever lived in settled homes; rather, they lived as pilgrims.[44] It is a curious thing that they never had more

of Noah must be seen as a preview of eschatological judgment for God's enemies and salvation for God's people; see Kline, *Kingdom Prologue*, 214–8.

43. For N.T. Wright, "The main point of 'faith' in this chapter . . . is that it looks forward to what has been promised but not yet granted"; Wright, *The Resurrection of the Son of God*, 458.

44. Johnson makes an interesting connection between the pilgrim-people of God

stable, permanent homes. They did not lack the financial resources to build them, nor had God forbidden them from doing so. Rather, their living in tents throughout the entirety of their stay in the land of promise is indicative of the fact that their true, permanent home was elsewhere. It was in heaven with God. To say this is not speculative; it is exactly what Hebrews 11:10 says, "For he was looking forward to the city that has foundations, whose designer and builder is God." The contrast could not be clearer: living in man-made, earthly tents is one thing; but living in the eternal city *that has foundations* and is built by God is something entirely different. The author of Hebrews is demonstrating that the lives of each of the patriarchs were shaped in such a way as to reveal the fact that their true, permanent and abiding city was in heaven with God.[45] Though they were blessed with wealth and prosperity while living in the land of Canaan which God had promised them, they knew that they belonged to a better country—a heavenly city, and this would be the focal point of their gaze, that constantly lead them forward and upward.

Again, we see a symbolic display, not simply of the faith of the patriarchs, but of the reality of the better things that have come with the person and work of Christ. Though Abraham and the other patriarchs looked forward to and awaited that better city to come, they would not see it in the days of their flesh. They would have to wait for a future day in which they would be perfected alongside the many other saints who would join the patriarchs in their pilgrimage of faith (Heb 11:39–40). But more importantly, even Jesus himself came into this world knowing that his kingdom was not to be found here (John 18:36). He was the consummate pilgrim, the one who came in order to bring all those who would follow him by faith into the city that his Father had prepared, and that he would go away to complete after the resurrection (John 14:2). The city to which Abraham and the patriarchs looked forward is the city that Christ alone could bring, and to which the author of Hebrews is referring.[46] Their earthly homes became the stage upon which their heavenly home was being revealed. Thus, their forward-

---

living in tents, and God himself dwelling in one in the incarnation, indicating that both were moving forward to a more permanent eschatology and communion with one another; Johnson, *Him We Proclaim*, 347, esp. n15.

45. For a helpful comparison of the city of God in Hebrews with the eschatological city descending from heaven in Revelation, see Van Bruggen, "Het apostolische evangelie als geloofsbelijdenis," 135–41.

46. Van Houwelingen, "For Jesus, Jerusalem was no lasting city. He was no longer welcome there"; Van Houwelingen, "Wij hebben hier geen blijvende stad," 49 (trans. mine). This article helpfully shows the way in which, from the time of the crucifixion, Jerusalem is clearly no longer the city of Jesus; he was himself seeking a better, eternal home, and this is the ultimate hope of the patriarchs and the church alike.

looking faith in Hebrews 11 is ultimately a part of God's revelation of the substance of the covenant—a heavenly city that can only be apprehended by those whose gaze of faith is fixed forward and upward.[47] For them, God is not only the builder and designer of their eternal home, but is also the designer of their dramatic roles in the history of redemption.

SARAH'S MIRACULOUS CONCEPTION (HEBREWS 11:11–12)

In the midst of the Hebrews 11 hall of faith is the story of Sarah's miraculous conception of Isaac.[48] God made promises to Abraham, and by extension, to Sarah. At the heart of God's promises is a progeny that would be as innumerable as the sands on the seashore and the stars in the sky.[49] Decades passed since God made those promises and yet Abraham and Sarah remain childless. Sarah, in the weakness of her faith, conjures up the Hagar plan, and pleads with Abraham to sleep with Hagar as a means of bringing about an heir.[50] Hagar conceives, and immediately begins to despise Sarah, and Sarah treats Hagar with scorn. This was not God's plan; it was Sarah's. But both Abraham and Hagar capitulate to Sarah's request, and this patriarchal family begins to look more like a test case in familial dysfunctionality than the fountainhead of God's covenant people.[51] In spite of Abraham and Sarah's weakness, God gives them a covenant son—Isaac. By the time of Isaac's birth, Abraham is one hundred years old, and Sarah is ninety. Hebrews 11:11–12 highlights this by noting that not only was Sarah herself past the age of child-bearing, Abraham was "as good as dead" (verse 12) as far as fathering children is concerned. This "as good as dead" language is

---

47. Kline, *Kingdom Prologue*, 181.

48. Dirk Visser makes a plausible argument that Heb. 11:11 should be translated, "Through faith he [Abraham] received the power to conceive a child, although Sarah herself was barren, even when he was actually too old, and this because he trusted in the one who had made the promises." He bases this argument on the text variant discussions, the potential of reading Σάρρα (nominative case) as Σάρρα (dative case, implying means), as well as the express language of Rom 4:18–22 (cf. Gen 18:10–14); Visser, "Verwekte Sara een kind?," 131–3 (trans. mine). The effect of this would be to eliminate Sarah as the subject of Heb 11:11, replacing her with Abraham.

49. Gen 12:2,7; 15:5.

50. As with their laughter at God's promise of Isaac to come, this is, as J. Smelik puts it, an expression of "pure and unashamed disbelief"; Smelik, "Sara," 2.

51. 1 Pet 3:4–5 makes the point that not only was Sarah the matriarch of Israel, but also of faithful women in the church who by faith do good and replace fear with faith in God.

noteworthy as it shows God's intentional plan to bring about his promises in a way that would display his power through their weakness.[52]

Still, at the time of God's appointment, Sarah conceives. Her barren, lifeless womb suddenly swells with the child that God had promised so long ago. God tells Abraham to name the child "Isaac" which means "laughter." This is often interpreted as God's chiding reaction to both Abraham's and Sarah's laughter when God reaffirmed his promise to give Abraham a son through Sarah at such an old age.[53] While this is plausible, it is likely that the point of emphasis is God's ability to laugh in the face of his and his people's enemy—death itself. The fact that Abraham and Sarah are literally taken to the point of death before conceiving Isaac is God's way of dramatically displaying his power over both the grave and the barren womb. When Isaac is born, tears of barrenness are transformed into the fullness of joy. God's triumph over Sarah's womb is a preview of his triumph over death itself. "He who sits in the heavens *laughs* . . ." (Ps 2:4) at his enemies and the enemies that threaten his people. This is the profound lesson that Abraham and Sarah must learn—God's promises are stronger than death. It is the point that God is also dramatically revealing in their own faith-experience, so that their very struggle to walk by faith and trust God's promises becomes a display of his resurrecting power—even over the grave-like womb of Sarah, where life takes the place of death and the son of promise is climactically born at the time of God's appointment.

It would be regrettable to isolate the story of Sarah's conception of Isaac from Mary's conception of Jesus and his birth in the fullness of time (Gal 4:4). As Ohmann puts it, "It is He [Jesus] who redeemed Abraham and the patriarchs from so many awkward predicaments and delicate situations, but most of all, it is by his work that the promise is fulfilled in making the promised seed appear on the stage of history."[54] Isaac is not the only son of promise born to an empty womb in the history of redemption. God appears to Mary and promises the unexpected coming of Jesus in much the same way in which he came to Sarah. Each child's miraculous conception is forecasted by a visit from God and attended by the ministry of angels. Both children are God's answer to long-made prayers for the fulfillment of God's covenant promises. Both children also speak clearly to the greatest of all God's promises, his promise to triumph over death itself and spread eschatological blessings to the nations.[55] Whereas Isaac's birth is in the

---

52. Horton, *Christless Christianity*, 150.

53. Gen 17:17; 18:12, respectively.

54. Ohmann, "Redemptive Historical Preaching," 209.

55. Wright, *The Mission of God's People*, 69.

context of a barren womb and a father who is "as good as dead," Jesus is born to triumph over death through his own death and resurrection. In this respect, the coming of Jesus is not only more miraculous than that of Isaac, but the life and ministry of Jesus far exceed that of Isaac as he overcomes that which Isaac never could—the power of sin which is death itself. In the birth narrative of Isaac, we see a powerful, dramatic preview of the coming of the greater Son of Abraham who will bring about the eschatological fulfillment of the Abrahamic covenant. In this sense, the ministry of Christ is both present to Abraham and yet to come. Von Balthasar, commenting on the forward-looking nature of Abraham's faith states, "Thus, the time of Jesus also embraces and contains the time of Old Testament—and in a way beyond all we can imagine."[56]

PARENTHETICAL COMMENTARY (HEBREWS 11:13–16)

Most commentaries see Hebrews 11:13–16 as being a significant pause in the author of Hebrews' list of heroes.[57] Some see in it a form of parenthetical application.[58] Suggestively, no one person is in view, but a general collection of "all these." Some have suggested that those in view are Abraham and the patriarchs, to whom the author of Hebrews has just referred. Others see it as a broad-sweeping generalization of all those listed in the hall of faith.[59] Both suggestions seem to make sense, with the obvious exception that Enoch never dies, and thus would be excluded from the list of those who "died in faith" (11:13). However, it would appear in our view that the former option is to be preferred, not only for the exception of Enoch, but more importantly for the flow of the chapter. The fact that the author returns to his treatment of Abraham and subsequently to the other patriarchs would seem to underscore the idea that it is the early patriarchs who are in view. This also has an interesting pastoral contribution. If the original audience included

---

56. Von Balthasar, *Theo-Drama*, 5.24.

57. O'Brien, "The central position of vv. 13–16 gives prominence to these reflective comments: they are not simply a parenthesis"; O'Brien, *Hebrews*, 418. Skarsaune, "The central message of Hebrews' retelling of the OT narratives is powerfully articulated in a summary excursus that our author inserts in the middle of his discussion"; Skarsaune, "Does the Letter to the Hebrews Articulate a Supercessionist Theology?," 163. Rhee, as was mentioned before, represents a creative, if not strained, attempt to locate this section in Hebrews 11 as the chiastic center; Rhee, "Chiasm and the Concept of Faith in Hebrews 11."

58. Grosheide, *De brief aan de Hebreeën en de brief van Jakobus*, 266; Pink, *An Exposition of Hebrews*, 727; Bruce, *The Epistle to the Hebrews*, 299.

59. For a persuasive argument for the former, see Lane, *Hebrews 9–13*, 356; see also Hughes, *A Commentary on the Epistle to the Hebrews*, 467.

some who were being tempted to return to the nostalgic and familiar paradigms of the Old Covenant, the author of Hebrews would be exercising a
stroke of pastoral brilliance by showing that even the patriarchs evidenced
a faith that was looking forward to an eternal city in the heavens, and that
their gaze was fixed forward and upward toward heaven. Those among the
Hebrews who were being tempted to return to the preparatory ministry of
the Old Covenant were fixing their gaze backward and downward, and were
effectively walking the *opposite* direction of the patriarchs. They were succumbing to the temptation to walk by sight rather than by faith, and were
looking for an eternal city of peace here on earth rather than in heaven.
Their eschatology was upside down (more earthly than heavenly) and their
pilgrim route was reversed (more backward than forward).

The patriarchs, by contrast, saw these eschatological realities to which
their lives testify by faith. They "saw them and greeted them from afar" (Heb
11:13).[60] In John 8:56, Abraham is said to have seen Christ's day and rejoiced.[61] In his own day, however, Abraham was a proto-pilgrim, paving a
path for future pilgrims to follow. He was joined by the other patriarchs in
declaring that on earth they were "strangers and exiles" (Heb 11:13),[62] who
were determined not to go backward in the covenant, as evidenced in their
unwillingness to return to their prior homeland (Heb 11:14).

The last comment made in the parenthetical commentary is on the
one hand a high note of praise for the patriarchs, and on the other a stern
warning to those in the community who depart and *shrink back* to those
things that were all designed to lead forward to Christ and be fulfilled in
him. God, we are told, is "not ashamed to be called their God, for he has
prepared for them a city" (Heb 11:16). The language of not being "ashamed"
(ἐπαισχύνεται) is used of Christ in Hebrews 2:11, where Christ is "not
ashamed to call them brothers" who have been sanctified by himself, as they
all have the same Father in heaven. Christ is the ultimate reason that God is
not ashamed of those whom he names as his own, including the patriarchs.
The inheritance *they* were ultimately awaiting is the same inheritance *Christ*
has earned by becoming the "founder and perfecter" of faith—the faith that

60. The word for "greeted" (ἀσπασάμενοι) in this context implies the idea of embrace. It is used in Heb 13:24 for the greeting the members of the community are to
give to their leaders. It is done with a "holy kiss" in 1 Pet 5:14, and it occurs at the end
of numerous New Testament books.

61. Van Houwelingen suggests that the day that Abraham saw and rejoiced over
was the day of Christ's birth, which Abraham saw by faith; Van Houwelingen, *Johannes*,
203–5.

62. Van den Berg notes the similarity between the pilgrim-confession of Abraham
in Gen 23:4 and that of Jacob in Gen 47:8; Van den Berg, "Hoopvolle asielzoekers," 6.

the patriarchs were actively revealing as they spoke and acted out the drama of redemption.[63]

THE SACRIFICE OF ISAAC (HEBREWS 11:17)

Thus far, we have been contending that the hall of faith is not simply given to emphasize the subjective faith of the individual heroes, but also to reveal the better things to come in Christ. Perhaps nowhere in Hebrews 11 is this emphasis more clear than with Abraham's offering up of Isaac. Abraham's faith in this most remarkable trial in Genesis 22 is exemplary in the best sense of the term. The book of James underscores the fact that Abraham's obedience in the face of such unthinkable pressure was evidence that Abraham's faith in God was living and active. It was neither dead nor superficial (Jas 2:21; cf. Rom 4). While this is a truly remarkable moment of sacrifice in the history of redemption, it is still the case that this is not *the* most remarkable moment in the history of redemption.

Abraham's offering up of Isaac is suggestively the "John 3:16 of the Old Testament."[64] Few events in the Old Testament rival it for its unmistakable RH anticipation of the most dramatic event of the New Testament—when God the Father gives up his only beloved Son as a sacrifice. The parallels are numerous. Isaac is not simply *a son* to Abraham, he is *the son*, the only son of Sarah, granted by God to Abraham and Sarah when they are ninety and one hundred years old respectively. Isaac's miraculous birth from the yet unopened womb of Sarah is second only to the miraculous birth of Christ to the Virgin Mary. Both children are long-awaited sons of promise. Both sons are clearly loved by their fathers.[65] Both are the progenitors of the Abrahamic covenant, but whereas Isaac is the first son through whom the

---

63. As noted above, there are important theological and pastoral parallels between the "city" promised to those who persevere by faith in Hebrews, and the city promised to those who overcome by faith in Revelation. For a fuller treatment of the subject, see Van Houwelingen, "Contouren van een nieuw Jeruzalem," 186–203; see also Schelling, "De enige troost in de belofte van God," 36.

64. We suggest this in the light of clear RH parallels between Gen 22 and John 3:16. In each, the uniquely-begotten and beloved son is offered up as a means of perpetuating the covenant. But whereas Abraham's love-demonstration for God in the sacrifice of Isaac is stayed off at the moment of death, God's love for Abraham, and for "the world" was carried through with the cutting off of Jesus at the cross. By this, God guaranteed for Abraham and his spiritual descendants what they could not secure for themselves—eternal life.

65. Cf. Gen 22 with Matt 3:15.

promise shall descend, Jesus is the ultimate Son in whom the promises find their yes and amen.[66]

Genesis 22 sets the stage for Abraham's offering up of Isaac by highlighting not only the test of Abraham's faith, but also the genuine predicament created by the reality that if Isaac is laid to rest under a shroud of death, the promise of the covenant is broken. Nevertheless, Abraham trusts and obeys God in a way that far exceeds the limits of our imagination as he binds his son Isaac upon an altar, and in one of the most climactically staged moments of the Old Testament, prepares to kill Isaac in an act of other-worldly trust. Exactly at the pinnacle of the drama, God stops Abraham, and applauds Abraham's uncontestable faith and obedience. A ram is providentially caught by its horns in a thicket nearby—nothing less than the gift of God. Isaac is unbound, and the ram takes Isaac's place in death. God then swears to Abraham the full-measure of his blessing upon Abraham and his descendants (Gen 22:17).[67] The place where this redemptive event occurs (Mt. Moriah) will later become the place where Israel's temple will be built.[68] Thus, the sacrifice of Isaac is a multi-faceted preview of God's plan to bless his covenant people, as well as a preview of the liturgical and sacrificial system connected to the temple. Yet there is still more.

The sacrifice of Isaac by Abraham is bettered by God's offering up his own Son in the fullness of time. The difference between the two events is more striking than the similarity. In the Genesis 22 narrative, Abraham is spared the agony of having to take his own son's life, and Isaac is spared the fate of death. In the New Testament counterpart to this story, God the Father "did not spare his own Son, but gave him up for us all" (Rom 8:32; John 3:16). Just as striking is the difference for Christ, the incarnate Son of the eternal covenant (Heb 13:20). Whereas for Isaac, a substitutionary ram is found to take his place under the knife intent on circumcising him from the land of the living; for Jesus, no such substitute is found. He is the substitute. He is the one who must take the place of all other sacrificial victims, and even more importantly, he must take the place of his people and be cut off from the land of the living in order that they might find everlasting life in him. And the Father actually goes through with it. In his love, he offers his beloved Son a sacrifice for many, thus securing for his people what they could never secure for themselves—an everlasting share in the eschatological promises made to Abraham. Søren Kierkegaard captures this very well:

---

66. 2 Cor 1:20.

67. This promise also previews the blessing that would later be pronounced prophetically over Rebekah in Gen 24:60.

68. Cf. 2 Chr 3:1.

Venerable Father Abraham! When you went from Mount Moriah, you did not need a eulogy to comfort you for what was lost,
for you gained everything and kept Isaac—was it not so? The
Lord did not take him away from you again, but you sat happily
together at the dinner table in your tent, as you do in the next
world for all eternity.[69]

The drama of this story is clearly the drama of redemption. To reduce
the events of Genesis 22 to simply a remarkable display of human faith and
divine intervention would be to flatten the text out and drain it of all its
redemptive vitality.[70] Abraham's offering up of Isaac and Isaac's active and
passive obedience to his father are a divinely shaped preview of God the
Father offering up Jesus, as well the active and passive obedience of Christ
to fulfill the typological offering up of Isaac. That typology is appropriately
applied in this context is evident in Hebrews 11:19, which states that Abraham, "considered that God was able even to raise him (Isaac) from the dead,
from which, figuratively (ἐν παραβολῇ) speaking, he did receive him back."
Genesis 22 and the death and resurrection of Christ (i.e., John 3:16) cannot
be properly understood apart from one another. The former grows into the
latter and the latter finds its necessary backdrop against the former.

That such a relationship exists between the Old Testament event and
its New Testament counterpart is not unique to the Genesis 22 narrative.
As we have already suggested, this appears to be the pattern of Hebrews 11
from beginning to end. The pastoral significance is anchored in the exegetical significance. Not only were the Old Testament saints listed in Hebrews
11 looking forward by faith to the better things that would come in Christ
with the New Covenant; perhaps even more importantly, their very own
lives were revelations of the things to which they were looking forward to by
faith. God so shaped the story of these saints to preview in them the realities
of the covenant that would later appear on the dramatic stage of history, and
thus they became witnesses to the better things that Hebrews contends have
come in Christ.

ISAAC, JACOB, AND JOSEPH (HEBREWS 11:20–22)

Less attention is given to the other pre-Exodus patriarchs in Hebrews 11
than to Abraham or Moses, who follows them. But their contribution to

69. Kierkegaard, *Fear and Trembling*, 22–23; cited in Bartholomew and Goheen,
The Drama of Scripture, 57.

70. For additional ways to preach Christ from this text, as well as certain cautions,
see Greidanus, *Preaching Christ from Genesis*, 201–5.

the progressively unfolding drama of redemption is still significant. Each of them demonstrates the same principle we have seen thus far: their lives and faith testify to a longing for the future realities that will come about in the person and work of Christ. It is interesting to contemplate, given the long lives of each of the men of faith listed here, why the author of Hebrews selects *these* particular aspects of their lives to reflect on in Hebrews 11. In other words, how do these particular pieces of their testimony further the pastoral and apologetic argument of the book of Hebrews, and is that testimony consistent with the other witnesses in the hall of faith? We will bear these questions in mind as we look briefly at each of them.

Isaac, mentioned ever so briefly in Hebrews 11:20, is noted for the future orientation of the "blessings" he pronounces on both Jacob and Esau concerning future things (περὶ μελλόντων εὐλόγησεν). It is unusual that Esau is described as having been *blessed* by Isaac, as the customary thought is to imagine that he was only cursed, as would appear to be the case from Romans 9:10–12. But it is not as though Esau's life was utterly and only cursed. He was permitted by God to marry, have children, and even occupy a land.[71] Perhaps more optimistically, some of his descendants, the Edomites, would eventually be adopted into the messianic family and share in its blessings. Yet Esau is still cursed in the sense that he, as the older son, personally loses both his birthright and his inheritance from Isaac. In this sense, he is excluded from the covenant line through which the Abrahamic blessings will descend and through whom the Messiah himself will actually come.

Jacob, by contrast, will inherit the blessing. Even though he is the younger son, and not even the favored son of Isaac (Gen 25:28), he is the son whom God has chosen to bless, and the son who will receive, reveal, and perpetuate the messianic blessing. In Jacob we see the principle of God's electing purposes, which defies human reason or expectation. This principle is most clearly seen in the New Testament in God's electing purposes by which he chooses some as his soteriological objects of blessing and leaves others to remain his eschatological objects of wrath (cf. Rom 9). In Jacob and Esau, God's electing purposes are plainly revealed. The clear accent of God's blessing will fall upon Jacob, and therefore he is listed first (even in Heb 11:20), though Esau is the firstborn. Isaac's testimony of faith and the things promised regarding his two sons are previews of greater realities that will come to perfection in the future age of the Christ and his kingdom. In that age, the unexpected Son of promise will inherit all that his Father has

71. See Gen 33 and 36, respectively.

promised him, and his kingdom will not come by human strength, skill, or design, but by the covenant-keeping faithfulness of God himself.

The reference to Jacob in Hebrews 11:21 is, in some ways, one of the more enigmatic verses in Hebrews 11. This is particularly due to the awkwardness of the phrase, "bowing in worship over the head of his staff" (προσεκύνησεν ἐπὶ τὸ ἄκρον τῆς ῥάβδου αὐτοῦ).[72] Beyond the exegetical difficulties,[73] the intention of the text is discernible. As Jacob lies dying, he summons the sons of Joseph, Manasseh and Ephraim, to bless them. To Joseph's surprise and dismay, Jacob inverts his hands, thus placing the right hand upon Ephraim (the younger) and his left hand upon Manasseh (the older). This move would make no sense, except for the fact that this is Jacob "the supplanter" who at various stages of his life supplanted his older brother Esau. More importantly, in spite of Jacob's many foibles, it was God's intention to bless Jacob, thus fulfilling his promise that the "older shall serve the younger" (Gen 25:23). This unexpected nature of the coming kingdom and in particular its king becomes a theme that runs through Genesis from Jacob to Joseph, and now to his sons. It will later re-emerge in King David, and will ultimately be perfected in Jesus Christ, the unexpected king of Israel whose kingdom comes not by human design or expectation, but through the miraculous display of the power of God. It is a fitting irony that the manner of Jacob's departure from this world, and more importantly, the history of redemption, is reminiscent of Jacob's birth into it.

This brings us to Joseph. It is interesting that of the many good things that could be said about Joseph, the author of Hebrews chooses to highlight Joseph's request at the end of his life to have his bones carried out of Egypt (Gen 50:24–25). Why did the author of Hebrews not highlight the way in which Joseph refused Potiphar's wife, or endured a long stay in prison, or forgave the betrayal of his brothers? Each of these might have been helpful, especially with a "by faith" introduction, but that is not what is emphasized. In fact, what is emphasized could easily be seen as enigmatic and odd, yet it is profoundly consistent with the pastoral and theological goal of the book of Hebrews.[74]

72. Gen 47:31. The difficulty lies in that the LXX, which Hebrews follows, has "καὶ προσεκύνησεν Ισραηλ ἐπὶ τὸ ἄκρον τῆς ῥάβδου αὐτοῦ," whereas the Hebrew text portrays Jacob as worshipping at the head of his bed, "וַיִּשְׁתַּחוּ יִשְׂרָאֵל עַל־רֹאשׁ הַמִּטָּה."

73. For a concise interaction with the difficulties, see Ellingworth, *The Epistle to the Hebrews*, 603–4.

74. Summarizing the life of Joseph, R. Kent Hughes argues rightly, "We have to willfully close our eyes not to see bold hints of Jesus in the life of Joseph . . ."; Hughes, *Genesis*, 459.

At the end of Joseph's life, he makes "the sons of Israel" (his brothers) swear to him that when God visits them to bring them up from Egypt, they must carry the bones of Joseph back to the land God swore to Abraham and the patriarchs. The Hebrew word for "visit" (פָּקַד) is a theologically rich term, echoed numerous times throughout the Bible as an expression of God entering into history in order to bring blessings upon his people or judgment upon his enemies.[75] It is also a term with which the beginning of the Exodus is introduced in Exodus 4:31. Joseph's request that his bones be carried up out of Egypt is fulfilled when God's promise to visit his people takes place (Ex 13:19). The fact that Joseph requested that his bones be carried up displays his confidence in the fact that God would indeed keep his promise to redeem and deliver his people to the promised land of Canaan. It is a prophetic promise of the future with typological significance. Yet beyond this, it also displays Joseph's faith in God, who is the God of the living, and a resurrecting God. The bringing up of Joseph's bones is a symbolic portrait of the hope of the resurrection.[76] Joseph knows that he is only sojourning in Egypt, and that soon his people will be in bondage there just as he once was. God promised as much. But he has also seen God redeem Joseph's life from the pit of despair on more than one occasion, and even in death, his faith looks beyond the grave in Egypt to God's promised redemption. Joseph's request that his bones be permanently settled in Canaan is indicative of his faith and hope in a better exodus to the Canaan above. This future-oriented faith in the eschatological things to come is not simply the testimony of Joseph, but of the patriarchs before him as well. It is this future-oriented faith that the author of Hebrews highlights, and through it shows the way in which their lives also display, in seed form, the very things to which they were looking by faith.

MOSES (HEBREWS 11:23-28)

The introduction of Moses in Hebrews 11 is rather provocative, as it does not so much focus on the faith of Moses, but the faith of Moses' parents.

75. Thus Brueggemann, "The main character in the drama is Yahweh"; Brueggemann, *Genesis*, 298.

76. This is discernable first in that the term ἔξοδος ("exodus") is used of Jesus's departure from this world through death in Luke 9:31, and 2 Pet 1:15. Koester notes, "Joseph's confidence of being taken to the promised land after his death reinforces the hope that the believer's final rest will be in the place that God has promised (Hebrews 12:22–24)"; Koester, *The Dwelling of God*, 500, cited in O'Brien, *The Letter to the Hebrews*, 427. See also Phillips, *Hebrews*, 486; Hughes, *A Commentary on the Epistle to the Hebrews*, 491–2.

Moses is only a child, passive in the event described in verse 23. Hebrews says that Moses' parents "saw that the child was *beautiful*." The word "beautiful" (ἀστεῖον) follows the LXX of Exodus 2:2, where in the Hebrew text טוֹב (good) is used.[77] The point of emphasis in the narrative is not simply the physical appearance of Moses, but suggests the special place his parents believed, by faith, that Moses would have in the future of Israel's salvation history. As with several of the peculiar birth narratives recorded in Genesis and commented upon in Hebrews 11, the birth of Moses is a proleptic anticipation of God's redemptive plan for his people. Moses is born under the evil star of persecution; a persecution of the Hebrew people so great that it involves a decree of infanticide from Pharaoh himself. Yet God will rescue Moses from Pharaoh's death-decree by the fearless plan of his mother to set Moses adrift on the Nile River in the hope that God might somehow spare his life.

We note with interest that the ark in which Moses is placed by his mother is taken from the same Hebrew word תֵּבָה (ark), which is also used of the ark built by Noah for the salvation of him and his household.[78] As the fate of Noah and his family is bound to the ark of their salvation, so also is the fate of Moses, and arguably the family of Israel, bound to the ark that providentially carries its future leader safely across the waters of judgment safely into the care of Pharaoh's daughter. Within moments, Moses goes from being the object of Pharaoh's death-decree to being a son in Pharaoh's house. Even better, his own mother is providentially selected to be his nurse until he is weaned (Ex 2:8–9). The details of the text clearly illustrate that much more is going on here than simply a display of the king-defying faith of Moses' parents for the sake of their good-looking baby boy. God is at work in the story, setting the stage for the exodus of Israel through Moses. Yet just as Moses is born under a star of persecution and narrowly rescued by the providence of God, so also is the Redeemer who is greater than Moses. Jesus is born under a similar star of persecution, culminating in a similar death-decree from Herod to kill all the male children born in that time and vicinity and, ironically, Jesus is bravely carried by his parents to Egypt of all places, and is providentially preserved by the hand of God. This stage setting is thematically intentional, and it shows the harmony between Moses and the first exodus, and Jesus who is clearly portrayed in Hebrews

---

77. Cf. Acts 7:20, where ἀστεῖος is also used to describe Moses.

78. Though the ark in which Moses traversed the Nile river is not mentioned in Hebrews, the comparison here helps to fill in the picture of how Moses' preservation is about more than the faith of his parents—it is revelation of how God will preserve his covenant people through a mediator who is greater than Moses.

as being better than Moses, who brings with himself a better redemption (=exodus) into a better land.[79]

The next episode in Moses' life referred to in Hebrews 11 is his departure from Pharaoh's house to identify with the people of Israel in their suffering. It is very clear that Moses is willingly abandoning his earthly inheritance in Pharaoh's home, and its "fleeting pleasures of sin" (verse 25) for the sake of a better, eternal inheritance (verse 26).[80] What is quite remarkable is that Hebrews 11:26 says that Moses "considered *the reproach of Christ* greater wealth than the treasures of Egypt, for he was looking forward to the reward." How exactly Moses understood his own sufferings as being a form of participation in "the reproach of Christ" is the subject of much discussion in commentaries.[81] It would appear that part of what Moses' faith apprehended was similar to that of Abraham, who saw Christ's day and rejoiced.[82] The details of what Moses truly understood are unclear, yet what is clear is that in some way, Moses understood that a messianic redeemer would come and suffer reproach on behalf of his people. His later ministry also clearly reveals that he understood the promises God made to the patriarchs, particularly the Abrahamic promise. Somehow, Moses was able to put these things together and see in his own trials an identification with and preview of the reproach of Christ. Commenting on this idea, Pink says, "There was a communion between Christ and his people [then], as real and as intimate as that union and communion which exists between him and his people now."[83] In addition, Moses seemed to understand by faith that a certain reward lay ahead of him, and that this reward would greatly exceed in value any treasure or pleasure he had known as a son in Pharaoh's house. The reward (μισθαποδοσίαν) he was looking to, according to Hebrews 11:26, is the same reward that has already been referenced in Hebrews 10:35 and 11:6, and appears to be the eternal city of God which he has created for those who love him and walk by faith toward that heavenly city. It is equivalent to the better rest or inheritance mentioned in Hebrews 3–4.

79. For further discussion of this idea, and in the way in which Matt 2:15 interprets Hos 11:1, see Kwakkel, "Out of Egypt I Have Called My Son," 171–88.

80. Cf. an analogous use of "reproach" (ὀνειδισμὸν) in Heb 13:13.

81. See the list provided by Ellingworth, *The Epistle to the Hebrews*, 613–4.

82. Attridge, "Such an awareness of Christ is attributed to other figures of the Old Testament by early Christians, and it would not be impossible within the Christological framework of Hebrews"; Attridge, *Hebrews*, 341.

83. Pink, *An Exposition of Hebrews*, 801. While this statement borders on pneumatological and Christological hyperbole, it highlights the continuity between Old and New Testament believers in a helpful way.

Moses' faith is further described in reference to the Exodus during which he not only was unafraid of the anger of the king of Egypt, but also, more importantly, rested his faith firmly in "him who is invisible" (11:27). This verse, in our view, is more likely a general reference to the Exodus itself, and not Moses' first identifying himself with his people prior to his departure into the wilderness.[84] The faith and fearlessness of Moses, as well as his constant intercession on behalf of Israel, preview the faith and fearlessness of Christ who did the same. The ministry of Moses (typifying the work of Christ) culminates in the Passover event, where the sprinkled blood of the lamb stands as a substitute for the life of the people whom it covers. Few events in the Bible more clearly and effectively preview the work of Christ than the shedding of the blood of the Passover lamb. The New Testament, in numerous other places outside of Hebrews 11, clearly portrays Jesus as the eschatological lamb whose once and for all sacrifice puts an end to all need for further sacrifice.[85]

Thus, when we summarize the life and ministry of Moses in Hebrews 11, we are not simply left with a portrait of a mighty man of faith; far more importantly, we see the way in which God has designed aspects of the life of Moses to be a preview of the life of Christ. What the author of Hebrews highlights is not only the Christ-typology in the life of Moses, but also the way in which Moses' faith was oriented to the future work of God in which he would bring about the one who is much better than Moses, and whose salvation and promises will be much better as well. Thus, Moses' own life, just as with the other heroes in Hebrews 11, becomes a glimmering reflection of the very things to which his own faith was looking. Moses is not only a witness to the "things to come" of Hebrews 11:1, but also, by faith, his very life becomes revelation of the messianic sufferings that would be perfected in Christ.

THE FAITH OF THE ISRAELITES (HEBREWS 11:29)

It is a curious thing that the faith of the Israelites coming out of Egypt is held up as an example of faith, especially given that they "greatly feared" the Egyptians, and grumbled against Moses and against the Lord.[86] In addition, the majority of that generation died in the wilderness due to unbelief. Here

---

84. We base this on two reasons: the first is that Exod 2:14 says that Moses "was afraid" when he learned that Pharaoh knew that he had killed an Egyptian; the second reason is the language of Moses "seeing him who is invisible." This is likely a reference to seeing God work in the midst of the plagues that staged Israel's departure from Egypt.

85. Heb 9:12, 14; 10:19; 12:24; John 1:36; 1 Cor 5:7; 1 Pet 1:9; Rev 5:12.

86. Exod 14:1–11.

again we see that it is not simply the subjective faith of individuals that is
being emphasized in Hebrews 11, but the particular way in which God is
shaping the faith-experiences of those listed in Hebrews 11 to be displays of
redemptive realities that were still future.[87] So it is with the crossing of the
Red Sea. In the Bible, seas (or bodies of water) are often places of judgment.
The New Testament refers to both the flood of Noah's day and the crossing
of the Red Sea as baptisms (1 Pet 3:21 and 1 Cor 10:2, respectively). Baptism
is generally associated with a positive theology of salvation (Titus 2:5) and
union with Christ (Rom 6:1–4), but it also carries in Scripture an implied
theology of judgment as well.[88] Not all baptisms end well for those who
are baptized, as is evident in the flood. Jesus himself spoke of going to the
cross as a baptism that he had to undergo but to which he was not looking
forward (Luke 12:50). In this connection between baptism and judgment,
we note also that at the end of history, Satan and all who belong to him are
cast eternally into the lake of fire (Rev 20:10,15). There they are eternally
baptized into God's all-consuming and insatiable, fiery judgment. This is
likely the same judgment referenced in Hebrews 10:29 (cf. Deut 4:24) as the
final outcome of those who apostatize. For believers, however, the absence
of any sea in the new heavens and earth (Rev 21) suggests that upon their
eschatological arrival, judgment is a thing of the past, as it was climactically
experienced for them by Christ, through his death on the cross (Col 2:11).

Thus, to return to the crossing of the Red Sea, we cannot ignore what
God is revealing in the faith-experience of the people of Israel—a preview of
the substance of things to come. The absence of water on the seabed is noteworthy. Water does not even dampen the soles of their shoes as the people
of Israel pass through on "dry ground" (Exod 14:22). The water is walled
up on either side of them in an episode that reminds us of the creation
narrative where God also "divided the waters" (Gen 1:6; Exod 14:21). Only
here the purpose is not creation but a redemptive re-creation of the people
of Israel and a dramatic display of God's judgment upon his enemies. Thus,
his chosen people of Israel pass through the waters of judgment completely
untouched by the water, whereas when the Egyptians enter the same water,
God calls the waters down upon them like soldiers being ordered to execute
offending criminals. The Egyptians are wholly consumed, wholly drowned,
wholly baptized into their watery grave. This episode in Israel's history is
clearly a preview of God's final judgment, as well as the journey his people

---

87. N.T. Wright notes that, " From at least the time of the letter to the Hebrews,
the Wilderness has been used in Christian writings as an image for the dark side of the
spiritual journey"; Wright, *The Way of the Lord*, 36.

88. For an excellent and concise treatment of this subject, see Kline, *By Oath Consigned*, 65–73; see also Fesko, *Word, Water and Spirit*, chapters 9–10.

must undertake into a redemption that carries them not *around* judgment, but *through* it. They too must pass through God's waters of judgment, only to be found alive on the other side. The intercession of Moses on the basis of God's promises to the patriarchs is the basis for the salvation of Israel at the Red Sea. In like manner, the intercession of Christ will be the basis for the salvation of the true household of faith that cannot circumvent judgment, but must rather pass through it by being united to Jesus, who undergoes the judgment to which baptism pointed on their behalf. Being vindicated due to his own righteousness, his people will share in his victorious life on the other side of judgment with him. In conclusion, the Red Sea crossing is not so much about the faith of the Israelites as it is about the faithfulness of God. What is typologically previewed at the Red Sea will be later fulfilled when the consummate event comes with Christ and his return in glory.

THE DESTRUCTION OF JERICHO AND SALVATION OF RAHAB (HEBREWS 11:30-31)

The Greek grammar is peculiar in that it is the walls of Jericho (not the people walking around them) that stand in the nominative case and take the main verb. At best, the faith of the people who encircle the walls is implied, while the real focus of the verse is on what happened to the walls in particular. It is true that it is the people of Israel who walk obediently around the walls after the Lord promises that he has given the city and its inhabitants into the hands of the Israelites (Josh 6:2). Of peculiar interest is the fact that God, according to the Joshua narrative, tells the Israelites to encircle the city of Jericho for six days, and then on the seventh day to circle it seven times, followed by the blowing of the priest's trumpets (Josh 6:15–16). When this occurred, the walls of Jericho fell down and, with the exception of Rahab and her family, all the inhabitants of Jericho were killed. This is made emphatic by the language of Joshua 6:21 which says, "Then they devoted all in the city to destruction, both men and women, young and old, oxen, sheep, and donkeys, with the edge of the sword."

One could easily wonder how a redeeming message of grace could be preached from such a devastating story of judgment. This type of total judgment is referred to as "cherem" judgment, and is taken from the Hebrew word חָרַם which is employed a number of times in the Old Testament in reference to the Canaanite cities.[89] In Jericho, God employs the very unusual

---

89. A list of such cities is given in Deut 20:17; cf. Josh 2:10 where Rahab references the peoples west of the Jordan (the Amorites, Sihon and Og) who were devoted to the same manner of destruction.

tactic of having the truncated army of Israelites encircle the city seven days, with seven trumpets being blown on the last day. It is well noted that the coupling of the sevens is intended to echo the structure of the creation week. Israel's first conquest in the land of Canaan is Jericho. They will enter God's rest (or as Heb 3–4 puts it, God's "Sabbath"), only through the conflict of war. The same God who created all things is on their side, and will give them victory over their enemies, thus guaranteeing their acquisition of the promised land of rest. The fact that everything from man to beast is destroyed in Jericho represents a virtual reversal of the creation blessings.[90] In other words, everything from man to beast is destroyed on the seventh day when Jericho's walls fall down. Just as God once judged his own creative work, calling it good, and then entered his rest; even now he will again judge, but this time the outcome will be the polar opposite of creation and rest—it will be utter destruction.

Jericho becomes a theater of judgment. Its inhabitants become unwilling performers in one of the saddest displays of God's wrath in history. Yet the black cloth of death that hangs over their heads proves to be at the same time the backdrop for one of the most tender, redemptive stories in all of Scripture—the salvation of Rahab the harlot. Rahab is a prostitute in a pagan land filled with idolatry and rebellion. She is the antithesis of faithful Israel, yet in God's redemptive plan, she is not only physically spared the destruction of her fellow-citizens; she is ultimately listed in the hall of faith. Even beyond Hebrews 11, Rahab is included in the genealogy of Christ in Matthew 1:5, and is also held up as an example of one whose faith is evidenced to be genuine by the works that accompany it (Jas 2:25). Her faith is not merely commendable, it is illustrative of those who believe the future promises of God. Like the rest of those listed in Hebrews 11, she forsakes many of the familiar things of her native city in order to embrace the better things that God has promised to his people in the everlasting city. Her actions not only commend her faith, they also demonstrate in the earliest stages of Israel's entering the land, that God's mercy will seek and save some of the most unlikely candidates to inherit the promises with faithful Israel.[91] Rahab, the Gentile prostitute, will become Rahab, the adopted daughter of Israel and heir of the promises to come in Christ. Not only will she be delivered from the destruction of Jericho, but so also will all of those within her family who are found in the house with her. While the strength

---

90. A similar reversal of the creation paradigm is seen in the plagues in Egypt, where all of creation turns upon the Egyptians one plague at a time, culminating in their being thrown into a chaotic, watery abyss that bears striking similarity to the watery, chaotic darkness of Gen 1:2.

91. De Leede and Stark, "Protestantse preken in hun kracht en zwakheid," 94.

of all the men of Jericho fails to save the city, the faith of a lowly, female prostitute saves an entire family. Thus, we find here not only the blossoming flower of covenant representation; we also see the continuing plan of God to incorporate Gentiles into his covenant family. Rahab is the only Gentile mentioned in Hebrews 11, yet her role is stunning for what it contributes to an understanding of the true nature of God's kingdom and the recipients of his promises.[92]

Rahab is a diamond on a black cloth, set in brilliant contrast to the destruction of the rest of the inhabitants of Jericho. She testifies to the future realities of God's redemptive promises, and in this sense, she becomes a diamond set in a ring alongside other diamonds—the inclusion of the Gentiles. It is perhaps for this significant reason that the author of Hebrews not only includes Rahab in his list of heroes, but also lists Rahab last (in the sense of being the last to receive exclusive treatment). Her faith experience is both a preview and promise of the better things to come when God brings not only his day of judgment that is greater than the seventh day of Jericho, but also a greater salvation that is previewed in the salvation of Rahab and her family. Her voice still speaks, and it continues to testify to the better things that have come in Christ.

SUMMARY AND CONCLUSION (HEBREWS 11:32-40)

What follows the description of Rahab is a listing of faith heroes from the time of the judges through the time of the prophets. The author's "what more shall I say? For time would fail . . . " (verse 32) implies that he could go on like this for quite a while. His enumeration of Old Testament saints could become nearly endless, so he opts for a summary instead of in-depth particulars. A quick overview reveals some surprise, as the author refers even to saints whose reputation is somewhat mixed. Of the judges, Samson is not known for his commendable morality, but rather for the way in which God grants him his climactic request to bring down irrepressible judgment upon the enemies of God (the Philistines) and himself, in the final moments of his life. The power of God's kingdom is displayed, even in the weaknesses of the judges. The theme of the resurrection is also in view, as many of those alluded to stared into the face of death, only to walk away alive. Some literally "received back their dead by resurrection" (11:35). Others embraced the resurrection through martyrdom, and experienced such painful treatment as mocking, flogging, imprisonment, stoning, the saw, and the sword (verses 36-37). Through their faithful enduring of such horrid mistreatment, they

---

92. Teunis, "Rachab en de verspieders," 19.

proved that they were those "of whom the world was not worthy" (verse 38). They belonged to another world—the heavenly city above whose builder and maker is God (verse 10), and through their faith, they showed not only the means of entrance into the city of God (persevering faith) but also revealed the realities of God's redemptive plan in their very own lives (even their sufferings).[93]

This brings us to the author's climactic summary of the hall of faith,[94] verses 39–40, which we quote at length: "And all these, though commended through their faith, did not receive what was promised, since God had provided something better for us, that apart from us they should not be made perfect." Here, more than anywhere else in Hebrews 11, we get a clear sense of the author's intention to show how the faith of the Old Testament saints, while commendable, was at the same time revealing something "better." There is no question that he commends their faith, and in this respect we must do the same. Yet, as Horton argues, Hebrews 11 is not just "a collection of brief stories that end with a moral principle."[95] Much more is going in this chapter than simply commending their faith in an exemplary fashion.[96] Though they were faithful in one manner or another, still they *did not* receive what was promised. The point seems to be that in their earthly lives, they died in a state of anticipation instead of fulfillment, and were thus awaiting the "better" things to come in Christ.[97] This is a remarkably comprehensive and provocative statement, as many of the heroes of faith mentioned in Hebrews 11 did indeed at least appear to have received something of what was promised to them. Noah saw the destruction of the world and the salvation of his family. Abraham had children and lived in the land. Moses saw the Exodus. Israel inherited the land. Rahab lived. On we could go, but the point is that even though the Old Testament saints received some manner of earthly fulfillment of the promises, they did *not*

93. Horton suggests this is one of the greatest ironies in history, that those who belong to God are aliens and strangers in this world because of the offense of the gospel of God; Horton, *Covenant and Eschatology*, 276.

94. For discussion of this as the final marker and summary of Heb 11, see Köstenberger and Patterson, *Invitation to Biblical Interpretation*, 595.

95. Horton, *Christless Christianity*, 149. Similarly, Vanhoozer says, "The canon is not a de-historicized sourcebook of faith but a theo-drama: a record of the words and acts of God"; Vanhoozer, *The Drama of Doctrine*, 223; see also 231.

96. Trimp, *Heilsgeschiedenis en prediking*, 91–92. Huijser, while advocating the exemplaristic approach to Heb 11, suggests an analogy is to be seen between their faith-experience and our own. In the following chapter we will demonstrate that while this is approach is not altogether wrong, it may yet be too reductionistic; Huijser, "'Exemplarische' prediking," 11.

97. Van Bruggen, *Apostelen*, 211.

receive the true reality. Rather, they received a down payment through the types and shadows revealed in their own faith experiences. Noah learned by faith to await another day of judgment and salvation. Abraham learned to look to the coming of his greater Son whose sacrifice would exceed that of Isaac. The other patriarchs learned with Abraham to live as pilgrims and to await a land that would far exceed the earthly Canaan. Moses learned to anticipate a better Exodus. Israel learned to expect a better Passover, a better baptism than the crossing of the Red Sea, a better salvation from judgment that includes Gentiles like Rahab . . . and on we could go.

This is what the author means by suggesting that the heroes of Hebrews 11 did *not* receive what was promised. The promise that awaited them in the future was truly "better." This same promise, according to the author of Hebrews, belongs to the church today, as she is bound to the same promise with them by faith. Both the Old and New Testament saints awaited and embraced the same eschatological realities in the coming of Christ and his kingdom, and as they could not be "perfected" (τελειωθῶσιν) apart from us, neither can we be perfected apart from them. The Old Testament saints, however, have completed their dramatic faith-performances on the stage of world history, while the New Testament saints are still on stage, still working out their salvation, still performing the drama of redemption. They all await the closing of the final curtain, when each supporting actor in God's story of redemption will stand back and allow God to receive all the applause as the one who has both inspired this dramatic narrative, and has also performed its greatest act in the theater of his glory—the coming of the Son to offer the climactic act of sacrifice and triumph through his own death and resurrection.

This is the something "better" that the Old Testament as a whole was leading to and awaiting. It is the "better" reality that God has provided "for us" (verse 40) in the New Testament, as the church no longer lives in the time of shadows and expectation (stage-setting and back-story), but rather in the era of climactic fulfillment and consummation.[98] The church lives in the era of the already inaugurated, but not yet consummated kingdom of God, brought about through the death and resurrection of Christ, the "founder and perfecter of faith."[99] What is awaited now is the closing of the curtain, and the gathering of the entire cast on the stage of God's glory, with himself at the center. This is not simply the story of the Bible; it is the drama of redemption—the drama of Hebrews 11.

98. WCF 7.5.
99. Heb 12:2.

5

Application or Imitation?
Reconsidering the *Sine Qua Non* of Preaching

WHAT EXACTLY IS *APPLICATION* in preaching? If one were to do a broad survey of what might be considered the recognized, standard homiletic works currently available, there is one essential ingredient that would run throughout each of them. That essential ingredient is *application*. Nearly every homiletic work will reflect on the topic (usually the methodology) in one fashion or another.[1] Some even offer definitions. Jay Adams, for instance, defines application in preaching as follows, "Application is the word currently used to denote that process by which preachers make scriptural truths so pertinent to members of their congregations that they not only understand how those truths should effect changes in their lives but also feel obligated and perhaps even eager to implement those changes."[2] Similarly, Köstenberger suggests, "Application then, is the believer's obedience to the correct interpretation of God's Word."[3] Hoekstra, representing the traditional Reformed homiletic approach, opines, "Without application the sermon is no longer the true ministry of the Word."[4] What sermon can

1. Adams, "All homileticians insist on the necessity for application but argue for widely differing methods of applying truth"; Adams, *Truth Apparent*, 76. For a helpful interaction with Adam's view of application in preaching, including a juxtaposition of it to the exemplaristic approach, see Johnson, *Him We Proclaim*, 39–43.

2. Adams, *Truth Applied*, 17.

3. Köstenberger and Patterson, *Invitation to Biblical Interpretation*, 785.

4. Hoekstra, *Gereformeerde homiletiek*, 299; De Ruijter, *Horen naar de stem van God*, 161 (trans. mine).

appropriately do without application and still be found faithful and edifying? What theological seminary's homiletic department would do without
significant reflection on the role of application within the sermon? And just
as importantly, how many churches and congregants would be satisfied with
sermons that neglect this homiletic *sine qua non*?

The following is proposed as a working definition of homiletic application: authoritative commands or imperatival language that is exegetically
derived from the text for the purpose of instructing hearers in their proper
response to the redemptive message indicated by the text. Though this definition is neither exhaustive nor satisfying in every way, it embodies in general
terms the structure of covenant theology: namely, that who God is and what
he has done for his people is the basis of the faith and obedience of God's
people.[5] In this respect, and as shall be developed in this chapter, all biblical
commands are based on something done by God in history. At the same time,
a weakness of the definition given above is the potential for a reductionist
approach to preaching that pretends that one part of the sermon is application, and by implication, the rest of the sermon apparently *does not apply*.
This bifurcation is not our intent, for we believe the whole sermon should be
perceived as application in a nuanced sense. That said, a sermon that remains
purely *de*scriptive and is in no way *pre*scriptive suffers from a lack of pastoral
emphasis. This particular pastoral emphasis is what is captured by the idea of
sermonic application. Thus, while the definition of application given above
will not settle a number of issues, it may serve as a reference point for discussing what other homileticians have said about application in preaching.

In this chapter we intend to give particular attention to the idea of
application in preaching, both by raising certain biblical, historical, and
theological questions about it, and by proposing a nuanced approach to application that we hope will advance and enhance the notion of application
in preaching *without abandoning it*, particularly by looking at the biblical
idea of imitation. We intend to do this by first establishing the importance
of application as seen in a cross-section of standard homiletic works. Then
we will consider something of the historical development of the idea of
homiletic application. Third, we will argue for the idea of imitation as a
nuanced, biblical approach to the homiletic idea of application, particularly
as it is anchored to the concept of union with Christ. Fourth, we will employ
several examples from Hebrews 11 as test cases for our proposal of imitating
the saints in a way that is sensitive to both RH and DR concerns. Lastly, we
will conclude by suggesting a few cautions regarding the idea of application
in preaching.

5. It also accords well with WSC 3.

THE IMPORTANCE OF APPLICATION

In this section we will look at some of the standard homiletic works that es-
tablish the importance of application in contemporary homiletic reflection.
For Haddon Robinson, the idea of application is essential to his definition of
expository preaching. He says, "Expository preaching is the communication
of a biblical concept, derived from and transmitted through a historical-
grammatical, and literary study of a passage in its context, which the Holy
Spirit first applies to the personality and experience of the preacher, then
through him to his hearers."[6] The same primacy of application is affirmed
by Willhite and Gibson in their perpetuation and expansion of Robinson's
work.[7] Stott sees the absence of application in preaching as part of the reason for the undermining of the Bible's authority.[8] Olford, following the
Webster's New World Dictionary definition of application as "relevance,"
argues that such homiletic relevance "is an indispensable component of
biblical preaching."[9]

Chapell gives a thoroughly nuanced definition of expository preaching
that also includes clear reference to application:

> A sermon that explores any biblical concept is in the broadest
> sense 'expository,' but *the technical definition of an expository
> sermon* requires that it expound Scripture by deriving from
> a specific text main points and sub-points that disclose the
> thought of the author, cover the scope of the passage, and are
> applied to the lives of the listeners.[10]

Clowney, who advocates a RH preaching model, says this about application
in preaching: "As we have already seen, preaching in the biblical sense cannot be limited to bare proclamation. It is also teaching and it embraces *every
mode of application* from the sternest rebuke to the tenderest entreaty and
comfort."[11] Clowney also does not believe that there is a necessary tension

---

6. Robinson, *Biblical Preaching*, 20.

7. In this volume, Josh Stowell, following in the train of Robinson, suggests that
the most important aspect of effective preaching is a concise, memorable application
statement; Stowell, "Preaching for a Change," 141.

8. Stott, *Between Two Worlds*, 59–60.

9. Olford, *Anointed Expository Preaching*, 251; see also Pierre Marcel who argues
the same in his *The Relevance of Preaching*, 61, 70.

10. Chapell, *Christ-Centered Preaching*, 129 (emphasis original). Chapell refers to
Broadus, *On the Preparation and Delivery of Sermons*, originally published in 1870, as
the "seminal volume for the codification and popularization of the expository method
as we now know it"; Chapell, *Christ-Centered Preaching*, 129n6.

11. Clowney, *Preaching and Biblical Theology*, 73 (emphasis added).

between the RH approach to preaching and application. So he says, "The redemptive-historical approach necessarily yields ethical application, which is an essential part of the preaching of the Word."[12]

In a slightly different vein, Van Dusseldorp describes the contemporary importance of the application question in Holland against the backdrop of certain failures within the RH preaching model to address the issues of the current ecclesiastical climate.[13] His resolve is to suggest that every sermon is to have a moral effect upon the hearer because the preached word brings the story of the gospel into contact with the realities of this life.[14] Against this backdrop, it is noteworthy that older Dutch homileticians, such as Hoekstra, argued for the necessity of preaching Christ in every sermon, while advancing the expository model and the particular necessity of application in preaching.[15]

A similar definition of expository preaching with application at the center is found in Mohler's explanation, "Expository preaching is that mode of Christian preaching that takes as its central purpose the presentation and application of the text of the Bible."[16] In Lloyd-Jones's widely embraced view of expository preaching, application is not only essential, it is something which must be done throughout the entire sermon, not merely at the end of the sermon or even at punctuated points.[17] MacArthur expresses a similar view when he says, "I prefer to say that all of a sermon should be applicable. If I preach the Word of God powerfully and accurately, everything I say should apply."[18] Later in this chapter we shall return to the idea of application throughout the sermon in the RH preaching debate in the Netherlands.

Dabney's well-known *Evangelical Eloquence* is replete with references to the language and importance of application in preaching. In one definitive place he says, "The object of application is to bring the truth which has been established in the discussion to bear immediately upon the conscience

---

12. Ibid., 80.

13. Van Dusseldorp, "De moraal van het verhaal," 85.

14. Ibid., 102.

15. Stark, *Proeven van de preek*, 153. Stark, interacting with empirical examples of contemporary preaching in Holland, notes that an "application-centric" paradigm exists among the types of preaching currently in vogue; Ibid., 229–31.

16. Mohler, *He Is Not Silent*, 66. He also says, "applying biblical truth to the church's life is a necessary task of expository preaching"; Ibid., 67. Stephen Lawson's definition is nearly identical; Lawson, *Famine in the Land*, 18.

17. Lloyd-Jones, *Preaching and Preachers*, 77–78. Stuart Briscoe refers to this necessity of application as addressing the "so-what hump" in preaching; Briscoe, "Hooting Owls on Tombstones," 76.

18. MacArthur, "Frequently Asked Questions about Expository Preaching," 281.

and the will."[19] Piper notes that, "Application is essential in the normal course of preaching."[20] In a similar vein, commenting on the long sections of application that were typical of Jonathan Edwards' sermons, Piper states, "It is a tragedy to see pastors state the facts and sit down. Good preaching pleads with people to respond to the Word of God."[21] Thus, well-recognized thinkers on the subject of preaching seem to broadly, yet equally, affirm the indispensable role of application in preaching. Still, an important question remains: from where did the idea of homiletic application come?

HISTORICAL DEVELOPMENT OF THE IDEA OF APPLICATION

Retracing the trail of the idea of application in preaching is not a simple thing. There is no question that the term "application" has been extensively employed throughout the church's homiletic history, yet the precise origin of the term is unknown.[22] In short, the idea of "application" in preaching is a virtually unchallenged part of the church's homiletic history,[23] yet its exact trail apparently has not been clearly retraced by any one homiletician or school of homiletics. If the homiletic theory of the church's past might be likened to stepping-stones traversing a wide pond, each stone (period of church history) has some form of homiletic application within its purview, though they are not all identical. We believe this to be an important nuance, as application has not necessarily meant the same thing in each period of church history, nor has it been approached the same way from every text of Scripture.[24] This is perhaps nowhere better illustrated than in the massive seven-volume history of homiletics by Hughes Oliphant Old, *The Reading and Preaching of the Scriptures*. We will shortly refer to his volume that covers the biblical period, where he alludes to the homiletic practice of application emerging as early as the books of the Pentateuch (though not referring

19. Dabney, *Evangelical Eloquence*, 174; first published as *Sacred Rhetoric* in 1870.

20. Piper, *The Supremacy of God in Preaching*, 14.

21. Ibid., 96. The particular feature of this paradigm is that it is not primarily text-centric, nor does it self-consciously wed the idea of "exposition" or "doctrine" to the application; the focus is simply on application.

22. This writer has searched numerous homiletic texts and consulted with numerous homiletic professors as well, and no one seems to have a direct line to the origin of the term "application" as it relates to preaching.

23. See, for contrast, C.G. Dennison, "Preaching and Application," 44–52.

24. Jeffrey Arthurs notes that there is no "one form" of the expository sermon, in so far as each text, as well as the varying genres of Scripture implies a variety of homiletic forms, and thus varying approaches to application; Arthurs, *Preaching with Variety, 16*.

to its precise inception). Forgoing that for the moment, we would highlight the fact that every one of his volumes alludes to the presence of application in preaching. In other words, in the view of Old, each age of the church's homiletic history is replete with sermon examples that include some form of homiletic application.

The story of preaching is peppered with applicatory sermons of one fashion or another. Well-recognized, contemporary pastor-theologians like Bryan Chapell, Ed Clowney, Martyn Lloyd-Jones, John Piper, and Jay Adams represent this time tested homiletic commitment to application as found in various Reformed theological traditions. Carrick is right in noting that, "Traditionally, of course, Reformed theology has viewed preaching as *explicatio et applicatio verbi Dei* [the explication and application of the Word of God].[25] Hoekstra, in a similar vein states, "The reformed homileticians of the seventeenth century have repeated again and again in their handbooks that the ministry of the Word consists in the explication and application of the text."[26] Puritanism followed and developed this paradigm, as is well represented in the classic work of Williams Perkins, *The Art of Prophesying*.[27] Pipa, in his PhD dissertation on Perkins' contribution to Puritan preaching in the Reformed tradition, notes that Perkins' view of preaching was "the chief method by which the new Reformed method [of preaching] was adopted universally by the seventeenth-century Puritans."[28] He additionally suggests that Perkins was the first English Protestant to write a book on homiletics. The "new method" to which Pipa refers is one that emphasized application in preaching, in contrast to a perceived over-emphasis on theological content, i.e., the dogmatic formulations of Protestant Scholasticism.[29] This sentiment is well captured in the words of the Puritan preacher, Robert Burns, "Christianity should not only be known, and understood, and believed, but also felt, and enjoyed, and practically applied."[30] It is equally important to note the emphasis in Puritan preaching on making the sermon accessible to common people (thus the "plain style") as a means of revival. It

25. Carrick, *The Imperative of Preaching*, 112.

26. Hoekstra, *Gereformeerde homiletiek*, 299 (trans. mine).

27. Perkins, *The Art of Prophesying*. On Perkins' "plain style" which emphasized application as "preaching to the heart" see Beeke and Jones, *A Puritan Theology*, 690.

28. Pipa, "William Perkins," 170; see also Lewis, *The Genius of Puritanism*, 20–21.

29. The significant influence of Peter Ramus, lecturer at Cambridge, upon Perkins' view of preaching has been noted by many. See, for instance, Beeke and Pederson, *Meet the Puritans*, 471.

30. Cited in Beeke, *Puritan Reformed Spirituality*, 426; see also Richard Baxter's chapter titled "Application" in *The Reformed Pastor*, esp. 134.

is for this reason that the Puritan era is sometimes referred to as the "golden age of preaching."[31]

While we recognize and appreciate certain "new" (quoting Pipa) aspects in the Puritan approach to preaching, it ought to be observed that application in preaching is *not* something that the Puritans invented. They may have been reacting, in certain ways, to the somewhat doctrinaire preaching of Protestant-Scholasticism.[32] Still, application was *re*-discovered at best, not discovered, *de novo*. Muller helpfully notes that this "plain style" was, in many respects, the style of the Reformers,[33] and adapted from perspicuous forms of classical rhetoric, devoid of philosophical sophistication.[34]

Calvin, as one clear and familiar example of Reformed homiletics predating the Puritans, described his own preaching in the following words, "I shall enforce myself to follow as briefly as I can the plain and true meaning of the text and without continuing in long exhortations . . . that the most ignorant shall easily acknowledge and confess that I mean nothing else but to make open and plain the simple and pure substance of the text."[35] Like those in his day, Calvin believed in application and called for such responses in his preaching.[36] Calvin defines a pastor as one who is gifted "for interpreting Scripture, but also for *applying it wisely to the present use*."[37] Similarly, according to Calvin, a pastor is one who "makes known the will of God, by applying with dexterity and skill, prophecies, threatenings, promises, and the whole doctrine of Scripture, to the present use of the church."[38] In Thomas's dissertation on Calvin's sermons on Job, he notes that the focus

31. Park, "The Sacred Rhetoric of the Holy Spirit," 4.

32. For an excellent expression of caution about the oft-expressed caricature of Protestant-Scholastic preaching as being dry and lacking application, see Ryken, "Scottish Reformed Scholasticism," esp. 204–8. Samuel Rutherford is used as an example of a "Protestant Scholastic" whose sermons also evidence a warmth and clear concern for application.

33. At one point during the Reformation of the 16th century, pastor-theologian Henry Bullinger's *Decades* were more influential than Calvin's Institutes. These sermons also evidence a consistent concern for application, and for a plain style that would resurface in Puritan preaching; see Beeke, "Introduction," lxxiii.

34. Muller, *Post-Reformation Reformed Dogmatics*, 340. Muller frequently employs Bullinger as an example of the Reformed homiletic approach, both for its plain style and applicatory approach to doctrine. "Bullinger . . . evidences a concern to link the past history of the Word with its present day use"; Ibid., 464; see also pg. 83 in connection with the Second Helvetic Confession's articulations about preaching.

35. Calvin, sermon on Psalm 119:5, cited in Koster, *Light for the City*, 81.

36. Schaefer, "Protestant 'Scholasticism' at Elizabethan Cambridge," 155.

37. Calvin, *Commentary on the Epistles of Paul the Apostle to the Corinthians*, 415 (re. 1 Cor 12:28).

38. Ibid., 416.

of Calvin's sermons is that we "'learn from,' 'profit from,' and 'apply' God's providence."[39] Parker describes Calvin's sermons on Ephesians as going "straight into application,"[40] and says that more generally, in all of Calvin's sermons, "the application is direct and immediate."[41]

Thus, application was clearly a concern in Calvin's preaching, and not something that was lost on such notable Reformers in his era. Likewise, Calvin's commitment to simplicity in preaching is perhaps nowhere better expressed than in his final testament, which he wrote shortly before his death. In this he indicated that his style of preaching and teaching was aimed at scriptural fidelity and rhetorical simplicity (apart from any appearance of sophistry) either with his congregants or his theological adversaries.[42] Thus, as illustrated by Calvin, a concern for simplicity and relevance in preaching was neither invented nor discovered by the Puritans, though the emphasis may have been revived with certain nuances and pastorally contextualized sensitivities. Preaching throughout the centuries is not always easily categorized, especially if these categories are being pitted sharply against other eras of church history. That there are trends and notable emphases is evident, but, as Hughes Old has ably demonstrated, many of the concerns of one generation of preachers (namely, application and simplicity of style) can be found both in previous and subsequent generations if one looks carefully enough.[43] This is especially the case with the idea of application in preaching.

A BIBLICAL PERSPECTIVE OF APPLICATION AND IMITATION

In this section we would like to give attention to what the Bible has to say about the very important ideas of application and, in particular, *imitation*. Our concern here is that our homiletic method (which is both a science and an art) should be as biblically based as possible. Old contends that the idea of application permeates the church's preaching, beginning as early as the Pentateuch itself. Regarding the way in which the Deuteronomic law undergirds the roots of the Christian ministry of the Word, he says, "As we find in Deuteronomy, the law is interpreted and applied to the situation

39. Thomas, *Calvin's Teaching on Job*, 226.

40. Parker, *Calvin's Preaching*, 82.

41. Ibid., 88–89.

42. Calvin, *Letters*, 250, 259; see also Calvin's rather convicting comments on 1 Cor 1:17, and particularly, "As for myself, I do not simply confess that my preaching has been conducted in a rude, coarse, and unpolished style, but I even glory in it"; Calvin, *Commentary on the Epistles of Paul the Apostle to the Corinthians*, 74.

43. Old, *The Reading and Preaching of the Scriptures*, 1.172.

at hand. The interpretation is not a matter of historical reconstruction but contemporary application."[44] Clowney also notes that the ministry of the Word in Deuteronomy was not simply meant to be understood, but also internalized and obeyed.[45]

Certain authors have suggested that Nehemiah 8 is the biblical foundation of expository preaching. Mayhue, for instance, argues that the expository method of explaining and applying the Scripture is exemplified particularly in Nehemiah 8:8, which says, "They read from the book, from the Law of God, clearly, and they gave the sense, so that the people understood the reading."[46] Arthurs contends that the model of explanation and application ". . . is at least as old as postexilic Israel when Ezra read the Law aloud . . . "[47] Stitzinger is perhaps more guarded and correct in suggesting that it is simply the explanation of the text that is in view in Nehemiah 8:1–8, and not application per se.[48]

Though the role of Nehemiah 8 is not decisive, we can nonetheless infer from the earliest inception of biblical interpretation that biblical explication implies something along the lines of homiletic application.[49] The internal hermeneutic of the Bible (interpreting and applying) itself would seem to require as much. Thus, though the homiletic term "application" does not occur in the Bible, ideas that relate to it abound.[50] The commands and exhortations of Scripture are clearly intended to be obeyed. The Bible's own view of itself would seem to require as much, both in the Old and New Testaments, and that from beginning to end.[51] Following this, the practice of the synagogue during the biblical period seems to function along similar lines. Again, we look to Old for guidance. In his view, "The preaching of the synagogue had as its aim the interpretation and application of the lessons read in worship . . . the translation was only the first level of the sermon.

---

44. Old, *The Reading and Preaching of the Scriptures*, 1.39.

45. Clowney, *Preaching and Biblical Theology*, 49.

46. Mayhue, "Rediscovering Expository Preaching," 10. Mayhue also employs Acts 20:26–27 to further illustrate his point.

47. Arthurs, "John 3:16 in the Key of C," 42.

48. Stitzinger, "The History of Expository Preaching," 29. For similar emphasis on the singular idea of interpreting or explaining the text, see Yamauchi's comments in "Ezra-Nehemiah," 724–5.

49. McCartney and Clayton, *Let the Reader Understand*, 205.

50. To the imperatives of Scripture could be added the implications of man being made in the *imago Dei*, as well as the rhetorical implications (often left unstated) in the parabolic stories of Scripture, told in both the Old and New Testaments.

51. Familiar verses that support this idea would include, but not be limited to, Ps 1; Ps 119; 2 Tim 3:16; Jas 1:22, all emphasizing the importance of *doing* the word.

The sermon was supposed to be a learned interpretation and application of the text."[52]

The thornier issue has not so much been to deal with the direct commands of Scripture, though even these must be understood through the lenses of a careful hermeneutical grid. Although all the word of God is profitable for the church's understanding and growth in grace, not all commands transcend time. To put it differently, many of the Bible's commands were to be obeyed within a certain historical context. The command to circumcise, for instance, eventually grew through New Testament decrees into the command to baptize. The command to kill the pagan nations in the land of Canaan and drive them out with the edge of the sword under Joshua's commission was eventually replaced by the command to lead the nations to eternal life with the sword of the Spirit which is the word of God, and to bring them into the new temple which God is building—his church. The Levitical laws have been repealed under the administrations of the New Covenant, and even the judicial laws of the Old Covenant are not to be applied and obeyed beyond the "general equity" of their intentions.[53] Thus, it is fair to say that while the biblical commands were meant to be obeyed, obedience to them was intended to occur within the context of a proper hermeneutical understanding of the text. This proper understanding is not only in its grammatical-historical context, but its RH context as well.[54]

The second, and perhaps more difficult issue, is that of using the individuals and nations described in the Bible as ethical examples, whether positive or negative. We would quickly suggest that a simple "yes" or "no" would not be helpful. As with the previously alluded to commands of the Bible, the same must be said of the narratives of individuals or groups. While the narratives of Scripture serve to aid our instruction in the ways of God and even help in our understanding of how to relate to him in faith and obedience, the question of application is not as simple as could be hoped. To state the matter positively, Scripture is replete with occasions where people or narrative events are used as moral examples.[55] This is demonstrable through

---

52. Old, *The Reading and Preaching of the Scriptures*, 1.103; cf. Dargan, *A History of Preaching*, 1.39. On the prominence of the synagogue's ministry throughout the post-exile lands, see Pattison, *The History of Christian Preaching*, 9. Edersheim also affirms this dynamic in his extensive treatment of synagogue preaching in his *Life and Times of Jesus the Messiah*, 307–12.

53. WCF 19:4.

54. Goldsworthy, *Gospel-Centered Hermeneutics*, 200–201. Goldsworthy later refers to this as the "macrotypology" of which Christ is the hermeneutical lens and climactic fulfillment; Ibid., 252. See also Williams, *How to Read the Bible Through the Jesus Lens*, 232–323.

55. Schilder, "Modern exemplarisme I," 41.

the language of typology. It is customary to think of typology foremost as a category of Christocentric revelation, i.e., contrasting the types and shadows of the Old Testament with the eschatological realities that have come in Christ.[56] While it is appropriate to think of typology in this way, the New Testament also employs the language of typology as a pastoral means of illustrating ethical norms being lived out in one fashion or another in the lives of people *and events.*[57]

The classic example of this, well employed in the RH debates in the Netherlands, is 1 Corinthians 10:6 which says, "Now these things took place as examples (τύποι) for us, that we might not desire evil as they did."[58] It would appear difficult to argue against at least some form of exemplaristic use in this verse. The question is: *which is the type, the people, or the event itself?*[59] Paul is clearly making a comparison between the Israelites who rebelled against God due to the shallowness of their faith and the lusts of their flesh, and the particular pastoral challenges that beset the Corinthians. We would argue that he does so with a proper hermeneutical filter that sees a RH parallel to the situation of the Israelites and the situation of the church. The Israelites were already brought out of Egypt in the Exodus but were not yet in the land of promise. During that stage, they were required to walk by faith and not by sight, and to resist the various temptations that surrounded them, including the temptation to turn against God and against his servants in a form of spiritual rebellion.

Certain points of comparison between the situation of the Israelites and the situation of the church are evident. Bos, in discussing what he refers to as the *Sensus Israeliticus,* notes that while the Old Testament was given primarily *to* Israel, it was not simply given *for* Israel.[60] The church lives in the *already* of having been brought out of the slavery of her sins,

---

56. Cf. Rom 5:14; Heb 8:5; see also HC 19; cf. WCF 19:3. Geerhardus Vos has a particularly helpful discussion of typology as it relates to preaching Christ from Hebrews in chapter three of his *The Teaching of the Epistle to the Hebrews,* esp. 55–68.

57. Daniel Treier helpfully notes the varying definitions and uses of biblical typology and the importance of not being overly simplistic; Treier, "Typology," 823.

58. Van 't Veer, "Christologische prediking," 157. The tendency for such exemplarism to disintegrate into abstract moralism has been often noted. See Schilder, "Modern exemplarisme I," 41–42.

59. Both Holwerda and Van 't Veer believed that it was the event itself and not the people referenced by the term (τύποι) in 1 Cor 10:6. The exegesis of the text would seem to be on their side. Cf. Renninger, "The New Testament Use of the Old Testament Historical Narrative," 49.

60. Bos, *We Have Heard That God Is with Us,* 168–71, esp. 170. Of particular help is the suggestion that while situational differences abound between the church and Israel, existential points of contact also proliferate.

and is also a mixed congregation, in the sense of there being varying levels of faith expressed among her. But the church has also *not yet* arrived at her final destination—the promised land of eschatological rest.[61] The life of the church in this present evil age is marked by her citizenship in two worlds—the land above that she can only see by faith and the land below that she sees by sight. In this world below, there are many temptations to sin and unbelief. God's dealing with Israel serves as a sober warning to those who are tempted to fall away from the faith by rebelling against God and his servants. But the context is also positive. It shows that Christ was among the Israelites, though strangely through the presence of a rock from which life-giving water streamed.[62] Mercy and judgment flowed together, just as they did at the cross of Christ. Thus, insofar as the Corinthians might experience greater mercy than Israel did, they could also experience greater judgment if they fell away.[63]

These correspondences, in our view, vindicate the use of the idea of application, generally speaking. The comparisons between Israel and the church are clear, demonstrable, and are anchored in the over-arching DR theme of God's redemptive metanarrative as that which binds not only Scripture together, but also binds the faith experiences of God's people *back then* with God's people *now*. Thus, we agree with Bos when he says, "When the apostles and evangelists open the books of Moses and the prophets, they are not mere spectators of past events. They become aware that they too are part of these stories and books."[64] The correspondences that existed between the Israelites and the Corinthians also exist between the Corinthians and those today who are a part of the same church, united in the resurrection, upon whom the end of the ages has come.[65] The correspondences are not arbitrary or without notable contextual points of similarity. We belabor this point in order to highlight the fact that the Bible does indeed hold up particular faith and experiential aspects of the lives of people as ethically instructive examples for New Testament believers. At the same time, this does not imply that *everything* done or experienced, even by the most upright people in the Bible, should be "applied." Aspects of their particular situa-

61. Cf. Heb 3–4. For a thorough treatment of the "already and not yet" aspects of eschatological rest in Heb 3–4, see Gaffin, "A Sabbath Rest Still Awaits the People of God," 34–36.

62. 1 Cor 10:2.

63. In language similar to Bos, Phillip Cary argues for an "Israelogical" reading of the text, noting particularly how the story of Jonah "represent[s] not only Christ, the church and Christians, but also Israel and Judah"; Cary, *Jonah*, 19.

64. Bos, *We Have Heard That God Is with Us*, 144.

65. 1 Cor 10:11.

tions may be unique to them alone, while the call to identify with their faith is transcendent. We shall illustrate this in the next section when we look at specific examples from Hebrews 11.

Another intriguing use of the language of typology (τύποι) is found in the way in which the leaders in the New Testament (Jesus, the apostles, church leaders, etc.) are used as positive examples. In 2 Thessalonians 3:9, Paul holds up himself and the other apostles as examples (τύποι) in the eyes of the church, in that they did not take advantage of the saints, but worked hard to provide for themselves and proved to be models of servanthood, sacrifice, and contentment. Their examples were clearly intended to be followed by the Thessalonians. In a similar vein, Paul instructs Timothy, the young pastor of the church in Ephesus, to be an example (τύπος) of the fruit of the Spirit before the church (1 Tim 4:12). Paul gives the same instruction, in remarkably similar language, to Titus, the young pastor of the newly formed church in Crete (Titus 2:7). Again, the positive use of examples (types) in serving the church as a form of ethical instruction is evident, whether those types are the apostles or leaders in the local church. To deny that Jesus himself functions at some level as an ethical example would be to deny the very goal of Christian discipleship—becoming like Christ.[66] At the same, time, we would continue to assert the caution that employing biblical characters, episodes, and even Jesus himself as normative examples requires nuancing. For instance, Jesus raised the dead (John 1), cast out demons (Mark 1:37), and walked on water in the midst of a turbulent storm (Mark 6:49). Are these normative examples to be followed by all believers? A positive answer dies the death of too many qualifications. But a negative answer only illustrates the fact that these texts need to be understood in their RH context in such a way as not to create a one-to-one transfer—i.e., Jesus did a particular thing, and so also should we.[67]

This brings us to the important biblical language of imitation. As has been well pointed out by others, the language of imitation is often abused or misunderstood.[68] Hood has demonstrated the variety of abuses and over-reactions that have overshadowed discussions about the language of imitation in the context of biblical discipleship or practical theology. He says, "There has been, and still is, a crisis in contemporary preaching of

66. Samra, "A Biblical View of Discipleship," 223.

67. For a good discussion of such cautions, see Köstenberger and Patterson, *Invitation to Biblical Interpretation*, 786–7.

68. John Webster expresses this concern well when he says, "The language of imitation appears to detach moral obligation from the objective accomplishment of human righteousness in Christ, in this way cutting the Christian life adrift from election and justification"; Webster, "The Imitation of Christ," 99.

moralistic sermons and church-based education for children and adults that present characters—and even Jesus—merely as behavioral models."[69] Yet these realities ought not to divert our attention from language that is replete throughout the New Testament, and from the way in which the language of imitation brings us, in many respects, to the heart of Christian disciple-ship—conformity to the image of Christ. In the New Testament, Christians are positively commanded to imitate the following: God (Eph 5:1); Jesus (1 Cor 11:1); the apostles (1 Cor 4:16; 11:1; 2 Thess 3:7, 9; Phil 3:17); church leaders (Heb 13:7); other saints (1 Thess 2:14; Heb 6:12); and good behavior (3 John 11). It is remarkable that the mimetic word group is employed so broadly and explicitly. Even where the mimetic word group is not explicitly used, the idea is nonetheless implicitly present.[70]

Jesus tells his disciples in Luke 9:23, "If anyone would come after me, let him deny himself and take up his cross daily and follow (ἀκολουθείτω) me." This command implies not simply going where Jesus went, but going in the same manner or pattern. As Jesus denied himself daily and took up his own cross, so also those who follow him in Spirit-inspired discipleship are to do the same. As Vanhoozer has pointed out, mimicking Jesus is not sim-ply doing everything that he did the same way, but also performing our own script in a creatively spirited manner in the particular dramatic contexts into which God has placed us.[71] In other words, a carefully nuanced, biblical hermeneutic needs to be applied even to the life of Christ (and others) in order to understand in exactly what ways we are to follow and imitate him. We are on the same stage as the biblical saints, yet we are in different scenes; and not every action of a previous scene was intended to be repeated. Care-ful exegesis of the biblical text must be employed in order to arrive at fitting conclusions. At the same time, a proper exegesis of *our own* lives must take place in order to understand how we ought to imitate Christ most faithfully in a given context. The Bible does not live out each scene of our lives for us, so as to give us a preview of exactly how we ought to act in each scene. Yet it does give us hermeneutical guidance as to how we are to live out our lives in a way that reflects the theological and ethical commitments of Jesus

69. Hood, *Imitating God in Christ*, 178.

70. The verses referenced here are only those which explicitly use a form of the word "imitate." Hood has competently proven that the imitation pattern is encompassed in a variety of other phrases such as "be perfect as," "walking after" and the idea "putting off and putting on"; Ibid., 84, 91, 104, respectively.

71. Wells, "Christian identity is first and foremost a matter of acting in light of the larger story"; Wells, *Improvisation*, 130–1. See also Vanhoozer, *The Drama of Doctrine*, 240, 456. For a similar expression in the context of "incarnational ministry" see Van de Kamp, *Hart voor de stad*, 299–300.

himself, as revealed in Scripture and properly understood. This leads us to an important idea—the relationship of sonship to imitation.

We would suggest that the language of imitation, at least biblically conceived, is based upon the doctrine of creation and re-creation in Christ.[72] In Genesis, we are told that Adam was created in the image of God (Gen 1:26). God entered history to speak and act. His crowning achievement in the creation week was the creation of Adam on the sixth day. God spoke and acted for his own glory and man's good. Adam was to do the same. He was to speak and act, and his speaking was a reflection of the fact that he had been made in the image of a speaking God. Likewise, all that he did was to be a reflective mimicking of his Father in heaven who was perfect.[73] Adam was to work because in doing so, he would reflect and imitate the work of God. Adam was to rest because in doing so, he would reflect and imitate God's resting. It is remarkable that in Luke 3:38 Adam is called "the son of God." This term is not ontological in the sense of suggesting any sort of equality with the persons of the Trinity *in se*, but rather to suggest that Adam enjoyed son-like status, in that in his creation he was fashioned in the image of God, and enjoyed the privileges of fellowship in the presence of God. From a theological point of view, that Adam was patterned *after Christ* is clear from Romans 5:14 and 1 Corinthians 15:45. As a son to a father, Adam was to imitate the one who had created him in righteousness, holiness, and with dominion over the creatures.[74]

To the extent that Adam was created within the context of an intimate relationship with God, the fall of Genesis 3 also brought a tragic interruption to that relationship. The image of God in Adam was now a marred painting or cracked mirror, forever scarred by the original and actual sins of Adam and the sons and daughters of Adam. But this was not the end of the drama. God continued to preserve mankind, upon whom the image of God had been indelibly imprinted, even after the fall. A pattern of redemptive adoption begins to develop, as is illustrated by the hall of faith in Hebrews 11. This comes, perhaps, to its clearest expression in Abraham and Israel. With Abraham, God shows his particular plan both to redeem (and especially) to conform his adopted covenant people into his own glorious image. Abraham was called out of a world which he knew in order to embrace one which he did not yet know. He was given not only promises to cherish in his heart, but also obligations to keep in his life. God specifically commanded

72. For a helpful treatment of this, see Van de Kamp, *Verhalen om te leven*, 104–7, esp. 107, where particular attention is given to the "reeds en nog niet" (already and not yet) aspects of our being re-created in the image of Christ (trans. mine).

73. Kline, *Kingdom Prologue*, 62–63.

74. WSC 10.

Abraham to "walk before me and be blameless" (Gen 17:1), and it is later said by God of Abraham that he had "obeyed my voice and kept my charge, my commandments, my statutes and my laws." To walk with God meant for Abraham (and others in Heb 11) to walk in righteousness as a servant and friend of God in a lively relationship.[75] Walking with God also meant imitating what was learned from God by obeying the specific things God commanded.[76]

Related to the imitation idea, a peculiar pattern emerges in Abraham that is repeated in the later patriarchs, and then in Israel as a nation. The pattern is that of thematic recapitulation, in which particular details in the story of one person clearly anticipate the life of someone to come later in the biblical story. As an example, each of the patriarchs at one point will reside in the land of promise, then make pilgrimage to the south into a particular context of trial, only to ascend again to the land of promise richer than they were when they originally left. Both Jacob and Joseph complete their earthly pilgrimages in Egypt (a long way from the promised land), and yet cling to a promise that God will bring them out of that land and return them to the land of promise. Joseph, though not making the same geographic trek in his lifetime as the patriarchs, nonetheless experiences something similar as he descends from the house of Potiphar into the pit of despair in the Egyptian prison, only to rise up again to become second to Pharaoh himself in Egypt.[77] Following the death of Joseph, the twelve tribes that descended from Jacob's twelve children will eventually come up out of the land of Egypt, and through great trial and temptation in the wilderness, will eventually arrive in the land of promise.

A remarkable statement is made about this in Hosea 11:1, "When Israel was a child I loved him; out of Egypt I have called my son." Israel's being called the "son" of God implies that the narrative of the nation was in some ways an anticipation of the narrative of Jesus, the greater Son of Adam, Abraham, and Israel, who was yet to come in the fullness of history. Clear evidence of this typological correspondence between Israel as God's son and Jesus as the incarnate Son of God is found in Matthew 2:15, which applies Hosea 11:1 to Christ, particularly in the context of Jesus descending

75. Noordzij, "This is also the scarlet cord of Hebrews 11 and also of the letter: God will live with his children in a lively and cordial relationship"; Noordzij, "In het geloof draait alles om het hart," 7 (trans. mine). As Johnson notes, "Truth proclaimed is both to be embraced in faith and translated into a worthy 'walk' (the biblical metaphor for conduct of life)"; Johnson, *Him We Proclaim*, 84.

76. The language of "walking with God" is also rightly seen as anticipating the New Testament idea of discipleship. See Ryken, *Dictionary of Biblical Imagery*, 922.

77. Interestingly, Joseph's bones did return to the Promised Land as noted in Gen 50:24–25, cf. Exod 13:19 and Josh 24:32.

into Egypt under a star of persecution only to come up again under a star of protective deliverance.[78] The ascent of Jesus out of Egypt as an infant, according to Matthew, is seen as the fulfillment of the theme embodied in Israel.[79] The pattern of thematic recapitulation moves progressively through the patriarchs to Israel, and from Israel to Christ, thus progressively revealing more and more about God's redemptive plan and the promised seed of redemption.

These statements about the patriarchs and Israel together illustrate the way in which the adoption-like dynamic informs God's relationship with Israel and her patriarchal predecessors.[80] Thematic recapitulation and imitation seem to go hand in hand, thus wedding the RH hermeneutic with a very preachable form of application imbedded in the dramatic concept of imitation.[81] This is due to the fact that God's plan to adopt a family for himself to be conformed to his own glorious image was not abandoned with the fall of Adam. It was redeemed and perpetuated by the promises made to and embodied in the patriarchs and the nation of Israel. Abraham is not simply the father of Israel, he is a preview of the adoptive relationship God will have with Israel through the covenant promises. As history progresses so also does the unfolding revelation of God's redemptive promises to his people.

Israel is not only an outgrowth of God's adoptive plan in Abraham, she also serves as a large-scale prototype of the Son of God who is *not* adopted, but is actually the same in substance and equal in power and glory to God himself.[82] This is perhaps nowhere more evident than in the macro-structure of the life of Israel and the life of Christ. Of each it could be said that they were foreknown, predestined, called, baptized, commissioned, tested, exiled, and restored. While the symmetry is not perfect, it is remarkably

---

78. An important backdrop to these verses is Exod 4:22 where God refers to Israel as "my son."

79. Vos suggests that the key to resolving the difficulty of discerning legitimate typology lies in whether or not there is a clear, direct correspondence in New Testament history that becomes the antitype; Vos, *Biblical Theology*, 145.

80. For a helpful discussion of Israel as "God's son" see Wright, *Knowing Jesus through the Old Testament*, 118–32.

81. Abraham Kuruvilla, though dismissive of the RH hermeneutic, recognizes the use of "role-duplication" or thematic "recapitulation" in Genesis and its value for application. See particularly this idea applied to the Joseph narrative in his homiletic commentary; Kuruvilla, *Genesis*, 518, 522–3.

82. Fairbairn notes that typology is not particular to one dispensation of Scripture or another; it flows through them all, but that, since the goal of the Christian life is conformity to Christ, he is "emphatically and pre-eminently *the type* of the church"; Fairbairn, *Typology of Scripture*, 43 (emphasis original).

similar and intriguing.[83] One cannot easily miss the intentional ways in which God previewed the life of Jesus in the life of Israel. Add to this the clear ways in which God refers to Israel as his "son,"[84] and it becomes clear that in a sense, Israel was imitating Jesus *before* Jesus came into the world via his incarnation, even though they could not have known it.[85] If such a statement might be made of Israel in the Old Testament, how much more is it true of the church—the adopted children of God and heirs of the Abrahamic promise in the New Testament?

The New Testament is filled with the idea that the church has now received a share in the Abrahamic promises, and these promises include being conformed to the image of Christ—Abraham's greater Son and Lord. For textual support of this idea, we might consider Romans 8:28–30:

> And we know that for those who love God all things work together for good, for those who are called according to his purpose. For those whom he foreknew he also predestined to be conformed to the image of his Son, in order that he might be the firstborn among many brothers. And those whom he predestined he also called, and those whom he called he also justified, and those whom he justified he also glorified.

This classic text has often been seen as undergirding the *ordo salutis*. While affirming that, we wish to highlight a few things related to the idea of imitation. First, what God is doing in his people is clearly anchored in what God had already done in Christ; the one was to be reflective of the other.[86] According to Paul, God is working all things in the lives of his people together for a particular good. This "good" is regrettably too often misunderstood in simplistic terms and applied to material things. Rather, the particular good that God seems to have in mind for his beloved people is conformity "to the image of his Son." This makes sense in the light of a chapter that is dealing both theologically and pastorally with the reality of suffering in the Christian life. Paul is effectively answering the question, "If God loves us,

83. We must also recognize here that as a nation, Israel sinned and failed in many ways, and thus, while there is continuity, there is also discontinuity. This is where the typology clearly breaks down (like all analogies). Thus Clowney, "Preaching Christ from All the Scripture," 174. At the same time, we agree with Clowney that, "The whole history of redemption before the coming of Christ has a symbolic dimension"; Ibid., 178.

84. Cf. above, as well as Ps 103:13.

85. Vanhoozer, *The Drama of Doctrine*, 223.

86. Trimp helpfully notes how more careful attention to this inter-relationship between the *ordo salutis* and the *historia salutis* might have prevented unnecessary dichotomies from developing in the RH preaching debates; Trimp, *Heilsgeschiedenis en prediking*, 93–95.

why are we still suffering?" The answer is found in Jesus. God has loved him most, and yet even Jesus had to make his way through "this present evil age" (Gal 1:4) on a trail from suffering to glory. And all along the way he learned obedience and was perfect as his father in heaven is perfect.[87]

The church is thus called to follow a similar path, dramatically imitating Jesus along the way to heaven. If Jesus, the Son of God and the Lord of Glory, was not above bearing a cross in this world, how can his adopted sons and daughters think of themselves as exempt from mimicking him in the yet-unfolding drama of redemption? Even more so, to suffer in this present evil age is, pastorally speaking, clear evidence of belonging to God and not to the world. It is the Christian badge of honor to suffer for Christ's sake and to have his or her life conformed to the image of Christ through the means of the cross.[88] In this context we note that the history of the church, in many ways, reflects the pattern seen in Israel and in Christ.[89] The church also is foreknown before the foundation of the earth, is called, baptized, commissioned, tested in this world, exiled, and climactically enters the eternal land of promise. Again, while not wanting to press these analogies too far, it is important to observe the fact that there are overlapping patterns in the lives of Israel, Jesus and the church.[90] To ignore these would be like watching a drama on a stage, all the while pretending not to see the backdrop against which the specific performances are rendered, or divorcing one scene from the next.

Ultimately, union with Christ is the necessary, non-negotiable foundation of the New Testament idea of imitating Christ.[91] It is the grounding indicatives of God's redemptive work in Christ, apart from which the imperatives of Scripture are neither attainable nor meaningful.[92] This indispensable

87. Cf. Matt 5:48; Luke 24:26; 1 Pet 1:11.

88. This seems to be the point of Heb 12, that through loving discipline, God is conforming us to the image of Christ, who himself learned obedience through the things he suffered (cf. Heb 5:8).

89. Herbert Bateman IV, appropriately recognized this as one of the greater tensions within Dispensationalism, and his hope that "Progressive Dispensationalism" would be able to advance this question of the relationship between Israel and the church, without capitulating to the vagaries of postmodern hermeneutics. See his particular interaction with Darrell Bock in Bateman, "Dispensationalism Tomorrow," 312.

90. Robertson sees this as part of the "drama" of God in redefining the Israel of God so as to include both Jew and Gentile, who receive the blessings and benedictions promised to Israel in eschatological form; Robertson, *The Israel of God*, 45.

91. On this foundational aspect of union with Christ, see Gaffin, *Resurrection and Redemption*, esp. 51.

92. Ad de Bruijne argues that overly separating the indicative from the imperative leads to an ethical theological orientation that is sterile and inadequate; De Bruijne,

relationship between the indicative and the imperatives of the Christian life is perhaps nowhere better articulated than by Herman Ridderbos when he says, "The new life in its moral manifestation is at one time proclaimed and posited as the fruit of the redemptive work of God in Christ through the Holy Spirit—the indicative; elsewhere, however, it is put with no less force as a categorical command—the imperative."[93] Ridderbos sees this indicative/ imperative relationship in Paul as being "a matter of the inner relationship and structures of his [Paul's] preaching and doctrine."[94] Johnson sees this as the apostolic paradigm of Christian obedience, and is worth quoting on this point at length, "The apostolic model of *parenesis* (exhortation) in the New Testament grounds believers' obligations in the gospel itself, showing how the indicatives describing Christ's saving work precede and entail the imperatives that define our believing response to his mercy."[95] Apart from this indicative/imperative relationship, whether preaching from the Pauline Epistles or Hebrews, homiletic imitation is reduced to a form of legalism.[96] Yet grounded in the idea of union with Christ, imitating Christ becomes the right, privilege, and responsibility of every believer.[97] It is a tangible expression of being adopted into a right relationship with God through union with Christ and receiving all his benefits, including the privilege of following him and bearing his cross. Imitating Christ is also evidence that we have undergone the transition of being recreated anew through union with Christ in his death and resurrection.[98]

As we have seen, imitating God is by no means simply a New Testament idea. Persons in the Old Testament imitated God in various forms, and some even imitated, or perhaps better put, symbolically previewed particular aspects of the work of Christ. For Adam, Abraham, and the saints of old, imitating God was required, and meant doing not only what God

"Christelijke ethiek tussen wet, schepping en gemeenschap"; see section 2.2.2 in particular.

93. Ridderbos, *Paul*, 253.

94. Ibid., 253.

95. Johnson, *Him We Proclaim*, 42.

96. Horton, "Our default setting is law rather than gospel, imperatives (things to do or feel) rather than indicatives (things to believe)"; Horton, *Christless Christianity*, 131. While we appreciate the sentiment here, equating the indicatives of Scripture with "things to believe" seems ironically to confuse indicatives with imperatives.

97. Burger rightly notes that, "Imitation does not necessarily imply participation," as is evidenced by the commands to do so in the book of John, prior to the resurrection. However, as Burger notes, after the resurrection, to live in Christ implies participating in his relationship to the Father, imitating his love for others, as well as his sufferings and mission to the world; Burger, *Being in Christ*, 174.

98. Hood, "Evangelicals and the Imitation of the Cross," 125.

said, but also what God did in a spirited fashion. God spoke and acted in a certain way, and part of God's plan of redemption for man as the *Imago Dei* is to continue this mimetic expectation.[99] The pattern of speaking and acting a certain way that reflects God's righteousness and holiness continues well into the history of Israel and God's relationship with her. It lies at the heart of what it meant for Old Testament saints to walk with God. But nowhere is this idea clearer than when God sends Christ into the world, the one who is both the word and work of God incarnate (John 1). His work on our behalf is not only the basis of our reconciliation with God; it is also the pattern of Christian reconciliation with one another (Eph 5:1-2). As the love of God is what caused him to effect reconciliation with sinners in and through Christ, so also are his adopted children commanded to imitate this pattern of life, and to walk in love as his beloved people. This pattern of imitation and conformity to the image of Christ is what we have seen to a certain extent in Hebrews 11, and is that to which we now more fully turn our attention.

99. Earlier we noted that Adam, after the fall, was to imitate the pattern of atoning sacrifice instituted by God himself in Gen 3:21. This helps us to understand the rejection and acceptance of Cain and Abel and their respective sacrifices.

6

Imitating the Saints

A Case Study in Hebrews 11

IN WHAT WAY SHOULD the saints of Hebrews 11 be imitated? This is foremost a hermeneutical question, and secondly a pastoral one. It has been demonstrated that the author of Hebrews has a particular hermeneutical paradigm in view in Hebrews 11. The heroes of the chapter have been called upon not merely as role models to be imitated, but as those whose very lives testify to the better things that would eventually be fulfilled in Christ. Thus, their lives theatrically display the veritable realities for which their faith is hoping. In this sense, there is a measure of typology anchored in the RH continuity of Scripture, underlying the "by faith" references.[1] Thus, each scene in Hebrews 11, from creation to the perfection of the saints (11:39–40), is part of a larger dramatic narrative encompassing all of redemptive history. Hebrews 11, in this respect, is comparable to a compact summary of the entire Old Testament. Following their lead, the church (those now living at the end of the ages) is included in this drama of redemptive history insofar as her pilgrimage arrives at the same eschatological goal as Old Testament believers. This goal has been inaugurated in Christ but shall not be consummated until the closing scene of the arrival of the kingdom of God in all of its perfected glory (Hebrews 11:39–40).

1. We find Vanhoozer's definition of typology here to be particularly helpful. In his view, "Typology is the mainspring of theo-dramatic unity, the principle that accounts for the continuity in God's words and acts, the connecting link between the history of Israel and the history of the church, the glue that unites the Old and New Testaments"; Vanhoozer, *The Drama of Doctrine*, 223.

What then are we called to imitate in Hebrews 11? The particular point of emphasis appears to be the imitation of the faith and perseverance of the saints, as through faith they not only endured a variety of trials and temptations, but more importantly, embraced and witnessed to the redemptive promises of God. In this respect, their faith is worthy of imitation. This emphasis on imitation is related to Hebrews 6:11–12, which says, "And we desire each one of you to show the same earnestness to have the full assurance of hope until the end, so that you may not be sluggish, but imitators of those who through faith and patience inherit the promises." The language of imitation is obvious, and appears to have the Old Testament saints in view.[2] The hermeneutical reasoning is significant. The Old Testament saints, like the church that received this "word of exhortation" (13:22), needed grace to persevere. Their earthly circumstances were, in many ways, a discouragement to their faith. They professed faith in the promises of God, only to find those promises remaining at a distance that seemed harder and harder to overcome. The historical gap which separated their present experiences from the promises of God threatened to diminish their confidence in God's word. Just as the Old Testament saints were tempted to spiritual despair and sluggishness, so also are the New Testament saints, both in the first century and even today. The call to persevere by faith is not new, just as the same gospel that was preached to them has also been preached to "us" (Heb 4:2).

The mixed metaphor of Hebrews 12:1–3 also compels a proper form of imitation. In as much as the "great cloud of witnesses" has testified to the veracity of the promises of God in Christ through their faith, they set in place a pattern that is worthy of imitation. They looked to Christ as they ran their race, and now we too are called to do the same—to run our race while "looking to Jesus, the founder and perfecter of our faith" (12:2). Thus, to deny the idea of imitating both the saints of Hebrews 11, and even more so, Jesus himself, would seem to do hermeneutical and pastoral violence to the intention of the text.[3] Not only have the Old Testament saints finished their race, but more importantly, that which their faith embraced and which their faithful lives revealed, has been perfected in Christ.[4] In comparison to

2. Ellingworth suggests, "The examples must be Old Testament figures, and more specifically the patriarchs such as Abraham, who believed God's promise to multiply their descendants and ultimately give them possession of Canaan"; Ellingworth, *The Epistle to the Hebrews*, 333. Lane sees the reference as including all of those referenced in Heb 11:1–12:3; Lane, *Hebrews 1–8*, 145; cf. also Grosheide, *Hebreeën*, 152.

3. Van de Kamp suggests not only that the "imitation" theme of Heb 6:12 corresponds to the intentions of Hebrews 11, but also that this idea of imitating those who, through faith, inherit the promises is the "deepest motive" of the book of Hebrews; Van de Kamp, *Hebreeën*, 168 (trans. mine).

4. Samra "A Biblical View of Discipleship," 223.

whatever things they inherited from God during the Old Testament times, Jesus is better, because he is both the founder (or author) and perfecter of their faith stories. Jesus was not above the sufferings that were endured by his people as they ran their race of faith. The book of Hebrews goes to great length to show the tender and intimate ways in which the humanity of Jesus was embodied. Accordingly, Jesus was humbled for us (2:7–9); became a loving sibling (2:11–12); sympathized with our weakness and was tempted in every way that we are yet without sinning (4:15); learned obedience through what he suffered (5:8); offered himself as our substitute (9:28; 10:10); endured the cross (12:2); triumphed over all his and our foes through the resurrection (12:3); continues to intercede so as to guarantee our inheritance in the kingdom of God (12:22–24); and inspires our worship of God in his heavenly sanctuary (12:28–29).[5] Jesus is the object of our faith, and the ultimate pattern of life that is worthy of imitation.[6] In as much as the Old Testament saints were revealing aspects of the pilgrimage and perseverance of Jesus, they are suitable exemplars for us. But again, this requires some nuanced qualification.

Simply put: *not everything about the saints in Hebrews 11 is meant to be imitated.* Thus, we underscore the vital importance of a cautious hermeneutical approach, and the way in which only the analogy of faith can help to determine ethical implications that are normative from those that are not. As noted earlier, just because something in the Bible is *described* does not mean that it is *prescribed.* While certain nuances of the lives of the Old Testament saints are worthy of imitation, others are either less than blameless, or so historically unique as to be clearly non-normative. A brief review of the saints in Hebrews 11 should clearly illustrate both the imitability of the heroes as well as certain ways in which their particular circumstances were unique and thus not imitable.

While Abel's martyrdom is unique, the reality of resurrection through martyrdom is not. All the saints of God who experience martyrdom will, like Abel, continue to speak in the resurrection. Additionally, that God is pleased with and commends Abel's sacrifice is made clear by Hebrews 11:4, and picked up again in Hebrews 12:29. We too, in a manner of imitating Abel, should seek to offer God acceptable worship through faith and

5. For an insightful treatment of how Jesus not only fulfills the cry of Ps 22:1 at the cross, but also is leading his people in heavenly worship, see Clowney, "The Singing Savior," 40–42.

6. We mean this not in a reductionist "What Would Jesus Do?" manner but, as Horton puts it, "Through the gospel, the Spirit clothes us with Christ's righteousness (justification) and renews us (regeneration), conforming us daily to the image of Christ (sanctification)"; Horton, *Christless Christianity*, 107.

obedience to God's word. And, if worshipping God acceptably should result in martyrdom at the hands of her enemies, the church must learn to submit to the Lord of her script, and through martyrdom, join the perfected heavenly choir (12:24–26) of which Abel is a part. Thus, we are able not only to imitate the faith of Abel, but also share in aspects of his fate. This proves to be the case with other saints listed in Hebrews 11 as well.

Enoch's situation, by contrast, is unique.[7] Though he too is a man of faith, and that faith is to be imitated, some aspects of his dramatic scene will not be experienced by all believers. Enoch was taken up and did not see death (11:5), but this fate of not seeing death served a unique function in the history of redemption, and as such is a preview of the particular fate of those who are alive at Christ's coming and are caught up alive with Christ on that day.[8]

Noah's faith-experience is also a mixture of unique and normative qualities. God's particular command to Noah to build an ark was not a "timeless truth"[9] to be obeyed or imitated by all God's people; but having faith in God's promises, enduring mockery and rejection from a hostile world, and becoming an heir of the righteousness of God that comes by faith—these are all normative aspects of the life of all God's people in every age. More importantly, the depiction of God's judgment as that from which only he can deliver his redeemed people is clearly the goal of the text. Thus, God entering the drama of history in an episode of redemptive judgment is the real sermon theme, not simply or moralistically imitating the particular actions of Noah himself.

In a similar vein, Abraham's faith journey has many imitable as well as non-imitable aspects. To obey God's commands by faith, as Abraham did, is always commendable. More importantly, to inherit Abraham's blessings clearly implies inheriting his responsibility to *be a blessing* to the nations.[10] But many of the commands God gave to Abraham were unique in their

---

7. See the discussion of Enoch's situational uniqueness above in the previous chapter.

8. 1 Thess 4:13–18.

9. Köstenberger and Patterson, *Invitation to Biblical Interpretation*, 789. For a similar proposal of employing "universal principles" to form a homiletic bridge, see Krabbendam, "Hermeneutics and Preaching," 236–40. Though this approach is well intended, it seems to die the death of too many qualifications: namely, how does one clearly and systematically identify the "universal principles" of the text. This "universal principles" or "timeless truth" approach seems to be more of a western, rational hermeneutic than one actually found in Scripture itself. Rein Bos helpfully warns against the dangers of the "timeless truth" approach, which potentially de-historicizes the text; Bos, *Identificatie-Mogelijkheden*, 127; see also Greidanus, *Preaching Christ from Genesis*, 106.

10. Wright, *The Mission of God's People*, 81.

place in redemptive history. God does not continue to command everyone to abandon their homeland and move to a foreign land (11:8) or to live in physical tents as Abraham, Isaac, and Jacob did (11:9). God certainly does not command us to physically offer up our children in sacrifice (11:17). While there may be some form of spiritual symbolism that accrues to the particular commands given to Abraham, it must be observed that Abraham's place in redemptive history was unique, and many of the commands (circumcision, etc.) were for a particular time, place, and people.[11]

Our point here is that too often a "direct line" is drawn between something a person does in the Bible and our being called to do that same thing.[12] Careful exegesis does not always support such conclusions, and a hermeneutic of convenience sometimes regrettably trumps the hermeneutic of the text, and particularly the analogy of faith. As Haddon Robinson puts it, "More heresy occurs in application than in any other part of the sermon."[13] Eisegesis is often unknowingly exchanged for exegesis, especially in the application section of sermons.[14] Ironically, in our view, to the extent that RH preaching is often (and sometimes rightly) accused of venturing into typological speculation that easily turns into allegory,[15] the very same thing often happens in non-RH sermons, especially in the application portions of the sermon, where illegitimate connections are frequently made. In either case, as Vanhoozer appropriately warns, disregarding the author's intended meaning of the text, whether willful or unintentional, borders on a form of bearing false witness.[16] It is regrettable that sermons on Genesis 22 (Abraham offering up Isaac), too quickly degenerate into sermons on tithing,[17] asking inappropriate questions such as, "Abraham was willing to

11. While arguing in favor of the "timeless truth" approach to application, Murray Capill helpfully suggests, "Truths that God revealed to Abraham, Moses, or David, for example, come to us via Jesus Christ and the full realization of the gospel in his redeeming work. In handling 'always' (=timeless) truths, therefore, we must not leapfrog from the past to the present, ignoring the progress of redemptive history and the climactic work of the Messiah"; Capill, *The Heart is the Target*, 47.

12. Peterson, *Leap over a Wall*, 4, cited in Mathewson, *The Art of Preaching Old Testament Narrative*, 99.

13. Robinson "The Heresy of Application," 21.

14. Horton, *Christless Christianity*, 145.

15. See Abraham Kuruvilla's critique of Clowney and Greidanus on Gen 22, which he states rather forcefully with, "All of these typological explorations render the narrative a tangled skein of anachronistic references, especially for preachers"; Kuruvilla, *Privilege the Text!*, 218–9.

16. Vanhoozer, *Is There a Meaning in This Text?*, 398.

17. Benny Hinn for instance, says of Genesis 22, "This passage teaches us much about tithing. You see, the Father's demand that Abraham sacrifice Isaac was in essence

give up his son; are you willing to do the same?" Or, "What are you willing to give to God today?" We would question whether these fairly represent the theological and pastoral intentions of Genesis 22.[18]

A similar reservation could be stated about the Sarah narrative in Hebrews 11. While the call to imitate her faith is a natural exegetical deduction from the text, not every aspect of her story is imitable (or even commendable). Would it be right to say to barren women today that if one of them has enough faith (like Sarah), she too might conceive as Sarah did—perhaps even at ninety years old? Such an interpretative application would seem nonsensical, yet a similar approach clearly exists in the "health and wealth" or "prosperity gospel" preachers.[19] The hermeneutics of such an approach fail to take into account what is unique about Sarah and her particular place and function within redemptive history. Drawing straight lines between the Old Testament saints and believers today is not just the occasional or extreme mistake embodied by some; it is frequently the temptation to which many preachers succumb. Indeed, knowing when to and when not to draw such lines is one of the interpretive difficulties faced by preachers week after week, and why proper hermeneutics are essential to faithful preaching— particularly the unique role a text plays in its place in redemptive history, and the light other texts might shed upon the specific sermon text.[20]

When coming to the patriarchal blessings of Isaac and Jacob, we are again confronted with the question of which lines to draw. Isaac, we are told, invoked future blessings upon Jacob and Esau (11:20) and the two boys subsequently became two mighty, warring nations (Israel and Edom). Jacob, following in the footsteps of his father, blessed each of the sons of Joseph

---

a demand that Abraham give Isaac to the Father as a tithe, for Isaac represented the first and the best"; Hinn, *The Biblical Road to Blessing*, 66.

18. Sidney Greidanus refers to this as "biographical preaching" which "tends to look for attitudes and actions of biblical characters which the hearers should either imitate or avoid"; Greidanus, *Preaching Christ from the Old Testament*, 292.

19. Old documents such trends in prosperity preachers such as T.D. Jakes; Old, *The Reading and Preaching of the Scriptures*, 7.388–99. See Horton's critique of "prosperity gospel" proponents such as Joel Osteen, in *Christless Christianity*, 80–91, esp. 86. The lack of sensitivity to RH hermeneutics in Charismatic/Pentecostal theology is discernable through the conspicuous absence of any reference in the section discussing "hermeneutics," in Burgess and McGee, *Dictionary of Pentecostal and Charismatic Movements*, 376–89.

20. Duane Litfin notes that on top of the exegetical challenges to preaching, few commentaries offer much help with how to appropriately connect the text to the sermon audience; Litfin, "New Testament Challenges to Big Idea Preaching," 57. See also Childers, "Homiletics is about the discovery of the proper means of interpretation of an authoritative text and its appropriate proclamation for a situation"; Childers, "A Critical Analysis," 28.

with prophetic blessings (11:21) and the twelve boys became the twelve tribes of the nation of Israel. The point of this section, as with the rest of Hebrews 11, is not duplicating the specific actions of the saints. Sermons from Genesis and Hebrews 11 often seem to adopt a pick and choose hermeneutic of application, at times recognizing the unique place in redemptive history that a particular scene embodies; yet at other times, drawing a straight line between the Old Testament saint's faith experience and our own.[21] Our plea is for hermeneutical caution and consistency.

Drawing a straight line between Joseph's unusual request at the end of his life that his bones should be carried up from Egypt to Canaan (11:22) would seem equally nonsensical if directly applied today. There is clearly symbolism involved here in what Joseph requests "by faith." Joseph's faith was in the hope of an even greater Exodus, one from earth to heaven, and having his bones carried up from Egypt was symbolic of where his true hope lay—in the land of God's promised rest.[22] The fact that there is such easily recognized symbolism in this text provokes the tension of application and illustrates a methodological inconsistency in preaching—which is to treat some texts one way and other texts differently. Some heroes might be treated as direct examples to be imitated with little qualification or sensitivity to the uniqueness of their place in redemptive history; others treated with a fairly different hermeneutic, viewing the text (and particularly the application drawn from the text) symbolically, if not allegorically. Yet all of this would come from the same book of the Bible (Genesis or Hebrews) and perhaps even the same chapter (e.g., Heb 11). Whether or not it is fitting to employ a different hermeneutic for two side-by-side verses is difficult to ascertain. The troubling reality is that often preaching, especially as it relates to application, does exactly that.

Moses' parents by faith hid their child from infanticide, and thus preserved his life. But as we saw earlier, the parallels between this text and the birth narrative of Jesus (cf. Matt 2) force us to dig deeper and to wrestle with whether or not the point of the text is what parents ought to do in order to protect their kids, or what God is doing in order to protect his covenant

---

21. We agree with Pamela Eisenbaum's opening comments to her PhD dissertation, suggesting that the majority of exegesis on Hebrews 11 has devolved into "illustrations of faith, rather than on the way the chapter functions as a retelling of the scriptural story"; Eisenbaum, "The Jewish Heroes of Christian History," 1.

22. Trimp seems to suggest the breadth of the scope of Hebrews 11 when he says, "Hebrews 11 wants to show the New Testament Community from all sides what the experimental power is of faith in the promise of God"; Trimp, *Heilsgeschiedenis en prediking*, 92 (trans. mine); see also Greidanus, *Sola Scriptura*, 113.

people.[23] Again, the answer is not so much of an either-or, but a matter of arriving at a proper application of the text through the lens of a hermeneutical process that is sensitive to the particular details of the text and its place in redemptive history.[24] In this context, there are certainly ways in which the life-saving faith of Moses' parents is worthy of imitation, but the primary focus ought rather to be upon the way in which God was preserving the life of Israel's future mediator from death not just for his sake, but also for the sake of God's people—a promise Moses' parents embraced by faith.

This point flows nicely into the section dealing with Moses himself, and his resisting various temptations for the sake of God's covenant people and ultimately for Christ. When Moses grew up, he refused to embrace the worldly pleasures to which he was entitled as an adopted son of Pharaoh, and chose rather to endure affliction with the people of God. While this posture is certainly worthy of imitation, it is inseparable from the fact that Moses did so with the eyes of his faith fixed upon Christ (11:26). Whatever he might have forfeited in this world was not worth comparing with what he was to inherit in Christ. In this light, we might suggest that Moses was imitating Christ, well before Christ had come in the flesh. Though we doubt that this was in any way something about which Moses was clearly self-conscious, it was nevertheless the way in which God was shaping the life of Moses—to reflect the life of Christ. That God continues to shape the lives of his people this way *today* is clear even from the book of Hebrews (particularly chapter 12). Thus, to imitate the faith, righteousness, and separation of Moses from the world is consistent with what it means to imitate those who through faith and perseverance inherit the promises.[25] To speak this way is neither arbitrary nor exegetically untenable. More importantly, it is not abstract from the gospel itself, but is self-consciously anchored into the RH unfolding of God's redemptive drama.[26]

How does one apply the Passover or the crossing of the Red Sea? The crossing served a unique point in redemptive-history, while the Passover was

23. On the similarities between the birth narrative of Christ and Moses, including an interesting discussion of their mediatorial roles, see Morales, "The Rebirth of Moses," esp. 2, 38–39 (unpublished, used by permission).

24. Many have recognized that this may be something of a false dilemma; see Kranendonk, *Vital Balance*, 138; Trimp, *Heilsgeschiedenis en prediking*, 93–96. For an excellent summary of this false dilemma and a balanced proposal for going forward, see Johnson, *Him We Proclaim*, 177–8.

25. Heb 6:12.

26. In this context, Mees te Velde says, "Man is not the passive object of the developments that God, in his providence, has caused to occur. But he [man] is an actor, participant, mandated that in everything that he does he is to accomplish a certain task"; Te Velde, "Vrijgemaakte vreemdelingen," 186 (trans. mine).

more about what God was doing to bring about the redemption of his people. Yet to be identified with the blood of the lamb was to be identified with the redemptive promises of God.[27] Outside of that lamb, there was no salvation from God's judgment. In this light, we not only hear the gospel, but also hear the pastoral implications of this text both for the first-century community of Hebrews and today, as the same gospel that saved them is the gospel that still saves. Outside of the Lamb of God who is Jesus, there is no salvation (10:26–31). Likewise, the nation of Israel crossing the Red Sea was unique. It is impossible to imitate their actions directly, yet the call to trust God at his word, and to walk by faith and not by sight, is consistent with the overall pastoral message of Hebrews. Likewise, the implicit imperative that we will either follow the Israelites into redemption or the Egyptians into judgment is evident (Cf. 1 Cor 10). The members of Israel passed through the Red Sea safely, yet died in the wilderness due to a lack of faith, and thus did not inherit the promises. Similar realities abide, even during the *today* in which God is still speaking a promise to those who keep the covenant by faith and those who abandon it through unbelief. The promises of salvation and judgment remain as living and active as the word of God itself (Heb 4:10).

The events at Jericho are unique on the one hand in terms of their place in redemptive-history. On the other hand, they reveal not only God's sovereign power over his enemies but also the need of his people to follow after him, however awkward or perilous that may be for them. We can only imagine the reaction of the Israelites being told to march around Jericho for seven days, blowing trumpets. While their faith is imitable in a general sense, the saving faith of Rahab is even more so. Like Moses, she identified herself with the people of God, only she had little to lose and much to gain. The effect of her faith led not only to her own salvation but also to the salvation of her household. As James 2:25 declares, the genuineness of her faith was dramatically evidenced in the reality of her works. This is an example worthy of imitation to be sure, even though some of the details of her story are obviously unique.

"And what more shall I say?" The question of the author of Hebrews (11:32) is very much our own. Highlighting these points of continuity as well as RH discontinuity could go on and on. They well represent both the problem and the promise of an exegetically derived hermeneutic that leads to an exegetically derived homiletic application, or better put, a quality worthy of emulation. This fast and furious race through the prophets in Hebrews 11 who endured martyrdom for the cause of the faith only underscores the idea

27. Clowney makes an interesting connection between the Passover and the sacrifice of Isaac in Gen 22 as a principle of redemption through the firstborn, which would ultimately culminate in Christ; Clowney, *Preaching and Biblical Theology*, 86.

that the hermeneutic employed by Hebrews might be applied to other places in the Old Testament as well. The implication is that this pastorally rich, exegetically sensitive hermeneutic articulated in Hebrews 11 is consistent with the book of Hebrews as a whole, and thus suggests a promising means of addressing certain exegetical and pastoral questions about preaching the Old Testament in general. Thus, not only are the saints of Hebrews 11 imitable in a nuanced sense, so also is the *hermeneutic* of Hebrews 11 as it guides us in the proper pursuit of homiletic application (imitation).[28]

It is, no doubt, for this reason that both sides of the RH controversy in the Netherlands appealed to Hebrews 11. The RH side could rightly look to Hebrews 11 and see within it a rich, Christ-centered hermeneutic that was not primarily anthropocentric; though as Trimp has pointed out, this strength may have been overemphasized to the point of becoming a weakness in the position.[29] Nor did it cave in to cheap, artificial application or abstract exemplarism.[30] The RH concern for reductionism in preaching (reducing the sermon to moralistic character sketches) would appear to be supported from our study of Hebrews 11. Too many nuances arise from a careful study of Hebrews 11 to suggest that a perpetual one to one application can be consistently derived from the text. Their purpose in the drama of redemption was not simply to give us atomistic character-sketches to be moralistically imitated, but to show how their particular faith episodes were ultimately mini-dramas in the great metanarrative of God's drama of redemption.[31] Their individual stories could not be properly understood apart from the bigger story of which both they and we are a part (11:39–40), a dramatic story in which Jesus Christ is not only the center, but also the founder and perfecter.[32]

---

28. Thus Anderson, "Preaching through Hebrews offers us a course in Christian Hermeneutics"; Anderson, "The Challenge and Opportunity of Preaching Hebrews," 140.

29. Trimp, *Klank en weerklank*, 52–57. See also Trimp's particular critique of Holwerda and Van 't Veer for overemphasizing the progress ("voortgang") of redemptive history, at the expense of God's fellowship ("omgang") with his covenant people; Trimp, *Heilsgeschiedenis en prediking*, 96–100.

30. From a pastoral perspective, T. David Gordon has rightly noted that "Faith is not built up by introspection, moralism, or even cultural pre-occupation, but by focusing on the person and work of Christ"; Gordon, *Why Johnny Can't Preach*, 76.

31. De Ruijter, *Horen naar de stem van God*, 77; Arthurs, "Preaching from the Old Testament Narratives," 84.

32. Horton, "When we allow Christian preaching to drift from this plot, it easily becomes a pretense for other dramas, whether that takes the form of moralism, pragmatism, consumerism, or therapy"; Horton, *Covenant and Eschatology*, 268. See also Johnson, *Him We Proclaim*, 53.

The suggestion of some within the RH camp that creating too great a divide between explication and application can have a numbing effect upon congregants is well noted. This was illustrated by the common practice within many of the older Dutch churches, in which the sermon was liturgically divided between doctrine and application so starkly that the sermon would literally be interrupted half-way through at the end of the *doctrine* section, at which point the church would stand up, sing a hymn, and then sit down again for the *application* portion of the sermon. We would also echo at this point the sentiment of many who would not be aligned with the RH preaching paradigm (Piper, Lloyd-Jones, MacArthur, etc.) who implicitly agree with Schilder's point that the entire sermon ought to be application, not simply a portion that stands in stark contrast to the rest of the sermon.[33] At the same time, we wish to be careful not to entirely dismiss the *explicatio et applicatio* paradigm; rather, we would suggest that it needs nuancing, just as much as the RH and other paradigms of preaching do as well.[34]

On the other side of the RH debate, we would agree with those who argue that some form of mimesis is certainly implied in Hebrews 11. This was explicitly stated in 6:12, and seems to be implicitly echoed throughout the book. And just as the bookends of Hebrews 11 (chapters 10 and 12) seem to imply a Christocentric approach to Hebrews 11, so also do they imply that it is those who "live by faith" (10:38) with whom God is well-pleased, whose lives are dramatically illustrated in chapter 11, and thus form the "cloud of witnesses;" (12:1) whose testimony is to be heeded, and whose example of faith is, in some way, to be imitated. In light of these statements, an either/or approach to Hebrews 11 cannot be affirmed, as the book as a whole does not seem to advocate such a view, nor does a careful exegesis of the chapter appear to arrive at such a conclusion. Furthermore, worth underscoring is the value of the DR metaphor as it particularly relates to Hebrews 11, thus highlighting both the primacy of the divine performance of God in and through

33. We have grown to appreciate the fact that this sentiment—the idea of the whole sermon as application—runs through the homiletic theory of many authors, both RH preachers and others. It is a subject worthy of further inquiry.

34. John Carrick suggests, "It is this indicative-imperative pattern of New Testament Christianity that constitutes the tacit theological rationale for the Puritan concept of preaching as *explicatio et applicatio verbi Dei*; it constitutes the tacit theological rationale for the Puritan division of the sermon into Doctrine and Application"; Carrick, *The Preaching of Jonathan Edwards*, 317. While we appreciate the sentiment, it needs to be pointed out that indicative and imperative is the structure of covenant theology; the *explication et application* approach to paradigm is a rhetorical style. Again we would ask, does Carrick's suggestion imply that the "doctrine" sections of Scripture do not "apply"? Or do they apply in different ways than the imperative sections of Scripture (our view)? Ultimately, the whole sermon ought to be considered as "application."

the saints listed in the chapter, as well as the secondary way in which the role of individuals in the dramatic story of God's redemption draws *us* into the drama. In this drama we are not mere spectators, but living, vital, active performers who continue to participate the drama of redemption in history.[35] Horton summarizes the pastoral intention of Hebrews 11 by describing it as, "A drama in which the covenant establishes performances that generate not only passively transformed readers, but a new reality outside of the text-script in which covenant partners actively participate in the ongoing and unfolding performance on the world stage."[36]

The book of Hebrews (and chapter 11 in particular) is as balanced as the covenant formula, "I will be your God and you will be my people" (Exod 6:7; Lev 26:12; Jer 30:22; Ezek 26:28). Each plays their part in Hebrews 11. This summary of the covenant is embodied in Hebrews 11 as God fulfills his role of being their God through the redemptive work of Christ. Christ is the fulfillment of all that God spoke through the fathers and the prophets in time past, and in these eschatological days is the climactic word of God in the flesh (1:1–3). He is the dramatic epicenter of redemptive-history and all the promises find their yes and amen in him. On the other side of this coin is the role of God's people, who are dramatically called to walk by faith in the promises of God through a variety of trials and temptations with their eyes fixed upon Christ, thus manifesting that through faith, they are the sort of people of whom God is not ashamed to call his own (11:6).

Hebrews 11 is also as equally balanced in its pastoral sensitivity as the summary of Scripture given by the Westminster Shorter Catechism, which says, "What do the Scriptures principally teach? The Scriptures principally teach what man is to believe concerning God, and what duty God requires of man."[37] Hebrews 11, on the one hand, is primarily interested in revealing what we ought to believe concerning God and his promises. His faithfulness to his word and to his people is explicitly manifest in the legal testimony of the "witnesses" (12:1) of Hebrews 11. The primacy of faith in God's words and works is obvious in Hebrews 11, but also present is the call to imitate those whose duty it was to follow God by faith, thus making their calling and election sure. As some of those who were attached to the community of the Hebrews had fallen away during a time of trial and adversity, the duty of the church presently is not only to imitate those who persevere by faith, but also *not to imitate* those who fall away unto destruction (10:39).

---

35. Vanhoozer, *The Drama of Doctrine*, 255.

36. Horton, *Covenant and Eschatology*, 14–15.

37. WSC 3.

A similar foil of pastoral imitation is expressed in Hebrews 13:17 which says, "Remember your leaders, those who spoke to you the word of God. Consider the outcome of their way of life, and *imitate their faith*." Earlier we concluded that these "leaders" are most likely the local church leaders who were caring for the Hebrew community. However, even with this stated, it is interesting to note the almost vague way in which the language used here sounds sublimely like that of Hebrews 11. By faith, the heroes of the Old Testament participated in revealing the word of God, and the outcome of their faithful way of life was to inherit the promises of God, whether through persecution, martyrdom, or otherwise. The command to imitate the faith of the Old Testament leaders is also already expressed in the book. But in this context, it is the local church leaders who are viewed as those who are speaking the word of God, some of whom have set an example not only of piety but possibly of martyrdom as well. In light of this, their faith is held up as something to be imitated. Thus, the recipients of the exhortation to the Hebrews are encouraged not only to imitate the faith of the Old Testament saints (6:12), but also their local church leaders (13:17).[38]

From these statements we conclude that the idea of dramatic imitation is unambiguously at work in the book of Hebrews from a pastoral perspective. To deny it would appear, in our view, to do violence to the exegetical and homiletic intentions of the text, and to ignore what we would refer to as the RH and DR concerns expressed in the book of Hebrews. The two ideas grow up together like seeds planted in the same plot of soil.[39] Together they set the book of Hebrews, and particularly chapter 11, in a warm, pastoral context that is full of Christ-centered exegesis and rich pastoral exhortation. If these conclusions are correct, it also suggests that in certain respects, the impasse reached by the RH homiletic debates in the Netherlands, while generating very important discussions, was also quite regrettable.[40] In our view, it is helpful to learn from, and also to move beyond that debate to the fresh herme-

38. B. Holwerda, in a sermon on Heb 13:9–14, seems to recognize and apply something of an imitation approach in the context of preserving through sufferings related to the war; Holwerda, "Het altaar zonder tafel," 48–72, esp. 54.

39. To our knowledge, the only person to attempt a clear homiletic synthesis of these ideas thus far is C. J. de Ruijter in his 2013 *Horen naar de stem van God*. The same year, Abraham Kuruvilla published his *Privilege the Text*. This homiletic work also develops some of the DR themes in helpful ways. However, it seems to lean more toward a dispensational direction, and is regrettably dismissive of many of the RH authors and insights.

40. We heartily appreciate Dennis Johnson's balanced treatment of both sides of this debate and his concern not to develop overly striated dichotomies, as is evidenced in his *Him We Proclaim*, esp. 53–54. See also the conciliatory reflections of Runia, *Het hoge woord in de Lage Landen*, 123–4.

neutical insights that have been advanced not only by more recent advocates of the RH paradigm, but also by advocates of the DR and similar paradigms.[41]

CROSSING THE BRIDGE OF HISTORY?

Before concluding this chapter, we would like to draw brief attention to what we believe is an important common denominator in much of contemporary homiletic discussion, particularly as it relates to sermonic application. This issue is the tension of history. How do we who live in this present time make a genuine point of contact with the biblical world? How do we traverse the bridge of history across Lessing's ditch?[42] That this question is of great importance is demonstrated in one way or another by nearly every book on homiletics. It is particularly evidenced in the titles of books such as *The Modern Preacher and the Ancient Text, Between Two Worlds, The Relevance of Preaching,* and in the very popular approach of building "application bridges"[43] in preaching. The tension of historical distance is always felt in the sermon, as the great chasm between the world of the text and the world of today must be crossed by something in the sermon. Is it timeless truth? Circumstantial similarity? The same sin struggles? Moralistic application? Perhaps the gospel alone? How one answers these questions will greatly affect the approach to preaching particular texts. In other words, these are questions whose answers come with great consequences.[44]

It is here that we have found the DR paradigm to make a helpful contribution to homiletics, especially against the backdrop of the RH preaching

41. Te Velde, "Vrijgemaakte vreemdelingen," 198. Outside the immediate field of homiletics, we could list here the works of Timothy Keller, Christopher Wright, Craig Bartholomew, and Michael Goheen as those who, in one way or another, are trying to work out nuanced approaches to practical theology with an eye both to RH and DR themes.

42. As Lessing himself asked, "This is the broad and ugly ditch which I cannot get across, no matter how often earnestly I have tried to make the leap. If anyone can help me over it, I beg and implore him to do so. He will earn a divine reward for his service"; Nisbet, *Gotthold Lessing,* 87.

43. See Adams, *Truth Applied,* 48–52. For an insightful critique of the "application bridge" paradigm, see Findley, "Bridges or Ladders?"

44. It is worth suggesting that while the gospel is the main "bridge" that binds the Old Testament and the New Testament, from a homiletic perspective there may be more than one means by which we draw people into the text. On this note, we appreciate the sentiment of Frances Young who suggests, "In order to improvise these essential new cadenzas, which will inevitably be somewhat ephemeral, the preacher needs skills, philological skills, hermeneutical theories, imaginative insights, and a lot of sensitivity to context. The bridge has to be flexible or it will crack under pressure"; Young, *The Art of Performance,* 161–2.

debates over Christocentricity and application. The DR paradigm, first seeing Scripture as the living speech-act of the Triune God, allows for the text of Scripture to then function as the performance-directing script that guides the church not only into a right knowledge of God, but also of a rightly practiced performance of the text of Scripture itself. In this way, it is God himself who is capable not only of inspiring, but also preserving his word. He makes it homiletically relevant to the actual needs of contemporary hearers. De Ruijter, while helpfully synthesizing the fruits of Vanhoozer's work in particular, also acknowledges that the drama metaphor does not erase all the hermeneutical problems created by the historical distance between the text and hearer.[45] Very promising, however, is the DR approach with its sensitivity to a canonical reading of Scripture within a Trinitarian framework. At the same time, it implies a provocative form of application in preaching that is sensitive to the hermeneutical nuances and challenges found in the varying contexts of redemptive history.

It has already been suggested that one of the reasons that such an emphasis on the tension of history (and thus some form of bridge-building) exists in so many homiletic works is due to an overstatement of the historical distance between the world of today and the world of the text. Having granted that there is an obvious distance between the days of the New Testament and our time, we would also suggest that in a provocative sense: *there is no distance*. Building again on Wright's use of the drama metaphor, we who are alive today are in the same act as those who live on this side of the resurrection, looking for the close of the eschatological curtain.[46] From the New Testament's perspective, we are just as much in the final act of the drama of redemption as were Peter, Paul, and the people of the time of the New Testament Canon. The days since the resurrection are the "last days" according to the New Testament, to be followed only by the climactic consummation of the end of the age.[47] Rather than strenuously apologize for the historical *distance* between then and now, our proposal is to strenuously emphasize (with nuances) the *continuity* between those alive today and historical era of the New Testament church.[48] The same Holy Spirit who first inspired the Bible has also preserved it through the ages, and in this light, God *continues*

---

45. De Ruijter, *Horen naar de stem van God*, 105.

46. Wright, "How Can the Bible be Authoritative?," 11.

47. Vos sees the coming of Christ into the world as the dramatic "denouement" of history, moving toward an "intensely dramatic," climactic consummation. Yet we who live in "this age" also live in the "last days" of the age of the Spirit, between the resurrection of Christ and consummation of his kingdom; Vos, *Pauline Eschatology*, 26.

48. C.G. Dennison, "Some Thoughts on Preaching," 3–9.

to speak to us in his word and through his Son.[49] It is his promise to be with his church until the end of the age (Matt 28:20) that establishes continuity between the then and the now of history.

Additionally, the New Testament views the church today as being caught up in the same RH moment of the sending of the Holy Spirit as was the case in New Testament times, and while historical nuances obviously exist, the assumption is continuity *first*, nuances *second*.[50] The same Spirit that raised Jesus from the dead is still acting out his part in the drama of redemption by gathering and sanctifying a church that forms the living theatre on the world stage of God's glory.[51] God continues to speak to and through his church, particularly as the church creatively, yet faithfully, echoes his words and imitates his deeds. Preaching in this New Testament era is the divinely appointed means by which God's Spirit continues to direct our performances. We can agree with Pasquarello, who says, "Preaching as a pilgrim practice calls the church to remember and to hope, thus forming its identity as an end-time people whose witness is in 'looking for the city which is to come.'"[52]

While the lives of the saints contribute varying nuances to the history of redemption (as is the case of Hebrews 11), they are yet bound by a common faith, common confession, and common hope. The same tension of history that we often highlight between the world of today and the world of the New Testament already existed in biblical times, and is even spanned by Hebrews 11 from the time of Abel to the time of the prophets. Importantly, the author of Hebrews does not apologize for that tension, nor does he build an artificial application bridge in order to unite Abel and Joshua (who lived in very different times and with different covenantal nuances). Rather, the author of Hebrews assumes a certain exegetical and homiletic continuity between the experiences of Israel and New Testament believers, as they both looked to the promises that culminate in Christ. The consequences of those who disobey in unbelief are of greater eschatological consequence today than for ancient Israel (Heb 10:26–31). Similarly, the promises of salvation

49. 2 Tim 3:16–17; Heb 1:1–3.

50. On this point Geerhardus Vos says, "Still, we know full well that we ourselves live just as much in the New Testament as Peter and Paul and John"; Vos, *Biblical Theology*, 325–6. We appreciate the way Trimp nuances this when he says, "It is a distance within a continuum, but nevertheless quite a respectable distance"; Trimp, *De preek*, 59 (trans. mine).

51. Calvin, in his comments on 1 Cor 7:31 suggests that Paul is using theatrical language in describing the consummation of the age as the closing of a curtain before the eyes of its spectators; Calvin, *Commentary on the Epistles of Paul the Apostle to the Corinthians*, 258.

52. Pasquarello, *Christian Preaching*, 183.

in these last days (Heb 1:1–2; 9:26) are even "better" (Heb 12:24). Thus, history is not to be treated as the archenemy of homiletics that must be slain in every sermon before application can happen. Rather, history is that which has been transcended by the living word and Spirit of God himself and Jesus, who is the same yesterday, today, and forever" (Heb 13:8). There are varying scenes in this drama to be sure, and again, we are not suggesting that each scene is the same any more than each actor's part is the same; but we are suggesting that the continuity of the drama is anchored in the transcendent God of history.[53]

CAUTIONS AND CONCLUSION

In this chapter it has been argued that the idea of imitation when properly understood, may offer helpful nuances to the homiletic idea of application. First, imitation has the advantage of being an explicitly biblical concept expressing the practical side of the Christian life. The idea of imitation has Old Testament roots in the relationship between God and his people, going all the way back to the creation of Adam in the *imago Dei*. Even after Adam, man continues to imitate God in various ways, and the progress of redemption reveals also the progress of God sanctifying man in the image of God. The book of Hebrews (in harmony with the New Testament as a whole) seems to develop this imitation idea, suggesting that while Jesus is the ultimate one to be imitated (12:1–2), he is not the only example granted to us for imitation (6:12; 13:7). Yet this idea must always be nuanced or cautioned by the analogy of faith. Many of the acts performed by the saints in Hebrews 11 are imitable, but some of them are obviously not. The same could be said of Christ, as he serves as an example to be imitated in many points; yet much of what he does is unique and non-imitable. Thus, particularly regarding Hebrews 11, one could suggest that faith is the main theme of the chapter, and that each hero is an example of a faith that reveals a measure of imitable perseverance, as well as something of the things to come in Christ.[54] In this light, what we are to imitate is their forward-looking faith in general, not necessarily the *specific acts* by which their faith was expressed. Such an approach is relatively satisfying, but still underscores the very important issue of the need to develop a properly balanced, biblical hermeneutic that synthesizes the best fruit of the DR and RH (and potentially other) paradigms.

53. More on this will follow in the next chapter, dealing with preaching in a postmodern context.

54. Von Balthasar, *Theo-Drama*, 2.112.

Our performances are to be directed by exegetically sound, pastorally rich sermons which have the power to show us our part not only in the particular scenes of life, but also in the over-arching drama of redemption itself.[55] The right and responsibility of the church is to be united to Christ and imitate him as his redeemed, adopted, children. Sermon after sermon ought to remind us of this: that history is ultimately *His*-story (the story of the Messiah and his kingdom) and thus not an adversary of the church. As surely as the church can be confident of God's part in the history of redemption, speaking and acting his will into the reality of time and space, so also can the church follow his example, dramatically imitating (however imperfectly) God in Christ, thus filling the earthly theater with the knowledge of his glory.

---

55. Kevin Vanhoozer argues for the necessity of studying our culture because, "We need to know where we are in the drama of redemption. The world is our stage, but culture is the setting for our next scene"; Vanhoozer, "What is Everyday Theology?, 34.

7

Preaching the Christ-Centered Drama of Redemption in the Postmodern Scene

IN MANY RESPECTS POSTMODERN thought sets the stage for contemporary preaching. It is a significant part of the context in which we live, and in which preaching occurs. Likewise, postmodernism is not simply a field of thought outside the church, but one that has influenced the thinking of those inside the church in one fashion or another. It is for these reasons that we suggest that postmodernism sets the stage of contemporary preaching, and why our climactic chapter focuses on homiletics within a postmodern context.[1] How does the preacher meaningfully address a generation whose confidence in history and meaning has been shaken? How does the pulpit address issues of morality amidst a generation that stands on the brink of losing its moral compass and redefining its most basic values? Lastly, from a rhetorical point of view, with what language shall preachers address those with changing concepts of the very meaning of language? These are only a few of the challenges faced by those who preach in the context of postmodernism's ever changing scenery—including the particular challenge of defining postmodernism, a movement which elastically resists definition. Still, there are certain defining characteristics that we believe are identifiable, and

1. It is important to note here that there are many faces of and expressions to postmodernism, from blatantly secular to evangelical adaptations; not all of which do we wish to portray in a starkly negative light. There are numerous benefits to be found in postmodern thought, yet there are also serious concerns with significant implications for homiletics. Our focus in this chapter, generally speaking, is on the ideas and influences of secular postmodernism.

may serve as a frame of reference for making homiletic suggestions in a postmodern context.

In this chapter, we would like to bring together the fruit of our study thus far and propose a few ways in which the homiletic model developed in this monograph, while not a silver bullet for postmodernism and its dilemmas, may yet be of service to those who preach in the contemporary scene. The thesis of this chapter is that a homiletic synthesis of the RH and DR ideas may indeed help address some of the critical challenges for preaching raised by postmodernism. The particular challenges we wish to address are the problem of history, the problem of authorial intention, and the problem of morality (the practical consequence of the first two issues). Having stated these three issues, we shall then propose homiletically sensitive responses to each of them with nuances taken from the RH and DR models as articulated in previous chapters. The first is how the RH emphasis on history and the DR emphasis on the Bible as revealing an unfolding historical drama are juxtaposed. The second is how both the RH and DR model help to preserve the idea of God as the living author and completer of history. The third is how the RH and DR rhetorical emphases might compel the postmodern hearer of sermons to see her life both lived within and formed by the drama of redemption in history, in a manner similar to what was seen in our study of Hebrews 11. Lastly, we will conclude by summarizing the chapter and stating particular cautions.

POSTMODERNISM AND THE PROBLEM OF HISTORY

In this section, we would like to address the challenge of history from a postmodern perspective, and propose that there are nuances from both the RH and DR paradigms that may be helpful to bear in mind for homiletic purposes. The first of these is the importance of history. "What is the source of history?" asks Foucault.[2] The answer he proposes embodies the historical skepticism of secular postmodernism. In his view, historians are biased, selective, discriminating, and unreliable. Since no one person is existentially able to jump across Lessing's famous "ugly, broad ditch"[3] of history, no one can be sure of what *actually* happened, and thus historical investigation, as a matter of scientific enterprise, is an illusory goal.[4] The consequence of

2. Rabinow, *The Foucault Reader*, 91.

3. Lessing, "On the Proof of the Spirit and of Power," 53–55, cited in Kapic and McCormic, *Mapping Modern Theology*, 23. Lessing's point, more precisely, is that historical facts are hard to discover and always the subject of debate. Thus, they cannot form the objective basis of faith, reason, or morality; see O'Neill, *The Bible's Authority*, 20.

4. Rabinow, *Foucault Reader*, 79. Hassan summarizes the nature of the postmodern

this, in Foucault's view, is that certain value judgments regarding the good and the evil of history are artificially imposed renderings without legitimate authority. But again, Foucault asks, who gets the right to interpret history and impute moral value to its happenings? Who can even say for sure what actually happened in history? These are trappings of a former day, according to postmodern thinkers such as Foucault. Such a pursuit of "true history," he suggests, is a fading memory, ready not only to be forgotten, but to be replaced by an openness to the possibility that there is no genuine history, only *perceptions* of history. "Truth, and its original reign," writes Foucault, "has had a history within a history from which we are barely emerging . . ."[5]

French postmodernist Jean Baudrillard provocatively suggests that what we describe as reality (history) is an illusion in that no one can know what has really happened or is happening. In Baudrillard's words, "History is our lost referential, that is to say our myth. It is by virtue of this fact that it takes the place of myths on the screen."[6] History, for Baudrillard, is equivalent to the experience one has in the cinema. It is not altogether real, nor is it altogether false. It is genuinely experienced, and yet projected at the same time, by the images of the camera angle defined by the subjective preferences of the historian (the cinematographer). For Baudrillard, and the recently *awakened* postmodern, this realization is utterly traumatic; it is both a tremendous discovery and a tremendous loss at the same time.[7] According to Baudrillard, the truth of this reality is what sets the awakened postmodern mind free. It is liberated. It now realizes the suppressing controls that have been imposed upon it by those who created the illusion of history, and by implication, the artificial story of meaning and morality.

How did such a dire situation come about? In many respects, the answer to this question does not lie in postmodernism alone but in modernism, and in its predecessor, Enlightenment philosophy. From cosmology to morality, the Enlightenment project concluded that things could not be naïvely assumed and trusted; they must be questioned.[8] On the one hand,

---

dilemma by highlighting the "laughable" conundrum of the triumphant existentialist who sleeps in the illusion of history but is awakened to stand and run in the reality of his own existence—a real story which is nothing other than the implied story of history; Hassan, *The Postmodern Turn*, 166.

5. Ibid., 80.

6. Baudrillard, *Simulacra and Simulation*, 43. Baudrillard's existential theory forms the premise of the famous movie trilogy *The Matrix* in which the main character (Neo) is violently awakened to the reality that his entire life is a fabricated delusion, a manufactured dream, created by a machine that has the singular desire to control him by controlling his perceptions of reality, values, and history.

7. Ibid., 44.

8. Vuyk, "De zoon met de vader weggooien?," 115–20.

the Enlightenment embraced an overly optimistic view of the human mind and its ability to see and discover truth through the eyes of reason. The mind was elevated in some ways above the soul (the classic tension of faith and reason), with the rational mind emerging victoriously. Education, one of the broad goals of Humanism, was deemed to be the way forward in the progress of human development.[9] The more the mind was enlightened through education, reason, and scientific discovery, the more human civilization, it was hoped, would advance.

An intellectual and philosophical chain of events followed that would further jeopardize confidence in history. While Enlightenment philosophy supposedly broke free from blindly accepted tradition, notable thinkers such as Immanuel Kant would ably criticize the alternative, as is found in his *Critique of Pure Reason*. Kant made an important distinction between what is actually knowable to the human mind and what is not. This was his famous noumenal/phenomenal distinction. For Kant, there were certain realities that could be known in this world, but when it came to making predications about things *above* (in the realm where God is, etc.), there could ultimately be only speculations.[10] Kant's epistemological conundrum was easily applied to history. All that can be genuinely known and meaningfully predicated is the phenomena of experience. Thus, a necessary chasm exists between the *now* of the knowable and experiential present, and the *then* of the historical past.[11] In a similar vein, philosophers such as David Hume contributed to this discussion by noting that even the things the human mind perceives in the present (including so-called scientific discovery, let alone historical deductions) cannot be truly objective. This is because every scientist, like the historian, looks at the facts through a subjective lens, influenced by his or her own biases and presuppositions. Thus, for Hume, there are no "brute facts," only perceived facts, whether in science, history, or elsewhere.[12]

As it relates to the key elements of biblical history (i.e., creation, miracles, the resurrection, etc.), many highly regarded modernist thinkers framed their theological arguments within the narrative of post-Enlightenment

9. We note, however, the postmodern critique of the university system of education, in that the university model was built upon the idea of a coherence between respective departments, creating something of an implied educational metanarrative within a university.

10. Kant, from the section "Pure Reason and the Question of God" in Allen and Springsted, *Primary Readings*, 197–202, esp. 202.

11. Stanley Grenz suggests that this hermeneutical antagonism between the "then" and the "now" goes back to the medieval times, forming a long dialectic debate; Grenz, *Primer on Postmodernism*, 8.

12. Hume, *Dialogues*, 30. Postmodern thinkers capitalized on this epistemological fault line, as is seen in Foucault, *The Archaeology of Knowledge*, 182.

skepticism.[13] A dualism of sorts developed between the objective facts of Scripture and the application of subjective ideas, particularly by a number of liberal critics of the Bible who were willing to sacrifice the veracity of Scripture on the altar of historical skepticism.[14] For Adolf von Harnack, this was illustrated in a significant distinction between the "kernel" of Scripture (the subjective applications or existential encounters with Scripture) and the "husk" of Scripture (the historical packaging of Scripture which comes along with the kernel). According to Harnack, one could separate the two: the history of Scripture, which was deemed errant and unreliable at best, from the kernels of Scripture, such as religious motivation, love for others, etc. The Jesus of history, in this train of thought, is reduced to a great religious example, while the essential facts of biblical history (whether or not Jesus was born of virgin, performed miracles, and rose from the dead) are all deemed to be highly questionable from a scientific point of view.[15]

Rudolf Bultmann employs a similar approach by suggesting the Bible's message could be divided into "kerygma" and "myth." The former, in Bultmann's view, is the subjective appropriation of the Bible's inspiring messages; the latter is what he refers to as the rationally unacceptable assertions made by the Bible. In Bultmann's view, "The Cosmology of the New Testament is essentially mythical in character."[16] To speak of heaven and hell, for Bultmann, is no different than echoing the fictitious lore of fables. His conclusion is forcefully stated, "Man's knowledge and mastery of the world have advanced to such an extent through science and technology that it is no longer possible for anyone seriously to hold the New Testament view of the world—in fact, there is *no one* who does."[17] Bultmann sought to rescue a form of piety from the Bible's dubious cosmology, history, and eschatology by straining from all of these nothing more than existential application.[18] This is nearly all that remains of Bultmann's (and subsequent liberalism's)

---

13. See Yarbrough, "God's Word in Human Words," 338.

14. This is perhaps best expressed in the subjectivism of Schleiermacher; see Braaten and Jensen, "The New Hermeneutics," 115–6. Schleiermacher is frequently dubbed the father of liberal theology, largely for his capitulation to Kantian epistemology on the one side and pietistic subjectivism on the other; cf. Sonderegger, "Creation," 109.

15. Machen notes the irony that the biblical miracles, given to strengthen faith, are deemed to be a hindrance to the skeptic's mind. In the end, to deny the miracles of Scripture reduces Jesus to simply an ethical example, not a resurrected Savior, and thus no real Savior at all; Machen, *Christianity and Liberalism*, 102, 109.

16. Bultmann, "New Testament and Mythology," 1.

17. Ibid., 4 (emphasis added).

18. Ibid., 15–16.

Bible: the existential application of religious ideals, apart from any reliable history or confident authority.[19]

In light of such modern skepticism about the historical integrity of the Bible, it is not difficult to anticipate postmodern disillusionment, even with the attempted intellectual compromises of modernism. It was only a matter of time before modernism's heirs raised obvious questions about a pick and choose, consumeristic approach to religion. In Craig Woelfel's words, "The defining characteristics of this age are a lack of naïveté, an immanent and humanist-influenced conception of reality, rationalism, and the default acceptance of a tremendous variety of positions ranging on a spectrum of belief to unbelief in which choice is accepted and, increasingly, unbelief is the default option."[20] Thus, the postmodern marketplace was born, in which belief and unbelief are equally valuable—a sophisticated panoply of intellectual and religious consumerism.[21]

We would hasten to assert here that there is much value in postmodern thought. It has created a renewed interest in the importance of viewing all of life through a narrative lens. It has also emphasized even more than its modern forerunners the importance of community and communal interpretation, and thus the necessity of incorporating multiple voices in theological conversation.[22] Other positive contributions will be addressed subsequently. At this point, however, we wish to particularly underscore its genuine recognition of certain epistemological tensions in the history of interpretation. Postmodern thinkers have rightly pointed out that modernism proved to be just as biased and presuppositional as the ecclesiastical sources they were critiquing. Even worse, modernism's somewhat idealistic claim to have an objective ability to determine truth from a rational point of view proved to be blatantly fallacious (a critique also made earlier by Kant and Hume). Postmodern thinkers have ably noted that subjective biases abound, both for those who accept the historical claims of Scripture and for those who reject them.[23] Thus, the Enlightenment and modernism each

---

19. This is embedded in the theology of Schleiermacher, and led to the "reader response" approach to the Bible. See Dingemans *Als hoorder onder de hoorders*, 71.

20. Woelfel, "The Varieties of Aesthetic Experience," 12.

21. Paas, "Nieuwe structuren," 149.

22. Grenz and Franke, arguing from a perspective of Evangelical postmodernism, suggest that this nuance within postmodern thought potentially creates a "place at the table" again for Scripture and tradition; Grenz and Franke, *Beyond Foundationalism*, 24. This idea will be returned to later in this chapter.

23. Peter Jones illustrates this point by noting that for many postmoderns, atheism is just as presuppositional and irrational as theism; Jones, *One or Two*, 134.

formed their own intellectual cage that was no less biased and restrictive than pre-Enlightenment thinking.[24]

Two intriguing examples of modern critical scholarship illustrate this point. The first is found in the so-called Jesus Seminar, which sought to determine which verses or stories in the New Testament were actually spoken by Jesus and which were not.[25] A committee of critical scholars was formed with the plan of ascribing a colored bead to texts by which they could cast their vote as to the level of confidence they had regarding whether or not a particular text actually originated with the historical Jesus.[26] It was observed, even by critics of the Bible's historicity, that the Jesus that was portrayed by the Jesus Seminar tended to look remarkably similar to the scholars themselves. In other words, they were projecting images of themselves, their value commitments, etc., onto what they believed Jesus actually would or would not have said.[27] The same dynamic was noted in the twentieth-century quest for the "historical Jesus." Critical scholars attempted to find the real Jesus through their own empirical methods, but as Pope Benedict (Joseph Ratzinger) properly observed, the picture of Jesus they painted "looked much more like the photographs of their authors and the ideals they hold."[28] This is the inescapable conundrum acknowledged by postmodernism—all interpretation is biased and presuppositional.[29]

History tells a difficult story. Many modernist philosophers and theorists envisioned a utopian society in which humanity would reach the zenith of civilized existence (a secular eschatology), but this utopia remains elusive and has staged, for some, a rather hard turn to postmodernism.[30] Nietzsche's "death of God" theology hoped to liberate humanity from the tyranny of ecclesiastical tradition and replace it with secular alternatives.[31]

24. Dekker, "Het evangelie," 43.

25. For a summary of this effort, see Strimple, *The Modern Search for the Real Jesus*, 1–3.

26. N.T. Wright concludes that such a methodology "had nothing whatever to commend it"; Wright, *The Contemporary Quest for Jesus*, 25.

27. Strimple later notes that such critical endeavors ended up creating a Jesus that reflected the critic's philosophical and religious prejudices more than the text itself; Strimple, *The Modern Search for the Real Jesus*, 79.

28. Ratzinger, *Jesus of Nazareth*, xii.

29. Wright, "Five Gospels but No Gospel," 23.

30. Pauline Rosenau argues that for some, the failure of Marxism and Liberalism as two unrealized ideologies further staged the turn for many to postmodernism; Rosenau, *Post-Modernism*, 160.

31. In this context, Dietrich Bonhoeffer feared a coming "world without God . . . in which people simply cannot be religious anymore"; Bethge, *Letters and Papers from Prison*, 139, cited in Paas, "The Making of a Mission Field," 66.

Marxism was likewise a secular metanarrative built on an idealistic view of man, wholly independent of God and thus not subject to biblical authority or morality, yet it also radically failed to affect its social utopia. The Soviet Bloc would crumble, the Berlin Wall would tumble, and thus the secular metanarratives that would supposedly replace the biblical metanarrative ended tragically in violent loss.[32] The failure of the secular metanarrative resulted in the empty space of secular postmodernism—where ultimately *nothing* matters because there is no longer any definitive, unifying story to history.[33] Thus, Foucault concludes, "There is no 'history' but a multiple, overlapping and interactive series of legitimate versus excluded histories."[34] Having lost its past (history), secular postmodernism is unsure of its present existence and quite skeptical about its future.[35]

In summary, the narrative from modern to postmodern thought reveals a heightening tension surrounding the reliability of history and its interpretation. Though many of those questions were raised prior to the advent of postmodernism, the punctuated turn towards subjective interpretations of history has left a vacuous hole in the place where objective interpretations once stood. Fearing the tyranny of the interpreter, many postmodern authors have notably entered a sea of historical/epistemological doubt without a life preserver.[36] These important concerns should not be dismissed out of hand; especially by those who preach. Postmodernism's historical conundrum raises crucial questions not simply about history in general, but biblical history in particular. Thus, the implications for preaching are numerous and of great consequence both inside and outside the church.

PREACHING INTO THE HISTORICAL VACUUM

We begin our response to this significant dilemma by referring back to the RH debate on preaching in the Netherlands. It must be reiterated that when

32. David Wells notes some of the particular ways in which Lenin and Stalin strove to adapt Marx's ideals to serve their own purposes, which again, ended in brutality; Wells, *Above All Earthly Powers*, 24. For an eloquently postmodern expression of the emptying effects of modern warfare, see James, "Georges Bataille," 22–23.

33. Slob, "Verily I Say unto Thee," 2.

34. Michel Foucault, cited without reference in Appignanesi and Garratt, *Introducing Postmodernism*, 83.

35. Jimmy Long suggests a defining trend of postmodernism is "a movement from belief in human progress to hopelessness . . . a pervasive sense of loss"; Long, "Generating Hope," 326.

36. This "sea of doubt" is a pun on modernism's "sea of faith" as described in Thiselton, *Interpreting God and the Postmodern Self*, 81.

the RH preaching paradigm emerged in the Netherlands, it did so against the backdrop of the modernistic, higher critical approach to the Bible.[37] The historicity of the Bible was under fierce attack, and part of the RH (redemptive-*historical*) response was concerned with emphasizing not only that the primary intention of the Bible was to reveal the redemptive plan of God that would culminate in the person and work of Christ, but also to emphasize the importance of *history*. Redemption happened *in history*. If the Bible's historicity could not be trusted, then the gospel itself was a dubious proposition and had no more authority than other cultural beliefs at any other time in history.[38] This apologetic context is often lost by those who tend to treat and criticize the RH preaching paradigm as simply being an overemphasis on theocentric history to the exclusion of homiletic application. The RH discussion, in many respects, cannot be properly and charitably understood without sensitivity to the battle for biblical history that contextualized so much of those debates.[39] The response for those within the RH vein of thinking was that history (even common grace history) was the story of Jesus and his kingdom. If this was true of general revelation, much more was it affirmed regarding special revelation (Scripture). Special revelation is the history of the incarnation, and as Christ himself was a historical person, special revelation must be both historical and Christ-centered by nature.[40] Bavinck saw the New Testament apostles affirming the historicity and authority of the Old Testament for the way in which it testified to the coming of God in the person of Jesus Christ, and his incarnation *into history* as that which bound together the two testaments (old and new) and the two peoples of God (Israel and the church).[41]

Thus, even though the immediate historical context of the development of the RH preaching paradigm is not postmodernism, it still makes a meaningful contribution to the discussion about contemporary preaching in a postmodern context as it focuses homiletic attention on the importance of biblical history from a narrative perspective. While its epistemology and methodology differ, secular postmodernism's suspicion of history is similar to the suspicion expressed in earlier, modernistic discussions about the

37. See De Ruijter, "Heil en historie," 46–49.

38. Outside the RH preaching discussion, the same point is made in the context of apologetics. See Feinberg, *Can You Believe It's True?*, 73.

39. Veenhof illustrates that the hermeneutical, theological, and ethical constructs of Herman Bavinck, upon whose shoulders the RH pioneers were standing, were themselves shaped by the reaction to rationalism's attempt to de-historicize Scripture; Veenhof, *Revelatie en inspiratie*, 11,19.

40. Ibid., 834.

41. Bavinck, *Gereformeerde dogmatiek*, 1.372–3.

reliability of the Bible's history.[42] As Paul Ricoeur has admitted, "Revelation is a historical process, but the notion of a sacred text is something anti-historical. I am *frightened* by this word 'sacred.'"[43] Thus, we would suggest that to the extent in which secular postmodernism is simply repackaging many of modernism's earlier concerns about the reliability of biblical history, preachers would do well to reconsider the way in which defenders of biblical history have responded to the similar challenges of modernism, as the former clearly builds upon the latter. This certainly includes the earlier first responders to the crisis, among whom were some of the RH pioneers.[44]

Additionally, we would suggest that this concern to defend the truthfulness of biblical history is what characterized much of the ministry of important figures that are not necessarily connected to preaching itself, such as Vos and Ridderbos.[45] Both men interacted heavily with the critics of biblical history and did so with a hermeneutical method that has been categorized as RH. It is quite likely that one of the reasons why there has been a surge of interest, especially in North America, in these Dutch theologians has to do with the challenges to biblical history, many of which stem from postmodern thought. Williams expresses this well in saying, "The Vosian insight that the Bible is, by its very nature, a narrative, telling of the drama of redemption, that the story the Bible tells is what unifies the biblical text, and that the Bible is to be read looking for that history, is essential to the new energy in evangelical theology."[46]

Thus, from a narrowly homiletic and broadly hermeneutic point of view, the RH paradigm of preaching and exegesis offers something apologetically helpful to the current discussion about preaching in a postmodern context. This is especially true as it highlights the historical unity and

---

42. J. Gresham Machen, with remarkable prescience, noted that for modernistic-liberal approaches to the Bible, "The only authority can be individual experience; truth can only be that which 'helps' individual man. Such authority is no authority at all"; Machen, *Christianity and Liberalism*, 78.

43. Ricoeur, *Figuring the Sacred*, 72 (emphasis added).

44. Trimp notes that the rejection of "exemplarism" of Holwerda and Veenhof was inseparable from the rejection of the religious subjectivism of the day, and that it was in the midst of this fray that the RH preaching paradigm arose; Trimp, *Heilsgeschiedenis en prediking*, 109–110.

45. This concern undergirds nearly all of Vos's writings. Gaffin sees it as the driving force of Vos's career; Gaffin, *God's Word in Servant Form*, xiv. See also Lints, *The Fabric of Theology*, 181; J.T. Dennison Jr., *The Letters of Geerhardus Vos*, 39–40. Ridderbos, *Studies in Scripture and its Authority*, 22–24; Ridderbos, *Redemptive History and the New Testament Scriptures*, 49–50.

46. Williams, "Theology as Witness," 1.72. See also Kleber, *The Influences of Theological Liberalism*.

continuity of the Bible via the gospel as the thread which binds together the pages of biblical history. This confidence in a unifying history is the message which needs to be echoed repeatedly and confidently in preaching, especially in our postmodern context. Telling and retelling the *historical* story of redemption lies at the heart of preaching. Though persuading listeners of the truthfulness of this account is ultimately not a purely intellectual issue (it is a matter of faith wrought in the heart by the Holy Spirit); nonetheless, the Bible's approach to cultivating faith is through the means of proclaiming the gospel through the lens of history.[47] This approach to preaching, though seemingly simplistic, is suggested by Larsen as an alternative to discussions about the Bible's origin, and a renewed focus on telling the story of Scripture itself in preaching.[48]

Biblical history, according to the RH point of view, is nothing less than the covenantal activity of God by which redemption is accomplished in space and time. The Bible, as a result, cannot be reduced to simple, timeless truths, apart from the historical context in which those truths were revealed and by which the same truths are contextualized. In a similar manner, neither can any sort of existential encounter with God be abstracted from the history of Scripture apart from a genuine respect for the actual history in which God first revealed himself to his people and the means by which he established a covenantal relationship with them. This is true for modern thinkers like Bultmann and Harnack, but also for postmodern thinkers, including evangelicals who too readily abandon the importance of biblical history for application oriented thinking, and thus sound strangely like Bultmann and Harnack.[49]

Creation, fall, and redemption remain the abiding historical context of biblical revelation. Not only is biblical history meaningless apart from a genuine recognition of these historical events; contemporary history, as secular postmodernism has rightly concluded, has lost its rudder as well. If the Bible's historicity is not preached and believed, the wandering roots of postmodernism will only grow wider and deeper, suffocating the very life (identity) out of its adherents. RH preaching, at its best, emphasizes the importance of seeing God as the Lord of history and the primary subject of the biblical text.[50] That there have been extremes and weaknesses within

47. This is well embodied in the preaching in the book of Acts (2, 6, 13, for example) and elsewhere. In this sense, we are affirming the language of Rom 10:17, "So Faith comes by hearing, and hearing by the word of God."

48. Larsen, *Telling the Old, Old Story*, 22.

49. Horton, *Covenant and Eschatology*, 265.

50. K. Schilder and many RH advocates emphasized that salvation happens *in history*, and thus there is a sense in which all history is ultimately part of redemptive

the movement (both old and new) is certain.[51] It might be suggested that a charitable way to judge the lasting benefits of the RH movement is not to measure it by its extremes, or at times immature expressions (many of which abound today), but by the pastoral context in which it arose and the extent to which it was able to meet the pertinent challenges of its day. The modernistic skepticism about the canon's historicity and objectivity that formed the backdrop of the RH discussion in the Netherlands has come to an even stronger expression in recent years.[52] Thus, it may prove helpful to suggest a renewed emphasis on the importance of biblical history and a wariness of attempts at homiletic application that abstract such applications from the text, rather than anchor them emphatically and self-consciously in the covenantal and *historical* details of the text. Imperatives apart from historically accomplished indicatives are simply abstracted, timeless moral-isms—the fodder of liberal preaching which will, in the end, lead to post-modern skepticism.[53]

Along these lines, as we have highlighted throughout this monograph, there is a thought-provoking measure of overlap between the RH and DR ideas. The former looks at the Bible as a unified historical narrative that focuses upon God and historical revelation from creation, to redemption, to consummation. The latter, we believe, overlaps but also develops the former. This is particularly evident in that the DR paradigm sees a profound unity in all of biblical history. It also argues that God is the primary actor revealed

---

history; see Veldhuizen, *God en mens onderweg*, 107–8.

51. In the Dutch debates, RH thinkers accused their "exemplaristic" opponents of fragmenting history into disconnected and arbitrarily imposed categories that violated the place in history of the biblical text; cf. Renninger, "The New Testament Use of the Old Testament Historical Narrative," 53. Greidanus has pointed out that the same cri-tique could be made against the Dutch RH advocates (i.e., Schilder) of Schematism, speculation, and objective preaching; Greidanus, *Sola Scriptura*, 211. For instance, K. Schilder argued strenuously for the importance of locating the line of history in preaching; Schilder, "Iets over de eenheid der 'Heilsgeschiedenis,'" 366. However, the Old Testament books do not form a straight historical line, so to speak; nor do the New Testament synoptic gospels tell the same stories in exactly the same order. Ironi-cally, the methodology employed by many in the Dutch RH camp was often no less guilty of schematizing than that of their exemplaristic counterparts; cf. Greidanus, *Sola Scriptura*, 203–5.

52. Schreurs, "Postmodern Bildung," 291.

53. Machen observed that liberal preaching that divorced historical indicatives from moral imperatives was, in reality, "rejecting the whole basis of Christianity"; Ma-chen, *Christianity and Liberalism*, 47. As Dorothy Sayers also noted in the same time period, such an emphasis on morality apart from history and doctrine would inevitably fail to convict and arouse; Sayers, *Creed or Chaos*, 20.

within the Bible's grand drama (covenant metanarrative), with the church playing a supportive, yet important role.

One of the most notable things frequently missing in the RH homiletic model is a greater sensitivity to the role of the reader/recipient of the biblical message in the context of preaching. This weakness has been acknowledged by both critics of the RH preaching paradigm and its advocates.[54] In many ways, nuances of postmodern thought have helped the homiletic discussion by forcing the question of the reader/hearer's role as part of the Bible's unfolding story, and by revitalizing the importance of seeing life from a narrative point of view.[55] We do not simply read stories; we live them. It is important to note that while the postmodern turn to the reader has had negative effects, at the same time, it has placed a helpful emphasis upon the role of the reader—a thought factor that is remarkably important in homiletic discussions.

In his development of the DR idea, Vanhoozer has been effective at creatively responding to the criticisms of postmodernism, and has also helpfully recognized that some of postmodernism's criticisms are legitimate and its advances helpful. Vanhoozer's critique of "epic" approaches to systematic theology (that it simply tells the Bible's content in an encyclopedic manner) might be leveled at the RH model of preaching (simply telling the story of redemption to passive readers/listeners, without giving due attention to the importance of the one hearing the sermon and the idea of *living the drama*). At the same time, Horton, perhaps as much if not more than Vanhoozer, has noted that the evangelical preoccupation with application in preaching has had the same effect as rolling the Trojan horse into the city of Troy. The abstraction of moralistic truths from their historical context, and the over-emphasis on man's response at the expense of God's prior activities, has caused conservative Protestant pulpits and their liberal-Protestant counterparts to sound remarkably similar. In much of evangelical preaching, "What would Jesus do?" has effectively taken the place of "What did Jesus do" *in history*. It is here again we find that the historical emphasis of RH preaching may be worth reconsidering, and the furthering nuances of the DR paradigm may also prove helpful, particularly the nuance of seeing the Bible as revealing not simply a story to be told in epical fashion, but a drama to be participated in upon the world stage of history. Where evangelical

54. De Ruijter, while noting the benefit of the RH method of preaching, also notes its dramatic failure to properly pay attention to the needs of the hearers of sermons. He thus argues that the preacher should remember the RH method, but also remember the hearers of sermons as well; De Ruijter, "Herkenning en heilshistorie," esp. 44; cf. Kuruvilla, *Privilege the Text*, 242.

55. De Ruijter, *Horen naar de stem van God*, 164–7.

preaching de-emphasizes history and over-emphasizes application, it stands poised to fuel the skeptical fire of postmodernism in much the same way that Protestant liberalism did. This leads us to consider whether or not the Bible's historical message can be trusted.

IS THERE AN AUTHOR BEHIND THIS TEXT?

Secular postmodernism and, in a nuanced way, evangelical postmodernism, have struggled with the idea of foundationalism, a problem that manifests itself in the issue of authorial intention. Grenz and Franke suggest that, "Among philosophers today, foundationalism is in dramatic retreat."[56] If the objective facts of history lie on the other side of a ditch which cannot be crossed, how can one be sure not simply about the authorship of various works, but perhaps more importantly, the authoritative meaning of the words authors have left behind? This question was not simply pressed upon theological discussions, but perhaps in an equally leveling way, manifested itself in literary criticism. Nietzsche's "death of God" theology and similar strands of deconstruction trickled down into what became known as the "death of the author" paradigm within the world of literature.[57] As Steiner notes, "For deconstruction, however, there can be no foundational speech-act, no saying immune from un-saying. This is the crux."[58] This important idea can be illustrated through a number of authors.

Roland Barthes, in his famous article "The Death of the Author," makes the point that the idea of an authoritative author is passé and futile. He says, "It is language that speaks, not the author."[59] The point is that an author, at most, is *behind the text*, in a world to which we do not have direct access, and therefore in a world of ideas of which we cannot be certain. All that we can be sure of is the immanent language of a text that is left behind by the so-called author, which is to be interpreted and applied by the reader. The reader remains, but the author is lost. Barthes faults the classical approach to literature for granting literary works Bible-like status of unquestioned authorship and discernible, implied meaning.[60] Even worse, according to Barthes, the classical model of literary criticism focused so strongly upon

56. Grenz and Franke, *Shaping Theology in a Postmodern Context*, 38.

57. Felperin, *Beyond Deconstruction*, 104. For a fuller treatment of Nietzsche in particular, see "Nietzsche, Genealogy and History," in Rabinow, *The Foucault Reader*, 76–100, esp. 78.

58. Steiner, *Real Presences*, 119.

59. Barthes, "The Death of the Author," 1323.

60. Ibid., 1324.

what the author *intended* a text to mean, that the reader was largely ignored (a problem postmodernism would seek to redress). Many authors have rightly noted that language is a two-sided engagement embodying the activity of the speaker as well as the activity of the reader/hearer.[61] The question remains: to what extent can the *author's* intention be known?

In a related manner, evangelical postmoderns have suggested that the concept of biblical inerrancy is derived from a post-enlightenment pursuit that sought to create an impenetrable (and logical) fortress from which orthodox truths might be defended.[62] From this flowed the idea that all that had to be done in order to properly understand the particular meaning of texts was to determine the "original meaning" of the text to the author and its readership. Yet according to postmodern theorists, to the extent that the intentions of an author might be *perceived* as knowable, they still remain elusive and subject to interpretation and revision.[63] The "world of the text," a term frequently employed by postmodern literary theorists,[64] is an unknowable world.[65] Gadamer, building on what Plato referred to as the "helplessness of the written word," says, "The understanding of something written is not the repetition of something past but the sharing of a present meaning."[66] In this rather extreme view, the present meaning of a text is defined not by the *authors* of texts but by the *readers* of texts. In like manner, Barthes proclaims not only the death of the author but also the birth of the reader. For him, "The birth of the reader must be at the cost of the author."[67] One must win the battle of textual control—either the author or the reader. For Barthes, it is clearly the latter, the consequence of which is that any attempt to confidently determine the authorial intention of a text is irrelevant. So he says, "Once the author is removed, the claim to decipher

---

61. McCartney and Clayton, *Let the Reader Understand*, 216.

62. Grenz, *Renewing the Center*, 190. Princeton theologians such as Charles and A. A. Hodge are often referenced as those who fortified the conservative "foundational" doctrine of inerrancy in the context of defending Scripture against the higher critics; Murphy, *Beyond Liberalism and Fundamentalism*, 16; see also a helpful summary on pg. 35. For a rebuttal of the idea that post-enlightenment thinkers (or Old Princetonians) invented a higher view of Scripture than was previously taught, see Carson, *The Gagging of God*, 153–4.

63. This point is repeatedly stressed by Derrida and the deconstructionists who followed him. See Harmon, *A Handbook to Literature*, 151.

64. See Ricoeur, "Hermeneutics and the World of the Text," 11–18, esp. 13.

65. Kuruvilla argues that while this world of the text is unknowable, the world "projected by the writer" is; Kuruvilla, *Text to Praxis*, 25.

66. Gadamer, *Truth and Method*, 392–3.

67. Barthes, "The Death of the Author," 1326.

a text becomes quite futile."[68] Intended meaning dies with the author. The shackles of fixed meaning have been loosed, and the reader is now free to *determine* the meaning of the text, rather than *discern* it.[69] From this comes the birth of the reader-response hermeneutic.[70]

In a similar vein, Michel Foucault in his "What Is an Author?" contends that the humanistic cry *ad fontes* was too optimistic. To say that we can return to the sources (i.e., authors) of texts and determine their meaning is wishful thinking in his view. He illustrates this by referring to the idea of the "complete works" of an author. Foucault raises the question: who gets to decide what an author's complete works are? Why are some included and others excluded? Why are they arranged certain ways? Is there not an implied interpretive strategy being forced upon the canonization of an author's works that effectively treats the works of an author with the same literary biases and assumed meanings that formed the canon of Scripture? So Foucault says, "Modernistic criticism, in its desire to recover the original author and text, is still effectively Christian in that it attempts to prove the value of a text by locating its author and the author's intentions."[71] It is interesting to note his proposed link between the objective goals of modernism (discerning the facts of history through rational process) and Christianity (discerning the meaning of texts through hermeneutics).[72] For Foucault, both modernism and Christianity are clearly flawed in their hope of getting *behind* the world of texts in order to determine their actual meaning (let alone authorship). "Authors" do not exist according to Foucault. In his view, "Authors are just projections of what we think."[73]

---

68. Ibid., 1325.

69. T.S. Eliot, anticipating the sentiments of postmodernism, captures this well by saying, "What a poem means is as much what it means to others as what it means to the author; and indeed, in the course of time a poet may become merely a reader in respect to his own works, forgetting his original meaning—or without forgetting, merely changing"; from "The Use of Poetry and the Use of Criticism," cited in Leitch, *The Norton Anthology of Theory and Criticism*, 1231.

70. E.D. Hirsch may have been one of the earliest to develop a thorough response to this reader-response approach, bridging the gap between general discussions in the area of literature with their overlapping discussions of biblical authority. His argument is based upon the idea of an author's consciousness, and the important distinction between a valid interpretation, and a certain interpretation; Hirsch, *Validity in Interpretation*, esp. 40, 47, 163.

71. Foucault, "What Is an Author?" 110.

72. Paul Ricoeur admits that the idea of *hermeneutics* is a biblical idea, adopted and adapted by secular, literary tradition. Thus, in his attempt to undo the one, he effectively undoes the other; Ricoeur, *The Conflict of Interpretations*, 64.

73. Foucault, "What Is an Author?" 110.

For Foucault, the only author that ultimately still exists is the *reader*, who searches the empty space left behind by the death of the author (or God). In a somewhat radical conclusion, he states:

> It is not enough, however, to repeat the empty affirmation that the author has disappeared. For the same reason, it is not enough to keep repeating (after Nietzsche) that God and man have died a common death. Instead, we must locate the space left empty by the author's disappearance.[74]

To "locate" is to study, contemplate, and seek; yet it would seem to avoid the idea of imputing fixed, objective meaning. Thus, the reader trumps the author, and the question "What does it *mean*?" is diminished. Seemingly, the question remaining is, "What does it mean *to you*?" So Foucault asks, "What difference does it make who is speaking?"[75] The implied answer: it does *not*. The question of who spoke or wrote a text and its fixed meaning is negligible in this literary perspective of secular postmodernism. The conclusion is rather that readers potentially create their own meanings, because the true author and his intentions cannot be identified, and thus the meaning of the text is neither fixed nor static.[76] This is the postmodern turn—the turn to the reader.

Evangelical postmodernism has mused over these issues while trying not to fall off the same cliff as secular postmodernism. As noted above, many of Evangelical postmodernism's adherents remain unpersuaded by the "foundationalist" expressions of inerrancy and infallibility in conservative communities, often suggesting that such formulations reflect an Enlightenment way of thinking.[77] At the same time, they are unwilling to abandon altogether the idea of biblical authority, opting for something of a synthesis of postmodern concepts.[78] Room is left for the author, and just as importantly for the ecclesial and canonical reading of the Christian community.[79] While the "reader-response" hermeneutic is rejected by Evangelical postmoderns,

---

74. Ibid., 105.

75. Ibid., 120.

76. We appreciate Vanhoozer's caution that, "It would be misleading to infer that the reader's liberation movement endorses interpretive anarchy"; Vanhoozer, *First Theology*, 245.

77. Woodbridge, "Some Misconceptions," 244.

78. John Franke argues that the Triune God is the only true "foundation" of authority, and that this authority is conveyed by the Spirit through Scripture and ecclesiastical tradition; Franke, "Scripture, Tradition and Authority," 205.

79. Webber, *Ancient–Future Faith*, 179.

the important place of the reader is preserved, and above that the priority of an ecclesial reading.[80]

By contrast, in more strident, secular postmodern expressions, communities of interpretation may be formed to share ideas, but none of these ideas can be granted authorial status, for that would effectively rebuild the interpretive "iron cage" of authorial intent and fixed, static meaning.[81] Thus, for Derrida, "There is no such thing as outside the text,"[82] implying a metaphysics of meaning. According to Derrida, texts, including religious texts, do not serve as windows to the past but more as mirrors of the present.[83] In his view, both reason and religion have "been shaped by a dishonest pursuit of certainty, i.e., the 'word made flesh' as a means of linguistic, historical, and moral oppression."[84] Freedom from this identity cage is the hermeneutical goal and conclusion of secular postmodernism.[85] Each of these intellectual issues shapes the challenging backdrop of preaching in today's postmodern context—the influence of which is constantly felt upon the church, both inside and out.

PREACHING THE AUTHOR'S MESSAGE

Do authors actually do anything with words, and *did God actually say* anything with his? Can there be any such thing as an authoritative message that stands on the other side of the biblical text? To the extent that such a thing as a singular intended meaning might have been inspired by God in the biblical author's mind, how can any reader today, or hearer of a sermon, actually have confidence that the message proclaimed is the *intended* message from God? In short, can God still speak through the ministry of his word? Questions such as these have in many ways invigorated postmodern discussions of literature and have surrounded contemporary discussions of biblical criticism.[86] Preaching in this current intellectual climate cannot help but

---

80. Gert Kwakkel notes the importance of resisting a privatized reading of Scripture on the basis of 1 Pet 1:10–11, while affirming the importance of recognizing the reader's role in the interpretation process; Kwakkel, "The Reader as Focal Point of Biblical Exegesis," 223.

81. This is the idea to which Vanhoozer is responding in *Is there a Meaning in this Text?*; cf. Fish, *Is There a Text in This Class?*.

82. Appignanesi and Garratt, *Introducing Postmodernism*, 76.

83. Derrida, "Faith and Knowledge," 23–24.

84. Appignanesi and Garratt, *Introducing Postmodernism*, 77.

85. Vuyk, "De zoon met de vader weggooien?," 116.

86. This is well embodied in what is referred to as the *intentional fallacy* in the arena of New Criticism. The *intentional fallacy* "refers to the mistaken belief that the author's

engage these issues. As John Stott has aptly put it, "Nothing undermines preaching more than skepticism about Scripture."[87]

We would suggest that even though postmodern thought has amplified such questions and their challenging implications, they are not altogether *new* questions. This epistemological conundrum did not begin with postmodernism, or even modernism, but with the Bible's first stated question, "Did God *actually* say . . .?" (Gen 3:1). From a biblical point of view, it is from that question that the long shadow of epistemological doubt has attempted to suppress the authority of God's spoken and written word.[88] The same epistemological question that plagued the historical Adam in the garden also plagued Israel, who needed to be reminded over and over that God had actually spoken, and that his Word once spoken *in the past* continued to be authoritative and guiding *into the present.*[89]

Israel's many episodes of covenant renewal were not simply a retelling of the historical story, but a re-vitalizing of the historical drama. Their feasts were designed around the idea of dramatically re-enacting redemptive history.[90] The covenant sign of circumcision was a reminder that something had been spoken and done *in history*, and that the promises and obligations that God had once spoken were still just as binding and authoritative as when they were first uttered. The warnings for failing to heed the word of God that were impressed upon Israel were repeated in the New Covenant context, as is seen throughout the New Testament canon, and particularly in the book of Hebrews.[91] Thus, building on an argument from Psalm 95 about the dangers of not hearing God's voice *today*, the author of Hebrews compels his audience to understand that the same word of God, once spoken in the past, continues to be ". . . living and active, sharper than any two-edged sword, piercing to the division of soul and spirit, of joints and marrow, and discerning the thoughts and intentions of the heart" (Heb 4:12). The same word of God, authored by God himself, continues to be effective, and is

intention is the same as the text's meaning"; Tyson, *Critical Theory Today*, 136. And similarly, "The confusion of the author's intended meaning with the actual meaning of the text"; Macey, *The Penguin Dictionary of Critical Theory*, 202.

87. Stott, "Biblical Preaching in the Modern World," 115.

88. Cornelius Van Til notes that, "The Bible does not appeal to human reason as ultimate in order to justify what it says. It comes to the human being with absolute authority"; Van Til, *A Christian Theory of Knowledge*, 15.

89. Vanhoozer, *The Drama of Doctrine*, 223.

90. Fairbairn, *Typology of Scripture*, 377–80.

91. Michael Kruger, in a manner similar to Vos, argues that this continuation of the Old Testament's message was one of the ways that New Testament authors and participants viewed canonicity; Kruger, *Canon Revisited*, 148–9. A similar point is affirmed by N.T. Wright in his *The Last Word*, 53.

the objective standard by which God's judgment will take place (Heb 4:13). Such a homiletic posture found in the book of Hebrews, and its emphasis on God's continued, dramatic speaking, is the stage upon which homiletics must continue to stand, even in this postmodern age of historical and authorial skepticism. The problem remains the same and so does its solution—the historical gospel dramatically revealed in the word of God.

For homiletic purposes, we would reiterate the point that there is nothing new under the sun (Ecclesiastes), including postmodernism's recalcitrance toward objective, transcendent truth. It is of peculiar interest that Jesus referred to himself as being singularly "*the* way, *the* truth, and *the* life."[92] It was for this very purpose that he had entered history (John 18:37). Truth, according to Jesus, is historical, incarnational, and redemptive. Though obviously in seed form, the epistemological doubts of secular postmodernism were latent in the minds of some of Jesus' antagonists. Pilate's dismissive response stands among the most infamous questions of Christian history, "What is truth?" (John 18:38). Notice that Pilate, in a way that previews the epistemological ambiguities of postmodernism, does not so much rebuke or deny Jesus' claims, but simply evades them through questioning. The answer to his remarkably important question stands before him—in Jesus—but Pilate has no desire to wait for or engage Christ's answer.[93] The same intellectual evasiveness pervades much of contemporary postmodern thought—not so much an outright rejection of truth based on historical evidence, but a sophisticated avoidance of authorial truth that is thinly veiled behind a veneer of intellectual skepticism.[94]

The difference between the Pharisees and Pilate is suggestively the same as the difference between modernism and postmodernism: the former sought to disprove the claims of Christ on the basis of historical and textual evidence, and the latter seeks not so much to objectively disprove the claims of Christianity, as to circumvent the claims of Christ through skeptical questioning. What Pilate accomplished with one question, strains of postmodernism enhance with an endless subdivision of the same question in malleable forms. Yet the end-goal is the same—freedom from the claim of singular, authoritative truth as embodied in the historical Jesus and proclaimed by the time-tested, biblical gospel. Postmodernism's claim to

---

92. John 14:6 (emphasis added). This is defended as the "correspondence view of truth" by Doug Groothuis in "Truth Defined and Defended," 68–73. See similarly, Phillips, "Can We Know the Truth?," 34–36.

93. Van Houwelingen, *Johannes*, 358.

94. Zack Eswine helpfully distinguishes "practical doubt" (dealing with words in the biblical text) and "philosophical doubt" (dealing with the question of whether "meaning" actually exists); Eswine, *Preaching to a Post-Everything World*, 16.

epistemological uncertainty is not a new *anti*-affirmation, but simply the sophisticated and enhanced revision of antiquated reservations about truth, history, and authority.

These observations offer the contemporary preacher a point of view from which to interact with the anti-foundational sentiment of postmodernism, and perhaps a sense of confidence that postmodernism is not as new or insurmountable as it may appear.[95] Postmodernism—even secular postmodernism—should not be simply portrayed as an epistemology without foundations; its critique of history and authority is just as foundational and presuppositional as those who defend the Bible as historical and authoritative.[96] Furthermore, postmodernism's struggle to embrace the truths of history is not simply an intellectual dilemma created by the confines of history, but is ultimately a question of spiritual and moral submission—a concern which preaching must constantly address.[97] From a biblical point of view, the reason why the secular postmodern skeptic cannot embrace biblical truth, history, and authority is not because she simply has not had the right facts objectively portrayed in the right way (the romantic view of rationalism), but because there is a sublime, if not overt *unwillingness* to submit to the Author of Scripture and his definitions of history, meaning, and morality.[98] Related to these ideas, 1 Corinthians 2:14 states, "The natural person does not accept the things of the Spirit of God, for they are folly to him, and he is not able to understand them because they are spiritually discerned." The decision as to whether or not to trust and accept the truth claims of the biblical story, and thus God as its author and completer, is both a spiritual and moral one.[99]

The role of the Holy Spirit cannot be underestimated at this point. The very ideas of biblical inspiration, authority, and even homiletic application are the work of the Holy Spirit. All three of these categories, including faith in the words and work of God, fall lifelessly to the ground apart from the work of the Holy Spirit.[100] From the perspectives of epistemology and

95. Rico Sneller provocatively likens postmodernism to the mythical Medusa, whose gaze turned many to stone; and yet, ironically, it was her own reflection that proved to be her undoing; Sneller, "Gebod, belofte, en de tentakels van het schrift," 52–53.

96. Guthrie, "New Testament Exegesis of Hebrews," 591.

97. Gamble, *The Whole Counsel of God*, 1.49.

98. We will engage the moral implications of this material in the next section.

99. John Frame helpfully suggests that biblically speaking, the knowledge of God "is obedience" and "produces obedience"; Frame, *Systematic Theology*, 705.

100. This function of the Spirit's role in the confession of the early church is referred to as the "*sine qua non*" of the Christian faith"; Grenz and Franke, *Beyond Foundationalism*, 170.

preaching, "The Holy Spirit creates hope where otherwise there is no reason for hope."[101] We should also readily admit that there is a bit of circularity in this argument. At the same time, there must be an honest recognition that all reasoning is somewhat circular. Preaching begins and ends with the work of the Holy Spirit. Logic, reasoning, and argumentation may have their place; but their place is decidedly secondary to the work of the Spirit.[102]

Thus, to the extent that preaching does not bear in mind the intellectual consequences of the fall of Adam and the necessity for the Spirit of God to renew not only the will but also the mind of those who hear sermons, it will regrettably deepen the romantic pitfall of modernism, which thought too highly of the natural man's intellectual abilities.[103] In something of an ironic overlap, secular postmodernism concedes an important biblical conclusion: the natural man cannot cross the bridge of history to understand what *really happened* nor can he enter the realm of heaven to see who really wrote the story of human existence.[104] Yet these are the very issues the Bible explicitly addresses by the drama of God entering into history via the gospel. Here we agree with the important observation of Von Balthasar that only a transcendent third party can truly bridge the gap between the past and present, granting authoritative interpretation and meaning to both—and that is God himself.[105] It is in responding to these quandaries that postmodernism and biblical Christianity differ. The former concedes the matter to the dire consequences of intellectual autonomy; the latter submits itself to the necessity and authority of divine revelation. Vanhoozer rightly summarizes these two views as being the contrast between "*over*standing" and "*under*standing."[106] The former (modern, postmodern, etc.) exalts itself over the biblical text and therefore postures itself de facto in the place of God; the latter finds it-

---

101. Gerkin, *The Living Human Document*, 69, cited in Thiselton, *Interpreting God and the Postmodern Self*, 78.

102. Vidu, "Can We Say Very Much?," 233.

103. Arturo Azurdia refers to this as the "unique work of the Holy Spirit" within the economic actions of the Trinity as it relates to preaching; Azurdia, *Spirit Empowered Preaching*, 34.

104. Cf. Rom 10:6–8.

105. Von Balthasar, *Theo-Drama*, 1.115.

106. This remarkably helpful section both concludes the book as well as captures, in our view, the essence of literary humility as it relates to biblical literature; Vanhoozer, *Is There A Meaning in this Text?*, 462–7. This "overstanding" that leads to skepticism is well-embodied by Bart Ehrman, who suggests, "There is only one way to know whether stories about Jesus were ever made up or modified. That's by looking at all the stories, comparing them with one another, and deciding for yourself"; Ehrman, *A Brief Introduction to the New Testament*, 130. With this method, how could one ever arrive at a confident conclusion?

self in the humble posture of a creature, created to be a submissive covenant partner with God, yielding to God and his transcendent authority—the foundation of homiletic proclamation.

Preaching is a unique literary-oral phenomenon in that it suggests that the veracity and intention of the text being preached has been "upheld" by its author—God himself through the work of the Spirit. Thus, the author of the biblical text is *author*itatively unique and thus the text itself is *author*itatively unique. The content of the sermon must, by implication, be unique and authoritative as well. As acknowledged above, this argument is admittedly presuppositional, and even somewhat circular, but it is explicitly biblical. For the preacher to proclaim the drama of redemption from this point of view is intellectually honest, helpful, and defensible. The postmodern realization that it is impossible to break out of the hermeneutical spiral, or to be free from presuppositions, may actually create a fertile environment for the reconsideration of the biblical story as a coherent metanarrative that makes sense out of the world in which we live as the marred yet redeemable *Imago Dei*. Ultimately, not only are we unable to write the story of our lives, the only real confidence we have in accurately interpreting ourselves and the world in which we live is found in submitting to the one who is capable of writing (and righting) it for us—the divine author who is the same yesterday, today, and forever (Heb 13:8).

It is in this context that we find the contributions of the RH and DR paradigms to be helpful for the purpose of preaching in a postmodern era. The RH emphasis demands careful attention to the narrative of Scripture in its historical setting and context, while appreciating the overall continuity of the redemptive story as it progressively unfolds. A Christ-centered preaching of the gospel from all of Scripture displays not simply the message of redemption (which alone has the power to work faith in its hearers); it also makes a secondary argument for the implicit harmony and authority of Scripture itself. It resists the temptation of succumbing to anthropocentric moralism. Wedded to this RH emphasis, particulars of the DR paradigm draw the postmodern hearer *into the drama* of Scripture, rather than letting her remain at a safe distance as a spectator to the text. She is drawn not simply into the process of interpretation, but also the important aspect of faithful participation. As preaching calls its hearers to subject their own disharmonized narratives to that of the biblical drama, the potential for replacing a posture of *over*standing with one of *under*standing the text is optimistically possible. Again, apart from the vitalizing work of the Spirit, none of these hermeneutic or rhetorical efforts will bear any fruit. Thus, the real hope of the preacher is embedded in the promise of Scripture itself: that insofar as Christ abides in him and he in Christ, he will bear much fruit (John 15:3–5).

POSTMODERNISM AND THE CHALLENGE OF MORALITY

We have saved this section for last, as in many ways it is the logical conclusion to secular postmodernism's skepticism regarding the certainty of history and the extent to which the authorial intention of texts—especially biblical texts— can be confidently known. The implications are significant for discussions regarding morality—an issue biblical preaching must constantly address. In light of the postmodern conundrums of history and authorship asserted above, who has the right to say that their moral interpretations of history and meaning are correct, normative, and especially authoritative?[107] Jacques Derrida, the founding father of deconstructionism and one of the chief architects of postmodernism, has observed that the authorial-intention approach to interpreting history and historical works has forged an iron cage of morality in which many unwilling subjects have been forced to live.[108] This "iron cage" could be illustrated through an endless list of moral issues currently in vogue, many of which are now vigorously discussed and contested.[109]

We would be careful at this point to distance postmodernism from its oft-earned reputation of relativism. As noted in chapter 3, not even secular postmodernism is arguing for total moral relativism, as such a view would die the death of too many qualifications. In other words, if all morality is relative—and thus equally acceptable—by what ethical standard would postmodern thinkers condemn the inhuman atrocities committed during World War II? In fact, postmodern thinkers have been careful to distance themselves from total relativism, arguing for something more along the lines of a contextual pragmatism based upon voluntary alliance.[110] This is an important nuance as we make the turn to the way in which the homiletic model advocated thus far seeks to address the concerns raised by

107. This point is readily conceded by many postmoderns, and is referred to as "self-positioning"; see Woelfel, "The Varieties of Aesthetic Experience," 292.

108. See Foucault "The Punitive Society," 23–38, esp. 30–31; see also Foucault, "Truth and Power," 51–75.

109. Our goal here is not to raise or attempt to settle these particular moral issues raised by postmodern thought, but rather to underscore the reality that postmodernism, despite its claims, is effectively a worldview with moral implications. In short, everyone is living out the consequences of what he or she believes.

110. Rorty, *Consequences of Pragmatism*, cited in Wells, *Above All Earthly Powers*, 81–82.

the postmodern skeptic. With that qualification noted, it is still true that there are ways in which secular postmodernism takes on a quasi-missional disposition, striving not so much for the *ending* of religion but for the *blending* of religion.[111] Secular postmodernism's indifference toward objective, transcendent truth has created a climate in which the absence of tolerance is intolerable. Thus, a strange new world of religious uniformity in which all truth claims are perceived as equally true is the pluralistic identity of postmodernity and the challenge before contemporary preaching.[112]

There is an ironic air of intolerance in certain expressions of postmodernism, casting a vision in which the new metanarrative discards older ones in place of pluralistic religious consumerism.[113] Robert Sellers describes this well when he defines the postmodern impulse as, "To seek 'spirituality' without necessarily practicing any one particular religion, or sometimes by blending several religions into one new constellation of beliefs and rituals."[114] This subliminally missional agenda within certain postmodern expressions of morality and (in)tolerance proves the point that it is impossible to live without some form of moral compass and societal metanarrative—one with missional implications.[115] The postmodern rejection of biblical tradition and modernism has only created a bronze cage in place of the iron one it set out to destroy. There is no such thing as life apart from a metanarrative. *Everyone is a part of some story*—something which is true of those inside and outside the church. Yet what does this imply for the moral aspect of preaching in a postmodern context?

PREACHING THE MEANING OF TEXTS AND THE MEANING OF LIFE

In many respects, this section draws together the application of the monograph as a whole, as it binds together many ideas previously stated in the context of addressing the postmodern moral conundrum from a homiletic perspective informed by RH and DR insights. The moral implications of the loss of confidence in history and thus any metanarrative (whether secular or biblical), as well as the so-called "death of the author" (whether secular

---

111. Chapell, "The Necessity of Preaching Christ," 61.

112. Paas, *De werkers van het laatste uur*, 273.

113. Netland and Johnson, "Why Is Religious Pluralism Fun—And Dangerous?," 51–53.

114. Sellers, "Is Mission Possible in a Postmodern World?," 395.

115. Jones, *Spirit Wars*, 53.

or biblical) has led to the inescapable collapse of moral objectivity.[116] This is, in many respects, the logical consequence of the previously addressed ideas. Without the "center" of metanarrative and meta-authorship, postmodern morality is often subjectively defined, except that which might be defined by varying "tribal" communities.[117] It is for this reason that we suggest that homiletic interaction with postmodernism should include not only an honest acknowledgment of the preacher's own presuppositions, but also a constant engagement of postmodern presuppositions. Can the postmodern skeptic truly make sense of a world without God? Is there such a thing as a story without an author? As Altena asks, can postmodernism find authentic meaning in life when God is "no factor in our life-story?"[118] Or has postmodernism effectively proven true the time-tested confession of Augustine, "You have formed us for yourself, O God, and our hearts are restless until they find their rest in Thee."[119]

To a certain extent, no one *actually* can, nor indeed does, live consistently with postmodernism's ideals—a truth which many postmodern skeptics need to be challenged to consider. What secular postmodernism is, in reality, is an intellectually sophisticated attempt to rewrite the script of individual and societal morality, without objective grounds for doing so, allowing the demise of empirical optimism to give way to the tyranny of epistemological skepticism. While, as noted above, there are many helpful features in postmodern thought, its skeptical core can often lead to cynicism for those who do not learn to discerningly separate the wheat from the chaff. Preaching that is sensitive to the questions of postmodernism stands poised to offer a message of hope to those who may have lost confidence in history, authority, and morality. Thus, proclaiming the redemptive drama of God in the gospel and its moral implications (application) is of vital importance in a postmodern context. Preaching from this perspective challenges the skeptic that the only way to make any sense of their life-story is by seeing it in the context of a larger story—the biblical one—and it reminds those inside the covenant community of their place in the biblical drama, just as each witness in Hebrews 11 uniquely played their part in the hall of faith.[120] It is for this reason that the pulpit, called to inform the moral conscience of

---

116. Mohler, "Truth and Contemporary Culture," 63.

117. Long, "Generating Hope," 325.

118. Altena, "Wolken gaan voorbij," 111 (trans. mine).

119. Augustine, *Conf.* 1.1 (*NPNF1* 1.45).

120. Alasdair MacIntyre interestingly notes the way in which stories form the script of meaning and morality, and that apart from confidence in those stories our lives become dramatic chaos, and the answer to the question "What am I to do?" becomes unanswerable; MacIntyre, *After Virtue*, 216–7.

the nations, has become the object of postmodern indifference, and in some environments, its scorn.[121]

Our proposal is that the sermon should not only display the drama of God's redemption in Christ, but also direct hearers in how best to perform the particular script of Scripture in faithfully improvised ways, thus displaying the truth of the gospel.[122] Not only is the biblical story unified,[123] but it is also the only story which makes sense of the world in which we live, both individually and corporately. As Vanhoozer summarily concludes, "The biblical drama is the only drama."[124] Postmodern thinkers today, inside and outside the church, yearn to be a part of a meaningful, relational story.[125] From this point of view, the biblical skeptic as well as the confident Christian living in a postmodern and "post-Christian"[126] age alike might be compelled to properly live out their part in the drama of history, and to do so in the context of covenant community—the church. Thus, the homiletic imperative is not, "This is the story; now believe it," but "this is the story; now live it."

The Bible does not simply reveal a story to be told, but a drama to be actively participated in and lived out, and this is most helpfully lived out in the context of the church. As Gert Kwakkel has noted, "people do not enjoy total freedom in assigning meaning to texts."[127] By contrast, they are called not only to a submissive reading of the biblical text in a posture of *understanding* rather than *overstanding,* they are particularly called into what the Bible designs as the primary community of biblical interpretation—the church. Again, Kwakkel helpfully states, "The church of Jesus Christ is still the most proper place for the Bible to be read."[128] This idea is suggested in Hebrews, where abandoning the community of the saints is insepara-

---

121. Blamires, *The Post-Christian Mind,* 163. We might suggest that this helps to explain why church attendance in countries where postmodernism's influence is strongly felt has waned in contrast to previous decades. The pulpit is the emblem of everything secular postmodernism decries—history, authority, and morality.

122. Carlson, "Drama Theory," 267–71.

123. Graeme Goldsworthy helpfully points out that this canonical unity is a "theological presupposition, not an empirically based construct"; Goldsworthy, *Gospel-Centered Hermeneutics,* 251; see also Kruger, *Canon Revisited,* 148.

124. Vanhoozer, *The Drama of Doctrine,* 82.

125. That even secular postmoderns have this yearning has been affirmed by Baudrillard, *Simulacra and Simulation,* 43.

126. For a helpful discussion of how this term does not simply imply secularization, but a change in "beliefs, motivations, and practices," including declining influence from the church, see Paas, 'Post-Christian, Post-Christendom, and Post-modern Europe," 11.

127. Kwakkel, "The Reader as Focal Point of Biblical Exegesis," 220.

128. Ibid., 219.

bly linked to misreading and thus mis-*living* the biblical story. Those who misread and abandoned the gospel were described as having spurned and rejected the promises in contrast to those who inherited them by faith and a right understanding of the gospel. Thus, in a very meaningful sense, everyone, Christian and non-Christian alike, is *already* in the biblical drama; the only question is whether her role is one of submission (i.e., like Jacob) to the Author of life who is at the same time the script-writer of history, or if she is living out a subversive role of rebellion, pointlessly abandoning the scripts that she was created to perform in favor of idolatrous scripts of her own design (i.e., like Esau).[129]

The historically informed and exegetically derived indicatives and imperatives of Scripture are bound to one another. Thus to divorce one from the other is to tear apart what God has joined together, and succumb to the foundationless piety of modern liberalism.[130] To reverse the order is potentially just as dangerous as it effectively inverts the order and priority of the biblical drama.[131] Thus, the search for meaningful morality is attainable because the author-God of Scripture is also the transcendent God of history. Everything between creation and consummation is part of the story, part of the drama of God in history, and is governed by the inspired script. In Young's words:

> Like music, the word of God is never just 'back there,' tied to an antiquated score in an unread library, experienced as alien, as discerned across a great gulf or hermeneutical gap: it is 'realized' in performance, a performance inevitably inadequate at present, yet an earnest of the great eschatological performance to come in God's good time.[132]

To pretend not to be part of the drama is to effectively deny one's very existence.[133] The Bible's message of truth is not an enslaving one, but a liberating one—as sermons must constantly proclaim. And the church, rather than a social prison, is a "theatre of love, reconciliation, and hope."[134] Believ-

---

129. Horton, *Christless Christianity*, 240.

130. As Machen stated, "Here is found the most fundamental difference between liberalism and Christianity—liberalism is altogether in the imperative mood, while Christianity begins with a triumphant indicative . . . Liberalism makes Christ an example for faith; Christianity, the object of faith"; Machen, *Christianity and Liberalism*, 47.

131. Webster, "The Imitation of Christ," 106.

132. Young, *The Art of Performance*, 182.

133. Horton notes the irony of postmodernism's willful abandonment of hope, making it the incarnation of the Beatles' "Nowhere Man"; Horton, *Covenant and Eschatology*, 275.

134. Vanhoozer, *The Drama of Doctrine*, 427.

ing that there is no absolute truth is not liberating, but rather a new form of slavery to a different master—skepticism. It is for this reason that Jesus said that knowing *the* truth would make one *free* (John 8:32). Knowing the truth of our stories is not only existentially honest, it also grants meaning and morality to our lives. This is what the biblical drama proclaims, and what the pulpit should proclaim week after week—not moralistic threats abstracted from the gospel but the saving and sanctifying work of Jesus.[135] The absence of this dramatic emphasis explains the negative reaction of Christians that have been influenced by postmodernism, and postmodern skeptics alike. Proclaiming the drama of redemption offers comfort and hope in that the meaning of life is found in the Author of life. It is he who has imprinted upon the human soul a deep impression that life only makes sense as we come to know the author of our script and his purpose for our lives.[136] Thus, the homiletic call is to draw the listener into the drama of redemptive history and to show her the way in which God has accomplished the grandest rescue mission of history in the gospel, and how she can now become a beautiful part of that drama as well.[137] Thus, the pastoral goal is never to leave the hearer of this message in a passive posture, but to show her what an actively fitting response to the *Missio Dei* should be.[138]

It is in this missional context that we reiterate the weakness in the development of the RH paradigm, and at the same time find an enhancement in the DR paradigm. The former, as we have noted in the historical survey, failed to produce a genuinely outward-facing, missional identity.[139] During the earlier stages of the RH developments, the posture of many of its advocates was understandably reactionary and protective of the church. In a sense, the mission came *to* the church. Critics of the RH paradigm should again remember that the movement developed in the context not only of apologetic battles with higher criticism, but also of the bitter realities of a World War and entrenched ecclesiastical struggles.[140] Still, as C. Trimp pleaded in the 1980s, there was

135. Horton, *Christless Christianity*, 224.

136. Henderson, *Culture Shift*, 147.

137. Christopher Wright summarizes the message and mission of the Bible well by saying, "The writings that now comprise our Bible are themselves the product of and witness to the ultimate mission of God"; Wright, *The Mission of God*, 48. This point is simple enough for children to understand; see Lloyd-Jones *The Jesus Storybook Bible*, 17.

138. Vanhoozer, *The Drama of Doctrine*, 21–22; see also 252–63 for fuller treatment.

139. Attempts to rectify this in recent times are noteworthy. Kees Haak, coming from an RH background, suggests ways in which missions amongst postmodernists may be advanced, particularly by emphasizing the importance of community; Haak, "Schaamte en schuld op Papua," 136–59, esp. 156.

140. See chapter 1 above.

a need to continue the discussions about preaching with new conversation partners and in new contexts. We are suggesting that this continuing of the conversation implies a focus not merely on inter-ecclesiastical homiletic questions, but on extra-ecclesiastical missional questions as well. In other words, the Bible's drama of redemption is not simply the drama of the church, but the dramatic interaction between God, the church, and the world. This is clearly embodied in the "witnessing" of the saints in Hebrews 11, who saw themselves as not only inheriting the promises of the gospel by faith, but also as commissioned to proclaim the gospel by faith. The gospel implies mission or, as Vanhoozer puts it, "The gospel is a missional statement—a statement of the divine mission of Son and Spirit."[141]

The gospel is what Christians need to hear week after week for the sake of their sanctification and comfort,[142] but it is also what non-Christians (including secular postmodern thinkers) need to hear in order to be reconciled with God and to find cognitive and existential rest from their skepticism.[143] Their part in the drama is an otherwise frustrated and hopeless role, and is in desperate need of redemption.[144] The church's continued role in the unfolding of the dramatic *Missio Dei* is to be God's covenant partner and servant, bringing the gospel to the ends of the earth until the kingdom of God is consummated in all of its climactic glory. The moral implications of the idea of walking with God while participating in the drama of redemption ought to be at the heart of preaching in a postmodern era, and is an important contribution of the DR paradigm.[145] Thus, we find the RH preaching paradigm deficient to the extent that expressions of it not only lacked application or explicit imperatives, but also lacked a particularly missional emphasis.[146] But deficient does not mean unhelpful or unredeemable.

141. Vanhoozer, *The Drama of Doctrine*, 69.

142. Thus, the time-tested and warm summary of Protestant theology as found in the first question and answer of the Heidelberg Catechism. Fred Klooster calls it the "song of the Reformation"; Klooster, *Our Only Comfort*, 1.23.

143. Frame, *Doctrine of the Knowledge of God*, 152–3; see also his *Systematic Theology*, 738, 1133.

144. An interesting contrast can be made between a *pilgrim* and a *nomad*. The former is passing through yet has a destination; the latter is wondering aimlessly without one. This homelessness of postmodernism is in stark contrast to the idea of eschatology—the goal of Christian pilgrimage, and the communal identity of the local church; see Beach, "The Local Church," 136.

145. For similar reflection on the unique contribution of the DR paradigm, see Jensen, Review of *The Drama of Doctrine*, 228.

146. Stefan Paas, writing within this Dutch Reformed tradition, argues that one of the greatest needs of preaching today is the reconsideration of the pulpit as a means of evangelistic mission to the unreached, not simply the building up of the saints; Paas,

Rather, we believe that by taking some of its best fruit and combining it with that of the DR paradigm, a homiletic model with a Christ-centered focus and an outward facing, missional imperative is attainable. This proposal has the potential of helping to respond to postmodernism's dilemmas, just as the early RH advocates responded to the crises created by higher criticism. The issues today are different than those of the last century, and yet the overlap is also striking and reminds us that there is nothing new under the sun. The church is still on stage, living out a witness role in history, proclaiming a message of truth that has yet to meet a genuinely *new* challenge. The church may refine and reform its thinking and homiletic rhetoric, but the message must remain the same.[147] Sermons, of necessity, constantly maintain some form of rhetoric. They are obliged to employ the most effective form of rhetoric.[148] This is the burden of the pulpit: to continue to proclaim an old message in new ways; to creatively yet faithfully tell the same story that began in an earthly garden and ends in a heavenly temple.[149]

This is effectively what we saw in Hebrews 11. God, who first spoke and acted, continues to speak and act through his word and Spirit to and through his church. God not only revealed the gospel by speaking in history, he embodied it by entering into history in the incarnation of Jesus Christ, the word made flesh. His life was one of faithfully performing the word of God in various contexts, thus creatively improvising the biblical script from one setting to another without ever compromising its morality. Facets of his person and work were revealed in the great hall of faith in Hebrews 11. A similar assembly of the faithful exists in the church today, which is called to perform the biblical script in this postmodern scene—faithfully *improvising*, yet never *compromising* in its application of Scripture to all of life.[150]

God not only walked with his people, he actively conformed them to his image through the drama of their lives, making them fittingly dressed actors on the stage of history for his glory. In this sense, the church today, influenced by the best and the worst of postmodernism, continues to

---

"Missionair preken," 16–22, esp. 22.

147. Thus, C.S. Lewis implores, "Our business is to present that which is timeless (the same yesterday, today, and tomorrow) in the particular language of our own time"; Lewis, *God in the Dock*, 91.

148. The inescapability of employing rhetoric in sermons is affirmed by secular rhetoricians; see Corbett, *Classical Rhetoric for the Modern Student*, 30.

149. See Beale, *The Temple and the Church's Mission*, 399–400.

150. Keller rightly observes that the question of whether preachers must "change for the culture or challenge it" will ever be before the church; Keller, *Preaching*, 96. He subsequently offers numerous suggestions on how to do so and suggests, "No one can present a culture-free formulation of biblical truth"; Ibid., 92. Being sensitive to the culture without being seduced by it is the tightrope upon which every preacher stands.

creatively embody the gospel according to authoritative script, speaking and acting as the *Imago Dei*.[151] As Richard Hays says, "Right reading of the New Testament occurs only where the Word is *embodied*."[152] The pulpit exists to speak with nothing less than the authority of God to these very issues. This includes hermeneutically informed, Christ-centered moral instruction that leads to a proper reading and embodying of the word of God.[153] Preaching calls the postmodern skeptic out of moral darkness and into the light of Christ.[154] It also directs the church, living in a postmodern age, in how to perform her missionary calling while walking with God en route to the heavenly city. The fact that God is "still speaking" (Heb 4:10) to us today, particularly through the ministry of his preached word, is the foundation of our confidence, confession, and commission—as well as our morality.

SUMMARY, CAUTIONS AND CONCLUSION

In this chapter we have attempted to state and address three important issues within postmodern thinking—the questions of history, authorship, and morality—from a homiletic perspective that synthesizes the DNA of the RH and DR paradigms. Though our treatment of many issues has been brief, we yet hope it may suggest ways in which the challenges articulated by strains of postmodern thought might be given a homiletic response. We have not suggested an overly specific homiletic model, per se, but rather have suggested particular nuances that ought to be considered in the current context of preaching, and the widespread influence of postmodernism. In particular, it has been suggested that viewing the Bible as revealing a redemptive drama is an enhancement over the idea of simply viewing it as a one-dimensional epic. Adding the dramatic emphasis causes us to see history under the light of the biblical story and reveals that God himself did not simply inspire a book but entered into a drama *in history*. The Bible, however, does not record the end of the drama, but rather forecasts how it will

---

151. Richard Hays has framed his ethical approach around this idea; Hays, *The Moral Vision of the New Testament*, esp. 212.

152. Ibid., 305 (emphasis added).

153. Jones, "The notion of reading and embodying Scripture in the community of faith means that we are participants in a company that includes all people who have sought to read and embody Scripture faithfully through the ages—for us as Christians, the church of Jesus Christ"; Jones, "Embodying Scripture in the Community of Faith," 147.

154. This is what D.A. Carson refers to as "worldview evangelism"; Carson, "Athens Revisited," esp. 386.

end.[155] In the meantime (post-biblical history), the drama is still unfolding as the church continues to perform its role of proclaiming and enacting the gospel before a watching world.[156]

In living out the gospel, the church joins the cast of characters from Abel and the cloud of witnesses in Hebrews 11, to the martyrs in Revelation, who all proclaimed the same redemptive message across the pages of history and various, dramatic scenes of redemption. The church today continues the drama of redemption in the context of preaching and living before a postmodern audience. Preaching with these thoughts in mind presses the claims of Christ not only upon the postmodern skeptic but also upon the church living in a postmodern context, sifting through its varying nuances. Arguably, no sermon is complete until God's part has been made clear (the accomplishment of the gospel), and the church has been told how to faithfully perform her script in the "theater of God's glory,"[157] and the unbelieving postmodern skeptic has been called to abandon her tattered script in order to take up the biblical script and follow Jesus.[158] Reflections on both the RH and DR paradigms should enhance homiletic commitment to these ideas. The common DNA of the two is not only notable, but can also be helpfully synthesized for homiletic purposes in a postmodern context.

A few cautions are in order as we conclude this chapter. The first is to reassert the difficulty of describing postmodernism as a singular coherent idea.[159] Additionally, in the eyes of some, we are no longer living in a postmodern age, but a *post*-postmodern age.[160] A number of suggestions have been made as to exactly what philosophical term would best express the intellectual climate that follows postmodernism, but none seem to have really stuck thus far. In other words, there is nothing even close to a consensus as to what age follows postmodernism, or whether or not we have

155. NWright, *The New Testament and the People of God*, 401.

156. Bartholomew and Goheen, "We who stand in historical continuity with the early church have also been taken up into its mission. Their story is also *ours*"; Bartholomew and Goheen, *The Drama of Scripture*, 172 (emphasis original). See also Nichols, *Welcome to the Story*, 132.

157. Calvin, *Inst.* 1.6.2.

158. Vanhoozer, *The Drama of Doctrine*, 115; De Ruijter, "Spreken met Gezag," 55.

159. Long notes that any definition of postmodern is itself technically "a *modern* definition of postmodernism, because postmodernists would say that postmodernism can't be defined"; Long, *Telling the Truth*, 325.

160. Jesse Lopez and Garry Potter argue for "critical realism" as the next movement to follow postmodernity, describing postmodernism consistently in the past tense, not so much because it *is* a thing of the past, but because the epistemological uncertainty of postmodernism, in their view, must lead to a more realistic epistemology—hence, their proposal of "critical realism"; Lopez and Potter, *After Postmodernism*, 4.

even truly exited postmodernism into the next intellectual climate. In each age of the church's history, she has had to rise up to meet certain challenges and the various rhetorical forms by which those challenges were expressed; from first-century polytheism to militant Islam, from the Enlightenment to atheism, from modernism to secular postmodernism. The pulpit does not speak into a vacuum, but into the historical context that shapes its pastoral address. While the gospel-cure remains the same from age to age, the complexities of sin, both moral and intellectual, continue to form a moving target, to which the pulpit must be ever-sensitive. Today it is postmodernism; tomorrow it will be . . .

Having affirmed the constantly changing environment in which the pulpit ministry is performed, we would also like to reiterate that the homiletic proposal in this chapter is aimed at addressing some of the genuine challenges of postmodernism in a meaningful way without demonizing it in every way. The faces of postmodernism are many and its expressions sophisticated, from stridently secular to selectively evangelical. Our focus has been largely on the former. Homiletic reflection needs to bear these varied nuances in mind as it seeks to know and address the nuances of its context. To the extent that postmodernism itself is a fairly elastic movement, so also should our rhetorical responses to it reflect some sort of pastorally discerning flexibility. In this light, we are suggesting that a sermon should bear in mind the way the same gospel reaches different people in different situations. On this point of improvisation, Stefan Paas notes, "In each new context the church must give a new answer, not primarily in regard to the changing social situation, but in regard to its universal calling to be a witness of the gospel."[161]

The homiletic imperative is to be always improvising yet never compromising. Thus, part of what we have found particularly helpful about the DR paradigm is the rhetorical way in which it calls the church to creatively embody the imperatives of the Great Commission. It is hoped that this might compel church members to see themselves as the "living application" of the sermon, embodying in specific ways what the sermon proclaims. While whole-heartedly affirming that the *ordinary* means by which God will work in the hearts of people to save them is through the preaching of his word from pulpits,[162] at the same time, we would not deny the way in which ordinary Christians, living out their lives in the context of their postmodern associations, will have creative opportunities to be salt and light before a watching, listening world.

161. Paas, "Missionair gemeente-zijn," 227 (trans. mine).
162. WSC 88.

Thus, not only should the sermon speak directly to the heart of post-modern issues (this is still the intellectual landscape of the day), but it should also equip Christians living in a postmodern age to figure out their part in embodying the redemptive drama of God in his *Missio Dei*. The church is thus enabled, through preaching, to embody "the drama of discipleship" as Vanhoozer puts it, effectively making the local church a "living Bible" which is formed by God's Spirit, directed by Scripture, and missionally focused.[163] Preaching, from this point of view, "Reminds disciples who they are, from where they have come, and why they are here."[164] We would add that this is not only what disciples of the church need to hear, but is also the vacuum created by secular postmodernism into which sermons must constantly proclaim the message of hope.

Lastly, we wish to underscore that in our view preaching is as much an *art* as it is a *science*. It tells the same "what" of the biblical story, while employing various rhetorical styles to communicate that message.[165] There is not a singular homiletic (rhetorical) method in the Bible. Rather, there is a singular message in the Bible (the gospel of God's dramatic redemption in Christ), and that message is preached by a diverse array of God's servants. That message is preached to God's people as well as those outside the covenant community (ecclesiastical preaching as well as evangelistic preaching) and is preached in a variety of ways.[166] The New Testament itself embodies a number of different homiletic styles and structures from the Sermon on the Mount, to Peter's preaching on the day of Pentecost, to the longest known sermon in the Bible—the book of Hebrews.[167] Each of these is obviously nuanced in its rhetorical structure and pastoral context, as we saw particularly in our treatment of Hebrews 11. We note that each of the New Testament's sermons was proclaimed in effectively the same age; yet stylistic nuances abound between them.

It is for these reasons that we have been careful not to attempt to present an *iron-clad* model for preaching in a postmodern age, but rather have suggested a model of preaching that creatively yet faithfully proclaims the biblical gospel as God has revealed it in his word, yet in ways that are

163. This is the theme of Kevin Vanhoozer's new book, *Faith Speaking Understanding*, 1.

164. Ibid., 131.

165. Brown, *Scripture as Communication*, 157.

166. We agree with Jeffrey Arthurs that, "there is no such thing as *the* sermon form"; Arthurs, *Preaching with Variety*, 16 (emphasis added).

167. On Acts, see Horton, *Covenant and Eschatology*, 268; on Hebrews, see Ellingworth, *The Epistle to the Hebrews*, 62.

sensitive to the issues created by our postmodern context.[168] We believe that nuances of the RH and DR paradigms will serve as helpful tools on the belts of preachers, enabling them to perform their homiletic task with greater ability in the particular contexts in which they find themselves. Thus, the *science* of homiletics is the exegesis of the text and of the people who hear sermons; the *art* of homiletics is crafting the sermon in the most rhetorically effective manner for the particular sake of those who hear it.[169] Proclaiming the redemptive-historical drama with a listening ear and a creative tongue may prove to be helpful and effective in the contemporary postmodern scene in which we find ourselves planting and pastoring churches. As Horton puts it, "Inasmuch as the redemptive-historical model works more like a drama . . . wherever the word is correctly preached and sacraments are correctly administered, there is no doubt a true church there."[170] Rhetoric and ritual are bound to one another in common service to the preached word. A common unity is found in the gospel that is preached; diversity is found in the rhetorical tools used to proclaim the redemptive-historical drama of redemption, along with the spirited role that each hearer of the sermon is called to perform in fitting response. Amid the changing scenes of postmodernism, one clear and climactic goal must be at the center of every sermon: all eyes on Jesus—the founder and perfecter of the drama of preaching.

---

168. Meyer, *Preaching*, 43.

169. Park, "Sacred Rhetoric of the Holy Spirit," 381.

170. Horton, *Covenant and Eschatology*, 243.

Summary and Overall Conclusion

What could be more full of meaning?—for the pulpit is ever this earth's foremost part; all the rest comes in its rear; the pulpit leads the world. From thence it is that the storm of God's quick wrath is first descried, and the bow must bear the earliest brunt. From thence it is the God of breezes fair or foul is first invoked for favorable winds. Yes, the world's a ship on its passage out, and not a voyage complete; and the pulpit is its prow.[1]

The pulpit leads the world. But how? Like a ship upon the sea, waves of doubt and darkness constantly beat against it and the way forward is not always easily discerned. The temptation to turn and be driven by the various winds of doctrine is ever-present. Yet Scripture calls those who preach to bear straight into the heart of the storm, mastering it, and trusting that from the pulpit, God will lead his people to the safe harbor which he alone can secure. Our proposal in this monograph has been that a homiletic model that synthesizes the common DNA of the RH and DR paradigms may have the unique ability to embody certain hermeneutical and homiletic commitments of Scripture, as well as be an effective rhetorical strategy for preaching in our postmodern context. We began by introducing the main ideas of the monograph, as well as offered a brief explanation of the purpose, necessity, and plan of the project.

Chapter 1 attempted to bridge the gap between the original discussion surrounding the RH preaching debates in the Netherlands and its contemporary expressions today, both inside and outside the Netherlands. It was noted that the older preaching debate focused largely on the question of preaching Christ from the Old Testament narratives, as well as the issue of proper homiletic application in preaching. In this context, the terms "redemptive-historical preaching" and "exemplaristic preaching" emerged.

---

1. Melville, *Moby Dick*, 39.

189

Both terms were and are easily subject to misunderstanding and misrepresentation. Regrettably, many caricatures and uncharitable portrayals of the debate abound, even within contemporary homiletic thought. Thus, the need for nuanced representation remains.

The RH view, at its best, sought to protect the idea that the Bible is foremost about God and his plan to accomplish redemption *in history,* and that to reduce sermons to moralistic, anthropocentric abstractions was not consistent with the purpose of special revelation, and effectively upstaged God from the drama of redemption. On the other side of the debate were those (labeled "exemplaristic" by RH advocates) who believed that Scripture required not only homiletic application, but often embodied this homiletic application in exemplaristic ways. Each side, in our view, was capable of making strong arguments with biblical support, and had pastoral motives behind them. Each side also had a general recognition of Christ as the tie that binds together all of Scripture. Regrettably, the two sides were unable to reach a mature, harmonious conclusion on issues of homiletic application— a state of affairs that remains to this day. This is likely due the fact that the original debate was not narrowly over homiletics, but occurred in the context of a World War, higher critical attacks on the historicity and authority of Scripture, and the fracturing of a denomination over issues of covenant theology, ecclesiology, and polity.

Numerous decades later, on several different continents, echoes of the debate are still heard. Recent interest in Dutch Reformed theologians such as Herman Bavinck, Geerhardus Vos, Herman Ridderbos, and Abraham Kuyper have helped to rekindle interest in the RH hermeneutic and homiletic, though driven by various concerns. The rise of postmodernity, in particular, has caused many to consider narrative approaches to history capable of defending historically confessional views of Scripture and morality, while being culturally relevant at the same time. All these ideas, in one way or another, have led to the revitalization, if not popularization of certain RH concerns.

In chapter 2 we introduced the *drama of redemption* (DR) paradigm, and juxtaposed it to the RH paradigm, noting overlapping concerns within each. Key among the two is the priority of God as the main speaker and actor in Scripture, as well as the idea that the Bible is bound together by a covenantal metanarrative that lends itself to a homiletically useful apologetic for the authority of Scripture, as well as a Christ-centered hermeneutic that harmonizes the message of the Old and New Testaments. At the same time, it was noted that the distinctions between the RH and DR models are just as important as their similarities. In particular, the DR paradigm, in our view, has been able to advance beyond the regrettable loggerheads at which the RH preaching debate remained entrenched—particularly as it relates to the important role of the hearer in preaching.

It is here that we find the DR paradigm remarkably helpful, as it *insists* that a faithful treatment of Scripture (i.e., preaching) include the way in which Scripture directs the hearer to understand how she is called to faithfully and fittingly respond to the ministry of the word. Numerous authors were employed to demonstrate the way in which the drama metaphor is a helpful way of thinking about Scripture, covenant, and homiletic application. The idea of *improvising the script* was also discussed as a provocative way of seeing scriptural drama as that which must be creatively performed in various scenes without departing from the script itself. Thus, the either/or dichotomy of Christ-centered versus application-driven preaching is overcome by the nuances of the DR paradigm, which both overlaps as well as surpasses, the RH preaching debate.

In chapters 3–4 we looked at Hebrews 11 as an exegetical case study of our proposal. In particular, the question we sought to explore was to what extent the overall narrative of Hebrews 11 reflects a redemptive drama in which each of the saints "by faith" reveals a facet of the person and work of Christ—the denouement of redemptive history. In other words, how do their individual scenes function as revelation within the drama of redemption that witness to the better things to come in Christ? Our conclusion was that God had shaped the lives of each of the saints in Hebrews 11 in such a way that they were not only looking to the fulfillment of the redemptive promises in the future, but that God was also displaying aspects of *how* those promises were to be later fulfilled in Christ. Thus, the "cloud of witnesses" of Hebrews 11 both *look to* and *reveal* the things to come in Christ by faith.

Their part in God's drama of redemption was not simply to embrace the promises of the covenant, but also to reveal them. Proof that this is the case is found in the ascription given to Jesus at the beginning of Hebrews 12, where he is referred to as the "founder and perfecter of faith." Jesus perfects, or eschatologizes, the revelation given through each of the saintly witnesses of Hebrews 11, as he is the one after whose image they are patterned. This is consistent with the *better word* hermeneutic of Hebrews 1:1–3, and seems to fit in with the overarching hermeneutic of the book of Hebrews, where nearly everything the author of the book touches on in the Old Testament is turned into a facet of God's revelation of the person and work of Christ. Related to this, we noted with interest that the author of Hebrews pastorally describes the suffering of the church, past and present, as a theater of martyrdom. Thus, the saints of Hebrews 11 performed their supportive roles as scripted by God; yet Jesus was the perfecter of their dramatic previews. This leads to considering how the church today continues to perform its role within the theater of

God's glory, and ways in which the sermon instructs the church in how to faithfully improvise the Scripture (application).

Chapters 5–6 sought to address this important question of homiletic application. While not wishing to abandon the traditional approach, we have suggested that it needs to be further developed, enriched, and enhanced. The traditional expository preaching paradigm has proven to be both useful and yet quite improvable. Several observations are worth summarizing. First, in our view, a rigid distinction between exposition and application is not consistently demonstrable from Scripture, nor is it, in our opinion, equally edifying. We agree with the many who have noted that the entire sermon is to be preached with an eye to application, and that application should always be anchored in faithful exposition. Secondly, we suggested that as the gospel is the tie that binds all of Scripture together, it must also be the glue that holds in place the entire sermon—especially the application of a sermon. The gospel implies Christian obedience, and to overly divorce the indicative from the imperative in preaching is to tear apart what God has joined together.

In this same chapter, we also proposed the idea of imitation as a potential improvement of the application idea. We favored the imitation paradigm as it seems to be built upon a clearer biblical vocabulary and is less fraught with some of the baggage of the modern critics who dismissed the history of Scripture in favor of subjective application, a trend that leads to a difficulty in distinguishing much contemporary evangelical preaching from its liberal counterparts. In other words, evangelical preaching that fails to anchor its application in *redemption* and *history* sounds dangerously similar to the anti-historical impulses of the modernism and postmodernism to which it often seeks to respond. Union with Christ, the foundation of our relationship with God, implies growing into the image of Christ as his adopted sons and daughters. Preaching is the primary means by which God instructs his church how to embody the drama of redemption into which we have been called. While creatively improvising our Christian obedience in the varying scenes of life is unavoidable, faithfulness to the script of Scripture is non-negotiable, and no sermon is complete until this homiletic requirement is fulfilled.

The final chapter of this monograph attempted to synthesize the fruit of the previous chapters with a particular eye to preaching in a postmodern context. We recognized the difficulty of defining postmodernism—a movement that self-consciously resists definition—yet at the same time, we believe that it remains possible to identify certain trends within the movement. Particular expressions of postmodernism have displayed a deep skepticism regarding the issues of history, authority, and morality, the effects of which have certainly been felt within the church. We surveyed the landscape of these developments in a way that, while admittedly brief, was hopefully still able to give a postmodern backdrop against which our homiletic proposal may be set. It is worth highlighting that our focus was primarily upon secular postmodernism, and not the various strains of Evangelical postmoderns and their mediating nuances.

Postmodernism is the inescapable context in which pastoral ministry currently happens. The church is both affected by it and responding to it, as it sets the stage for the church's carrying out of the Great Commission. Postmodernism is also not all bad; in fact, in many ways it has ironically created a narrative lens through which Bible believers and skeptics may read and discuss Scripture. It has highlighted the importance of the place of readers of texts, and by implication, hearers of sermons. Postmodernism has also offered devastating critiques of the failures of Enlightenment and modernism, and created a revival of interest in the biblical drama, at least in certain circles. Even more helpful is the way in which postmodernism has exposed the reality that there is no such thing as "presupposition-less" hermeneutics. Every theologian, preacher, congregant and critic reads the Bible through tinted lenses, and is informed by various presuppositions and social influences. The question is not "will there be presuppositions and social influences?" but *"which presuppositions will guide our interpretation?"* Are they biblical or secular, and why? Additionally, what role does the church play in aiding the understanding of Scripture, particularly through preaching? Our proposal, following Vanhoozer in particular, is that the homiletic method which places itself under the Scripture, rather than over it, will be the most faithful and profitable. This is so because only God himself is capable of transcending both the historical and ontological realities that the Enlightenment pursued, modernism proved unattainable, and postmodernism declared meaningless. No one can live a consistently postmodern, foundationless, and metanarrative-less life as everyone is a part of some drama. The question is: which drama? Thus the Bible continues to speak authoritatively, redemptively, and compassionately into a world that has lost its Way, denied the Truth, and declared meaningless its Life. The church thus remains the most fitting place to read and perform what Scripture teaches, and the means of grace (the preaching of the word, the sacraments, and prayer) remain at the center of the church, especially in an ever-changing world.

The pulpit continues to lead the world. Whether it does so well and faithfully is of vital importance now, just as it always has been. In this world, there will be controversy and confusion, and those who preach must constantly study the biblical script (Scripture)—for it alone is the sure chart across the turbulent sea. Careful study of the script and the world in which we live is a necessity, just as the old captain must know the boat and the seas upon which it sails. He who first spoke the theater of his glory into existence continues to speak and act within it—by the Word of his power. By that same powerful word, preached week after week, God continues to redeem a people for himself and conform them to his image. For this reason we happily join the chorus of those who sing, "How beautiful are the feet of those who bring the good news!" (Rom 10:15). The Triune God has entered history and fulfilled the drama of redemption in its principal actor—Jesus. All of history is thus moving toward the climactic scene for which it was created. The church's performance in history is not yet complete. She faithfully follows Jesus as she takes up her cross and walks wisely in this world according to her God-given Script. To declare such things is the privilege and responsibility of the pulpit. It is the drama of preaching.

Lo, what a cloud of witnesses
Encompass us around!
Men once like us with sufferings tried,
But now with glory crowned.

They reached the finish of the course
And thus obtained the rest.
We too—for God fulfills his word—
Shall be with victory blest.

Let us then full of confidence
run to complete the race
and put off sin and every weight
which could slow down our pace.

We look to Jesus even more
Than to all those around;
in him, the Author of our faith,
its Finisher is found.

He for the joy before him set—
unselfish in his love—
endure the cross, despised the shame,
and now he reigns above.

Let us, forgetting things behind,
Press on to God's right hand;
there, with the Savior and his saints,
triumphantly to stand.

"Lo, What a Cloud of Witnesses"
Hymn 43, *Book of Praise: Anglo-Genevan Psalter*

Appendix
Samenvatting (Dutch Summary)

DE CENTRALE STELLING IN deze dissertatie is dat een homiletisch model dat het gedeelde DNA van de heilshistorische methode in de prediking combineert met dat van de drama of redemption-methode zou kunnen dienen als een effectief model voor de prediking in een postmoderne context. Vanouds heeft de discussie over heilshistorisch preken zich gericht op een christocentrische hermeneutiek en toepassing. Onderdelen van het postmoderne denken hebben de interesse in aspecten van heilshistorische prediking doen herleven, terwijl de kritiek tegelijkertijd blijft voortgaan. Deze belangrijke thema's worden behandeld door Hebreeën 11 hermeneutisch en homiletisch te onderzoeken, met gebruikmaking van de drama of redemption-methode als veelbelovend middel om de discussie een stap verder te brengen. Omdat preken zowel een kunde (hermeneutiek) als een kunst (retoriek) is, hopen we dat een synthese van deze ideeën de kerk kan dienen: de kansel bevindt zich nu eenmaal in het spanningsveld dat wordt gecreëerd door de voordelen en uitdagingen van het postmodernisme.

We beginnen met een introductie van de belangrijkste thema's van dit onderzoek. Bovendien biedt het een korte uitleg van het doel, de noodzaak en het ontwerp van deze studie. Het introductie sluit af met een korte uiteenzetting van de vooronderstellingen van de auteur en zijn theologische uitgangspunt.

Hoofdstuk één tracht de kloof tussen de aanvankelijke discussies over heilshistorische prediking in Nederland en de hedendaagse verschijningsvormen van die discussies binnen en buiten Nederland te dichten. Geconstateerd wordt dat het vroegere debat over de prediking zich vooral richtte op de vraag naar het verkondigen van Christus vanuit de verhalen in het Oude Testament en op het thema van passende homiletische toepassingen in de prediking. In deze context ontstonden de termen 'heilshistorische prediking' en 'exemplarische prediking'. Deze termen werden en worden makkelijk misverstaan of verkeerd geïnterpreteerd. Helaas bestaan er van beide kanten van het debat veel karikaturen. Een genuanceerdere weergave blijft dus nodig.

De heilshistorische prediking probeerde het idee dat de Bijbel in de eerste plaats gaat over God en zijn plan om verlossing te brengen in de geschiedenis te beschermen. Het reduceren van preken tot moralistische, antropocentrische abstracties was volgens deze benadering dus niet consistent met het doel van de bijzondere openbaring. Sterker nog: hierdoor zou God verdwijnen uit het verlossingsverhaal. Aan de andere kant van het debat bevonden zich theologen (door de heilshistorici bestempeld als 'exemplarici') die geloofden dat de Schrift niet alleen homiletische toepassing nodig heeft, maar deze vaak zelf al in zich draagt in morele en exemplarische zin. Men kan stellen dat beide kampen sterke argumenten hadden en zich op Bijbelse gronden en pastorale motieven beriepen. Spijtig genoeg is men echter nooit tot een harmonieuze conclusie gekomen. Dit heeft waarschijnlijk te maken met het feit dat de discussie niet alleen over homiletiek ging, maar zich afspeelde in de context van de Tweede Wereldoorlog, kritische aanvallen op de historiciteit en autoriteit van de Schrift en een kerkscheuring rondom de thema's verbond, ecclesiologie en kerkbestuur.

Een aantal decennia later en op meerdere continenten klinken de echo's van dit debat nog altijd door. De recente interesse in Nederlandse theologen zoals Herman Bavinck, Geerhardus Vos, Herman Ridderbos en Abraham Kuyper binnen de Noord-Amerikaanse theologische discussies heeft bijgedragen aan een hernieuwde belangstelling voor heilshistorische prediking. Bovendien heeft de opkomst van het postmodernisme velen ertoe aangezet narratieve benaderingen van hermeneutiek en prediking te overwegen als een begaanbare homiletische weg. Al deze aspecten hebben op de één of andere manier bijgedragen aan een hernieuwde interesse in bepaalde onderdelen van heilshistorische prediking.

Hoofdstuk twee biedt een uitvoeriger introductie van de drama of redemption-methode en zet deze naast de heilshistorische methode met het oog op overlap tussen deze beide methodes. Een van de belangrijkste punten van overeenstemming is het idee van de prioriteit van God als belangrijkste spreker en actor in de Schrift, naast het idee dat de Bijbel een geheel vormt als verbondsnarratief. Deze nadruk past goed in een gereformeerde verdediging van de autoriteit van de Schrift en een christocentrische hermeneutiek die de boodschap van het Oude en Nieuwe Testament met elkaar in harmonie brengt. Tegelijkertijd worden ook verschillen opgemerkt tussen de heilshistorische methode en de drama of redemption-methode, die wel eens net zo belangrijk zouden kunnen zijn als de overeenkomsten. De drama of redemption-methode gaat verder waar de heilshistorische prediking spijtig genoeg tegen blokkades aanloopt – met name op de punten van toepassing en de rol van de hoorder in de prediking.

Juist op deze punten is de drama of redemption-methode opmerkelijk helpend, waar ze als voorwaarde stelt dat een betrouwbare behandeling van de Schrift (d.i. de prediking) het noodzakelijk maakt de Schrift te lezen met de vraag: hoe verstaat de hoorder door de Schrift zijn roeping het script van de Schrift uit te voeren? Diverse auteurs worden aangehaald om te laten zien op wat voor manier de drama-metafoor behulpzaam kan zijn om over Schrift, verbond en homiletische toepassing door te denken. Het idee van het improviseren van het script wordt hier ook besproken als een uitdagende manier om de eigen rol binnen het drama trouw, maar ook creatief uit te voeren; iets waartoe hoorders van preken door gedegen hermeneutiek worden opgeroepen. Zodoende kan het dilemma tussen christocentrische en toepasselijke prediking mogelijk worden opgeheven door de synthese die deze dissertatie voorstelt.

Hoofdstuk drie en hoofdstuk vier vormen twee zijden van één medaille. Beide hoofdstukken richten zich op Hebreeën 11 als case study rondom de centrale stelling in deze dissertatie. Hoewel in geen van beide hoofdstukken een diepgravend commentaar wordt gegeven op Hebreeën 11, behandelt hoofdstuk drie enkele exegetische nuances die bij uitstek te maken hebben met christocentrisch preken. In lijn met een heilshistorische hermeneutiek wordt gesteld dat de narratieve hoofdlijn van Hebreeën 11 facetten van het komende werk van Christus laat zien in de volheid van de heilsgeschiedenis. Verder wordt gesteld dat elke 'door het geloof'-uitspraak in Hebreeën 11 fungeert als openbaring van "het betere" (11:40) dat in Christus zou komen, die de "voorman en voltooier" (12:2) is van het geloof. De verlossingsbeloften van God werden niet alleen geopenbaard aan de heiligen uit het Oude Testament, maar ook door hen. Als ontvangers en getuigen leveren de heiligen van Hebreeën 11 "de grondslag en het bewijs" (11:1) van de komende werkelijkheid in Christus.

Aangetoond wordt, dat dit voorstel consistent is met de openingsthese uit Hebreeën 1:1-3 en de overkoepelende hermeneutiek van het boek Hebreeën, waarin alles wat de auteur van het boek uit het Oude Testament benoemt, wordt neergezet als een facet van Gods openbaring van de persoon en het werk van Christus. Het is interessant op te merken dat de auteur van Hebreeën op een pastorale manier schrijft over het lijden van de kerk als een vorm van publiek martelaarschap (10:33). Impliciet hebben de heiligen van Hebreeën 11 hun ondersteunende rol gespeeld naar het script van God;

maar Jezus was de voltooier van alles wat zij ontvingen en zelf weer open-
baarden "door geloof".

Hoofdstuk vier houdt zich bezig met de vraag hoe de kerk vandaag
doorgaat met het spelen van haar rol in het theater van Gods glorie en hoe
de preek de kerk instrueert trouw te 'improviseren' in lijn met de Schrift
(= toepassing). Voorgesteld wordt dit concept verder uit te werken, te ver-
rijken en nuanceren, zonder de traditionele benadering van homiletische
applicatie te verwerpen. De expository-preaching-methode heeft bewezen
bruikbaar te zijn, maar is ook voor verbetering vatbaar. Een aantal observa-
ties zijn het waard samen te vatten. Ten eerste wordt voorgesteld dat een
rigide onderscheid tussen 'expositie' en 'applicatie' niet vanuit de Schrift kan
worden aangetoond en evenmin effectief is in een postmoderne context.
Terecht hebben velen opgemerkt dat de hele preek op een bepaalde manier
'applicatie' is en dat die applicatie altijd verankerd moet zijn in 'expositie'.
Daarnaast wordt in deze dissertatie gesteld dat zoals het evangelie de band
is die de hele Schrift samenbindt, het ook de lijm moet zijn die het geheel
van de preek op zijn plek houdt. Het evangelie impliceert christelijke gehoo-
rzaamheid en door op een overdreven manier de indicatief en imperatief in
de prediking van elkaar te scheiden loop je het risico uit elkaar te trekken
wat God met elkaar verbonden heeft.

Voortbouwend op en verdergaand in de exegese zoals die gevon-
den is in hoofdstuk drie wordt het idee van 'imiteren' van de heiligen in
Hebreeën 11 voorgesteld als een middel om met de vraag naar de homiletische toepassing om te gaan. De gedachte van imitatie verdient daarbij
de voorkeur aangezien ze lijkt opgebouwd uit een duidelijker Bijbels vo-
cabulair en minder doortrokken is van de bagage van de moderne hermeneutiek (inclusief liberale hermeneutiek) en de verminderde aandacht voor
Bijbelse geschiedenis ten faveure van een subjectieve toepassing, een trend
die ertoe leidt dat het vaak moeilijk is hedendaagse evangelicale prediking
te onderscheiden van haar liberale tegenhanger. Eenheid met Christus is
het fundament van de relatie tussen een christen en God en deze eenheid
impliceert groeien naar het beeld van Christus, als zijn geadopteerde zonen
en dochters. Preken gaat de gemeente voor in een creatieve, maar getrouwe
manier om de Schrift te improviseren en geen preek is compleet zonder dat
deze homiletiek sine qua non is uitgevoerd.

Hoofdstuk vijf probeert een synthese te bieden van wat de voor-
gaande hoofdstukken hebben opgeleverd, met het oog op preken in een
postmoderne context. Een bevredigende definitie van postmodernisme is
niet te geven, aangezien het om een beweging gaat die zich bewust tegen
definiëring verzet. Tegelijkertijd is het wel mogelijk om bepaalde trends
in de beweging te identificeren. Bepaalde postmoderne uitingen laten een

diepe scepsis zien ten aanzien van historie, autoriteit en moraliteit. De gevolgen van deze scepsis zijn zeker voelbaar binnen de kerk. Deze ontwikkeling wordt kort geschetst teneinde een achtergrond te creëren waartegen het homiletische voorstel van deze dissertatie kan worden gepresenteerd. De primaire focus van dit hoofdstuk ligt op de invloed van seculier, sceptisch postmodernisme, en niet op de verschillende vormen van 'evangelicaal postmodernisme' in al zijn nuances.

Postmodernisme is de context waarin pastorale bedieningen tegenwoordig plaatvinden. Daar valt niet aan te ontkomen. De kerk wordt beïnvloed door postmodernisme en formuleert er antwoorden op, aangezien het de achtergrond van eigentijds preken vormt. De invloeden van het postmodernisme zijn niet alleen maar negatief: verschillende positieve bijdragen worden opgesomd. Postmodern denken, zo wordt betoogd, heeft vernietigende kritiek geleverd op het falen van Verlichting en modernisme en een hernieuwde aandacht voor het Bijbelse narratief teweeggebracht, in elk geval in bepaalde kringen. Nog behulpzamer dan dat is de manier waarop het postmodernisme de realiteit heeft ontdekt dat er niet zoiets bestaat als hermeneutiek zonder vooronderstelling. Het voorstel van dit hoofdstuk is, in lijn met Kevin Vanhoozer, dat een homiletische methode die zichzelf onder de Schrift stelt in plaats van erboven, de meest getrouwe en vruchtbare methode zal zijn. Alleen God zelf kan uitstijgen boven de historische en epistemologische werkelijkheid die de Verlichting najoeg, waarvan het modernisme aantoonde dat zij onbereikbaar was en die het postmodernisme voor betekenisloos verklaarde. Maar niemand kan een consistent postmodern leven leiden, zonder fundament en zonder meta-narratief, aangezien iedereen onderdeel is van een bepaald verhaal. De Bijbel blijft spreken met autoriteit, verlossing en compassie in een wereld die de Weg kwijt is, de Waarheid heeft ontkend en haar Leven als betekenisloos heeft bestempeld. De kerk blijft daarom de beste plek om, geleid door het ambt van de verkondiging, de Schrift te onderwijzen en in te oefenen.

Hoofdstuk zes biedt een samenvatting en conclusie. Ondanks de uitdagingen van het preken in een postmoderne context, blijft de prediking richting geven door het aloude verhaal van het evangelie te vertellen op creatieve, maar getrouwe manieren. Zo participeert de prediking in het verhaal van de verlossing door te verkondigen wie God is en wat Hij verwacht van zijn volk. Predikers in een postmoderne context moeten met aandacht het Bijbelse script (de Schrift) bestuderen – alleen dát biedt een betrouwbare kaart op de onstuimige zee. Tegelijkertijd moeten zulke predikers met aandacht de wereld waarin wij leven bestuderen, zoals een kapitein zowel zijn boot als de zee waarop hij vaart goed moet kennen. Hij die eerst het theater van zijn glorie in aanzijn riep, blijft daarin spreken en handelen – in het bijzonder door de prediking van zijn Woord. Door dat krachtige Woord, week na week gepredikt, blijft Hij een volk verlossen voor zichzelf en vormt Hij hen naar zijn navolgbare beeld. God is de geschiedenis binnengekomen en heeft het verhaal van verlossing vervuld in de persoon van de hoofdrolspeler: Jezus, die ook de voltooier is van zijn kerk. Van zulke dingen te getuigen is het voorrecht en de verantwoordelijkheid van de kansel. Het is het verhaal van de prediking: the drama of preaching.

Bibliography

Adams, Jay. *Truth Apparent: Essays on Biblical Preaching*. Phillipsburg: P&R, 1982.

————. *Truth Applied: Application in Preaching*. Grand Rapids: Zondervan, 1990.

Agan III, Clarence "Jimmy" DeWitt. "Toward a Hermeneutic of Imitation: The Imitation of Christ in the *Didascalia Apostolorum*." *Presbyterion* 37 (2011) 31–48.

Altena, Bert. "Wolken gaan voorbij: Een homiletisch onderzoek naar mogelijkheden voor de preek in een postmodern klimaat." PhD diss., Zoetermeer: Boekencentrum, 2003.

Anderson, Charles. "The Challenge and Opportunity of Preaching Hebrews." In *Preaching the New Testament*, edited by Ian Paul and David Wenham, 126–41. Downers Grove: InterVarsity, 2013.

Appignanesi, Richard, and Chris Garratt. *Introducing Postmodernism*. New York: Totem, 1998.

Arthurs, Jeffrey D. "John 3:16 in the Key of C: Why True Preachers Are Worship Leaders." In *The Art and Craft of Biblical Preaching: A Comprehensive Resource for Today's Communicators*, edited by Haddon Robinson and Craig Larson, 41–44. Grand Rapids: Zondervan, 2005.

————. "Preaching from the Old Testament Narratives." In *Preaching the Old Testament*, edited by Scott Gibson, 73–86. Grand Rapids: Baker, 2006.

————. *Preaching with Variety: How to Re-create the Dynamics of Biblical Genres*. Grand Rapids: Kregel, 2007.

Attridge, Harold. *The Epistle to the Hebrews: A Commentary on the Epistle to the Hebrews*. Philadelphia: Fortress, 1989.

Augustine. "Confessions." In *Nicene and Post-Nicene Fathers, Vol. 1*, edited by Phillip Schaff. Peabody: Hendrickson, 1999.

Azurdia, Arturo G. *Spirit-Empowered Preaching: The Vitality of the Holy Spirit in Preaching*. Geanies House: Christian Focus Publications, 2003.

Baars, Arie. "Heilshistorische prediking in deze tijd (1) & (2)." *Nader Bekeken* 18 (2011) 10–15.

Bailey, Kenneth. *The Cross and the Prodigal: Luke 15 Through the Eyes of Middle Eastern Peasants*. Downers Grove: InterVarsity, 2005.

Barcellos, Richard. *The Family Tree of Reformed Biblical Theology. Geerhardus Vos and John Owen: Their Method of and Contribution to the Articulation of Redemptive History*. Pelham: Reformed Baptist Academic Press, 2010.

Barr, James. *The Concept of Biblical Theology*. Minneapolis: Fortress, 1999.

Barth, Karl. *Church Dogmatics IV: The Doctrine of Reconciliation, Part 1*, edited by G.W. Bromiley and T.F. Torrance. Peabody: Hendrickson, 2010.

Barthes, Roland. "The Death of the Author." In *The Norton Anthology of Theory and Criticism*, edited by Vincent Leitch, 1466–70. New York: W.W. Norton & Company, 2010.

Bartholomew, Craig G., and Michael W. Goheen. *The Drama of Scripture: Finding Our Place in the Biblical Story*. Grand Rapids: Baker Academic, 2004.

Bartow, Charles L. *God's Human Speech: A Practical Theology of Proclamation*. Grand Rapids: Eerdmans, 1997.

Bateman IV, Herbert. "Dispensationalism Tomorrow." In *Three Central Issues in Contemporary Dispensationalism: A Comparison of Traditional and Contemporary Views*, edited by Herbert Bateman IV, 307–18. Grand Rapids: Kregel, 1999.

Bauckham, Richard. *Jesus and the God of Israel: God Crucified and Other Studies on the New Testament's Christology of Divine Identity*. Grand Rapids: Eerdmans, 2008.

Baudrillard, Jean. *Simulacra and Simulation*. Translated by Shelia Glaser. 1981. Ann Arbor: University of Michigan Press, 1994.

Baugh, S.M. "The Cloud of Witnesses in Hebrews 11." *WTJ* 68 (2006) 113–32.

Bavinck, Herman. *Gereformeerde dogmatiek, Deel 1*. Kampen: Kok, 1928.

———. *The Philosophy of Revelation: The Stone Lectures for 1908-1909*. Grand Rapids: Eerdmans, 1953.

———. *Reformed Dogmatics Vol. 1*, edited by John Bolt. Translated by John Vriend. Grand Rapids: Baker, 2003.

Baxter, Richard. *The Reformed Pastor*. Carlisle: The Banner of Truth Trust, 1997.

Bayly, Timothy. "Covenant Succession and the Emasculation of the Church." In *To You and Your Children: Examining the Biblical Doctrine of Covenant Succession*, edited by Benjamin K. Wikner, 135–56. Moscow: Canon Press, 2005.

Beach, Lee. "The Local Church: Postmodern Possibilities." In *The Church, Then and Now*, edited by Stanley E. Porter and Cynthia Westfall, 134–50. Eugene: Wipf and Stock, 2012.

Beale, G. K. *A New Testament Biblical Theology: The Unfolding of the Old Testament in the New*. Grand Rapids: Baker Academic, 2011.

———. *The Temple and the Church's Mission: A Biblical Theology of the Dwelling Place of God*. Downers Grove: InterVarsity, 2004.

Beeke, Joel R. "Introduction." In *The Decades of Henry Bullinger, Vol. 1*, edited by Thomas Harding. Grand Rapids: Reformation Heritage Books, 2004.

———. *Puritan Reformed Spirituality*. Grand Rapids: Reformation Heritage Books, 2004.

Beeke, Joel R., and Mark Jones. *A Puritan Theology: Doctrine for Life*. Grand Rapids: Reformation Heritage Books, 2012.

Beeke, Joel R., and Randall J. Pederson. *Meet the Puritans: With a Guide to Modern Reprints*. Grand Rapids: Reformation Heritage Books, 2006.

Berkouwer, G.C. "Verval der Exegese." *Gereformeerd Weekblad* 2 (1947) 271–9.

———. "Bijbel en Relativisme." *Gereformeerd Weekblad* 3 (1948) 243–52.

Biezeveld, K.E. *Wie God zegt: Spreken over God in een wereld zonder God*. Kampen: Kok, 2001.

Blaising, Craig. "Dispensationalism: The Search for Definition." In *Dispensationalism, Israel and the Church: The Search for Definition*, edited by Craig Blaising and Darrell Bock, 13–34. Grand Rapids: Zondervan, 1992.

Blamires, Harry. *The Post-Christian Mind*. Vancouver: Regent College Press, 2001.

Bloedhorn, Hanswolf. "Theatre." In *Brill's New Pauly: Encyclopaedia of the Ancient World Vol.14*, edited by Hubert Cancik and Helmuth Schneider. Leiden: Brill, 2010.

Boersma, Hans. "On Baking Pumpkin Pie: Kevin Vanhoozer and Yves Congar on Tradition." *CTJ* 42 (2007) 237–55.

Bonhoeffer, Dietrich. *Letters and Papers from Prison*, edited by Eberhard Bethge. Translated by Reginald Fuller. New York: Macmillan, 1967.

Book of Praise: Anglo-Genevan Psalter. Winnipeg: Premier, 2014.

Bos, C.G. "Gods getuigenis over Abels offer." In *Waarheid & Recht* 35 (1963) 3–14.

Bos, Rein. *Identificatie-mogelijkheden in preken uit het Oude Testament*. Kampen: Kok, 1992.

———. *We Have Heard that God is with You: Preaching the Old Testament*. Grand Rapids: Eerdmans, 2008.

Braaten, Carl E., and Robert W. Jenson, eds. *A Map of Twentieth-Century Theology: Readings from Karl Barth to Radical Pluralism*. Minneapolis: Augsburg Fortress, 1995.

Bray, Gerald. "Biblical Theology and From Where it Came." *SwJT* 55 (2013) 194–208.

Briscoe, Stuart. "Hooting Owls on Tombstones." In *A Passion for Preaching: Reflections on the Art of Preaching. Essays in Honor of Stephen F. Olford*, edited by David Olford, 68–78. Nashville: Thomas Nelson, 1989.

Broadus, John. *On the Preparation and Delivery of Sermons*, edited by J.B. Weatherspoon. New York: Harper and Row, 1944.

Brown, Jeannine. *Scripture as Communication: Introducing Biblical Hermeneutics*. Grand Rapids: Baker, 2007.

Brown, John. *Hebrews*. Carlisle: Banner of Truth Trust, 1994.

Bruce, F.F. *The Epistle to the Hebrews*. Grand Rapids: Eerdmans, 1990.

Brueggemann, Walter. *Genesis*. Louisville: John Knox, 1982.

Bullmore, Mike. "The Gospel and Scripture: How to Read the Bible." In *The Gospel as Center: Renewing Our Faith and Reforming Our Ministry Practices*, edited by D.A. Carson and Timothy Keller, 41–54. Wheaton: Crossway, 2012.

Bultmann, Rudolf. *Kerygma and Myth: A Theological Debate*, edited by Hans Bartsch. New York: Harper and Row, 1961.

Burger, Hans. *Being in Christ: A Biblical and Systematic Investigation in a Reformed Perspective*. Eugene: Wipf and Stock, 2009.

Calvin, John. *Institutes of the Christian Religion*, edited by John McNeill. Philadelphia: Westminster Press, 1960.

———. *Letters of John Calvin: Selected from the Bonnet Edition with an Introductory Biographical Sketch*. Carlisle: Banner of Truth Trust, 1980.

———. *Commentary on the Book of Psalms*. Translated by James Anderson. Grand Rapids: Baker, 1996.

———. *Commentary on the Epistles of Paul the Apostle to the Corinthians*. Translated by John Pringle. Grand Rapids: Baker, 1996.

———. *Commentary on the Gospel according to John*. Translated by John Pringle. Grand Rapids: Baker, 1981.

Capill, Murray. *The Heart is the Target: Preaching Practical Application from Every Text* Phillipsburg: P&R, 2014.

Carlson, Marvin. "Drama Theory." In *The Johns Hopkins Guide to Literary Theory & Criticism*, edited by Michael Groden, et al., 267–71. 2nd ed. Baltimore: Johns Hopkins University Press, 2005.

Carrick, John. *The Imperative of Preaching*. Carlisle: The Banner of Truth Trust, 2002.

———. *The Preaching of Jonathan Edwards*. Carlisle: The Banner of Truth Trust, 2008.

Carson, D.A. "Athens Revisited." In *Telling the Truth: Evangelizing Postmoderns*, edited by D.A. Carson, 384–98. Grand Rapids: Zondervan, 2000.

———. *Collected Writings on Scripture*. Wheaton: Crossway, 2010.

———. *The Gagging of God: Christianity Confronts Pluralism*. Grand Rapids: Zondervan, 2011.

Carson, D.A. and Timothy Keller, eds. *The Gospel as Center: Renewing Our Faith and Reforming Our Ministry Practices*. Wheaton: Crossway, 2012.

Cary, Phillip. *Jonah*. Grand Rapids: Brazos, 2008.

Chapell, Bryan. *Christ-Centered Preaching: Redeeming the Expository Sermon*. Grand Rapids: Baker Academic, 2005.

———. "The Necessity of Preaching Christ in a World Hostile to Him." In *Preaching to a Shifting Culture: 12 Perspectives on Communicating that Connects*, edited by Scott Gibson, 59–78. Grand Rapids: Baker, 2004.

Childers, Jana. "A Critical Analysis of the Homiletic Theory and Practice of Browne Barr: First Congregational Church, Berkeley 1960-1977." PhD diss., The Graduate Theological Union, Berkeley, CA, 1992.

Childs, Brevard. "Current Models for Biblical Theology." In *Biblical Theology of the Old and New Testaments: Theological Reflection on the Christian Bible*. Minneapolis: Fortress, 1992.

Clark, R. Scott. *Caspar Olevian and the Substance of the Covenant: The Double Benefit of Christ*. Edinburgh: Rutherford House, 2005.

Clowney, Edmund P. "The Singing Savior." *Moody Monthly* (1974) 40–42.

———. "Preaching Christ from All the Scriptures." In *The Preacher and Preaching*, edited by Samuel T. Logan, Jr., 163–91. Phillipsburg: P&R, 1986.

———. *Preaching and Biblical Theology*. Phillipsburg: P&R, 2002.

Cockerill, Gareth. *The Epistle to the Hebrews*. Grand Rapids: Eerdmans, 2012.

Corbett, Edward. *Classical Rhetoric for the Modern Student*. Oxford: Oxford University Press, 1990.

Croy, N. Clayton. *Endurance in Suffering: Hebrews 12:1-13 in its Rhetorical, Religious, and Philosophical Context*. Cambridge: Cambridge University Press, 1998.

Dabney, R. L. *Evangelical Eloquence: A Course of Lectures on Preaching*. Carlisle: The Banner of Truth Trust, 1999.

Dargan, Edwin. *A History of Preaching, Vol. 1*. Grand Rapids: Baker, 1974.

De Boer, E.A. "Tertullian on Barnabas' Letter to the Hebrews in *De Pudicitia* 20.1-5." *VC* 68 (2014) 243–63.

De Bruijne, Ad. "Christelijke ethiek tussen wet, schepping en gemeenschap: Een positionering naar aanleiding van Romeinen 12, 1 en 2." http://forumc.digibron.nl/artikel?uid=00000000013099139c915a312b2dc35a3&docid=267.

De Graaf, S. G. *Verbondsgeschiedenis: Schetsen voor de vertelling van de bijbelsche geschiedenis*. Kampen: Kok, 1935.

Dekker, W. "Het evangelie: Eigentijds en van alle tijden." In *Bruggen slaan: Communicatie van het evangelie in een postmoderne tijd*, edited by J. Hoogland. Barneveld: De Vuurbaak, 1999.

De Koster, Lester. *Light for the City: Calvin's Preaching, Source of Life and Liberty*. Grand Rapids: Eerdmans, 2004.

De Leede, Bert, and Ciska Stark. "Protestantse preken in hun kracht en zwakheid: Een quickscan." *Nederlands Theologisch Tijdschrift* 67 (2013) 85–100.

Dennison, Charles G. "Preaching and Application." In *Kerux* 4 (1989) 44–52.

————. "Some Thoughts on Preaching." In *Kerux* 11 (1996) 3–9.

————. "Geerhardus Vos and the Orthodox Presbyterian Church." In *History for a Pilgrim People: The Historical Writings of Charles G. Dennison*, edited by Danny E. Olinger and David K. Thompson, 67–87. Willow Grove: The Committee for the Historian of the Orthodox Presbyterian Church, 2002.

Dennison, James T. Jr. "The Bible and the Second Coming." In *The Book of Books: Essays on the Scriptures in Honor of Johannes G. Vos*, edited by John H. White, 55–65. Phillipsburg: P&R, 1978.

————. "Geerhardus Vos." In *Bible Interpreters of the Twentieth Century*, edited by Walter A. Elwell and J.D. Weaver, 82–92. Grand Rapids: Baker, 1999.

————. *The Letters of Geerhardus Vos*. Phillipsburg: P&R, 2005.

————. "Irenaeus and Redemptive History." In *Ordained Servant: A Journal for Church Officers* 17 (2008) 67–72.

Dennison, William D. *Paul's Two-Age Construction and Apologetic*. Eugene: Wipf and Stock, 1985.

Derrida, Jacques. "Faith and Knowledge." In *Religion: Cultural Memory in the Present*. Stanford: Stanford University Press, 1996.

De Ruijter, C.J. "Gods verbondswoord gaat van hart tot hart." In *Vrijmaking-wederkeer: Vijftig jaar Vrijmaking in beeld gebracht*, edited by D. Deddens and M. te Velde. Barneveld: De Vuurbaak, 1994.

————. "Herkenning en heilshistorie." *De Reformatie* 3 (1994) 41–44.

————. *Preken en horen*. Kampen: Kok, 1998.

————. "Ik geloof." *Waarheid & Recht* 55 (1999) 16–27.

————. "Spreken met gezag." In *Bruggen slaan: Communicatie van het evangelie in een postmoderne tijd*, edited by J. Hoogland, 49–57. Barneveld: De Vuurbaak, 1999.

————. *Meewerken met God: Ontwerp van een gereformeerde praktische theologie*. Kampen: Kok, 2005.

————. *Horen naar de stem van God: Theologie en methode van de preek*. Zoetermeer: Boekencentrum, 2013.

Dijk, K. *De dienst der prediking*. Kampen: Kok, 1955.

Dingemans, G.D. *Als hoorder onder de hoorders: Een hermeneutische homiletiek*. Kampen: Kok, 1991.

Doriani, Daniel, *Putting the Truth to Work: The Theory and Practice of Biblical Application*. Phillipsburg: P&R, 2001.

Douma. J. "Kerk zijn?" In *Het vuur blijft branden: Geschiedenis van de Gereformeerde Kerken (vrijgemaakt) in Nederland, 1944–1979*, edited by P Jongeling, et al., 136–62. Kampen: Kok, 1979.

————. *Hoe gaan wij verder? Ontwikkelingen in de Gereformeerde Kerken (vrijgemaakt)*. Kampen: Kok, 2001.

Douma, Jos. *Veni Creator Spiritus: De meditatie en het preekproces*. Kampen: Kok, 2000.

Dugdale, Eric. *Greek Theatre in Context*. Cambridge: Cambridge University Press, 2008.

Duguid, Iain M. "Introduction." In *Living in the Gap Between Promise and Reality: The Gospel According to Abraham*. Phillipsburg: P&R, 1999.

Edersheim, Alfred. *Life and Times of Jesus the Messiah*. Peabody: Hendrickson, 1995.

Eglinton, James. "Schilder als exportproduct." In *Wie is die man? Klaas Schilder in de eenentwintigste eeuw*, edited by M. van Rijswijk et al., 187–96. Barneveld: De Vuurbaak, 2012.

———. *Trinity and Organism: Towards a New Reading of Herman Bavinck's Organic Motif*. London: T&T Clark, 2012.

Ehrman, Bart, *A Brief Introduction to the New Testament*. New York: Oxford University Press, 2009.

Eisenbaum, Pamela. "The Jewish Heroes of Christian History: Hebrews 11 in Literary Context." PhD diss., Union Theological Seminary. Atlanta: Scholars, 1997.

Ellingworth, Paul. *The Epistle to the Hebrews*. Grand Rapids: Eerdmans, 1993.

Ellingworth, Paul, and Eugene A. Nida. *A Translator's Handbook on the Letter to the Hebrews*. London: United Bible Societies, 1983.

Eswine, Zack. *Preaching to a Post-Everything World: Crafting Biblical Sermons that Connect with Our Culture*. Grand Rapids: Baker, 2008.

Faber, Jelle. "Klaas Schilder's Life and Work." In *Always Obedient: Essays on the Teachings of Dr. Klaas Schilder*, edited by J. Geertsema, 1–17. Phillipsburg: P&R, 1995.

———. *American Secession Theologians on Covenant and Baptism*. Neerlandia: Inheritance Publications, 1996.

Fairbairn, Patrick. *Typology of Scripture: Two Volumes in One*. Grand Rapids: Kregel, 1989.

Feinberg, John. *Can You Believe It's True? Christian Apologetics in a Modern and Postmodern Era*. Wheaton: Crossway, 2013.

Felperin, Howard. *Beyond Deconstruction: The Uses and Abuses of Literary Theory*. Oxford: Oxford University Press, 1987.

Ferguson, Everett. *Backgrounds of Early Christianity*. Grand Rapids: Eerdmans, 1993.

Fesko, J.V. "The Antiquity of Biblical Theology." In *Resurrection and Eschatology: Theology in Service of the Church. Essays in Honor of Richard B. Gaffin Jr.*, edited by Lane Tipton and Jeffrey Waddington. Phillipsburg: P&R, 2008.

———. *Word, Water and Spirit: A Reformed Perspective on Baptism*. Grand Rapids: Reformation Heritage Books, 2010.

Findley, Gary. "Bridges or Ladders?" *Kerux* 17 (2002). http://www.kerux.com/doc/1702A1.asp.

Fish, Stanley. *Is There a Text in This Class? The Authority of Interpretive Communities*. Cambridge: Harvard University Press, 1980.

Foucault, Michel. *The Archaeology of Knowledge and the Discourse of Language*. New York: Pantheon, 1972.

———. "The Punitive Society." In *Michel Foucault. Ethics: Subjectivity and Truth*, edited by Paul Rabinow, 23–38. New York: The New Press, 1997.

———. "What is an Author?" In *The Foucault Reader*, edited by Paul Rabinow, 101–120. New York: Pantheon Books, 1984.

———. "Truth and Power." In *The Foucault Reader*, edited by Paul Rabinow, 51–75. New York: Pantheon Books, 1984.

Frame, John. *Doctrine of the Knowledge of God: A Theology of Lordship*. Phillipsburg: P&R, 1987.

———. *Systematic Theology: An Introduction to Christian Belief*. Phillipsburg: P&R, 2013.

France, R.T. "The Writer of Hebrews as Biblical Expositor." *Tyndale Bulletin* 47 (1996) 245–76.

Francke, John. "Scripture, Tradition and Authority: Reconstructing the Evangelical Conception of *Sola Scriptura*." In *Evangelicals & Scripture: Tradition, Authority and Hermeneutics* edited by Vincent Bacote et al., 192–210. Downers Grove: InterVarsity, 2005.

Furley, William D. "Mimos." In *Brill's New Pauly: Encyclopaedia of the Ancient World Vol.14*, edited by Hubert Cancik and Helmuth Schneider, 921. Leiden: Brill, 2006.

Gadamer, Hans. *Truth and Method*. New York: Continuum, 1994.

Gaffin, Jr., Richard B. "Geerhardus Vos and the Interpretation of Paul." In *Jerusalem and Athens: Critical Discussions on the Philosophy and Apologetics of Cornelius Van Til*, edited by E.R. Geehan, 228–37. Phillipsburg: P&R, 1980.

———. *God's Word in Servant Form: Abraham Kuyper and Herman Bavinck on the Doctrine of Scripture*. Jackson: Reformed Academic, 2008.

———, ed. *Redemptive History and Biblical Interpretation: The Shorter Writings of Geerhardus Vos*. Phillipsburg: P&R, 1980.

———. *Resurrection and Redemption: A Study in Paul's Soteriology*. Phillipsburg: P&R, 1987.

———. "A Sabbath Rest Still Awaits the People of God." In *Pressing Toward the Mark: Essays Commemorating Fifty Years of the Orthodox Presbyterian Church*, edited by Charles Dennison and Richard Gamble, 33–52. Philadelphia: Committee for the Historian of the Orthodox Presbyterian Church, 1986.

———. "Systematic Theology and Biblical Theology." In *The New Testament Student and Theology, Vol. 3*, edited by John Skilton, 32–50. Phillipsburg: P&R, 1976.

Gamble, Richard C. *The Whole Counsel of God Volume 1: God's Mighty Acts in the Old Testament*. Phillipsburg: P&R, 2009.

Geertsema, H.G. Review of *Sola Scriptura: Problems and Principles in Preaching Historical Texts* by Sidney Greidanus. *Mededelingen van de Vereniging voor Calvinistische Wijsbegeerte* (1971) 7–12.

Gerkin, Charles. *The Living Human Document: Revisioning Pastoral Counseling in a Hermeneutical Mode*. Nashville: Abingdon, 1984.

Gibson, Scott M. "Challenges to Preaching the Old Testament." In *Preaching the Old Testament*, edited by Scott M. Gibson, 21–28. Grand Rapids: Baker, 2006.

———, ed. *Preaching the Old Testament*. Grand Rapids: Baker, 2006.

Gleason, Ron. *Herman Bavinck: Pastor, Churchman, Statesman, and Theologian*. Phillipsburg: P&R, 2010.

Goldsworthy, Graeme. *The Goldsworthy Trilogy*. Carlisle: Paternoster Press, 2000.

———. *Gospel-Centered Hermeneutics: Foundation and Principles of Evangelical Biblical Interpretation*. Downers Grove: InterVarsity, 2006.

———. *Preaching the Whole Bible as Christian Scripture*. Grand Rapids: Eerdmans, 2000.

Goppelt, Leonard. *Typos: The Typological Interpretation of the Old Testament in the New*. Translated by Donald Madvig. Grand Rapids: Eerdmans, 1982.

Gordon, T. David. *Why Johnny Can't Preach*. Phillipsburg: P&R, 2009.

Greidanus, Sidney. *The Modern Preacher and the Ancient Text: Interpreting and Preaching Biblical Literature*. Grand Rapids: Eerdmans, 1988.

———. *Sola Scriptura: Problems and Principles in Preaching Historical Texts*. Toronto: Wedge, 1970.

————. *Preaching Christ from Genesis.* Grand Rapids: Eerdmans, 2007.

————. *Preaching Christ from the Old Testament: A Contemporary Hermeneutical Method.* Grand Rapids: Eerdmans, 1999.

————. *Preaching Christ from the Old Testament: Foundation for Expository Sermons.* Grand Rapids: Eerdmans, 2007.

Grenz, Stanley. *A Primer on Postmodernism.* Grand Rapids: Eerdmans, 1995.

————. *Renewing the Center: Evangelical Theology in a Post-Theological Era.* Grand Rapids: Baker Academic, 2000.

Grenz, Stanley, and John Francke. *Beyond Foundationalism: Shaping Theology in a Postmodern Context.* Louisville: Westminster John Knox, 2001.

Groothuis, Doug. "Truth Defined and Defended." In *Reclaiming the Center: Confronting Evangelical Accommodation in Postmodern Time,* edited by Millard J. Erickson et al., 59–79. Wheaton: Crossway, 2004.

Grosheide, F. W. *De brief aan de Hebreeën en de brief van Jakobus.* Kampen: Kok, 1955.

————. *De eerste brief aan de kerk te Korinthe.* Kampen: Kok, 1957.

Guthrie, George. "New Testament Exegesis of Hebrews and the Catholic Epistles." In *Handbook to Exegesis of the New Testament,* edited by Stanley Porter, 591–606. Leiden: Brill, 1997.

————. *The Structure of the Book of Hebrews: A Text-Linguistic Analysis.* Leiden: Brill, 1994.

Haak, Kees. "Schaamte en schuld op Papua: De schaamtecultuur als opmaat voor missionaire benadering in een postmoderne context." In *Instemmend luisteren: Studies voor Kees de Ruijter,* edited by Marinus Beute and Peter Van de Kamp, 136–59. Kampen: Kok, 2014.

Hagner, Donald. *Encountering the Book of Hebrews.* Grand Rapids: Baker, 2002.

Harinck, George. "Inleiding." In *Wie is die man? Klaas Schilder in de eenentwintigste eeuw,* edited by M. de Jong et al., 9–16. Barneveld: De Vuurbaak, 2012.

Harinck, George and Anne Jacob van Omme. "Schilders Amerikaanse reis van 1939." In *Wie is die man? Klaas Schilder in de eenentwintigste eeuw,* edited by M. de Jong et al., 261–323. Barneveld: De Vuurbaak, 2012.

Harmon, William. *A Handbook to Literature.* Upper Saddle River: Pearson, 2009.

Harris, Max. *Theater and Incarnation.* Grand Rapids: Eerdmans, 1990.

Hassan, Ihab. *The Postmodern Turn: Essays in Postmodern Theory and Culture.* Columbus: Ohio State University Press, 1987.

Hays, Richard. *The Conversion of the Imagination: Paul as Interpreter of Israel's Scripture.* Grand Rapids: Eerdmans, 2005.

————. *The Moral Vision of the New Testament: A Contemporary Introduction to New Testament Ethics.* New York: HarperCollins, 1996.

————. *Reading Backwards: Figural Christology and the Fourfold Witness.* Waco: Baylor University Press, 2014.

Henderson, David. *Culture Shift: Communicating God's Truth to our Changing World.* Grand Rapids: Baker, 1998.

Hinn, Benny. *The Biblical Road to Blessing.* Nashville: Thomas Nelson, 1997.

Hirsch, E.D. Jr. *Validity in Interpretation.* New Haven: Yale University Press, 1967.

Hodge, Charles. *1&2 Corinthians.* Carlisle: The Banner of Truth Trust, 1994.

Hoekstra, T. *Gereformeerde homiletiek.* Wageningen: Zomer & Keuning, 1926.

Holwerda, B. "Het Altaar zonder tafel." In *Tot de dag aanlicht,* 48–72. Goes: Oosterbaan & Le Cointre, 1950.

————. *Gereformeerd mannenblad* 18 (1940) 25–28.

————. "De heilshistorie in de prediking." In *Begonnen hebbende van Mozes*, 79–118. Terneuzen: D.H. Littooij, 1953.

Holwerda, D. *Hebreeën:Vertaling met korte aantekeningen en 18 bredere studies.* Kampen: Kok, 2003.

Holwerda, David E. *Jesus and Israel: One Covenant or Two?* Grand Rapids: Eerdmans, 1995.

Hood, Jason. "Evangelicals and the Imitation of the Cross: Peter Bolt on Mark 13 as a Test Case." *EvQ* 81 (2009) 116–25.

————. *Imitating God in Christ: Recapturing a Biblical Pattern.* Downers Grove: InterVarsity, 2013.

Horton, Michael S. *A Better Way: Rediscovering the Drama of God-Centered Worship.* Grand Rapids: Baker, 2002.

————. *The Christian Faith: A Systematic Theology for Pilgrims on the Way.* Grand Rapids: Zondervan, 2011.

————. *Christless Christianity: The Alternative Gospel of the American Church.* Grand Rapids: Baker, 2012

————. *Covenant and Eschatology: The Divine Drama.* Louisville: Westminster John Knox, 2002

————. *People and Place: A Covenant Ecclesiology.* Louisville: Westminster John Knox, 2008.

————. *Pilgrim Theology: Core Doctrines for Christian Disciples.* Grand Rapids: Zondervan, 2011.

Houtman, Piet. *This Is Your God! Preaching Biblical History.* Delhi: Cambridge Press, 2010.

Hughes, Graham. *Hebrews and Hermeneutics: The Epistle to the Hebrews as a New Testament Example of Biblical Interpretation.* Cambridge: Cambridge University Press, 1979.

Hughes, Philip. *A Commentary on the Epistle to the Hebrews.* Grand Rapids: Eerdmans, 1990.

Hughes, R. Kent. *Genesis: Beginning and Blessing.* Wheaton: Crossway, 2004.

Huijser. J. "'Exemplarische' prediking I." *Gereformeerd theologisch tijdschrift* 50 (1950) 163–82.

————. "'Exemplarische' prediking II." *Gereformeerd theologisch tijdschrift* 51 (1951) 1–18.

Hume, David. *Dialogues Concerning Natural Religion.* New York: Hafner, 1948.

Hyun, Yung Hoon. *Redemptive-Historical Hermeneutics and Homiletics: Debates in Holland, America, and Korea from 1930 to 2012.* Eugene: Wipf and Stock, 2015.

James, Craig. "Georges Bataille (1897–1962): Introduction." In *The Postmodern God: A Theological Reader*, edited by Graham Ward, 3–15. Malden: Blackwell, 1997.

Jensen, Michael. Review of *The Drama of Doctrine*, by Kevin J. Vanhoozer. *Anvil* 24 (2007) 227–8.

Jewett, Paul. *Letter to Pilgrims: A Commentary on the Epistle to the Hebrews.* New York: Pilgrim Press, 1981.

Johnson, Dennis. *Him We Proclaim: Preaching Christ from all the Scriptures.* Phillipsburg: P&R, 2007.

————. *Walking with Jesus through His Word: Discovering Christ in All the Scriptures.* Phillipsburg: P&R, 2015.

Johnson, Luke Timothy. *Hebrews: A Commentary.* Louisville: Westminster John Knox, 2006.

Johnson, Terry. "Preaching the Point." http://theaquilareport.com/preaching-the-point.

Jones, Hywell. *Let's Study Hebrews.* Carlisle: Banner of Truth Trust, 2002.

Jones, L. Gregory. "Embodying Scripture in the Community of Faith." In *The Art of Reading Scripture,* edited by Ellen Davis and Richard Hays. Grand Rapids: Eerdmans, 2003.

Jones, Peter. *One or Two: Seeing a World of Difference.* Escondido: Main Entry: 2010.

———. *Spirit Wars: Pagan Revival in Christian America.* Escondido: Main Entry, 1998.

Jongeling, P., J.P. de Vries, and J. Douma, eds. *Het vuur blijft branden: Geschiedenis van de Gereformeerde Kerken (vrijgemaakt) in Nederland, 1944-1979.* Kampen: Kok, 1979.

Jonker, W.D. Review of *Sola Scriptura: Problems and Principles in Preaching Historical Texts,* by Sidney Greidanus. *Gereformeerd weekblad* 25 (1969/1970) 350–1.

Josephus, Flavius. "Flavius Josephus Against Apion." In *The Works of Josephus: Complete and Unabridged,* translated by William Whiston. Peabody: Hendrickson, 1995.

Kaminski, Carol. "Preaching From the Historical Books." In *Preaching the Old Testament,* edited by Scott M. Gibson. Grand Rapids: Baker, 2006.

Kant, Immanuel. *Critique of Pure Reason.* Translated by Norman Kemp Smith. New York: St. Martin's, 1958.

———. "Pure Reason and the Question of God." In *Primary Readings in Philosophy for Understanding Theology,* edited by Diogenes Allen and Eric O. Springsted. Louisville: Westminster John Knox, 1992.

Kapic, Kelly M., and Bruce L. McCormic, eds. *Mapping Modern Theology: A Thematic and Historical Introduction.* Grand Rapids: Baker. 2012.

Keller, Timothy. *Preaching: Communicating Faith in an Age of Skepticism.* New York: Viking, 2015.

———. *The Prodigal God: Recovering the Heart of the Christian Faith.* New York: Dutton, 2008.

Keller, Timothy and Edmund Clowney. "Preaching Christ in a Postmodern World." https://itunes.apple.com/nl/itunes-u/preaching-christ-in-postmodern/id378879885.

Kierkegaard, Søren. *Fear and Trembling: Repetition.* Translated by H.V. Hong. and E.H. Hong. Princeton: Princeton University Press, 1983.

Kistemaker, Simon. *1 Corinthians.* Grand Rapids: Baker, 1993.

———. "The Psalm Citations in the Epistle to the Hebrews." PhD diss., Vrije Universiteit Amsterdam, 1961. Amsterdam: Wed. G. Van Soest N.V. 1961.

Kleber, Jason. *The Influences of Theological Liberalism and Postmodernism on Conservative Evangelical Preaching, with a Proposal for its Correction by the Implementation of a Lectio Continua, Redemptive-Historical Approach to Sermon Preparation and Delivery.* D. Min. Project, Temple Baptist Seminary, 2012.

Kline, Meredith G. *By Oath Consigned.* Grand Rapids: Eerdmans, 1968.

———. *Kingdom Prologue: Genesis Foundations for a Covenantal Worldview.* Overland Park: Two Age Press, 2000.

———. *The Structure of Biblical Authority.* Eugene: Wipf and Stock, 1997.

———. *Treaty of the Great King: The Covenant Structure of Deuteronomy.* Grand Rapids: Eerdmans, 1968.

Kloester, Fred. *Our Only Comfort: A Comprehensive Commentary on the Heidelberg Catechism Vol. 1.* Grand Rapids: Faith Alive, 1998.

Koester, Craig R. *The Dwelling of God: The Tabernacle in the Old Testament, Intertestamental Jewish Literature, and the New Testament.* Washington, D.C.: Catholic Biblical Association, 1989.

———. *Hebrews: A New Translation with Introduction and Commentary.* New Haven: Yale University Press, 2001.

Köstenberger, Andreas, and Richard Patterson. *Invitation to Biblical Interpretation: Exploring the Hermeneutical Triangle of History, Literature, and Theology.* Grand Rapids: Kregel, 2011.

Krabbendam, Henry. "Hermeneutics and Preaching." In *The Preacher and Preaching: Reviving the Art in the Twentieth Century,* edited by Samuel Logan, 239–45. Phillipsburg: P&R, 1986.

Kranendonk, D.H. *Vital Balance: The Pursuit of Professors J.J Van der Schuit, G. Wisse, and L.H. Van der Meiden.* Brantford: Free Reformed Publications, 2006.

Kruger, Michael. *Canon Revisited: Establishing the Origins and Authority of the New Testament Books.* Wheaton: Crossway, 2012.

Kuiper, R. "Vrijmaking of wederkeer." In *Vuur en vlam: Aspecten van het vrijgemaakt-gereformeerde leven 1944-1969,* edited by R. Kuiper and W. Bouwman, 11–44. Amsterdam: Buijten & Schipperheijn, 1969.

Kuruvilla, Abraham. *Genesis: A Theological Commentary for Preachers.* Eugene: Resource Publications, 2014.

———. *Privilege the Text! A Theological Hermeneutic for Preaching.* Chicago: Moody, 2013.

———. *Text to Praxis: Hermeneutics and Homiletics in Dialogue.* New York: T&T Clark, 2009.

Kuyper, Abraham. *Lectures on Calvinism: The Stone Lectures for 1898.* Grand Rapids: Eerdmans, 1931.

———. *Our Worship.* Translated by Harry Boonstra. Grand Rapids: Eerdmans, 2009.

Kwakkel, Gert. "Out of Egypt I Have Called My Son: Matthew 2:15 and Hosea 11:1 in Dutch and American Evangelical Interpretation." In *Tradition and Innovation in Biblical Interpretation: Studies Presented to Professor Eep Talstra on the Occasion of his Sixty-Fifth Birthday,* edited by W.Th. van Peursen and J.W. Dyk, 171–88. Studia Semitica Neerlandica 57. Leiden: Brill, 2011.

———. "The Reader as Focal Point of Biblical Exegesis." In *Correctly Handling the Word of Truth,* edited by Mees te Velde and Gerhard Visscher, 215–25. Eugene: Wipf and Stock, 2014.

Laansma, Jon C. "Hebrews." In *Theological Interpretation of the New Testament: A Book-by-Book Survey,* edited by Kevin J. Vanhoozer, 186–99. Grand Rapids: Baker, 2008.

———. "Hebrews: Yesterday, Today and Future; An Illustrative Survey, Diagnosis, Prescription." In *Christology, Hermeneutics, and Hebrews: Profiles from the History of Interpretation,* edited by Jon C. Laansma and Daniel J. Treier, 1–32. New York: T&T Clark, 2012.

Lancaster, Sarah Heaner. "Dramatic Enactment of Christian Faith: A Review Essay." *The Asbury Journal* 62 (2007) 119–26.

Lane, William L. *Hebrews 9–13.* Dallas: Word, 1991.

Larsen, David. *Telling the Old, Old Story: The Art of Narrative Preaching.* Wheaton: Crossway Books, 1995.

Lawson, Stephen. *Famine in the Land: A Passionate Call for Expository Preaching.* Chicago: Moody 2008.

Leitch, Vincent, ed. *The Norton Anthology of Theory and Criticism.* New York: W.W. Norton & Company, 2010.

Leon-Dufour, Xavier, ed. *Dictionary of Biblical Theology.* 2nd ed. Gaithersburg: The Word Among Us, 1995.

Lessing, Gotthold. "On the Proof of the Spirit and of Power." In *Lessing's Theological Writings: Selections in Translation*, 51–56. Translated by Henry Chadwick. Stanford: Stanford University Press, 1956.

————. *Philosophical and Theological Writings*, edited by H.B. Nisbet. Cambridge: Cambridge University Press, 2005.

Lewis, C.S. *God in the Dock.* Reprint. Grand Rapids: Eerdmans, 2014.

Lewis, Peter. *The Genius of Puritanism.* Sussex: Carey Publications, 1979.

Lints, Richard. *The Fabric of Theology: A Prolegomena to Evangelical Theology.* Grand Rapids: Eerdmans, 1993.

————. "The Vinyl Narratives: The Metanarrative of Postmodernity and the Recovery of a Churchly Theology." In *A Confessing Theology for Postmodern Times*, edited by Michael Horton, 91–110. Wheaton: Crossway Books, 2000.

Litfin, Duane. "New Testament Challenges to Big Idea Preaching." In *The Big Idea of Biblical Preaching: Connecting the Bible to the People*, edited by Keith Willhite and Scott M. Gibson, 53–66. Grand Rapids: Baker, 1998.

Lloyd-Jones, D. Martyn. *Preaching and Preachers.* Grand Rapids: Zondervan, 1971.

Lloyd-Jones, Sally. *The Jesus Storybook Bible.* Grand Rapids: Zondervan, 2007.

Long, Jimmy. "Generating Hope: A Strategy for Reaching the Postmodern Generation." In *Telling the Truth: Evangelizing Postmoderns*, edited by D.A. Carson. Grand Rapids: Zondervan, 2000.

Loonstra, Bertus. "Verkiezing-Verzoening-Verbond: Beschrijving en beoordeling van de leer van het pactum salutis in de gereformeerde theologie." Ph.D diss., Rijksuniversiteit te Utrecht. Gravenhage: Boekencentrum, 1990.

Lopez, Jesse, and Garry Potter. *After Postmodernism: An Introduction to Critical Realism.* New York: The Althone Press, 2001.

MacArthur, John. "Frequently Asked Questions about Expository Preaching." In *Preaching: How to Preach Biblically.* Nashville: Thomas Nelson, 2005.

Macey, David. *The Penguin Dictionary of Critical Theory.* London: Penguin, 2000.

Machen, J. Gresham. *Christianity and Liberalism.* Grand Rapids: Eerdmans, 1923.

————. *What Is Faith?* Carlisle: Banner of Truth Trust, 1991.

MacIntyre, Alasdair. *After Virtue.* Norte Dame: University of Norte Dame Press, 1984.

Macleod, David. "The Literary Structure of the Book of Hebrews." *Bibliotheca Sacra* 146 (1989) 185–97.

Marcel, Pierre. *The Relevance of Preaching.* Grand Rapids: Baker, 1963.

Mason, Matthew. "Back to (Theo-drama) School: The Place of Catechesis in the Local Church." *Scottish Bulletin of Evangelical Theology* 30 (2012) 206–22.

Mathewson, Steven. *The Art of Preaching Old Testament Narrative.* Grand Rapids: Baker Academic, 2002.

Mayhue, Richard. "Rediscovering Expository Preaching." In *Preaching: How to Preach Biblically*, edited by John MacArthur et al., 3–16. Nashville: Thomas Nelson, 2005.

McCartney, Dan, and Charles Clayton. *Let the Reader Understand: A Guide to Interpreting and Applying the Bible.* Phillipsburg: P&R, 2002.

McWilliams, David. *Hebrews*. Powder Springs: Tolle Lege Press, 2015.

Meijer, J. "Noach's geloof." *Waarheid & Recht*, 12 (1956) 3–17.

Melville, Herman. *Moby Dick*. Evanston: Northwestern University Press, 2001.

Meyer, Jason. *Preaching: A Biblical Theology*. Wheaton: Crossway, 2013.

Middleton, J. Richard, and Brian J. Walsh. *Truth Is Stranger Than It Used to Be: Biblical Faith in a Postmodern Age*. Downers Grove: InterVarsity, 1995.

Moffat, James. *A Critical and Exegetical Commentary on the Epistle to the Hebrews*. Edinburgh: T&T Clark, 1975.

Mohler, Jr., R. Albert. *He Is Not Silent: Preaching in a Postmodern World*. Chicago: Moody Publishers, 2008.

———. "Truth and Contemporary Culture." In *Whatever Happened to Truth?*, edited by Andreas Köstenberger, 53–73. Wheaton: Crossway, 2005.

Morales, Michael. "The Rebirth of Moses: Exodus 2:1-10." Unpublished paper, used by permission of the author.

Moyise, Steve. *The Latter New Testament Writings and Scripture: The Old Testament in Acts, Hebrews, the Catholic Epistles and Revelation*. Grand Rapids: Baker, 2012.

Muether, John. *Cornelius Van Til: Reformed Apologist and Churchman*. Phillipsburg: P&R, 2008.

Muller, Richard A. *Post-Reformation Reformed Dogmatics: The Rise and Development of Reformed Orthodoxy, ca. 1520 to ca. 1725, Vol. 2*. Grand Rapids: Baker, 2003.

———. "Preface." In *Louis Berkhof: Systematic Theology*. Grand Rapids: Eerdmans, 1996.

Murphy, Nancey. *Beyond Liberalism and Fundamentalism: How Modern and Postmodern Philosophy Set the Theological Agenda*. Harrisburg: Trinity Press International, 1996.

Murphy, Nancey and Brad J. Kallenberg. "Anglo-American Postmodernity: A Theology of Communal Practice." In *The Cambridge Companion to Postmodern Theology*, edited by Kevin J. Vanhoozer, 26–41. Cambridge: Cambridge University Press, 2009.

Murray, John. "Systematic Theology" In *Collected Writings of John Murray, Vol. 4*, 1–21. Carlisle: The Banner of Truth Trust, 1982.

Netland, A. Harold, and Keith E. Johnson. "Why is Religious Pluralism Fun--And Dangerous?" In *Telling the Truth: Evangelizing Postmoderns*, edited by D.A. Carson, 47–67. Grand Rapids: Zondervan, 2000.

Nichols, Stephen. *Welcome to the Story: Reading, Loving and Living God's Word*. Wheaton: Crossway, 2011.

Noordzij, D.W. "In het geloof draait alles om het hart." *Waarheid & Recht*, 57 (2001) 9–15.

O'Brien, P.T. *The Letter to the Hebrews*. Grand Rapids: Eerdmans, 2010.

O'Donnell III, Laurence R. *Kees Van Til als Nederlands-Amerikaanse, Neo-Calvinistisch-Presbyteriaan Apologeticus: An Analysis of Cornelius Van Til's Presupposition of Reformed Dogmatics with Special Reference to Herman Bavinck's Gereformeerde Dogmatiek*. Unpublished ThM thesis, Calvin Theological Seminary, 2011.

O'Neil, J.C. *The Bible's Authority: A Portrait Gallery of Thinkers from Lessing to Bultmann*. Edinburgh: T&T Clark, 1991.

Ohmann, H.M. "Redemptive Historical Preaching." In *Proceedings of the International Council of Reformed Churches*. Neerlandia: Inheritance Publications, 1993.

Old, Hughes. *The Reading and Preaching of the Scriptures in the Worship of the Christian Church. Vol. 1: The Biblical Period.* Grand Rapids: Eerdmans, 1998.

————. *The Reading and Preaching of the Scriptures in the Worship of the Christian Church. Vol. 7: Our Own Time.* Grand Rapids: Eerdmans, 2010.

Olford, Stephen. *Anointed Expository Preaching.* Nashville: Broadman and Holman, 1998.

Osborne, Grant. *The Hermeneutical Spiral.* Downers Grove: InterVarsity, 1991.

Paas, Stefan. "The Making of a Mission Field: Paradigms of Evangelistic Mission in Europe." *Exchange* 41 (2012) 1–24.

————. "Missionair gemeente-zijn in de postmoderne samenleving." In *Instemmend luisteren: Studies voor Kees de Ruijter,* edited by Marinus Beute and Peter Van de Kamp. Kampen: Kok, 2014.

————. "Missionair preken." In *Postille* 62 (2010-2011) 11–23.

————. "Nieuwe structuren voor de gereformeerde geloofsbeleving." In *Postmodern gereformeerd: Naar een visie op christen-zijn in de hedendaagse belevingscultuur,* edited by Pieter Beunder et al., 142–52. Amsterdam: Buijten & Schipperheijn Motief, 2009.

————. "Post-Christian, Post-Christendom, and Post-modern Europe. Towards the Interaction of Missiology and the Social Sciences." *Mission Studies* 28 (2011) 3–25.

————. *De werkers van het laatste uur: De inwijding van nieuwkomers in het christelijk geloof en de christelijke gemeente.* Zoetermeer: Boekencentrum, 2008.

Park, Tae-Hyeun. "The Sacred Rhetoric of the Holy Spirit: A Study of Puritan Preaching in a Pneumatological Perspective." PhD diss., Theologische Universiteit Apeldoorn, 2005.

Parker, T. H. L. *Calvin's Preaching.* Louisville: Westminster John Knox, 1992.

Pasquarello III, Michael. *Christian Preaching: A Trinitarian Theology of Proclamation.* Grand Rapids: Baker, 2006.

Pattison, T. *The History of Christian Preaching.* Philadelphia: The American Baptist Publication Society, 1903.

Peels, Eric. "In het teken van Kaïn: Een theologische exegese van Genesis 4." *Verbum et Ecclesia* 29 (2008) 172–93.

————. "The World's First Murder: Violence and Justice in Genesis 4:1–16." In *Animosity, the Bible and Us: Some European, North American, And South African Perspectives,* edited by John T. Fitzgerald et al., 19–40. Atlanta: Society of Biblical Literature, 2009.

Pelton, Randal. *Preaching with Accuracy: Find Christ-Centered Big Ideas for Biblical Preaching.* Grand Rapids: Kregel, 2014.

Perkins, Williams. *The Art of Prophesying.* Carlisle: The Banner of Truth Trust, 1996.

Peterson, Eugene. *Leap over a Wall: Earthly Spirituality for Everyday Christians.* New York: HarperCollins, 1997.

Phillips, Richard D. "Can We Know the Truth?" In *The Gospel as Center: Renewing Our Faith and Reforming Our Ministry Practices,* edited by D.A. Carson and Timothy Keller, 23–40. Wheaton: Crossway, 2012.

————. *Hebrews.* Phillipsburg: P&R, 2006.

Philo. *The Works of Philo: Unabridged in One Volume.* Translated by C.D. Yonge. Grand Rapids: Hendrickson, 1995.

Pink, Arthur. *An Exposition of Hebrews.* Grand Rapids: Baker, 1954.

Pipa, Joseph. "William Perkins and the Development of Puritan Preaching." PhD diss., Westminster Theological Seminary, 1985.

Piper, John. "Jesus Christ as Dénouement in the Theater of God." In *With Calvin in the Theater of God: The Glory of Christ and Everyday Life*, edited by David Mathis and John Piper, 133–46. Wheaton: Crossway, 2010.

———. *The Supremacy of God in Preaching*. Grand Rapids: Baker, 2004.

Poythress, Vern. *In the Beginning Was the Word: Language: A God-Centered Approach*. Wheaton: Crossway, 2009.

———. *Understanding Dispensationalists*. Phillipsburg: P&R, 1994.

Ratzinger, Joseph. *Jesus of Nazareth: From the Baptism in the Jordan to the Transfiguration*. New York: Doubleday, 2007.

Reeves, Michael. *Delighting in the Trinity: An Introduction to the Christian Faith*. Downers Grove: InterVarsity, 2012.

Renninger, William Jr. "The New Testament Use of the Old Testament Historical Narrative and the Implications for the Exemplary Interpretation of Old Testament Narrative." PhD diss., Evangelische Theologische Faculteit te Heverlee, Leuven, 2000.

Rhee, Victor (Sung-Yul). *Faith in Hebrews: Analysis within the Context of Christology, Eschatology, and Ethics*. New York: Peter Lang, 2001.

Ricoeur, Paul. *The Conflict of Interpretations*. Evanston: Northwestern University Press, 1974.

———. *Figuring the Sacred: Religion, Narrative, and Imagination*. Minneapolis: Fortress, 1995.

———. "Hermeneutics and the World of the Text." In *Hermeneutics: Writings and Lectures, Volume 2*, 11–18. Cambridge: Polity Press, 2013.

Ridderbos, Herman N. *Paul: An Outline of His Theology*. Translated by John De Witt. Grand Rapids: Eerdmans, 1975.

———. "The Redemptive-Historical Character of Paul's Preaching." In *When the Time Had Fully Come: Studies in New Testament Theology*, 44–60. Ontario: Paideia, 1957.

———. *Redemptive History and the New Testament Scriptures*. Phillipsburg: P&R, 1963.

———. *Studies in Scripture and its Authority*. Grand Rapids: Eerdmans, 1978.

Robertson, O. Palmer. *The Israel of God, Yesterday, Today and Tomorrow*. Phillipsburg: P&R, 2000.

Robinson, Haddon. *Biblical Preaching: The Development and Delivery of Expository Messages* Grand Rapids: Baker, 1980.

———. "The Heresy of Application." *Leadership Journal* 18 (1997) 20–27.

Rorty, Richard. *Consequences of Pragmatism*. Minneapolis: University of Minnesota Press, 1982.

Rosenau, Pauline. *Post-Modernism and the Social Sciences: Insights, Inroads, and Intrusions*. Princeton: Princeton University Press, 1992.

Rosscup, James. "Hermeneutics and Expository Preaching." In *Preaching: How to Preach Biblically*, edited by John MacArthur et al., 93–106. Nashville: Thomas Nelson, 2005.

Roukema, R. "Heilshistorische exegese: Herman Ridderbos." In *Profiel: Theologiebeoefening in Kampen, 1970-1990*, edited by J. Van Gelderen and C. Houtman, 52–74. Kampen: Kok, 2004.

Runia, K. *Het hoge woord in de Lage Landen*. Kampen: Kok, 1985.

Ryken, Leland, et al., eds. *Dictionary of Biblical Imagery: An Encyclopedic Exploration of the Images, Symbols, Motifs, Metaphors, Figures of Speech and Literary Patterns of the Bible*. Downers Grove: InterVarsity, 1998.

Ryken, P.G. "Scottish Reformed Scholasticism." In *Protestant Scholasticism: Essays in Reassessment*, edited by Carl R. Trueman and R. Scott Clark, 196–210. Carlisle: Pasternoster Press, 1999.

Samra, James. "A Biblical View of Discipleship." *Bibliothecra Sacra* 160 (2003) 219–34.

Sayers, Dorothy L. *Creed or Chaos?* New York: Harcourt, Brace and Company, 1949.

Schaefer, Paul. "Protestant 'Scholasticism' at Elizabethan Cambridge: William Perkins and a Reformed Theology of the Heart." In *Protestant Scholasticism: Essays in Reassessment*, edited by Carl Trueman and R.S. Clark. Carlisle: Paternoster Press, 1999.

Schelhaas, J. "Christus en de historische stoffen in de prediking." *Gereformeerd theologisch tijdschrift* 42 (1941) 107–28.

Schelling, P. "De enige troost in de belofte van God." *Waarheid & Recht* 53 (1997) 30–36.

Schilder, H. J. 'De kerk in het wereldtheater." *De Reformatie* 50 (1974) 44–45.

———. "Modern exemplarisme I." *De Reformatie* 50 (1974) 41–42.

Schilder, Klaas. "Americana (1942)." http://www.dbnl.org/tekst/schi008amer01_01/schi008amer01_01_0003.php.

———. *Christus in zijn lijden*. 3 vols. Kampen: Kok, 1930.=*Christ and His Sufferings*. Grand Rapids: Eerdmans, 1938.

———. *Heidelbergsche Catechismus, Vol. II*. Goes: Oosterbaan & Le Cointre, 1947.

———. "Iets over de eenheid der 'Heilsgeschiedenis' in verband met de prediking I." In *De Reformatie* 11 (1931) 365–66.

———. *Zur Begriffsgeschicte des "Paradoxon," Mit Besonderer Berücksichtigung Calvins und des Nach-Kierkegaardschen "Paradoxon."* Kampen: Kok, 1933.

Schreiner, Susan. *The Theater of His Glory: Nature and the Natural Order in the Thought of John Calvin*. Grand Rapids: Labyrinth, 1991.

Schreiner, Thomas. *Magnifying God in Christ: A Summary of New Testament Theology*. Grand Rapids: Baker, 2010.

Schreurs, Martin. "Postmodern Bildung." PhD diss., Universiteit Utrecht, 2003.

Selderhuis, H. J., ed. *Handboek nederlandse kerkgeschiedenis*. Kampen: Kok, 2010.

Sellers, Robert P. "Is Mission Possible in a Postmodern World?" *Review and Expositor* 101 (2004) 389–424.

Selvaggio, Anthony. "An Answer to the Challenge of Preaching the Old Testament: An Historical and Theological Examination of the Redemptive-Historical Approach." *The Confessional Presbyterian* 5 (2009) 170–84.

Skarsaune, Oskar. "Does the Letter to the Hebrews Articulate a Supersessionist Theology? A Response to Richard Hays." In *The Epistle to the Hebrews and Christian Theology*, edited by Richard Bauckham et al., 174–82. Grand Rapids: Eerdmans, 2009.

Slob, Wouter H. "Verily I Say unto Thee: Rhetorical Normativity after Postmodern Theologies." PhD diss., Rijksuniversiteit Groningen, 2002.

Smelik. J. "Sara, mede het zaad der belofte verwekkend door haar geloof." *Waarheid & Recht* 43 (1948) 2–12.

Sneller, Rico. "Gebod, belofte, en de tentakels van het schrift." In *Spiritualiteit en postmodernisme*, edited by Bart Voorsluis, 50–65. Zoetermeer: Meinema, 2000.

Sonderegger, Katherine. "Creation." In *Mapping Modern Theology: A Thematic and Historical Introduction*, edited by Kelly M. Kapic and Bruce L. McCormic, 97–120. Grand Rapids: Baker. 2012.

Stark, Ciska. *Proeven van de preek: een praktisch-theologisch onderzoek naar de preek als Woord van God*. Zoetermeer: Boekencentrum, 2005.

Stedeman, Ray. *Hebrews*. Leicester: InterVarsity, 1992.

Steiner, George. *Real Presences*. Reprint. Chicago: University of Chicago Press, 1991.

Stitzinger, James F.. "The History of Expository Preaching." In *Preaching: How to Preach Biblically*, edited by John MacArthur et al., 27–46. Nashville: Thomas Nelson, 2005.

Stott, John. *Between Two Worlds*. Grand Rapids: Eerdmans, 1982.

————. "Biblical Preaching in the Modern World." In *The Folly of Preaching: Models and Methods*, edited by Michael P. Knowles, 113–26. Grand Rapids: Eerdmans, 2007.

Stowell III, Joseph M. "Preaching for a Change." In *The Big Idea of Biblical Preaching: Connecting the Bible to People*, edited by Keith Willhite and Scott M. Gibson, 125–45. Grand Rapids: Baker, 1998.

Strimple, Robert. *The Modern Search for the Real Jesus: An Introductory Survey of the Historical Roots of Gospels Criticism*. Phillipsburg: P&R, 1995.

Teunis, E. "Rachab en de verspieders." *Waarheid & Recht* 32 (1976) 3–11.

Te Velde, Mees. "De Vrijmaking gepeild." In *1944 en vervolgens: Tien maal over vijftig jaar Vrijmaking*, edited by Mees te Velde and George Harinck, 17–24. Barneveld: De Vuurbaak, 1994.

————. "Vrijgemaakte vreemdelingen tussen verleden en toekomst: Een nabeschouwing." In *Vrijgemaakte vreemdelingen: Visies uit de vroege jaren van het Gereformeerd-vrijgemaakte leven (1944-1960) op kerk, staat, maatschappij, cultuur, gezin*, edited by Mees te Velde and Hans Werkman, 175–200. Barneveld: De Vuurbaak, 2007.

Thayer, J.H. *A Greek-English Lexicon of the New Testament*. New York: American Book Company, 1889.

Thiselton, Anthony. *The First Epistle to the Corinthians*. Grand Rapids: Eerdmans, 2000.

————. *Interpreting God and the Postmodern Self: On Meaning, Manipulation and Promise*. Grand Rapids: Eerdmans, 1995.

Thomas, Derek. *Calvin's Teaching on Job: Proclaiming the Incomprehensible God*. Geanies House: Mentor, 2004.

Thompson, James. *The Beginnings of Christian Philosophy: The Epistle to the Hebrews*. Washington: The Catholic Biblical Association of America, 1982.

Trimp, C. *Heilsgeschiedenis en prediking: Hervatting van een onvoltooid gesprek*. Kampen: Van Den Berg, 1988.

————. *Klank en weerklank: Door prediking tot geloofservaring*. Barneveld: De Vuurbaak, 1989.

————. *Preaching and the History of Salvation: Continuing an Unfinished Discussion*. Translated by Nelson Kloosterman. Dyer: Mid-America Reformed Seminary, 1996.

————. *De preek: Een praktisch verhaal over het maken en houden van preken*. Kampen: Van Den Berg: 1986.

————. "The Relevance of Preaching." *WTJ* 36 (1973) 1–30.

————. Review of *Sola Scriptura: Problems and Principles in Preaching Historical Texts* by Sidney Greidanus. *De Reformatie* 45 (1969-1970) 337–9.

Turretin, Francis, *Institutio Theologiae Elencticae* (= *Institutes of Elenctic Theology*), edited by James T. Dennison, Jr. Translated by George Musgrave Giger. Phillipsburg: P&R, 1992.

Tyson, Lois. *Critical Theory Today: A User-Friendly Guide.* New York: Routledge, 2006.

Van Bekkum, Koert. "Op de tweesprong van kerk en wereld." In *Wie is die man? Klaas Schilder in de eenentwintigste eeuw,* edited by M. de Jong et al., 17–34. Barneveld: De Vuurbaak, 2012.

Van Bruggen, Jakob. "Hermeneutics and the Bible." In *Proceedings of the International Conference of Reformed* Churches. Neerlandia: Inheritance Publications, 2001.

————. "Het apostolische evangelie als geloofsbelijdenis." In *Apostelen: Dragers van een spraakmakend evangelie,* edited by P.H.R. van Houwelingen, 168–216. Kampen: Kok, 2010.

————. "Sermon on Hebrews 1:1-2a." http://vanbruggenpreken.nl/.

————. "Vergeet de dinosaurussen: DENK LIEVER AAN ABEL! (sermon on Hebrews 11:4)." http://vanbruggenpreken.nl/.

Van de Kamp, H.R. *Hebreeën: Geloven is volhouden.* Kampen: Kok, 2010.

Van de Kamp, Peter. *Hart voor de stad.* Kampen: Kok, 2003.

————. *Verhalen om te leven: Levensverhalen in het pastoraat.* Kampen: Kok, 2013.

Van den Berg, H. "Hoopvolle asielzoekers." *Waarheid & Recht* 56 (2000) 3–9.

VanderKam, James. *Enoch: A Man for All Generations.* Columbia: University of South Carolina Press, 1995.

Van der Welle, M.A. "Preken. Ook voor leken?" *Caementarius Oboediens Recte Norma Utitur* 4 (2014) 10–17.

Van Deursen, Arie Theodorus. *The Distinctive Character of the Free University in Amsterdam, 1880-2005: A Commemorative History.* Grand Rapids: Eerdmans, 2008.

Van Dijk, Douwe, *My Path Toward Liberation: Reflections on My Life in the Ministry of the Work of God.* Translated by Theodore Plantinga. Neerlandia: Inheritance Publications, 2004.

VanDrunen, David, and R. Scott Clark. "The Covenant Before the Covenants." In *Covenant, Justification, and Pastoral Ministry: Essays By the Faculty of Westminster Seminary California,* edited by R. Scott Clark, 167–96. Phillipsburg: P&R, 2007.

Van Dusseldorp, Kees. *Preken tussen de verhalen: Een homiletische doordenking van narrativiteit.* Kampen, Kok, 2012.

————. "De moraal van het verhaal: een verkenning rond de morele relevantie van de preek." In *Instemmend luisteren: Studies voor Kees de Ruijter,* edited by Marinus Beute and Peter van de Kamp, 79–103. Kampen: Kok, 2014.

Vanhoozer, Kevin J. *The Drama of Doctrine: A Canonical-linguistic Approach to Christian Theology.* Westminster John Knox, 2005.

————. "A Drama of Redemption Model: Always Performing?" In *Four Views on Moving Beyond the Bible to Theology,* edited by Stanley Gundry, 151–199. Grand Rapids: Zondervan, 2009.

————. *Faith Speaking Understanding: Performing the Drama of Redemption.* Louisville: Westminster John Knox, 2014.

————. *First Theology: God, Scripture and Hermeneutics.* Downers Grove: InterVarsity, 2002.

———. *Is There a Meaning in This Text? The Bible, the Reader, and the Morality of Literary Knowledge*. Grand Rapids: Zondervan, 2009.

———. *Remythologizing Theology: Divine Action, Passion and Authorship*. Cambridge: Cambridge University Press, 2012.

———. "Typology." In *Dictionary for Theological Interpretation of the Bible*, edited by Kevin J. Vanhoozer and Daniel Treier, 823–7. Grand Rapids: Baker, 2005.

———. "What is Everyday Theology? How and Why Christians Should Read Culture." In *Everyday Theology: How to Read Cultural Texts and Interpret Trends*, edited by Kevin J. Vanhoozer et al., 15–60. Grand Rapids: Baker Academic, 2007.

Van Houwelingen, P.H.R. "Contouren van een nieuw Jeruzalem: Hebreeën en openbaring over de eschatologische wereldstad." In *Het stralend teken: 60 jaar exegetische vergezichten van Dr. D. Holwerda*, edited by K. Van der Ziel and H. Holwerda, 186–203. Franeker: Van Wijnen, 2010.

———. "The Epistle to the Hebrews: Faith Means Perseverance." *The Journal of Early Christian History* 3 (2013) 98–115.

———. *Johannes: Het evangelie van het Woord*. Kampen: Kok, 1997.

———. "Riddles Around the Book of Hebrews." *Fides Reformata* 16 (2011) 151–62.

———. "Wij hebben hier geen blijvende stad," *Reformatie* 79 (2003) 49–52.

Vanhoye, Albert. *La Structure Litteraire de L'Epitre aux Hebreux*. Paris: Desclee de Brouwer, 1963.

Van Reest, Rudolf. *Schilder's Struggle for the Unity of the Church*. Translated by Theodore Plantinga. Neerlandia: Inheritance Publications, 1990.

Van Rijswijk, M. "Voorwoord." In *Wie is die man? Klaas Schilder in de eenentwintigste eeuw*, edited by M. de Jong et al. Barneveld: Uitgeverij de Vuurbaak, 2012.

Van Til, Cornelius. *A Christian Theory of Knowledge*. Phillipsburg: P&R, 1969.

Van 't Veer, M. B. "Christologische prediking over de historische stof van het Oude Testament." In *Van den dienst des Woords*, edited by R. Schippers, 117–67. Goes: Oosterbaan & Le Cointre, 1944.

Veenhof, C. "Church Polity in 1886 and 1944." In *Schilder's Struggle for the Unity of the Church*, by Rudolf van Reest, 459–64. Translated by Theodore Plantinga. Neerlandia: Inheritance Publications, 1990.

———. *Revelatie en Inspiratie: De openbarings- en schriftbeschouwing van Herman Bavinck in vergelijking met die der ethische theologie*. Amsterdam: Buijten & Schipperheijn Motief, 1968.

Veldhuizen, P. *God en mens onderweg: Hoofdmomenten uit de theologische geschiedbeschouwing van Klaas Schilder*. Leiden: J.J. Groen en zoon, 1995.

Veyne, Paul. *A History of Private Life: From Pagan Rome to Byzantium*. Harvard: Harvard University Press, 1987.

Vidu, Adonis. "Can We Say Very Much? Evangelicals, Emergents, and the Problem of God-Talk." In *Renewing the Evangelical Mission*, edited by Richard Lints, 226–49. Grand Rapids: Eerdmans, 2013.

Visser, Dirk. "Verwekte Sara een kind?" In *Ongemakkelijke teksten van de apostelen*, edited by P.H.R. van Houwelingen and Reinier Sonneveld, 131–3. Amsterdam: Buijten & Schipperheijn Motief, 2013.

Von Balthasar, Hans Urs. "*Dramatis Personae*: Man in God." In *Theo-Drama: Theological Dramatic Theory Vol. II*. San Francisco: Ignatius Press, 1990.

———. "*Dramatis Personae*: Persons in Christ." In *Theo-Drama: Theological Dramatic Theory Vol. III*. San Francisco: Ignatius Press, 1992.

————. "Prologomena." In *Theo-Drama: Theological Dramatic Theory Vol. I*. San Francisco: Ignatius Press: 1988.

————. *Theo-Drama, Theological Dramatic Theory Vol. V.* San Francisco: Ignatius Press, 2003.

Von Rad, Gerhard. *Genesis. A Commentary*. Philadelphia. Westminster Press, 1972.

Vos, Geerhardus. *Biblical Theology*. Grand Rapids: Eerdmans, 1980.

————. *Gereformeerde Dogmatiek*. 5 vols. Grand Rapids: 1896.

————. "The Doctrine of the Covenant in Reformed Theology." In *Redemptive History and Biblical Interpretation: The Shorter Writings of Geerhardus Vos*, edited by Richard B. Gaffin, Jr., 234–67. Phillipsburg: P&R, 1980.

————. "The Eschatological Aspect of the Pauline Conception of the Spirit." In *Biblical and Theological Studies*, edited by the Members and the Faculty of Princeton Theological Seminary, 209–59. New York: Charles Scribner's Sons, 1912.

————. "The Idea of Biblical Theology as a Science and Discipline." In *Redemptive History and Biblical Interpretation: The Shorter Writings of Geerhardus Vos*, edited by Richard B. Gaffin, Jr., 3–24. Phillipsburg: P&R, 2001.

————. *The Pauline Eschatology*. Phillipsburg: P&R, 1991.

————. *Reformed Dogmatics*, edited by Richard B. Gaffin, Jr. 5 vols. Bellingham: Lexham Press, 2014–2015.

————. "Running the Race of Faith." In *Grace and Glory*. Carlisle: The Banner of Truth Trust, 1994.

————. *The Teaching of the Epistle to the Hebrews*. Eugene: Wipf and Stock, 1998.

————. "'True' and 'Truth' in the Gospel of John." In *Redemptive History and Biblical Interpretation: The Shorter Writings of Geerhardus Vos*, edited by Richard B. Gaffin, Jr., 343–51. Phillipsburg: P&R, 1980.

Vuyk, C.M. "De zoon met de vader weggooien? De toekomst van christelijke traditie in een cultuur van neo-religiositeit." In *Het beloofde land? Christelijk belijden in een postmoderne eeuw: Een verkenning*, edited by J. Hoogland et al., 115–20. Leiden: Panoplia. 2003.

Wallace, Ronald. "Homiletics." In *The New International Dictionary of the Christian Church*, edited by J.D. Douglas, 479–80. Grand Rapids: Zondervan, 1978.

Waltke, Bruce. *Genesis: A Commentary*. Grand Rapids: Zondervan, 2001.

Webber, Robert. *Ancient-Future Faith: Rethinking Evangelicalism for a Postmodern World*. Grand Rapids: Baker, 1999.

Webster, John. "The Imitation of Christ." *Tyndale Bulletin* 37 (1986) 95–120.

————. "Principles of Systematic Theology." *International Journal of Systematic Theology* 2 (2009) 56–71.

Wells, David. *Above All Earthly Pow'rs: Christ in a Postmodern World*. Grand Rapids: Eerdmans, 2005.

————. *No Place For Truth: or Whatever Happened to Evangelical Theology?* Grand Rapids: Eerdmans, 1993.

Wells, Samuel. *Improvisation: The Drama of Christian Ethics*. Grand Rapids: Brazos, 2004.

Westcott, Brooke. *The Epistle To the Hebrews: The Greek Text With Notes and Essays*. Grand Rapids: Eerdmans, 1965.

Westfall, Cynthia Long. *A Discourse Analysis of the Letter to the Hebrews: The Relationship Between Form and Meaning*. New York: T&T Clark, 2005.

Wielenga, D.K. "Openbare belijdenis van het geloof." *Waarheid & Recht* 29 (1973) 25–33.

Williams, Michael D. *How to Read the Bible Through the Jesus Lens: A Guide to Christ-Focused Reading of the Scripture.* Grand Rapids: Zondervan, 2012.

————. "Theology as Witness: Reading Scripture in a New Era of Evangelical Thought Part 1: Christopher Wright, *The Mission of God*." *Presbyterion* 36 (2010) 71–85.

————. "Theology as Witness: Reading Scripture in a New Era of Evangelical Thought Part II: Kevin J. VanHoozer, *The Drama of Doctrine*." *Presbyterion* 37 (2011) 16–30.

Wilson, John. *Introduction to Modern Theology: Trajectories in the German Tradition.* Louisville: Westminster John Knox, 2007.

Woelfel, Craig. "The Varieties of Aesthetic Experience: Religious Experience and Literary Modernism." PhD diss., University of Norte Dame, 2012

Woodbridge, John D. "Some Misconceptions on the Impact of the 'Enlightenment' on the Doctrine of Scripture." In *Hermeneutics, Authority, and Canon*, edited by D.A. Carson and John Woodbridge. Eugene: Wipf and Stock, 2005.

Wright, Christopher. *Knowing Jesus through the Old Testament.* Downers Grove: InterVarsity, 1992.

————. *The Mission of God: Unlocking the Bible's Grand Narrative.* Downers Grove: InterVarsity, 2006.

————. *The Mission of God's People: A Biblical Theology of the Church's Mission.* Grand Rapids: Zondervan, 2010.

Wright, N. T. *The Contemporary Quest for Jesus.* Minneapolis: Fortress, 1996.

————. "Five Gospels but No Gospel: Jesus and the Seminar." In *Authenticating the Activities of Jesus*, edited by Bruce Chilton and Craig Evans, 83–120. Leiden: Brill, 1999. http://ntwrightpage.com/Wright_Five_Gospels.pdf.

————. "How Can the Bible be Authoritative?" *Vox Evangelica* 21 (1991) 7–32.

————. *Jesus and the Victory of God.* Minneapolis: Fortress, 1996.

————. *The Last Word: Scripture and the Authority of God. Getting Beyond the Bible Wars.* New York: HarperCollins, 2005.

————. *The New Testament and the People of God.* Minneapolis: Fortress, 1992.

————. *The Resurrection of the Son of God.* Minneapolis: Fortress, 2003.

————. *Simply Christian: Why Christianity Makes Sense.* New York: HarperCollins, 2006.

————. *The Way of the Lord: Christian Pilgrimage Today.* Grand Rapids: Eerdmans, 1999.

Yamauchi, Edwin. "Ezra-Nehemiah." In *The Expositor's Bible Commentary*, edited by Frank Gaebelein, 4.565–771. Grand Rapids: Zondervan, 1988.

Yarbrough, Robert. "God's Word in Human Words: Form-Critical Reflection." In *Do Historical Matters Matter to Faith? A Critical Appraisal of Modern and Postmodern Approaches to Scripture*, edited by James K. Hoffmeier and Dennis R. Magary, 327–44. Wheaton: Crossway, 2012.

Young, Frances. *The Art of Performance: Towards a Theology of Holy Scripture.* London: Darton, Longman and Todd, 1990.

NAMES INDEX

Adams, Jay, 114nn1–2, 119, 148n43
Altena, Bert, 178, 178n118
Anderson, Charles, 66, 144n28
Appignanesi,Richard, 170n82
Arthurs, Jeffrey D., 118n24, 122, 122n47, 144n31, 187n166
Attridge, Harold, 74n42, 106n82
Augustine, Saint, 45, 178, 178n119
Azurdia, Arturo, 174n103

Baars, Arie, 1, 1n2, 8n27, xvin10
Bailey, Kenneth, 36, 36n50
Barcellos, Richard, 12n54, 18, 18n74
Barr, James, 15n62
Barth, Karl, 4, 33n37
Barthes, Roland, 166–168, 166nn59–60, 167–168n67-68
Bartholomew, Craig G., 32–33, 32n35, 33n36, 148n41, 185n156
Bartow, Charles, 51n130
Bateman, Herbert, IV, 132n89
Bauckham, Richard, 79n70
Baudrillard, Jean, 155, 155n6–157, 179n125
Baugh, S.M., 70n21, 72n32, 75n46, 76, 76nn53–54
Bavinck, Herman, 9–10, 9n30, 28n18, 60, 72n33, 161, 161n39, 161n41, 190
Baxter, Richard, 119n30
Bayly, Timothy, 14n60
Beach, Lee, 182n144
Beale, G. K., 16, 30n24, 85n14, 183n149

Beeke, Joel R., 119n27, 119nn29–30, 120n33
Benedict, Pope (Joseph Ratzinger), 159
Berkhof, Louis, 9, 9n34
Berkouwer, G.C., 7n23
Bethge, Eberhard, 159n31
Biezeveld, K.E., 51n130
Blaising, Craig, 11n46
Blamires, Harry, 179n121
Bloedhorn, Hanswulf, 38n59, 39
Bock, Darrell, 132n89
Boersma, Hans, 3n8, 51, 51n126
Bonhoeffer, Dietrich, 159n31
Bos, C.G., 88n24
Bos, Rein, 2n3, 7n26, 19n75, 124–125, 124n60, 125nn63–64, 138n9
Braaten, Carl E., 51n127
Bray, Gerald, 21n88
Briscoe, Stuart, 117n17
Broadus John, 116n10
Brown, John, 40n67, 187n165
Bruce, Frederick Fyvie, 41n68, 84n10, 88n25, 97n58
Brueggemann, Walter, 87n19, 87n21, 104n75
Bullinger, Henry, 120nn33–34
Bullmore, Mike, 56n150
Bultmann, Rudolf, 52–53, 52n134, 157, 157nn16–18, 163
Burger, Hans, 48n115, 133n97
Burgess, Stanley, 140n19
Burns, Robert, 119–120
Buschel, Friedrich, 72–73, 72nn34–35

Calvin, John, xvin12, 28n18, 45–46,
  45nn92–96, 46nn99–100,
  120–121, 120n35, 120nn37–38,
  121n42, 185n157
Capill, Murray, 139n11
Carlson, Martin, 179n122
Carrick, John, 19, 19n77, 119, 119n25,
  145n34
Carson, Don A., 27n12, 167n62,
  184n154
Cary, Phillip, 125n63
Chapell, Bryan, 13, 13n56, 22, 116,
  116n10, 119, 177n111
Childers, Jana, 140n20
Childs, Brevard, 15n62, 20n84, 20n86
Clark, R. Scott, 33n37, 71n28
Clayton, Charles, 122n49, 167n61
Clowney, Edmund P., 12, 12n49, 83n3,
  116–117, 116–117nn11–12,
  119, 121–122, 122n45, 131n83,
  137n5, 139n15, 143n27
Cockerill, Gareth, 40, 40n66
Congar, Yves, 61n166
Corbett, Edward, 183n148
Croy, N. Clayton, 40, 40n65

Dabney, R.L., 117–118, 118n19
De Boer, E.A., 65
De Bruijne, Ad, 132–133n92
De Graaf, S.G., 27–28nn13–14, 56,
  56n153
De Jong, M., 3n8
De Leede, Bert, 110n91
De Ruijter, C. J., 2, 2nn3–4, 5n15,
  6–7n21, 28n18, 50n123, 54,
  54n140, 58, 58n157, 78n63,
  144n31, 147n39, 149, 149n45,
  161n37, 165n54, 185n158
De Vries, J.P., 4n11
Dekker, W., 159n24
Delling, G., 78
Dennison, Charles G., 12n48, 118n23,
  149n48
Dennison, James T., Jr., 9–10n35,
  10n37, 12n48, 12n54, 20n86,
  162n45
Dennison, W.D., 13–14n59, 13n55

Derrida, Jacques, 167n63, 170, 170n83,
  176
Dijk, K., 77n61
Dingemans, G.D., 158n19
Doriani, Daniel, 20n84
Douma, Jos, 2, 2n4, 2n6, 4n11
Dugdale, Eric, 39n56
Duguid, Iain M., 16n63

Edersheim, Alfred, 123n52
Edwards, Jonathan, 118
Eglinton, James, 10n39, 22n93
Ehrman, Bart, 174n106
Eisenbaum, Pamela, 141n21
Eliot, T.S., 168n69
Ellingworth, Paul, 41n68, 69n12, 77,
  77n60, 77n62, 80n74, 84n10,
  103n73, 106n81, 136n2,
  187n167
Eswine, Zack, 172n94

Faber, Jelle, 3n8, 5n16, 21n90
Fairbairn, Patrick, 130n82, 171n90
Feinberg, John, 161n38
Felperin, Howard, 166n57
Ferguson, Everett, 39n55
Fesko, John, 18n74, 20, 20n85, 108n88
Findlay, Gary, 148n43
Fish, Stanley, 170n81
Foucault, Michel, 154–155, 156n12,
  160, 160n34, 168–169, 168–
  169nn73–76, 168n71, 176n108
Frame, John, 173n99, 182n143
France, R.T., 65
Franke, John, 158n22, 166, 166n56,
  169n78, 173n100
Furley, William D., 42n80

Gadamer, Hans, 52n132, 167, 167n66
Gaffin, Richard B., Jr., 10n37, 12, 12n53,
  16n66, 125n61, 132n91, 162n45
Gamble, Richard C., 16n67, 173n97
Garratt, Chris, 170n82
Geertsema, H.G., 13n59
Gerkin, Charles, 174n101
Gibson, Scott M., 11n44, 32–33, 56,
  56n152, 116

Goheen, Michael W., 32–33, 32n35, 33n36, 148n41, 185n156
Goldsworthy, Graeme, 11, 11n45, 13, 13n57, 50n123, 56n149, 56n151, 123n54, 179n123
Goppelt, Leonard, 82, 82n1
Gordon, T. David, 144n30
Greidanus, Sidney, 2n3, 7n24, 13–14, 13n58, 14n60, 19, 19n75, 19nn78–80, 56n149, 66n5, 82–83, 83n2, 101n70, 138n9, 139n15, 140n18, 141n22, 164n51
Grenz, Stanley, 156n11, 158n22, 166, 166n56, 167n62, 173n100
Groothuis, Doug, 172n92
Grosheide, F.W., 40n63, 97n58, 136n2
Guthrie, George, 65, 74n40, 173n96

Hagner, Donald, 42n73, 181n139
Harinck, George, 5n13, 12n54, 21, 21n89
Harmon, William A., 167n63
Harnack, Adolf von, 52–53, 52n134, 157, 163
Harris, Max, 43n81, 45, 45n90
Hassan, Ihab, 154–155nn4–5
Hays, Richard, 55n146, 81n75, 184, 184nn151–152
Henderson, David, 181n136
Hinn, Benny, 139–140n17
Hirsch, E.D., 168n70
Hodge, A.A., 167n62
Hodge, Charles, 167n62
Hoekstra, T., 6n18, 114, 114n4, 117, 119, 119n26
Holwerda, B., 5n15, 9, 11, 11n42, 19–20, 19n81, 71n23, 124n59, 144n29, 147n38, 162n44
Hood, Jason, 126–127, 127nn69–70, 133n98
Horton, Michael S., xiiin1, 16n67, 24–26, 25–26nn1–5, 28–30, 29n19, 35n39, 37n52, 48, 53–54, 53nn135–136, 58, 58nn155–156, 87n23, 92n41, 96n52, 112n93, 112n95, 133n96, 137n6, 139n14, 140n19,

144n32, 146n36, 163n49, 165, 180n129, 180n133, 181n135, 187n167, 188, 188n170
Houtman, Piet, 15n61
Houwelingen, P.H.R. van, 70n19, 88n27
Hughes, Graham, 70n20
Hughes, R. Kent, 42, 42n76, 97n59, 103n74, 104n76
Huijser, J., 19, 66n7, 112n96
Hume, David, 156, 156n10, 156n12
Hyun, Yung Hoon, 5n14, 19n75, 22n92

Jakes, T.D., 140n19
James, Craig, 160n32
Jensen, Michael, 28nn15–17, 51n127, 53n135, 54n142, 59n160, 157n14, 182n145
Jewett, Robert, 69n14
Johnson, Dennis, 12, 12n50, 18n73, 37n53, 47n104, 57, 57n154, 93–94n44, 114n1, 129n75, 133, 133n95, 142n24, 144n32, 147n40
Johnson, Keith E., 177n113
Johnson, Luke, 40n64, 41, 41n69
Johnson, Terry, 14n60
Jones, Hywell, 40n67
Jones, L. Gregory, 184n153
Jones, Mark, 119n27
Jones, Peter, 158n23, 177n115
Jongeling, P., 4n11
Jonker, W.D., 13n59
Josephus, 42n75

Kallenberg, Brad, 53n138
Kaminski, Carol, 11, 11n44
Kant, Immanuel, 156, 156n10
Kapic, Kelly M., 154n3
Keller, Timothy, 12, 12nn51–52, 148n41, 183n150
Kierkegaard, Søren, 100–101, 101n69
Kistemaker, Simon, 39, 40n62, 73n36
Kleber, Jason, 162n46
Kline, Meredith G., 47, 47n107, 84n9, 88n28, 90n36, 92–93n42, 95n47, 108n88, 128n73
Klooster, Fred, 182n142

Koester, Craig R., 72, 72n31, 89n31, 104n76

Köstenberger, Andreas, 33–34, 34n38, 112n93, 114, 114n3, 126n67, 138n9

Krabbendam, Henry, 7n22, 138n9

Kranendonk, D.H., 142n24

Kruger, Michael, 171n91, 179n123

Kuiper, R., 3n7

Kuruvilla, Abraham, 87n22, 130n81, 139n15, 147n39, 165nn54–55, 167n65

Kuyper, Abraham, 3–4, 9, 9n31, 9n33, 22, 190

Kwakkel, Gert, 106n79, 170n80, 179–180, 179nn127–128

Laansma, Jon C., 65, 83n6

Lancaster, Sarah Heaner, 53n135, 61n166

Lane, William L., 42, 42n74, 65n2, 69, 69n11, 97n59, 136n2

Larsen, David, 163n48

Lawson, Stephen, 117n16

Leitch, Vincent, 168n69

Lessing, Gotthold, 52–53, 52n133, 148, 148n42, 154n3

Lewis, C.S., 183n147

Lewis, Peter, 119n28

Lindbeck, George, 26n7

Lints, Richard, 12n47, 61n169

Litfin, Duane, 140n20

Lloyd-Jones, Martyn, 117, 117n17, 119, 181n137

Long, Jimmy, 160n35, 178n117, 185n159

Longman, Tremper III, 36n47, 39n57

Loonstra, Bertus, 33n37

Lopez, Jess, 185n160

MacArthur, John, 117, 117n18

Macey, David, 171n86

Machen, J. Gresham, 73, 73n37, 157n15, 162n42, 164n53, 180n130

MacIntyre, Alasdair, 178n120

Marcel, Pierre, 116n9

Marx, Karl, 160

Mason, Matthew, 59n162

Mathewson, Steven, 139n12

Mayhue, Richard, 122, 122n46

McCartney, Dan, 122n49, 167n61

McCormic, Bruce L., 154n3

McGee, Gary, 140n19

McWilliams, David, 78n64, 81n76

Meijer, J., 92n40

Melville, Herman, 189n1

Menander, 39, 39n56

Meyer, Jason, 188n168

Michaelis, John David, 42–43

Middleton, Richard, 33–34,, 33n36

Moffat, James A., 41, 41n68, 41n70

Mohler, R. Albert Jr., 117, 117n16, 178n116

Morales, Michael, 142n23

Muether, John, 12, 13n55

Muller, Richard A., 9n34, 120, 120n34

Murphy, Nancey, 53n138, 167n62

Murray, John, 16n66

Netland, A Harold, 177n113

Nichols, Stephen, 32, 32n34, 54–55, 54n145

Nida, Eugene, 69n12, 77, 77n60, 80n74

Nietzsche, Friedrich, 159–160, 166

Nisbet, H.B., 148n42

Noordzij, D.W., 129n75

O'Brien, Peter.T., 41, 41n68, 71n25, 77, 77n59, 97n57, 104n76

O'Donnell III, Laurence, 9n30

Ohmann, H.M., 96, 96n54

Old, Hughes Oliphant, 118–119, 121–123, 121–122nn43–44, 123n52, 140n19

Olford, Stephen, 116, 116n9

O'Neill, J.C., 154n3

Osborne, Grant, 53n137

Osteen, Joel, 140n19

Paas, Stefan, 158n21, 159n31, 177n112, 179n126, 182–183n146, 186, 186n161

Park, Tae-Hyeun, 18n73, 120n31, 188n169

Parker, T.H.L., 121, 121nn40–41

Pasquarello III, Michael, 150
Patterson, Richard, 112n93, 114n3, 126n67, 138n9
Paul, 39–40, 43, 124, 126, 131, 133
Pederson, Randall J., 119n29
Peels, Eric, 87n20, 88n26
Pelton, Randal, 11n43, 51n125
Perkins, William, 119, 119n27, 119n29
Peterson, Eugene H., 139n12
Phillips, Richard D., 16n63, 41, 41n72, 91n38, 104n76, 172n92
Philo, 42, 42n75
Pink, Arthur, 97n58, 106, 106n83
Pipa, Joseph, 119–120, 119n28, 120
Piper, John, 56n147, 118–119, 118nn20–21
Plato, 45
Potter, Garry, 185n160
Poythress, Vern, 10n41, 84n11

Rabinow, Paul, 154–155n4, 154n2, 166
Radius, Marianne, 9–10n35
Ramus, Peter, 119n29
Ratzinger, Joseph, 159n28
Reeves, Michael, 36n48
Renninger, William, Jr., 7n23, 76n51, 124n59, 164n51
Rhee, Victor, 70–71, 70n15, 71n22, 73, 73–74, 73–74n39, 74n40, 75n44, 97n57
Ricoeur, Paul, 51, 51n129, 162, 162n43, 167n64, 168n72
Ridderbos, Herman, 9, 9–10n35, 9n32, 20, 133, 133nn93–94, 162, 162n45, 190
Robertson, O. Palmer, 132n90
Robinson, Haddon, 116, 116nn6–7, 139, 139n13
Rorty, Richard, 176n110
Rosenau, Pauline, 159n30
Rosscup, James, 11n43
Roukema, R., 9n32
Runia, K., 147n40
Rutherford, Samuel, 120n32
Ryken, Leland, 36, 36n47, 38–39, 38n54, 39n57, 120n32, 129n76

Samra, James, 126n66, 136n4

Sayers, Dorothy, 49–50, 49–50nn118–121, 61–62, 61n168, 164n53
Schaefer, Paul, 120n36
Schelhaas, J., 78n67
Schelling, P., 99n63
Schilder, H.J., 5n15, 41n71, 83n5, 124n58
Schilder, Klaas, 3–5, 4n12, 5n15, 7n23, 9, 19, 19n76, 21, 46, 47n103, 145, 163–164n50, 164n51
Schleiermacher, Friedrich, 51n127, 52n132, 157n14, 158n19
Schreiner, Susan, 45nn97–98
Schreiner, Thomas, 75n49, 79n71
Schreurs, Martin, 164n52
Selderhuis, H.J., 4n10
Sellers, Robert, 177, 177n114
Selvaggio, Anthony, 17–18, 18n72
Skarsaune, Oskar, 97n57
Slob, Wouter H., 160n33
Smelik, J., 95n50
Sneller, Rico, 1773n95
Sonderegger, Katherine, 157n14
Stark, Ciska, 110n91, 117n15
Stedman, Ray, 87–88, 88n25
Steiner, George, 166, 166n58
Stitzinger, James F., 122, 122n48
Stott, John, 116, 116n8, 171, 171n87
Stowell, Josh, 116n7
Strimple, Robert, 159n25, 159n27
Swain, Scott R., 33–34, 34n38

Te Velde, Mees, 4n11, 8n28, 142n26, 142n36, 148n41
Teunis, E., 111n92
Thayer, J.H., 78n67
Thiselton, Anthony, 40, 40n63, 160n36, 174n101
Thomas, Derek, 120–121, 121n39
Thompson, James, 69n13
Treier, Daniel, 124n57
Trimp, C., xiv, 1n1, 5n15, 7n25, xivn9, 13n59, 19, 20nn82–83, 46n102, 59n158, 83n7, 112n96, 131n86, 141n22, 142n24, 144n29, 150n50, 162n44, 181–182
Turretin, Francis, 72n33
Tyson, Lois, 171n86

Van Bekkum, Koert, 5n16
Van Bruggen, Jakob, 42, 42n74,
    42nn77–78, 68n9, 74n41,
    77, 80n73, 87–88n24, 94n45,
    112n97
Van de Kamp, H.R., 3n8, 42n74, 42n77,
    68n9, 74n41, 77n58, 127n71,
    128n72, 136n3
Van den Berg, H., 98n62
VanderKam, James, 90n36
Van der Welle, M.A., 17n71, 61n171
Van Deursen, Arie Theodorus, 3n9
Van Dijk, Douwe, xivn8, 9, 6, 6nn19–
    20, 9
VanDrunen, David, 33n37
Van Dusseldorp, Kees, 2, 2n5, 117,
    117nn13–14
Vanhoozer, Kevin, 24, 26–31,
    26–27nn6–11, 30n22, 31n31,
    43n81, 48, 51, 51n128,
    52n134, 54, 54n139, 54n141,
    54nn143–144, 59–61, 59n161,
    60n163, 61n166, 61n170,
    112n95, 127, 127n71, 131n85,
    135n1, 139, 139n16, 146n35,
    152n55, 165, 169n76, 170n81,
    171n89, 174n106, 179,
    179n124, 180n134, 181n138,
    182, 182n141, 185n158, 187,
    187nn163–164
Van Houwelingen, P.H.R., 70n19,
    76n50, 89n32, 94n46, 98n61,
    99n63, 172n93
Vanhoye, Albert, 73–74, 73–74n39,
    77n58
Van Omme, Anne Jacob, 21n89
Van Reest, Rudolf, xivn8
Van Rijswijk, M., 3n8
Van 't Veer, M.B., 5n15, 9, 66n5,
    124nn58–59, 144n29
Van Til, Cornelius, 12, 171n88
Veenhof, C., 4n10, 5n15, 161nn39–40,
    162n44
Veldhuizen, P., 164n50
Veyne, Paul, 41n72
Vidu, Adonis, 174n102
Visser, Dirk, 95n48

Von Balthasar, Hans Urs, 45, 45n91,
    48–49, 48nn109–114, 49n116–
    117, 97, 97n56, 151n54, 174,
    174n105
Von Rad, Gerhard, 87n23
Vos, Geerhardus, 3n8, 9–11, 10n36,
    10n38, 11–13, 12n53, 15–16,
    15n61, 16n65, 17n68, 21–22,
    21n87, 29, 29n20, 33, 33n37,
    36, 36n49, 44, 44n89, 46–47,
    46n101, 47n105, 77n61, 83n4,
    85n12, 90n34, 124n56, 130n79,
    149n47, 150n50, 162, 162n45,
    190
Vuyk, C.M., 155n8, 170n84

Walsh, B,, 33–34, 33n36
Waltke, Bruce, 87n23, 90n37
Webber, Robert, 169n79
Webster, John, 47, 47n106, 126n68,
    180n131
Wells, David, 160n32
Wells, Samuel, 32, 32n33, 48n108, 56,
    56n148, 127n71, 176n110
Wenham, Gordon, 87n19
Westcott, Brook, 77n57
Westfall, Cynthia, 75n45
Wielenga, D.K., 79–80n72
Wilhoit, James C., 36n47, 39n57
Willhite, Keith, 116
Williams, Michael, 30–31, 31n30, 52,
    52n131, 59n159, 60, 60nn164–
    165, 123n54, 162, 162n46
Wilson, John, 52n134
Woelfel, Craig, 158, 158n20, 176n107
Woodbridge, John D., 169n77
Wright, Christopher, 148n41, 181n137
Wright, N.T., 31–32, 31–32n32, 35n44,
    50, 50n122, 93n43, 96n55,
    108n87, 130n80, 138n10, 149,
    149n46, 159n26, 159n29,
    171n91, 185n155

Yamauchi, Edwin, 122n48
Yarbrough, Robert, 157n13
Young, Frances, 148n44, 180, 180n132

SUBJECT INDEX

Abel
  dramatic arc, 89n30
  as first martyr and witness, 78, 86,
    88, 134n99, 137
  links to resurrection, 89
Abraham
  eschatological vision, 94, 97–98,
    98n61
  faith-experience, applying
    homiletically, 96 , 99–100,
    138–39
  focus on in Hebrews, 93
  God's covenant promise to, 37,
    128–31, 130n78
  impotence, and Sarah's conception
    of Isaac, 95–96, 95n48
  journey, pilgrimage, 93–95, 98,
    98n62
Acts, and hearing God's Word, 163n47
Adam
  creation of in *imago Dei*, 35
  Enoch as descendent of, 90, 90n36
  exclusion from the Garden of Eden,
    79
  garden covenant, Christocentric
    nature, 85
  New Testament perspectives, 128,
    130
  and pattern of atoning sacrifice,
    134n99, 171
  typological approach to, 85
Adams, Jay, 114, 114n1
Altena, Bert, 178
Anderson, Greg, 66n4

anti-Semitism, in Hebrews, 42
application in preaching. *See* homiletic
    application
ark
  building of, and Noah's forward-
    looking faith, 92–93, 138
  Moses's, language used for, 105,
    105n78
Arthurs, Jeffrey D., 122
Article 31 of the Church Order, 4n1
The Art of Prophesying (Perkins), 119,
    119n27
atheism, postmodern views, 50n123,
    158n23, 186
Attridge, Harold, 106n82
Augustine of Hippo (St. Augustine), 45
authorship, authority associated with
  and evangelical postmodernism,
    169–70
  New Testament doubts about, 172
  and the postmodern "death of the
    author" paradigm, 166–69

Baars, Arie, 1, 8n27
Bailey, Kenneth, 36
baptism
  Jesus's, and crucifixion, 34, 41,
    108–9
  and water symbolism, 92n42, 108,
    113
Barcellos, Richard, 18
bare exemplarism, 67
Barth, Karl, 4
Barthes, Roland, 166–68

Bartholomew, Craig G., 32–33, 148n41
Bartow, Charles, 51n130
Bateman, Herbert, IV, 132n89
Baudrillard, Jean, 155
Baugh, S.M., 76
Bavinck, Herman
    criticisms of, 60
    on historical continuity and
        authority of Scripture, 161,
        161n39
    influence outside the Netherlands, 9
    organic metaphor, 10, 10n39
Bayly, Timothy, 14n60
Beale, G. K., 16
Belgic Confession of Faith, xviii
Benedict, Pope (Joseph Ratzinger), on
    the Jesus Seminar, 159
Berkhof, Louis, 9, 9n34
A Better Way: Rediscovering the Drama
    of God-Centered Worship
    (Horton), 23
the Bible. See Scripture, the Bible
biblical theology. See also Scripture, the
    Bible
    and absolute authority/strict
        adherence to Scripture, xviii
    and dualistic understandings of
        Scripture, 156–57
    as foundation for the RH paradigm,
        18
    and the historicity of the Bible, 159,
        161, 161n39
    and nuanced application of biblical
        texts, 127
    and systemic theology, 16–17
    and the themes of creation, fall and
        redemption, 163
    varying definitions of, 15, 15n61,
        16n66
Biblical Theology (Vos), 9–10, 16n66
Biezeveld, K.E., 51n130
biographical preaching, 140, 140n18
Blaising, Craig, 11n46
Bloedhorn, Hanswulf, 39
blood sacrifice, 87–88, 87–88nn23–24
Boersma, Hans, 51
Bonhoeffer, Dietrich, 159n31

Book of Praise: Anglo-Genevan Psalter
    (Hymn 43), 195
Bos, Rein
    on dormancy of discussions of RH
        preaching, 2n3
    on Israelogical reading of Scripture,
        124–25, 124n60
    on universalist approach to
        Scripture, 138n9
"bread of life" message, 36
Briscoe, Stuart, 117n17
Brown, John, 40n67
Bruce, Frederick Fyvie, 84n10
Brueggemann, Walter, 87n19, 87n21
Bullinger, Henry, 120nn33–34
Bultmann, Rudolf, 52–53, 157n14
Burger, Hans, 133n97
Burns, Robert, 119–20
Buschel, Friedrich, 72–73

Cain
    God's rejection of, scholarly
        discussions, 87–88, 87nn20–23
    Lamech as descendent of, 90, 90n36
    murder of Abel, 88
    sacrifices of, 86, 134n99
Calvin, John
    final testament, 121
    preaching approach, 120–21,
        121n42
    "theater" vocabulary, xvi, 45–46
canonical-linguistic theology
    the continuity of the Old Testament
        message, 171n91
    "cultural-linguistic" approach vs.,
        51n124
    and the language of God in
        Scripture, 26–27, 26n7
    overlaps with the DR paradigm, 31
Canons of Dordt, xviii
Capill, Murray, 139n11
Carrick, John
    on application in Reformed
        theology, 119
    on origins of the RH debate, 19
    on the Puritan explicato et applicatio
        paradigm, 145n34
Carson, Don A., 27n12

Cary, Phillip, 125n63
catechisms, as theological standards,
        xviii, 17
Chapell, Bryan
        Christ-centered preaching
                approach, 13, 22
        expository preaching, 116, 116n10
        homiletic application, 119
Charismatic/Pentecostal theology,
        140n19
cherem (total) judgment, and the
        destruction of Jericho, 109–10,
        109n89
chiastic structure, Hebrews 11, 73–74,
        97n57
Christ
Christ/Jesus. See also the drama of
        redemption (DR) paradigm;
        Jesus, historical
        as "anchor" for souls in Hebrews 6,
                71n29
        birth narrative, parallels with
                Moses, 142, 142n23
        centrality of in both Old and New
                Testaments, 8, 11, 55, 83–84
        command to disciples to mimic
                him, 127
        crucifixion, as form of baptism, 108
        crucifixion, as God' sacrifice,
                comparison with Abraham, 99,
                99n64, 100–101
        as the consummate pilgrim, 94
        as ethical model, 126
        first Adam as prototype for, 85
        genealogy of, Rahab's role, 110
        as human, and the dramatic
                unfolding of God's redemptive
                plan,
        incarnation and resurrection of, as
                the climax of the redemptive
                drama, 30, 35–36, 35–36n46,
                46–47, 96, 117, 172, 172n92,
                183
        leadership in heavenly worship, xiv,
                94, 137n5
        locating within the Old Testament,
                11, 20, 65, 70
        as perfecter/fulfillment of faith, 78,
                79–81, 93, 136–37
        response to shame and suffering, 40
        role in the creation, 84n10, 86n15
        role in the DR paradigm, 25, 54
        as truly faithful son of Eve, 89
        union with, as anchor for homiletic
                application, 115, 132–33
        use of parables, 36–37
Christ-Centered Peaching (Chapell), 13
Christian church, as actor on world
        stage, 43
Christians, early
        disdain for the theater, 45
        martyrdom, suffering, and displays
                of faith, 41–42, 112n93
        parallels with the Israelites, 124,
                124nn59–60
Christocentric theology. See also
        covenant theology
        and communicating hermeneutic
                and homiletic meaning of
                Scripture, 151–52
        Greidanus's homiletic focus on,
                13–14
        and integrating the RH and DR
                paradigms, 149, 175–76
        and typological understanding of
                Scripture, 124
Christus in zijn lijden (Schilder), 7, 19
the church
        as context for the drama of
                redemption, 53–54, 53nn137–
                38, 132, 179, 185, 185–87
        existence between Old and New
                Covenants, 125
        historic development, continuity
                of, 132
        importance of local leadership, 147
        including in the sermon, 57
        role as covenant partner and
                servant to God, 182
        role as a witness to history, 183
        as sacred theater, Calvin's view, 46
circumcision, 37, 123
cities, destruction of in the Old
                Testament, 109, 109n89

city of God
    in Hebrews compared with
        Revelations, 94n45, 99n63
    Moses's understanding of, 106
    and the promise of God to
        Abraham, 94
Clowney, Edmund P.
    on ministry of the Word in
        Deuteronomy, 121–22
    on redemption prior to Christ's
        coming, 131n83
    RH preaching model, 12, 116–17
    on the sacrifice of Isaac, 143n27
Cockerill, Gareth, 40
comedy, in Greek theater, 39n56
conception/birth, miraculous, 95–96
confessional theology, 61–62, 190
congregation. See hearers
consumerist approach to religion, 158
1 Corinthians
    eschatological parallels to Adam 85
    and obedience to God, 173
    typological approach in, 124,
        124n59
correspondences, typological,
    interpreting, 89n29, 125–26,
    129, 130n79, 172n92. See also
    imitation (typos)
Covenant and Eschatology: The Divine
    Drama (Horton), 23
covenant theology, covenant of
    redemption (pactum salutis)
    and the Bible as manifestation of
        redemption in space and time,
        86n15, 163
    Christ as the foundation for, 71
    covenant obedience, 25, 29, 146
    discussions about, 33n37
    and the doctrine of creation and
        re-creation, 128
    and the exclusion of Esau from, 102
    and the garden covenant with
        Adam, 85
    and God's adoptive relationship
        with Israel, 130–31, 130n78
    and God's promise of redemption
        after the fall, 86–87

    and God's promise to Abraham, 37,
        93, 99–100
    and God's supreme sacrifice, 100
    Kuyper's perspective, 3
    and mutual promises and
        obligations of God's covenant,
        146, 171
    and the prescriptive purpose of
        sermons, 115, 145n34
    Vos's perspective, 21–22, 21n87
    and the "Vrijmaking" (liberation)
        controversy, 3–4
the creation
    and the biblical language of
        imitation, 128–29, 128n72
    dramatic history of, 35
    echoes of in the destruction of
        Jericho, 110, 110n90
    and the garden covenant with
        Adam, 85
    and redemption, 133
    revelatory promise inherent in,
        84–85
    understanding of, in Hebrews 11,
        84–86
Creed or Chaos (Sayers), 49
creeds, importance of adhering to, 62
critical realism, 185n160
Critique of Pure Reason (Kant), 156
Croy, N. Clayton, 40

Dabney, R.L., 117–18
David, King, 103
de Bruijne, Ad, 132–33n92
Decades (Bullinger), 120n33
deconstructionism, 166, 167n63, 176
De Graaf, S.G., 27n13, 56
Delling, G., 78
Dennison, James T. Jr., 12n48
Derrida, Jacques, 170, 176
De Ruijter, Kees (C.J.)
    and God's call to participate in
        Scripture, 54
    homiletic synthesis of RH and DR
        themes, 147n39
    on problems associated with the
        historical gap between Scripture
        and hearer, 149

on purpose of sermons, 58
on RH approach to preaching, 2n3,
    165nm54
views on preaching, challenges to,
    2, 2n4
Deuteronomy, on application of the law,
    121–22
discipleship, and walking with God,
    127, 129n76
dispensational hermeneutics/
    homiletics, 10–11, 10n41,
    132n89
"The Doctrine of the Covenant in
    Reformed Theology" (Vos),
    21–22
Dogmatiek (Vos), 12
doubt/hopelessness, and the
    postmodern vision, 160,
    160n35, 172–73
Douma, Jos (Veni Creator Spiritus), 2,
    2n4, 2n6
drama, drama metaphor
    dogma juxtaposed against, 49
    epic vs., 28
    limitations of, 59
    Paul's use of, 43
    in postmodern rhetoric, 60–61
    story/narrative vs., 27
    value of, for homiletics, 23, 45, 175
    as valid metaphor for biblical truth,
        44
The Drama of Doctrine (Vanhoozer),
    28, 61
drama of redemption (DR)
    paradigm. See also imitation
    (typos); participation, active
    engagement
    acts and scenes in, 31–35
    as all inclusive, universal
        participation of humanity in,
        42, 142, 142n26, 180–82
    and Calvin's use of the theater
        metaphor, 45n92
    continuous unfolding of, 28,
        31, 34–35, 44, 149, 185–87,
        185n156
    as counterargument to
        postmodernism, 53, 178

defined, 25
development of within a
    postmodern context, 50
and the doctrine of creation and re-
    creation, 86, 86n15, 128–29
dramatic comedy, 89n30
epic (prepositional) theology
    contrasted with, 27–28, 27n13
and the faith of the Israelites,
    107–9, 125
and finding meaning in one's life
    story, 178
Holy Spirit as initiator of, 30, 55
homiletic value, 56–58, 62–63,
    62n169, 62n171, 135, 144,
    147–49, 150–51, 175–76, 179,
    187–88
Horton's theological exposition of,
    23–24
integrating/synthesizing with
    RH paradigm, summary and
    conclusions, 22, 25, 30–31, 51,
    56–57, 65–66, 66n5, 181–83,
    148n41, 154, 189–94
role of Abel, 88, 89n30
role of Abraham, 37, 93–95
role of Cain and Abel, 86–89
role of the creation and the fall,
    84–86, 86n15
role of the destruction of Jericho/
    salvation of Rahab, 109–11
role of Enoch, 89–91
role of historical context, 34–35
role of Isaac's sacrifice, 99–101
role of Israel, 35, 35n44
role of Moses, 104–7
role of Noah, 91–93
role of Sarah's miraculous
    conception, 95–97
roles of Isaac, Jacob, and Joseph,
    101–4
and slow and ever-unfolding plot
    development, 31, 47–49, 84, 129
theological limitations, 59
value of applying to Hebrews 11,
    145–46
Vanhoozer's goal in developing, 51
Dutch-Reformed theologians, 9, 145

Edersheim, Alfred, 123n52
education as path to truth,
    Enlightenment faith in, 156
Edwards, Jonathan, 118, 145
Ehrman, Bart, 174n106
Eliot, T.S., 168n69
Ellingworth, Paul, 69n12, 77, 84n10
Enlightenment rationalism, 51–52,
    51n130, 155–57
Enoch
    as descendent of Adam, 90, 90n36
    faith, 91
    imitating, 138
    Lamech's counterpoint to, 90
    as prototype for resurrection apart
        from death, 89–90
Ephesians, Calvin's sermon on, 121
Ephraim, Jacob's blessing of, 103
epic (prepositional) theology, 27–28,
    27n12
Esau, depiction of in Hebrews, 102
Eswine, Jack, 172n94
Evangelical Eloquence (Dabney),
    117–18
evangelical postmodernism
    approaches to biblical authority,
        167, 167n62
    and author's perspective on the RH
        debate, xviii
    dispensationalism in, 10–11
    emphasis of application over
        history, 165–66
    historical-critical approaches to the
        Bible, 51
    rejection of biblical inerrancy,
        169–70
evidence (ἔλεγχος) ("élenchos"), 68–69,
    72–73, 72n32
exegetical theology, 14–16
exemplarism (exemplarische) approach
    to Scripture
    bare exemplarism, 68
    cautions related to, 124n58
    criticisms of, 164
    Holwerda's use of term, 19
    as primary approach to Hebrews,
        66–67

and typological understanding,
    123–24
exodus
    as act in the drama of redemption,
        34
    as faith-journey, 107, 113, 124
    of Israel, and Moses-Jesus parallels,
        105–6
    Joseph's, and promise of ultimate
        return, 104, 141
    use of as term to describe Jesus's
        death, 104n76
explicato et applicatio paradigm
    RH approach contrasted with, 6,
        6n18
    value of, and need for nuanced
        approach to, 145, 145n34
expository preaching
    Chapell's definition, 116
    Nehemiah 8 as foundation for, 122
    role of application in, 116–17

Fairbairn, Patrick, 130n82
faith. See also drama of redemption;
        participation, active
        engagement
    Abel's compared with Cain's, 87–88,
        87n24, 88n25
    and hearing the Word, 163, 163n47
    Christ as fulfillment of, 12, 80–81,
        81n74
    Enoch's, and promise of
        redemption, 91, 138
    exemplaristic view, 66
    and homiletic emphasis on
        application, 115
    justification by, 14n60, 66, 131
    lived faith, 11, 26–29, 61, 86, 145
    and moving from protology to
        eschatology, 85
    Noah's, 92
    subjective and objective meanings,
        72–73
    and walking with God, 129nn75–76
    words used for in Hebrews, 69–73,
        73n38, 80, 136
faith heroes (Hebrews 11), 111–13,
    112n96. See also hall of faith

the fall, and God's role as rescuer, 34–
    35, 86, 128, 130, 134n90, 174
Fesko, John, 20
Foucault, Michel, 154–55, 160, 168–69
foundationalism, 166, 167n62, 173
Franke, John, 169n78
Furley, William D., 42n80

Gadamer, Hans, 52n132, 167
Gaffin, Richard B. Jr., 12
Genesis
    confession of Lamech in, 90
    and the exclusion of Adam from the
        Garden of Eden, 78–79
    lesson of tithing in, criticisms,
        139–40, 139–40n19
    thematic recapitulation in, 128–30,
        130n81
    unfolding of history in, 90, 90n36
    and the unified meaning of
        Scripture, 30
Gentiles, salvation offered in the story
    of Rahab, 111
Gereformeerde Kerken (GKv), 3, 4n1,
    6–7, 19–20, 23, 23n24
Gereformeerde Kerken in Nederland
    (GKN), xivn8, 3, 6
Gibson, Scott, 116
God's Word. See covenant theology;
    drama of redemption (DR)
    paradigm; Scripture, the Bible
Goheen, Michael W., 32–33, 148n41
Goldsworthy, Graeme
    on canonical unity of Scripture,
        56n151
    on macrotypology of RH approach,
        123n54
    on moralistic nature of Christ-
        centered approach to Old
        Testament, 11
    and revitalization of interest in RH
        paradigm, 13
    on the theological implications of
        postmodernism, 50n123
Goppelt, Leonard, 82
the gospel. See also New Testament;
    Scripture, the Bible
    mission in, 182

as vehicle for God's entry into
    history, 174
Gospel in the Old Testament series, RH
    approach in, 16
Greek theater, 39
"greeting" language, in Hebrews 13:24,
    98n60
Greidanus, Sidney
    biographical preaching, 140n18
    critiques of, 14, 14n60
    impact on Christ-centered
        preaching, 13–14
    on importance of Hebrews, 66n5
    on the RH debate, 2n3, 13, 19
    Sola Scriptura, 13
    on typological approach to the Old
        Testament, 82–83
    warnings about exaggerated
        Christology, 56n149
Grenz, Stanley, 156n11
Groothuis, Doug, 172n92
Grosheide, F.W., 40n63

Hagar, 95
hall of faith (Hebrews 11), xv, 84, 112,
    183
Harinck, George, 12n54
Harnack, Adolf von
    dualistic understanding of Scripture
        as "kernel" and "husk," 157
    influence of, Wilson's view, 52n134
    modernist approach to Scripture,
        52–53, 60
Harris, Max, 45
Hassan, Ihab, 154–55n4
Hays, Richard, 55n146, 81n75, 184
hearers. See also homiletics; preaching
    making sermons accessible to,
        119–20
    and purpose of homiletic
        application, 115
    role of, in preaching, 2
Hebrews
    christological focus, 71n29, 79,
        79n70, 81
    Christ as 'anchor' of souls,
        covenantal theology in, 171–72
    emphasis on imitation, 43

Hebrews (cont.)
  faith-journeys in, 41–42
  on hearing and listening to God's
      voice, 84, 171
  importance of Rahab in, 111
  Old Testament references in, 73n36
  references to the tabernacle in,
      70n19
  view of a suffering church, 39–40
Hebrews 11. See also covenantal
    theology; hall of faith
  Abel as first martyr in, 86
  and Abraham's faith-journey, 93–94
  authorship, origins, 65, 65n1
  demonstrations of Jesus's humanity
      in, 137
  emphasis on New Covenant over
      Old Covenant, 101
  Enoch as prototype for resurrection,
      89–90
  and the eschatological goal of
      creation, 84
  exegetical study of, summary,
      191–92
  exemplaristic view of, 66
  the faith of the Israelites, 107–9
  hermeneutic and homiletic intent,
      64–66, 85, 95–98, 97n57, 135–
      37, 144, 146, 150–52
  importance of Moses in, Moses,
      104–7
  interpreting/imitating, and the
      importance of nuance, 67, 137,
      140–41, 145–48, 151–52
  Isaac, Jacob, and Joseph, 101–4,
      140–41
  Jericho and Rahab's salvation,
      109–11
  listing of faith heroes, 111–13
  Noah as prototype, preview of
      redemption, 91–92
  objective interpretation, consistency
      with rest of Hebrews, 70
  as Old Testament commentary, 91
  and priority of redemptive
      revelation in, 67, 113, 141n21,
      146, 183
  proposed structures for, 73–75

  RH approach to, xiv, 66–67, 144
  scope and breadth of, 141n22
  translations/subjective
      interpretations, 68–69, 71–72,
      76
  typological approach, 82–83,
      178–79
Hebrews 12
  cautions about use of "our" in
      translations, 80–81, 81n74
  Christ as founder and perfecter of
      faith, 12, 77–78, 80
Heidelberg Catechism, xviii, 182n142
Hirsh, E.D., 168n70
historical-critical movement of biblical
    criticism, 51, 55n146
history, Bible historicity
  abstraction of moral truths from,
      165
  and the DR paradigm, 7, 28–29, 46
  God's authorship of, and universal
      salvation, 33–34, 177, 180, 194
  and the Jesus Seminar, 159
  the "knowable" now vs. the
      unknowable past, 149, 156–57,
      156n11
  postmodern view of as myth,
      154–161
  RH emphasis on, and preaching in
      the postmodern context, xviii,
      8, 162–63
  unity, integrity, and continuity in,
      4, 21, 37–38, 48–49, 149, 156,
      163, 161
  and universalist approach to
      Scripture, 138n9
Hoekstra, T.
  on application in preaching, 114,
      119
  on emphasis on Christ the
      redeemer, 117
  the Hoekstra homiletic, 6n18
Holwerda, B.
  "De Heilshistorie in de Prediking,"
      19–20
  imitation approach to Hebrews 11,
      147n38
  on importance of Hebrews, 66n5

on interpreting1 Corinthians 10:6,
    124n59
on the interruption of Old
    Testament prophecy, 11
narrow view of the RH paradigm,
    9, 144n29
Holy Spirit, overriding role in drama of
    redemption, 2, 55–56, 149–50,
    173–74
homiletic application. *See also*
    drama of redemption (DR)
    paradigm; imitation; preaching;
    redemptive-historical (RH)
    paradigm
    Calvin's emphasis on, 120–21
    and Chapell's definition of
        expository preaching, 116
    and Charismatic/Pentecostal
        theology, 140n19
    definitions, 114–15
    and embracing continuities with the
        past, 121, 148–51, 148n44, 164
    emphasizing throughout the
        sermon, 117, 145, 145n33
    and ethics, 116–17
    and examination of postmodern
        presuppositions, 178
    and illegitimate connections to
        Scripture, 139–40
    importance of, scholarly
        considerations, 116–18, 116n6,
        125–26, 144n30
    and the indicative/imperative
        relationship, 132–34, 133n96
    and integrating Old and New
        Testaments, 122–23, 142–44
    and integrating RH and DR
        approaches, 22, 147–48,
        148n41, 175–76
    modern commitment to, 119
    nuanced approaches to, 115, 137–
        42, 151–52, 192
    origins of the term, 118–21, 118n22
    and overcoming the "so-what
        hump," 117n17, 142, 142n24,
        145
    preoccupation with, criticisms of,
        165

purpose, 115
and skepticism about Scripture,
    170–71n86
and the value of the DH paradigm
    in, xvii, 144, 148–49
homiletics
    and approaches to interpreting and
        applying Scripture, xvii, xivn9
    biographical preaching, 140,
        140n18
    and the challenges of the
        postmodern context, 153–54
    and clarity about dogma, 62
    and countering anti-foundational
        postmodern views, 173
    and covenant partnership with
        God, 174–75
    diversity of possibilities for, 187–88,
        187n166
    modern, Vos's influence on, 11–12
    and need to creatively embody the
        Great Commission, 186–87
    postmodern questioning of
        historical truth and, 160
    relationship with other theological
        disciplines, 14–17
    and the RH debate, xiv, xivn9,
        13–14, 161
    rhetoric in sermons, 183n148
    and the role of the reader/hearer,
        165
    Spirit-innovated purpose, 57–58
Hood, Jason, 126–27, 127n70
Horen naar de Stem van God (de
    Ruijter), 2
Horton, Michael S.
    on the church as participant in
        the drama of the Bible, 53–54,
        53nn137–38
    influence of Von Balthasar on, 48
    on the interactive nature of
        theology, 28–29
    on irony of the isolation of early
        Christians, 112n93
    on need to surrender to God's
        unfolding drama, 58
    on the pastoral intention of
        Hebrews 11, 146

Horton, Michael S. (cont.)
   on the preoccupation with
      application in preaching, 165
   on the RH model, 188
   on the unified meaning of
      Scripture, 30
   use of DR vocabulary, 24–26
Hosea, actions demanded of, 38–39
Houwelingen, P.H.R. van, 70n19
Hughes, R. Kent, 42, 103n74
Huijser, J., 19, 112n96
Humanism, and faith in education, 156
Hume, David, 156
Hymn 43 (*Book of Praise: Anglo-
   Genevan Psalter*), 195
hypocrite (ὑποκριτής) (*"hypocritu"*),
   43–44, 44n88
hypostasis (πόστασις) (confidence), 71
Hyun, Yung Hoon, 22n92

Illegitimate Totality Transfer (ITT),
   83n8
Imago Dei
   and the creation of Adam, 35, 151
   and embodied readings of gospel,
      184
   implications for humankind,
      122n50
   and redemption, 134, 174
   and submission to God as the
      author of our lives, 175
imitation, mimesis (μιμέομαι)
   (*"mimos"*), links to drama,
   42–43
imitation (*"typos"*). *See also* typological
   approach to Scripture
   and Abel's faith-experience, 137
   and Abraham's faith-experience,
      138–39
   and conforming to the image of
      God's Son, 131–32
   discipleship, and walking with God,
      129n75–76
   and the doctrine of creation and
      re-creation, 128–29
   and Enoch's and Noah's faith
      experiences, 138

   as ethical instruction, Paul's
      emphasis on, 126
   of faith and righteousness,
      emphasizing in sermons, 142
   and God's ongoing shaping of
      lives in their own redemptive
      dramas, 42
   homiletic applications, nuanced
      approaches, 126–27, 136–38,
      145, 151–52
   and the intertwining of the
      indicative and the imperative,
      132–33
   and Jacob's faith-experience, 140–41
   and Joseph's faith experience, 141
   and justification by faith, 131
   and living in Christ, 133n97
   of local church leaders, 147n38
   and moralistic reductionism, 144
   and Moses's faith-experience,
      141–42
   of the saints, cohesion and
      continuity of experience of, 150
   and Sarah's faith-experience, 140
   and thematic recapitulation, 129–30
   and the typology of the saints, 137
Institutes (Calvin), theater/drama
   metaphor in, 45
the intentional fallacy in New Criticism,
   170–71n86
Isaac
   as God's covenantal gift to Sarah, 95
   name given, meaning, 96
   offering of, implications, 99, 139–
      40n19
   relationship to the unfolding drama
      of redemption, 101–2
   sons, and the blessing/election of
      Jacob, 102
   triumph over death, Jesus's triumph
      compared with, 96–97
Isaiah, actions demanded of, 38–39
Israel, Israelites
   crossing of the Red Sea, 35, 108
   failures of, as a nation, 107–8,
      131n83
   as God's adoptive family, 130–31,
      130n78, 132n90

lessons regarding redemption/
covenant renewal, 108, 129–30,
171
parallels with the situation of the
church, 124–25, 124nn59–60
and ritual continuity between past
and present, 37–38, 129–30
as the "son" of God in Hosea, 129

Jacob, faith-journey, 102–3, 140–41
Jericho, judgment and destruction of,
42, 109–10, 110n90
Jesus, historical, 157, 159, 159n26,
159n27. See also Christ/Jesus
Jesus Seminar, 159, 159n26, 159n27
Jewett, Robert, 69n14
Jews, 42, 65
1 John, mention of Cain in, 88
Johnson, Dennis
on active participation in faith,
129n75
on apostolic model for Christian
obedience, 133
balanced treatment of historicity
debate, 147n40
on the Christocentric hermeneutic
of the Old Testament, 57,
57n154
influence of Vos on, 12
on pilgrims as people of God,
93–94n44
and RH preaching in a modern
context, 18n73
Johnson, Luke, 40n64, 41
Johnson, Terry, 14n60
Jones, L. Gregory, 184n153
Jones, Peter, 158n23
Joseph
demonstration of faith, 104, 104n76
depiction of in Hebrews, 103
desire to return to the promised
land of Canaan, 103–4
faith-experience, applying, 130n81,
141
as symbol of hope of resurrection,
return to God, 103–4, 103n74
judgement, final, 92, 108

judgement, total ("cherem" judgment),
109–10, 109n89

Kaminski. Carol, 11
Kant, Immanuel, 156
Keller, Timothy, 12, 148n41, 183n150
"kerygma," in Scripture, 52, 52n134,
157
Kierkegaard, Søren, 100–101
Kistemaker, Simon, 39, 73n36
Kline, Meredith, 47
Koester, Craig R.
on Hebrews 11-12:24 as single
literary unit, 89n31
on Joseph's return to the promised
land, 104n76
on objective interpretations of
'hypostasis,' 72n31
on patristic interpretations of
Hebrews, 11, 72
Köstenberger, Andreas, 33–34, 114
Krabbendam, Henry, 7n22
Kruger, Michael, 171n91
Kuruvilla, Abraham, 87n22, 130n81,
147n39
Kuyper, Abraham, 3–4, 9, 9n31
Kwakkel, Gert, 170n80, 179–80

Lamech, as antichrist and counterpart
to Enoch, 90, 90n36
Lancaster, Sarah Heaner, 61n166
Lane, William, 42, 69, 136n2
Lawson, Stephen, 117n16
leader/chieftain (ἀρχηγὸν)
("archegon"), meanings of, 78,
78nn67–68
Lessing, Gotthold
on debates about historical facts,
154n3
and gaps between the Bible and
modern readers, 52–53, 148,
148n42
Lewis, C.S., 183n147
liberalism, modern
contrast with Christianity, 180n130
failure of, and postmodernism,
159n30
foundationless piety of, 180

liberalism, modern (cont.)
    Modernist theology, 157n14
    utopian thinking, 159–60, 160n32
Lindbeck, George, 26n7
Lints, Richard, 62n168
Litfin, Duane, 140n20
Lloyd-Jones, Martyn, 117
Long, Jimmy, 160n35, 185n159
Lopez, Jesse, 185n160
Luther, Martin, 20, 72

MacArthur, John, 117
Machen, J. Gresham, 73, 157n15,
    180n130
MacIntyre, Alasdair, 178n120
Manassah, Jacob's blessing of, 103
martyrdom, suffering
    Abel's, 86
    Christ's, 137
    of early Christians, 41–42, 112n93
    emphasis on in Hebrews, 40–43
    imitating, nuanced approaches,
        136–38, 147n38
    of the Israelites in Egypt, 106
    and the need to walk by faith, 146
    and participation in drama of
        redemption, 39–42, 40n63,
        131–32, 132n88
    and the promise of redemption,
Marxism, failure of, and turn to
        postmodernism, 159–60,
        159n30, 160n32
The Matrix (movie trilogy), 155n6
Mayhue, Richard, 122, 122n45
McWilliams, David, 78n64, 81n76
Menander (Thais), 39, 39n56
Michaelis, John David, 42
Middleton, Richard, 33–34
miracles, viewing as myth, 156–57,
        157n15
modernist approaches to Scripture
    emphasis on the individual, 174
    impact on preaching, 4
    and rationalist biases and
        presuppositions, 158
modernist approach to Scripture,
        theological limitations, 53–55
Moffat, James A., 41

Mohler, R. Albert Jr., 117, 117n16
moralistic/subjective preaching, 18, 144
morality, moral values
    and moralism, cautions about,
        126–27
    moral relativism, 176
    postmodernist perspectives, 176–78
    as relative, postmodernist views,
        155
Moses
    birth story, 104–5, 142
    faith-experience, vision, 106–107,
        106nn82–83, 107n84, 141–42
    life of, as preview of the life of
        Christ, 107, 142
    and the Passover event, 107
Muether, John, 12
Muller, Richard A., 120, 120n34
Murray, John, 16n66
myth, in Scripture, Bultmann's view,
        157

Nehemiah 8, 122
Neo-Kuyperian school of thought, 9
the Netherlands, and the RH preaching
        debate, xiv, 1, 3, 7–9, 164n51
New Covenant communities, 77–78,
        78nn63–64
New Criticism and the intentional
        fallacy, 170–71n86
New Testament. See also covenant
        theology; Scripture, the Bible
    allusions to Greek theater in, 39–40
    affirmations of the historicity and
        authority of the Old Testament,
        56, 85, 97, 123, 131, 161,
        161n39, 164n51
    as climax of covenant drama, Von
        Balthasar's view, 48–49
    discipleship, and walking with God,
        127, 129n76
    diverse homiletic styles in, 187–88
    and the doctrine of creation and
        re-creation, 128–29
    doubts about Jesus's authority,
        echoes of in secular
        postmodernism, 172–73
    gospel mission in, 182

gospel as vehicle for God's entry
into history, 174
"last days," continuous shift in
through time, 149–50, 149n47
and the unified meaning of
Scripture, 30
Nichols, Stephen, 32, 54–55
Nida, Eugene, 69n12
Nietzsche, Friedrich, 159–60, 166
Noah, 91–93, 92n40, 138
nomads *vs.*pilgrims, 182n44
Noordzij, D.W., 129n75
North American churches, homiletic
debates in, xivn9

obedience, Christian. *See also* God's
Word
apostolic model for, 133
and God's loving discipline, 132n88
and homiletic emphasis on
application, 115
O'Brien, Peter T.
interpretation of Hebrews 11, 77,
97n57
interpretation of 'hypostasis,' 71n25
on theatrical language of shame, 41
Ohmann, H.M., 96
Old, Hughes Oliphant
on application in the Pentateuch,
121–22
on historical continuity in
homiletics, 118–19, 121
on purpose of Old Testament
preaching, 122–23
Old Covenant ministries, warnings to,
65, 79–80, 98–99
Old Testament. *See also* New
Testament; Scripture, the Bible
allegorical *vs.* historical
understanding, 83
as Christocentric, and the unified
meaning of Scripture, 11,
11n43, 20, 30, 48
examples of application in, 121–22
historical context, and continuity
between past and present, 7,
37–38, 137–41, 161, 161n39,
164n51

perspective on by gospel writers,
55n146
preaching from, challenges, 11,
11n42, 65
saints, as witness and models,
66–67, 81, 81nn75–76
theological interpretation in
Hebrews, 70, 73n36, 83, 144
typological reading, 82–83, 136, 147
Olford, Stephen, 116
Orthodox Presbyterian Church, xviii
orthodoxy and orthopraxy, 26–27, 61
overstanding *vs.* understanding, 174–
75, 174n106

Paas, Stefan, 182–83n146, 186
parables, as dramatic teachings, 36–37
parishioners. *See* hearers
Park, Tae-Hyeun, 18n73
Parker, T.H.L., 121
participation, active engagement
and Christ's use of parables, 36–37
de-emphasis on in the RH
paradigm, 165
examples of in Hebrews, 37–38
and God's requirements of man,
xiii, 44, 48–49
and homiletic application, 57–58,
142, 142n26
integrating with imitation, 58,
133–34, 133n97
and lived faith/theology, 26–29, 61
and living in the "last days," 149–50,
149n47
and the Lord's Supper, 37
Paul's emphasis on, 39–40
and personal context for
experiencing Scripture, 53–54,
53nn137–38
sermons as summons to, 57–58, 181
the Passover, 37, 142–43, 143n27
patriarchs. *See* saints, patriarchs
Paul, apostle
emphasis on imitation, 126
and God's good work, 131
the indicative and imperative in
teachings of, 133
typological understanding of, 124

Paul, apostle (cont.)
  use of term "*mimos*" (imitate), 43
  use of term "*theatros*," 39–40
The Pauline Eschatology (Vos), 10
Peels, Eric, 87n20, 88n26
perceived facts *vs.* absolute truths, 156
perfector (τελειωτὴν) ("*teleiotes*"),
    eschatological connotation,
    79–80, 79n71
Perkins, William, 119, 119n29
persecution. *See* martyrdom, suffering
Pharisees, questioning of historical
    authority of Jesus, 172
Phillips, Richard D., 41
Philo, 42
Pilate, 172
pilgrims. *See also* Israel, Israelites
  Abraham as, 93–94, 98, 98n62
  Jesus as, 94
  nomads *vs.*, 182n44
  as people of God, 93–94n44
Pilgrim Theology (Horton), 26
Pink, Arthur, 106, 106n83
Pipa, Joseph, 119–20
Piper, John, 118, 118n21
"plain style" preaching (Perkins),
    119n27
Plato, 45
postmodernism
  as anchorless, 160
  and canonical-linguistic theology,
    26n7, 51n124
  and consumerist approach to
    religion, 158
  and "critical realism," 185n160
  defining, intrinsic challenge of,
    185n159
  and despair, hopelessness, cynicism,
    178
  destruction of concepts of history
    and authorship, 51, 55, 162,
    167, 170
  and the DR paradigm, 50–51, 53,
    60–61
  homiletics/pastoral ministry
    within context of, xv, 153–54,
    161, 163–64, 173, 179n121,
    179n126, 193

identifying future intellectual
    movements, 185–86
  moral implications, 176–78,
    176n107, 176n108
  multiple faces and expressions of,
    153n1, 185–86
  New Testament parallels, 172
  positive contributions, 158, 158n22
  and the replacement of God by the
    individual, 50n123, 55, 165, 174
  roots in modernism and
    Enlightenment philosophy,
    155–56, 172–73
Potter, Garry, 185n160
Poythress, Vern, 10n41
practice, religious. *See* participation,
    active engagement
preachers/pastors. *See also* homiletics;
    preaching
  Calvin's definition, 120
  and the importance and value of
    diversity, 6
  improvisation by, 185–86
  role of, in DR paradigm, 59,
    59n160, 59n172, 62n169
  skills needed by, 148n44
preaching. *See also* homiletic
    application; imitation
  and the application bridge, 148–49,
    148n44
  as an art as well as science, 187–88
  and communication of ultimate
    meanings, 189
  and the creation as starting point,
    86
  definitions, xiii, xiiin1
  as a dramatic action, xiii, 50–51
  effective, and adherence to
    theological traditions, 56n151,
    62–63, 62n171, 69n169, 163,
    170–76
  emphasizing participation in and
    living faith, 44, 178, 179, 181,
    185
  as a manifestation of God's word,
    xiii
  and Moses's ministry, 107

in postmodern context,
contributions of RH paradigm,
161
responsibility of, xiii
RH vs. the exposition and
application approach, 6
and the role of culture in, 183n150
and the role of the reader/hearer,
165
simple, in the Puritan tradition,
119–21
and stale orthodoxy, 49–50
and value of typological approaches,
83
and the "Vrijmaking" (liberation)
controversy, 3–4
Preaching and Biblical Theology
(Clowney), 12
Progressive Dispensationalism, 132n89
Prolegomena (Bavinck), 9
propositionalist approach to theology,
16–17, 51–54, 59–60
prosperity preachers, 140n19
Protestant Scholastic preaching, 119–
20, 120n32
Psalms 68:3, 71n24
Puritan tradition, Puritanism, 18n73,
119–21, 145n34

Rahab, salvation of, 110–11
Ramus, Peter, 119n29
rational biblicism, 158
reader-response hermeneutic, 166–69,
168n70, 169n76, 169n78. *See
also* postmodernism
The Reading and Preaching of Scriptures
(Old), 118–19
reason, faith in, 155–56, 170, 174
redemption, salvation, *See also
the* Christ, Jesus; drama of
redemption (DR) paradigm;
redemptive-historic
redemptive-historical (RH) preaching
paradigm/movement
complexity of, 5–6, 131n86
contemporary expressions, 12–13,
18–19, 18n73

critiques, 2–8, 7n22, 8n28, 14n60,
124, 145, 147n40, 161
Dutch version *vs.* broader
expressions, 1, 8–9
focus on historic continuity within
Scripture, 5, 8, 31, 83, 130, 135,
161
Greidanus's influence, 13–14
historical background/origins, 5,
5n15, 8, 10, 20, 161, 162n44
homiletics and, 11, 15, 56–57, 116–
17, 147–48, 165, 175–76
interpretations of Hebrews, 11,
66–67, 69n10, 144
judging, context for, 164, 164n51
as manifestation of biblical/
covenantal theology, 4, 11,
16–18, 22, 55, 161, 163, 190
and "neo-orthodox" approaches,
4–5, 4n11
newness of, 17–22
nod to in the *Gospel in the Old
Testament* series, 16
nod to in the *Reformed Expository
Commentary* series, 15
synthesis with DR paradigm,
xvi–xvii , 22, 30, 56–59, 65–66,
66n5, 147–48, 148n41, 154,
181–83, 189–94
and the understanding of biblical
commands, 123
Red Sea crossing, 38, 41, 92n42, 108,
142–43
Reformation, Christocentric
hermeneutic during, 20
Reformed Theological Seminary,
Orlando, 12
Reformed theology/homiletics, 4, 10,
119–20, 120n34
religious subjectivism, 162n44
Renninger, William, Jr., 76n51
resurrection. *See also* imitation (typos);
martyrdom, suffering
Abel's links to, 89
Christ's, as theme linking all of
Scripture, 10, 30, 34, 36, 75,
101, 111–13, 125
Enoch's, 89–90

resurrection (cont.)
  in final verses of Hebrew 11, 111
  and God's promise to Abraham,
    94, 97
  and Joseph's return to Canaan,
    103–4, 103n74
  and living in the "last days," 149–50,
    149n47
RHD (Redemptive Historical Dutch),
  defined, 9n29
RH debate. See redemptive-historical
  (RH) preaching paradigm/
  movement
Rhee, Victor, 70–71, 70n15, 73–74
  97n57
Ricer, Paul, 51, 162, 168n72
Ridderbos, Herman, 9, 133, 162
Ridderbos, J., 20
Robertson, O. Palmer, 132n90
Robinson, Haddon, 116, 139
Romans, 85, 131
Rosenau, Pauline, 159n30
rose seed metaphor, 10
Rosscup, James, 11n43
Rutherford, Samuel, 120n32
Ryken, Leland, 36, 38–39

sacrifice, atoning. See also martyrdom,
  suffering
  Abel's compared with Cain's, 87
  and Abraham's sacrifice of Isaac,
    100
  and Adam, after the fall, 134n99
  blood, in the Old Testament, 87n23
saints, in Hebrews 11
  as belonging to the past, 113
  in exemplaristic interpretations,
    66–67
  imitating faith and perseverance
    of, 76–77, 82, 115, 136–37,
    136nn2–3
  as witness to and participants in the
    drama of redemption, 76– 78,
    78nn63–64, 81–82, 81nn75–76,
    97–98, 183
saints, patriarchs
  as audience/onlookers, Calvin's
    view, 46

and dramatic actions of the
  prophets, 38
faith and eschatological vision, 94
"salvation-historical" theology. See
  redemptive-historical (RH)
  preaching paradigm/movement
Samson, 111
Sarah
  demonstration of disbelief, lack of
    faith, 95, 95n50
  in Hebrews 11, 140
  and lesson of God's promise, 95–96
  as matriarch of the faithful and the
    church, 95n51
  relationship with Hagar, 95
Sayers, Dorothy, 49–50, 61–62
Schilder, H.J., 5n15, 41n71
Schilder, Klaas
  on application throughout the
    sermon, 145
  Christus in zijn lijden, 7, 19
  covenant theology of, 21–22, 21n90
  as the father of the RH movement, 5
  on the importance of history in
    preaching, 164n51
  leadership style, behavior, 3
  narrow view of the RH paradigm, 9
  orthodox, Protestant theology of, 21
  on paradox, 4–5
  on salvation as happening within
    history, 46–47, 163–64n50
  sermons, complexity and obscurity
    of, 5, 5n16
  and the "Vrijmaking" (liberation)
    controversy, 3–4
Schleiermacher, Friedrich, 52n132,
  157n14
Schreiner, Thomas, 79n71
Scripture, the Bible. See also dramatic-
  redemptive (DR) paradigm;
  homiletics
  applicability to all of humanity,
    138n9, 180
  commands in, obedience to, 115,
    122–23, 138–39
  confessional readings of, 62

covenantal continuity and integrity
of, 4, 31, 35, 47, 55, 115, 150,
161, 163–64
and the "death of the author
paradigm," 167, 167n62
divine authorship and authority of,
8, 26n7, 51, 55, 116, 138–39,
149, 168–71, 169n78, 171n88,
173
and the doctrine of creation and
re-creation, 128–29
dramatic structure, dramatic
metanarrative, 27n13, 32,
44–47, 125, 165, 175
dualistic understandings, 156–57
Enlightenment approaches,
evangelical criticisms, 51–52,
51n130
exemplars in, importance of
nuanced use, 123
existential perspectives, evolution
of, 155–58
God's call to become active
participant in, 28–29, 53–54,
53nn137–38
God as the primary subject of,
163–64, 174
God's message in, preaching in the
postmodern context, 170–76
hermeneutic and homiletic
purposes, xiv, 123n54, 170–76
historical unity and continuity,
51–53, 148, 161–63
as inclusive, Spirit-innovated
purpose, 58–59
interactive relationship with,
181–83
interpretive distinctions, 83–84,
83n8
message and mission, Wright's
summary, 181n137
metaphors in, 23
modernistic, critical approaches,
4–5, 52–53
moralistic interpretations, debates
about, 8–9
readers' role in interpreting, 170n80

rose seed metaphor for revelation,
10
separation of reader from,
modernistic methods, 52
as single, unified revelation, 15–16,
22, 30, 56, 149, 161, 161n39,
179
Spirit-directed, 25
thematic recapitulation in,
examples, 129–30
time markers in, 87n19
as tool for sustaining the
foundations of the church, 4
typological approach to, 8–9,
121–34
Von Balthasar's view of as unfolding
participatory drama, 48–49
sea/water imagery and metaphors,
92–93n42, 108–9
Second Helvetic Confession, xiii,
120n34
Sellers, Robert, 177
Selvaggio, Anthony, 17–18
sermons. *See* homiletics; preaching
shame, human, as part of the drama of
redemption, 39–42
Skarsaune, Oskar, 97n57
skepticism, modern/postmodern, 156–
58, 157n15, 158n19, 184
Sola Scriptura (Greidanus), 13
Stark, Ciska, 117n15
Statenbijbel, 69, 71, 71n24
Stedman, Ray, 87–88, 88n25
Steiner, George, 166
Stitzinger, James F., 122
Stott, John, 116, 171
Stowell, Josh, 116n6
struggle, adversity. *See* martyrdom,
suffering
subjectivism, 157n14. *See also*
postmodernism, secular
substance (ὑπόστασις) ("*hypóstasis*")
in Hebrews 11, 68–70
objective understandings, 72n30,
72n31
translations of, 69–72, 71nn24–27
suffering. *See* martyrdom, suffering
Swain, Scott R., 33–34

Swain, Scott R. (cont.)
the synagogue, preaching in, 122–23, 123n52
systematic theology. *See* propositionalist approach to theology

Te Velde, Mees, 8n28
textual meaning, as uncertain, postmodern perspectives, 166–67, 170
Thais (Menander), Paul's quotations from, 39
theater, Greek, New Testament allusions to, 39–40
thematic recapitulation, 129–30
theo-drama. *See also* dramatic-redemptive (DR) paradigm
lack of dogmatic clarity, 61–62
Sayers's views on, 49–50
Scripture as, 111–12, 112n95
Vanhoozer's rhetoric around, 61
Von Balthazar's views on, 48–49
Wright's views on, 50
Theo-Drama (Von Balthasar), 48–49
theological-rhetorical paradigm, 61
Thiselton, Anthony, 40
Thomas, Derek, 120–21
Thompson, James, 69n13
Three Forms of Unity, xviii
time, language related to in Scripture, 87, 87n19
Titus, Paul's instructions to, 126
Treier, Daniel, on uses and definitions of biblical typology, 124n57
Trimp, C.
on the Christological focus of RH interpretations of Hebrews 11, 144
concept of "omgang" (concourse, fellowship), 59n158
contributions to the RH debate, xiv–xv, 1n1, 19–20, 162n44
critiques of Holwerda and Van 't Veer, 144n29
on nuanced understanding of continuity with the past, 150n50

on relationship between *ordo salutis* and *historia salutis*, 131n86
on scope and breadth of Hebrews 11, 141n22
truth
historical, and questions about authorship and authority, 172, 172n92
objective, postmodernist intolerance for, 177
Turretin, Francis, 72n33
typological approach to Scripture. *See also* imitation
application to Hebrews 11, 82
and Christocentric revelation, 124
Fairbairn's comments on, 130n82
and "by faith" references in Hebrews, 135
and God's adoptive relationship with Israel, 130, 130n78
and imitation of New Testament leaders, 126
and the Israelites as God's adoptive family, 130–31
and Jesus as the ultimate type, 137
pitfalls, 139–40, 139n15
and selectivity in application of specific narratives and commands, 123–26
and thematic recapitulation of the creation, re-creation doctrine, 129–30
Vanhoozer's definition, 135n1

universalism, universalist principles, limitations of, 138n9
utopias, secular, failures of, 159–60, 160n32

Van Bruggen, Jakob
on interpretation of "*hypostasis*," 68n9
on martyrdom experienced by the newly converted, 42
on saints in Hebrews 11 as witnesses, 77, 80n73
Van de Kamp, H.R., 128n72
Van Dijk, Douwe, 6, 9

Van Dusseldorp, Kees, 2, 117
Vanhoozer, Kevin
  on the anarchy inherent in
    postmodernism, 169n76
  on the biblical drama as the only
    drama, 30, 179
  criticisms of propositional theology,
    59–60
  definition of typology, 135n1
  on demythologizing approaches to
    Scripture, 52n134
  de Ruijter's synthesis of, 149
  on epic approach to theology, 28
  on God as bridge between past and
    present, 174
  on the gospel as a mission
    statement, 182
  importance of understanding
    contemporary culture, 152n55
  influence of Von Balthasar on, 48
  lack of dogmatic clarity, 61–62
  meaning of the word "drama" for,
    27–28
  and narratives of redemption,
    30n22, 31
  on overstanding vs. understanding,
    174–75, 174n106
  on passive approaches to systematic
    theology, 165
  on the propositionalist approach to
    theology, 54
  on role of pastors, 62n169
  Scripture as historical theo-drama,
    112n95
  theological traditions advocated
    by, 61
  on using the DR paradigm, benefits
    and cautions, 24, 26–27, 51,
    61n166
Vanhoye, Albert, 73–74
Van Til, Cornelius, 12
Van 't Veer, M.B.
  cautions about exemplarism in
    preaching, 124n58
  on limitations of the RH paradigm,
    9, 144n29
  on RH meanings in Scripture, 10,
    66n5, 124n59

Veenhof, C., 161n39
Veni Creator Spiritus (Douma), doctoral
    thesis incorporating RH
    preaching, 2, 2n6
Veyne, Paul, 41n72
Visser, Dirk, 95n48
Von Balthasar, Hans Urs, 45, 48–49, 97
Von Rad, Gerhard, 87n23
Vos, Geerhardus
  on the coming of Christ as the
    denouement of the drama of
    redemption, 149n47
  and the contributions of the RH
    paradigm to reenergizing
    evangelical theology, 162
  covenant theology of, 21–22, 21n90
  on the dramatic structure of
    Scripture, 33, 44
  eschatological orientation, 33, 47,
    47n105
  emphasis on unity of Old and New
    Testaments, 11
  on the history of covenant theology,
    21
  impact on homiletics, 13
  legacy, 9–12, 15
  in living now in the New Testament,
    150n50
  on newness of biblical theology, 21
  orthodox, Protestant theology of,
    16n66, 21
  The Pauline Eschatology, 10
  on saints in Hebrews, 83n4
  seed metaphor, relationship to
    drama metaphor, 10, 46–47
  support for the covenant of
    redemption concept, 33n37
  on typology in Hebrews, 85n12,
    124n56
  use of term "biblical theology," 15,
    15n61
"Vrijmaking" (liberation) controversy,
    3–4

Walsh, B, 33–34
war, just, and God's judgment of
    Jericho, 110
Webster, John, 47, 126n68

Wells, Samuel, 32

Wenham, Gordon, 87n19

Westminster Confession of Faith, as theological standard, xviii

Westminster Shorter Catechism (WSC), 29n21, 35n40, 35n43

Wielenga, D.K., 79–80n72

Willhite, Keith, 116

Williams, Michael
on the contributions of the RH paradigm to evangelical theology, 162
on the dramatic history of redemption, 30–31
on evangelical critiques of enlightenment rationalism, 52
on propositionalist approaches to Scripture, 60, 60n165

Wilson, John, 52n134

witnesses. *See* saints in Hebrew 11

Woelfel, Craig, 158

Word of God. *See also* Scripture, the Bible
as basis for all creation, 84
Christ as, emphasis on in Hebrews, 81

communicating clearly, xiii, 184
as the foundational speech-act, postmodern struggles with, 166
hearing, as the basis of redemptive faith, 163, 163n47, 171, 181
and Scriptural application and imitation, 121–22, 122n51

worldview evangelism, 184, 184n154

Wright, Christopher, 148n41, 181n137

Wright, N.T.
on Abraham's journey of faith, 93n43
on the centrality of the story of Israel, 35n44
on the dramatic structure and language of Scripture, 31–32, 31–32n32, 50
on methodology of the Jesus Seminar, 159n26
on modern hearer's participation in the drama of redemption, 149
on wilderness metaphors, imagery, 107n87

Young, Frances, 180

SCRIPTURE INDEX

OLD TESTAMENT

Genesis

1-2	85n13
1:2	110n90
1:6	108
1:26	128
3, 79	128
3:15	30, 86n17, 88, 90–91, 171
3:17	87n22
3:21	87, 87–88n24
3:24	79
3:31	134n99
4:1	86
4:3	87, 89n29
4:4	86, 87, 87n20
4:4-6	87
4:8	86
4:10	86n16
4:15	90
4:24	90
5	91
6:9	91
12	93
12:2	95n49
12:7	95n49
15:5	95n49
17:1	91, 129
17:7	37
17:17	96n53
18:10-14	95n48
18:12	96n53
22, 99–100	99nn64–65, 101, 139–140, 139–140n17, 139n15, 143n27
22:17	100
23:4	98n62
24:60	100n67
25:23	103
33	102n71
36	102n71
40:4	87n19
47:8	98n62
47:31	103n72
50:24-25	103, 129n77

Exodus

2:2	105
2:8-9	105
2:14	107n84
4:22	130n78
4:31	104
6:7	146
12:26-27	37
13:19	104, 129n77
14:1-11	107n86
14:21	108
14:22	108

Leviticus

2:14	87n23
26:12	146

Numbers

1:16	78n68
2	78n68
3:32	78n68
7	78n68
9:2	87n19

Deuteronomy

4:24	108
20:17	109n89

Joshua

2:10	109n89
4	37
4:21-24	38
6:2	109
6:15-16	109
21	109
24:32	129n77

2 Chronicles

3:1	100n68

Nehemiah

8	122
8:1-8	122
8:8	122

Psalms

1	122n51
2:4	96

19	35n42, 86n15
22:1	137n5
68:3	71n27
95	171
103:13	131n84
119	122n51
19:5	120n35
138:1	46

Isaiah

20:1-6	38

Jeremiah

13:1-7	38
17:19-27	38
19	38
27	38
30:22	146
31	74
32:1-25	38
51:59-64	38

Ezekiel

12:11	38
26:28	146

Hosea

11:1	106n79, 129

Habakkuk

2:4	74-75, 86n16

NEW TESTAMENT

Matthew

1:5	110
2	141
2:15	106n79, 129
3-4	41
3:15	99
5:48	132n87
23:35	86
28:20	150

Mark

1:37	126
6:49	126

Luke

3:38	128
9:23	127n71
9:31	104n76
12:50	108

24:26   132n87   10:17   163n47

John

1	89, 126, 134
1:1-14	86n15
1:14	30n26
1:36	107n85
3:16	14n60, 99, 99n64, 100, 101
6	36
6:32	36
6:55	36
8:32	181
8:56	98
14:2	94
14:6	172n92
15:3-5	176
17:1	34
17:3	35n41
17:5	33
18:36	94
18:37	172
18:38	172

Acts

2	163n47
3:15	78
6	163n47
7:20	105n77
13	163n47
19:29-31	39
20:26-27	122n46
35:31	78

Romans

4	99
4:18-22	95n48
5:14	85, 124n56, 128
6:1-4	108
8:28-30	131
8:32	100
8:35	86
9	102
9:10-12	102
10:6-8	174n104
10:15	194

1 Corinthians

2:14	173
4:6	127
4:9	39, 39n57
4:16	40, 43
5:7	107n85
10	66, 143
10:2	41, 108, 125n62
10:6	124, 124n59
10:11	125n65
10:16	37
11:1	43, 127
15:33	39
15:45	85, 128

2 Corinthians

1:20	100n66
5:4	30n29
9:14	72n30
11:17	72n30

Galatians

1:4	132
3:26	37
4:4	30n23, 46, 88, 89n29, 96

Ephesians

1:11	35
3:10	46
5:1	43, 127
5:1-2	134

Philippians

2:5-8	30n27
3:17	127

Colossians

2:11	108
3:9-14	30n28

1 Thessalonians

1:6	43
	2:14, 127
4:13-18	138n8
4:17	90n35
6:12	43

2 Thessalonians

3:7	43n82
3:7	127
3:9	126, 127

1 Timothy

1:2	73n38
1:10	17n70
3:9	73n38
4:1	73n38
4:12	126
6:10	73n38
6:21	73n38

2 Timothy

2:15	xiiin1
3:16	122n51
3:16-17	150n49

Titus

1:9	17n70
2:1	17n70
2:5	108
2:7	126

Hebrews

1:1	69n10, 71n25, 76
1:1-2	81, 151
1:1-3	70, 70n18, 146,
	150n49, 191
1:2	69n12, 80
1:3	xiii, 69n12, 70, 71n25,
	73, 89
2:7-9	137
2:10	78
2:11	98
2:11-12	137
2:14	40

3-4	106, 110, 125n61
3:14	70-73
4:2	136
4:10	143, 184
4:12	171
4:13	172
4:15	137
5:8	132n88, 137
6:9	71n29
6:11-12	136
6:12	42, 43, 43n83, 127,
	136n3, 142n25, 145,
	147, 151
6:13	37
7:8	76
7:17	76, 76-77n55
8:5	124n56
9:11-14	74
9:12	107n85
9:14	107n85
10	74-76
10:1-18	74
10:5-10	35n41
10:15	76
10:19	107n85
10:19-25	74
10:26-31	143, 150
10:29	108
10:30-31	75
10:32-33	40
10:32-39	74
10:33	39n57, 43
10:35	106
10:38	145
10:39	146
11	xiv, 42, 42n75, 43n83,
	65-67, 66n4, 66n5,
	70n15, 73, 73n38,
	74-75, 77, 78n67,
	82-83, 92, 115, 126,
	128-129, 129n75,
	140, 141n22
11:1	69n13, 71, 72, 72n31,
	72n32, 78n66, 107
11:1-3	72, 73
11:1-12:2	70
11:1-12:3	136n2
11:2	65, 76, 76-77n55, 80

11:3	84–86, 84n10	13:7	127, 151
11:4	86–90, 86n16, 87n24, 137	13:8	151, 175
		13:12-13	40
11:4-5	76	13:17	147
11:5-6	89–91, 138	13:20	100
11:6	91, 106, 146	13:22	136
11:7	91–93, 92	13:24	98n60
11:8	139	19:26	151
11:8-10	93–95		

James

11:9	139	1:22	122n51
11:10	94	2:21	99
11:11-12	95–97, 95n48	2:25	110
11-12:24	89n31	2:5	143
11:13	98	5	66
11:13-16	97–99		
11:14	98		
11:16	98		

1 Peter

11:17	99–101, 139	1:9	107n85
11:19	101	1:10-11	170n80
11:20	140	1:11	132n87
11:20-22	101–104, 102	1:12	39n58
11:21	103, 141	3:4-5	95n51
11:22	141	3:21	92n42
11:25-26	106	3:31	108
11:26	142	5:14	98n60
11:27	107		
11:29	107–109		

2 Peter

11:30-31	109–111	1:15	104n76
11:32-40	111–113, 143	2:5	92
11:35	111		
11:36-37	111		

3 John

11:39	76, 85	11	127
11:39-12:2	74		
11:39-40	94, 112, 135, 144		
11:40	77, 87–88n24, 113		

Jude

12	74, 78, 132n88, 191	3	17n69, 73n38
12:1	145, 146	14-15	90n36, 91n39
12:1-2	65, 68, 75, 77–81, 79n72, 84n10, 151		
12:1-3	136		

Revelation

12:2	78n67, 80, 113n99	5:12	107n85
12:3-4	75, 137	20	85
12:22-24	104, 137	20:10	92n42, 108
12:24	86, 89, 107n85, 136, 137, 151	20:15	92n42, 108
12:24-26	138	21	108
12:28-29	137	21:3	85
12:29	137	22	85n13
13:1	39n58